# Grit, Noise, & Revolution

# Grit, Noise, & Revolution

## the birth of detroit
## rock 'n' roll

### david a. carson

University of Michigan Press    Ann Arbor

Copyright © by David A. Carson 2005
All rights reserved
Published in the United States of America by
The University of Michigan Press
Manufactured in the United States of America
⊗ Printed on acid-free paper

2008   2007   2006   2005      4   3   2   1

*A CIP catalog record for this book is available from the British Library.*

Library of Congress Cataloging-in-Publication Data

Carson, David, 1949–
Grit, noise, and revolution : the birth of Detroit rock 'n' roll /
David A. Carson.
    p.    cm.
Includes bibliographical references and index.
Discography: p.
ISBN 0-472-11503-0 (cloth : alk. paper)
1. Rock music—Michigan—Detroit—History and criticism. I. Title.
ML3534.C34   2005
781.66'09774'34—dc22                              2004030698

This book is dedicated to all the rock and R & B musicians who played and sang with a passion that would always be identified with Detroit. It could not have been written without the love & support of my wife Laura, and my daughter Erin.

# Contents

**Contents**
**viii**

# Preface

On April 7, 1969, over sixteen thousand fans turned out at Detroit's Olympia Stadium for a ten-hour rock concert event called the Detroit Pop Festival. Although there were no "national" acts on the bill, kids were lining up to see Motor City stalwarts such as the MC5, the Stooges, SRC, the Bob Seger System, the Amboy Dukes, the Rationals, and Frost.

Two years earlier, as Detroit burned during the urban riots in the summer of '67, San Francisco's music and cultural scene had drawn national attention with its laid-back image of "peace, love, and flowers in your hair." Now, hard-driving, high-energy Detroit bands were breaking through with major label record contracts. Their reputations were forged through performances that intimidated many of the touring acts forced to follow them onstage at venues such as the Grande Ballroom. It appeared to many observers, including those in the national press, that Detroit was on the verge of becoming the next big music scene.

There was no denying Detroit's reputation as a tough, gritty, unheralded industrial metropolis most associated with a colorful band of gangsters, automotive assembly lines, and a famous R & B music label. By the late sixties, the city's bands began to mirror that image, and fans began taking pride in it. Their attitude was, "Yeah, we make the cars, and the best damn rock 'n' roll anywhere—just try and outplay our bands."

Berry Gordy's Motown empire had emerged from the heart of the city to put Detroit on the music map. Now, influenced by their R & B heritage, the Motor City's aspiring rock musicians were redefining what *Time* magazine was describing as "a real Detroit sound, pulsating with the belch of its smokestacks and the beat of its machinery."

Fueled by the radical social and political stances of activist John

Sinclair, the controversial and quintessential Detroit band MC5 was at the center of what looked like a musical and cultural revolution at the height of the Vietnam War and the civil rights struggle.

Although it took place primarily during the period between 1965 and 1972, the roots of this explosive musical scene can be traced all the way back to the forties and fifties. And that's where we'll begin.

# Acknowledgments

I would like to express my appreciation to my wife Laura and to Chris Hebert at the University of Michigan Press for their assistance in editing. I would also like to thank my daughter Erin for her support and assistance with computer troubleshooting. Thanks also to Strother Bullins for his technical assistance with photos.

# 1. Boogie and the Beat

Before there was rock or R & B, there were blues. In Detroit the blues were personified in the music of John Lee Hooker, an artist whose "electrified sound" would influence future generations of rock and R & B musicians.

He arrived in Detroit by Greyhound bus in 1943, stepping down in Black Bottom, a section of town that rural French farmers had named for its rich soil.[1] The bustling sixty-six-block residential area, east of downtown, running from Brush Street east to Elmwood, and Larned north to Gratiot, was home to most of the city's African American population, at the time numbering more than 150,000.[2] Like Hooker, many of its residents had migrated from the South seeking steady employment in the city's automotive and steel plants. Adjacent to Black Bottom on the northwest was the mainly black-owned business and entertainment district known as Paradise Valley, a five-square-block neighborhood bordered by Vernor on the north, Gratiot on the south, Beaubien on the west, and Hastings on the east. In its prime during the 1930s, the Valley attracted huge mostly white audiences to see the country's top black entertainers. Duke Ellington, Cab Calloway, and Bessie Smith, among others, performed in lavish shows staged at upscale nightclubs such as the B&C, Club Plantation, and the Chocolate Bar.[3]

Although the race riots in the summer of 1943 signaled a decline, the Valley was still ripe with blues and jazz clubs in the mid to late forties. There was El Sino on St. Antoine, Sportree's Music Bar on Hastings, Club Three 666 and the 606 Horseshoe Bar on East Adams, and just down the street (replacing Club Plantation), Club Congo in the Norwood Hotel. Henry's Swing Club was nearby at 1700 Orleans.

As Hastings Street, Black Bottom's main artery, continued

north beyond the Valley, there was also plenty of action at spots such as the Ace Bar, the Three Star Bar, the Cozy Corner, and Sunnie Wilson's Forest Club, a huge entertainment center featuring a roller rink and bowling alley, located at Forest and Hastings. To the west was the Cotton Club at Livingstone and St. Antoine, and the Parrot Lounge on E. Canfield.[4] Along with the bars, there were poolrooms, ten-cent movie houses, plenty of after-hours joints, and jam sessions everywhere. Later, Hooker recalled Hastings Street, as being "rough, wide open," a place where "anything goes."[5]

John Lee Hooker was born just outside of Clarksdale, Mississippi, on August 22, 1917 (though other dates are often cited), the fourth of eleven children. His parents, William Hooker and Minnie Ramsey, were sharecroppers. His father was also a Baptist minister.[6] As a child John Lee sang in the church choir, but spirituals took a back seat to blues music after his sister Alice began dating a guitar player named Tony Hollins, who gave John Lee his first guitar, an old Silvertone model.[7]

Following a divorce, John Lee's mother married William Moore, a farmer highly regarded as a regional blues performer. Moore encouraged his stepson and allowed him access to his record collection, which included blues artists such as Charlie Patton, Blind Lemon, Blind Blake, and LeRoy Carr. Their recordings influenced Hooker, but it was the guitar style of his stepfather that made the greatest impression on the young musician.[8]

At fourteen, wishing to escape farm life, Hooker left home to live with aunts in Memphis, and then Cincinnati. Eventually, he decided to hone his musical skills in the Motor City, believing there would be less competition there than in Chicago, which had already developed a big blues scene. He found a place at a rooming house called Mom's and worked for a while at the Ford River Rouge Plant, before becoming an orderly at Receiving Hospital. From there, he took a daytime janitor's position at the Dodge Main Plant, while at night he played guitar and sang at various house parties, and occasionally had the opportunity to sit in with a club band.[9]

By 1948, after several tough years, Hooker, now married with children and working a day shift at Comco Steel, was still playing mainly for tips at "rent parties," but he was also performing more in nightspots such as Lee's Sensation Bar on Owen, and Club Carribee on East Jefferson.[10] Most often he could be found playing on the small stage at the Apex Bar on Oakland Avenue. It was there, according to Hooker, that a black record store owner named Elmer Barbee heard him playing and invited him down to his shop at 609 Lafayette, which housed a small recording studio in the rear. After cutting a few demos, Barbee introduced Hooker to Bernie Besman, the owner of a minor local label called Sensation Records, and co-owner, along with John Kaplan, of Pan American Music Distributors. As he listened to Hooker's demo tape, Besman was intrigued. He quickly signed him to a personal management contract.[11]

Shortly after the signing, Hooker closed a Saturday night show at the Broadway Capitol Theater, promoted by Bill Randle, a white jazz deejay at WJLB. Randle recalls that Hooker, like a lot of local musicians, used to come up to the WJLB studios on the thirty-first floor of the David Broadrick Tower downtown and "just hang around" during his late night show (the Interracial Goodwill Hour). "Then on Saturday nights we used to do a live jam session remote from Club Sudan (formerly Club Congo), from Midnight to 4 and John Lee would come down and play. The place was always packed."[12] Randle says the concert at the Broadway Capitol Theater in 1948 was Hooker's first major appearance. "It was a very eclectic show and there was a largely white audience. We had Milt Jackson on the bill as well as Tate Huston and Bill De Arango, one of the greatest jazz guitarists of all time. We also had Willie Anderson, a terrific jazz pianist, and then John Lee Hooker. At the end of the show everybody was out on the stage for a really wild jam session."[13] Bernie Besman later described witnessing Hooker's performance at the concert as "one of the most profound experiences" of his life.[14]

Besman arranged for Hooker to record at a session originally scheduled for band leader and pianist Todd Rhodes at United Sound Systems, Detroit's premier recording studio. Located in a two-story brownstone at 5840 Second Avenue, United Sound had been the first independent studio in the country when it opened in 1933. Owner Jimmy Siracuse, a former cinematographer working in the Detroit automotive ad business, had originally built the facility as a full-service film, recording, and design operation.[15] "There was a huge recording studio in the back on the main floor in an area that had first been constructed for film production," recalls Detroit musician and broadcaster Jack Surrell. "It had one of *the,* if not *the only* studio in town that could accommodate a full orchestra. There was also a smaller studio in the front."[16] Surrell, an accomplished pianist, had done sessions in both studios and says that Jimmy Siracuse and his son Joe ran the whole thing. "We didn't do too many takes back then. We'd talk about what we wanted to accomplish, and then Jimmy or Joe would run into the control booth and do the actual recording. It was quite a professional operation though, compared to some other little backroom studios around town."[17] Surrell had several releases on the Sensation label in the late forties, including "Detroit Boogie."

At the time, John Lee Hooker was usually accompanied in clubs by pianist James Watkins and drummer Curtis Foster, but on this occasion he was asked to record alone.[18] His technique, learned from his stepfather Will Moore back in Mississippi, made extensive use of "hammering" one-chord guitar figures, bare-fingered on the strings of an old Stella acoustic guitar with an electric pickup, while stomping his feet to the beat.[19] He had a nonrhyming singing style that was at times out of rhythm but nonetheless effective.

The initial United session on September 3, 1948, produced Hooker's first smash hit, "Boogie Chillen," which he had also written about his early days on Hastings Street. "The thing come into me. It was just a funky old lick I found. I heard Will Moore do a song like that when I was a little kid down South, but he didn't call it 'Boogie Chillen.' But it had that beat," recounted the musician in a later interview.[20] It was a driving but hesitant beat, with Hooker adding a stark, chilling vocal, and staccato guitar breaks, followed by the cry: "Boogie chillen!" According to the singer-composer, he had taken "boogie" from piano-driven boogie-woogie, and gave it an entirely new feel.[21]

Bernie Besman leased the song to Modern Records, a Los Angeles label owned and operated by the Bihari brothers. Released on November 3, 1948, the recording reached number 1 on the R & B charts at the start of 1949.[22] "When 'Boogie Chillen' first come out, everywhere you went you would hear that, 'cause that was a new beat to the blues then," said Hooker.[23] "Sally Mae" was featured on the flip side. As part of his recording deal, Hooker received a thousand dollars up front and the promise of a cent and a half royalty.[24]

He quickly followed up with a string of top 10 R & B hits on Modern, such as "Hoogie Boogie," "Hobo Blues," "Queen Bee," and "Crawling King Snake." His biggest was 1951's "I'm In the Mood," where over a slow, bluesy beat, Hooker's voice could be heard in an echo effect, singing the memorable line: "Nighttime is the right time . . . be with the one you love." The haunting sound had been created by Joe Siracuse using the new technique of over-dubbing Hooker's vocal onto the master.[25] The record spent four weeks at number 1. All these early classics were cut at United Sound in Detroit.

John Lee Hooker's music was in such demand that he released records for other labels using pseudonyms, such as Johnny Lee, John Lee Booker, Texas Slim, Delta John, and the Boogie Man.[26] "[Elmer] Barbee would come to me late at night and say, 'Man, I got a deal! This record company want to do something with you. I know you under contract, but we can change your name,'" claimed Hooker.[27] As he felt that he wasn't getting paid in a timely fashion by Modern Records, John Lee saw no problem with the clandestine midnight sessions that paid him cash "right on the spot."[28]

By mid-1952, as a result of serious health problems, as well as business differences with Modern Records, Bernie Besman relocated to Southern California. Hooker began working directly with Modern. Joe Bihari took over as producer, flying in from L.A. for the sessions at United Sound, still engineered by Joe Siracuse.[29]

When Hooker's contract with Modern expired at the end of 1954, he signed a recording deal with Vee-Jay Records of Chicago, but he continued to live in Detroit and perform locally with his own Detroit-based band, the Boogie Ramblers, which he had formed in 1953. "I spent all my best years right there in Detroit," Hooker told *Living Blues* magazine. "Yeah, they was real good to me."[30]

"Few musicians have been able to figure out what John is playing, let alone copy it," said writer Dave Sax.[31] Hooker had no imitators, and because of this, Detroit never developed its own identifiable blues style the way Chicago had. There were certainly talented blues artists in the Motor City, such as guitar and harmonica players Eddie Burns and Eddie Kirkland and pianists Boogie Woogie Red and Detroit Piano Fats, all of whom played with Hooker early on. There were also Little Sonny, Baby Boy Warren, Calvin Frazier, and Washboard Willie. But none were able to break out nationally.[32] In other parts of the country "Detroit blues" meant John Lee Hooker.

Many of these lesser-known blues artists made recordings in small backroom studios, such as Elmer Barbee's. There was also Sam's Record Shop at 3419 Hastings Street, run by Sam Taylor, and "Joe's Record Shop" nearby at 3530 Hastings. Owner Joe Battle, who liked to call himself Joe Von Battle, would lease many of his masters out to various national and regional labels. He would issue some locally on his own JVB label. Von Battle's biggest sellers, however, were the sermons of Reverend C. L. Franklin, recorded at the New Bethel Baptist Church at Linwood and West Pennsylvania, where the pastor's three daughters Carolyn, Erma, and Aretha Franklin sang in the choir each Sunday.[33]

Independent of Bernie Besman, Hooker had also cut some tracks for Von Battle that were leased to Chicago's Chess Records.[34]

One memorable Von Battle recording on JVB was a raucous piano-driven boogie-woogie track called "LeRoy Sent Me," by a Detroit outfit known as Joe Brown and His Kool Kats. It had been written in 1949 for LeRoy White, Detroit's first black deejay,[35] whose nightly show, *Rockin' with LeRoy* (successor to the *Goodwill Hour*), aired R & B from ten to midnight over WJLB: "Rock, rock, rockin' with LeRoy all night long," wailed the shouting chorus in a song that was a harbinger of things to come.

In the early fifties, vocal groups were the hottest craze in rhythm and blues. In Detroit, the Royals were street corner harmonizers from Dunbar High School. Members included Charles Sutton (lead and tenor), Henry Booth (tenor), Lawson Smith (baritone), and Sonny Woods (bass). Alonzo Tucker was their arranger and sometime guitarist.[36]

In November 1951, the Royals entered an amateur contest at the renowned Paradise Theater located at 3711 Woodward Avenue. Johnny Otis, at the time a band leader as well as a talent scout for King/Federal Records, the big Cincinnati-based independent label, was in the audience. In a later interview, he recalled that although the show was "supposed to have been an hour, it turned into three hours because there was so much talent in Detroit." Later, Otis put a call through to his bosses, telling them: "I sure found some people here."[37] His Detroit talent picks that night were Jackie Wilson, Little Willie John, and the Royals, but he remembers seeing "others with equal potential during that evening." When the King/Federal people arrived to audition Otis's talent discoveries, they passed on both Wilson and John, signing only the Royals, because, according to Otis, "they were a vocal group" at a time when, "suddenly—it was all vocal groups."[38]

The label chose a song Otis had written expressly for Jackie Wilson to sing at the audition, called "Every Beat of My Heart," for the Royals' first release in April 1952. The record wasn't much of a hit outside of Detroit, and the group's other releases failed to reach the charts. When Lawson Smith left to enter the service, he was replaced by a singer working in more of a gospel and country blues tradition. The singer's name was Hank Ballard.

Hank Ballard was born in Detroit in 1927, the son of a truck driver. At age seven, after the deaths of his parents, he was sent down to Bessemer, Alabama, to live with relatives. Country and gospel music had a profound influence on Ballard, but he also enjoyed listening to big band belters such as Jimmy Rushing and Al Hibbler as well as the smooth style of Nat "King" Cole.[39]

At age fifteen, he ran away and returned to Detroit. At the time, the city was teeming with aspiring rhythm and blues groups. According to Ballard, "You couldn't walk down the street without hearing groups that sounded like they should have a hit record."[40] He tried to sing in the style of high-voiced Clyde McPhatter, at the time the wildly popular lead vocalist with Billy Ward's Dominos, but after observing how difficult it was for solo artists to get signed by record companies, Ballard realized he needed to be part of a vocal group.

At the Ford plant where he worked, Hank would sing the harmonies of popular songs to the rhythm of the assembly line. Sonny Woods of the Royals also worked there, and, after hearing Hank, invited him to sing in several contests at the Paradise Theater. When Lawson Smith left for the army, Hank Ballard agreed to take his place, although he felt that the Royals were "singing for the older crowd," that they were "stuck in the Orioles mold." He told the other group members that they needed to "modernize" their sound. "It took me some time to convince these traditional rhythm and blues types to get with a modern, urban sound," Hank recalled.[41]

Ballard who had been writing songs for some time, pitched one of his tunes to the group as well as to Syd Nathan, the head of Federal/King Records. It was a slinky but upbeat number provocatively titled "Get It." Syd Nathan immediately recognized Ballard's writing skills and approved the song for a recording session. Hank would sing lead for the first time. Released in June 1953, "Get It" broke fast in Detroit, before jumping on the national R & B charts, rocketing up to number 6. By moving away from slow, syrupy ballads such as "Moonrise" and "The Shrine of St Cecilia," the Royals had finally come up with a national hit.[42]

The success of "Get It" gave Ballard the opportunity to submit more material for the group to record. Next up was a song that had started off as "Sock It to Me Mary." By the time it was finished, it had been transformed into "Work with Me Annie."[43] The recording, with its driving beat and raw, suggestive lyrics, quickly grabbed the attention of not only black listeners, but white teenagers searching for an alternative to Eddie Fisher and Kay Starr records. In the spring of 1954, "Work with Me Annie" zoomed to number 1 on the R & B charts.

As there was another recording outfit known as the 5 Royales, Ballard suggested that his group change their name to the Midnighters. He also convinced the group members to work on a series of choreographed dances to perform while he sang.[44]

"Work with Me Annie" was followed into the charts by "Sexy Ways," which rose to number 2 on the R & B chart. Then came "Annie Had A Baby," which explained why Annie was no longer able to "work." It climbed to number 1 R & B. The group's producer, Henry Glover, pushed for more of the same. He and Ballard then cowrote "Annie's Aunt Fannie" and "Henry's Got Flat Feet (Can't Dance No More)." "They were takin' the Annie thing to the bank," Ballard recalled. "I just couldn't get behind any more Annie songs. We had *done* it."[45] In the meantime, Detroit's Midnighters had become the hottest act in R & B, headlining across the country.

While the Midnighters were topping the national charts, back in Detroit there were other groups waiting for their chance at success. The Imperials started singing together in the choir at Sherrod Middle School, with Milton Harris and William "Mickey" Stevenson sharing lead tenor duties. As the Teen Toppers, they had performed one night out in front of the popular Flame Show Bar on John R Road, where they were seen by Phil Waddell, an entertainer who also worked as a booking agent. He placed them at the Graystone Ballroom at 4237 Woodward Avenue, and it was here that they met record shop owner Tony Vance, who offered to manage the group. Vance, along with recording engineer Kenneth Campbell, had formed the new Great Lakes record label and built a studio in the former ballroom of the Fairbain Hotel on Columbia Street, in the heart of Paradise Valley. Not wanting the group to be stuck with a "teen" name as they grew older, Vance renamed them the "Imperials," after his new Chrysler.[46]

Although the label was around for only a couple of years, it had some good talent. Detroit-born vocalist Della Reese waxed her earliest recordings there. When the Imperials entered the studio to record in November 1953, they were backed up by orchestra leader Sax Kari and his Ballin' the Blues Band. Of the six sides they recorded, "Life of Ease," written by Milton Harris, became a local hit in January 1954. The group performed the song at places such as the Chesterfield Lounge, the Sugar Hill Lounge, and the Garfield Lounge. Onstage at the Graystone Ballroom they would perform a wild version of the popular dance the Chicken.

Unfortunately, before the group could follow up with another hit, Great Lakes was closed down by two of its principals, who together formed the Boulevard and Avenue labels.

The first Boulevard release was "Runaround" by a white group known as the Three Chuckles, led by Teddy Randazzo. It became a national hit in November 1954, reaching number 20 in *Billboard*. As for the Imperials, they were lost in the shuffle, and that included losing their manager, Tony Vance. Unable to record and inexperienced at collecting money owed them, the various members went their separate ways.[47]

In 1951, a group of Northeastern High School students who called themselves the Serenaders liked to hang out over at Joe Von Battle's record shop on Hastings Street. They cut a few sides for his JVB label in 1952. Theron "T-Man" Hill was lead tenor. Other members included Noah Howell (baritone-tenor), Norman Thrasher (baritone), and Isaac "Ike" Reese (bass). They also recorded for some other small R & B labels, such as Roxy, and cut some sides for Decca's Coral label. "It's Funny" and "Misery," from 1952, were recorded in Detroit and shipped to New York, but the records didn't become big hits, and the Serenaders were dropped by Coral in May 1953.[48]

The following year, having no real success, they started calling themselves the Royals, after that group had become the Midnighters. Maurice King, the band leader at the Flame Show Bar, suggested that they change their name to the Royal Jokers. The reason according to Theron Hill was, " 'Cause we was funny, man. We did comedy routines on stage."[49] The Flame's manager, Al Green, became their manager and got them a deal with Atco, a new subsidiary of Atlantic Records in New York. In March 1955, the Royal Jokers finally picked up a national hit with "You Tickle Me Baby."[50]

While so many street corner artists of the time popped up on one label after another, a select few found a more permanent home as they sought success at a place called Fortune. The Royal Jokers would eventually land there after leaving Atlantic. It was, however, another group that would set the standard for the label.

# 2. Fame and Fortune

Of all the early Detroit groups, the Diablos, featuring Nolan Strong, may have been the most revered. Their entire recording career was spent with struggling, Detroit-based Fortune Records, owned by Jack and Dorothy Brown.

Jack was a former accountant, and Dorothy, who usually went by the name Devora, was a pianist, poet, and songwriter. In 1946, after unsuccessful attempts at breaking into New York's Tin Pan Alley, the Browns started their own music publishing company (Trianon Publications) and the Fortune record label, with the goal of getting Devora's songs recorded.[1] In the beginning, they worked out of their westside home at 11839 Twelfth Street, and tried to emulate the success of the major pop labels such as Columbia and RCA. "When we first started, we did everything wrong and lost about $3,000, which was all we had," Devora Brown recalled in a later interview.[2] Fortune did score one early regional pop hit in 1947 with her composition "Jane (Sweet As Summer Rain)," by a Bing Crosby–styled crooner named Russ Titus, backed by the Artie Fields Orchestra. "Devora came in to a club where I was playing and said she'd written hundreds of songs," recalls Fields. "They had hired a singer from Canada to record one and needed backing musicians, so we took the job."[3] According to Fields, the Fortune session took place at Tom Saffady's short-lived Vogue Record Company studios on Eight Mile Road near John R in Detroit. "That's the label that made those records with a colorful picture embedded in the disc," says Fields. "They recorded some well-known artists like Clyde McCoy, and they had a great studio but went out of business after just a year or so. Their sound quality was excellent, but the records were too expensive, and because they were so durable, they didn't get additional buys from jukebox operators." After ceasing production in April 1947, the parent company, Sav-Way Industries, began using the machines that trimmed the plastic records to make toilet seats.[4]

By 1951, the Browns had rented a storefront location at 11629 Linwood Avenue, in the middle of a block of other small shops just off Elmhurst, in a mixed black and Jewish residential neighborhood. They installed their own studio and turned to recording country music with such artists such as the York Brothers, Skeets McDonald, and Roy Hall, who appealed to the many white southerners who had moved north to work in automotive-related jobs. The Davis Sisters (including Skeeter Davis) made a few demos at Fortune before signing with RCA. Their recording of "Jealous Love" in 1952 gave the Detroit label another regional hit.[5]

Despite the various styles of music they recorded, the Browns had always favored classical music in their home.[6] Jack Brown had done a John Lee Hooker session at Toledo's Sweeney Sound Engineering, supposedly in 1948, prior to "Boogie Chillen," though the two sides ("Curl My Baby's Hair" and "609 Boogie") were not released until ten years later.[7] Aside from that session, the Browns were "absolutely ignorant of black records."[8] One day in the fall of 1953, some kids who attended Central High, just across the street from Fortune, came in to cut an R & B demo. Nolan Strong was the tall, handsome leader, as well as lead singer. He had named his five-man group the Diablos, after a book he was reading in school called *El Niño Diablo (The Little Devil)*.[9] The other group members included tenor Juan Guiterriez, baritone Willie Hunter, bass Quentin Eubanks, and guitarist Bob "Chico" Edwards. Born in Scottsboro, Alabama, on January 22, 1934, Nolan moved with his family to Detroit when he was very young. In 1950 he founded the Diablos. Like Hank Ballard, Nolan admired Clyde McPhatter.[10]

According to Devora Brown, her husband Jack was out of town the day the demo was recorded: "When he heard it, he said 'I never heard such a high singer, he might be too high.' I said, 'I don't think so, it might be an extra point for him that he sings so high.'"[11] The demo session won the Diablos a contract, and in the spring of 1954 they recorded "Adios My Desert Love," penned by Devora. It was a romantic, up-tempo number, driven by Latin rhythms under Nolan's lilting lead vocal. On the bridge, Strong is heard softly chirping high above the bass singer's spoken word part. Pianist George Annis, a white musician with a pop background, was musical director for the session.[12] The record became a big Detroit R & B hit. For their next release the Diablos were scheduled to record their own composition—"The Wind."

It was a hot August day when the group came through the door at Fortune, making their way down the narrow hallway past the little record shop at the front and into a cramped recording area in the middle of the building. There Jack Brown adjusted knobs and switches in a small, glass-paneled control room looking out on the
studio, where, for sound insulation, Persian rugs covered the wood floors and hung along the walls. Above, billowing sheets draped from the ceiling.[13] The Flame Show Bar's Maurice King was hired as musical director for the session, and as he went over the arrangement with the musicians, Jack and Devora moved around the studio, setting up microphones.[14] Nolan Strong stood before his mike while the other members huddled around theirs. After a short rehearsal, Jack punched the record button on Fortune's lone Magnecord PT-6 recording deck, and guitarist Bob "Chico" Edwards played the creeping, mysterious opening notes that ended with a slow reverberating chord. The group, anchored by bass singer Quentin Eubanks leaned in on their mike, solemnly harmonizing the opening line: "Wind, wind—blow, wind." From high above, Nolan Strong's silky falsetto sailed in, evoking memories of a lost love that were brought back like a "dream" by the wind. The haunting, mesmerizing arrangement featured Nolan not only on the melody but also on a talking bridge spoken over a background of the group, who continued to half-sing, half-chant "Blow, wind."

After a couple of takes, everybody jammed the doorway to the control room, anxious to hear the playback. Unhappy with his vocal, Nolan and the group returned to the studio, and after an additional five or six complete takes, they got it right.[15] Jack Brown rushed a tape of the unique recording to an outside cutter for mastering. Upon release in September, "The Wind" became a huge R & B hit not only in Detroit, but in a number of other important markets such as Chicago, Cleveland, Pittsburgh, and New York. Sadly, Fortune's spotty distribution prevented "The Wind" from reaching the national charts.[16]

Along with their early record successes, the Diablos were popular performers at spots such as the Warfield Theater, the Gold Coast Theater on Twelfth Street and at the Madison Ballroom, located at 4643 Woodward near Forest. It was at the Madison that they "bested the Midnighters" in one of the venue's "Battle of the Groups" competitions, usually held on Saturday nights. "No one could touch them, and the girls would just go crazy for Nolan," says Gary Banovetz, a member of a white fan club calling itself Diablo Dukes.[17] According to Banovetz, Jack Brown had been "happy to find out that there were potential white record buyers for his R&B recordings."[18]

In the spring of 1955, the Diablos scored another regional hit with Nolan's jumpin' and slightly risqué composition "Daddy Rockin' Strong." In the fall, Nolan displayed a grittier, more mature sound on "The Way You Dog Me Around," which he had also written. Despite Fortune's inadequate distribution network, the searing, bluesy ballad managed to climb to number 12 on the R & B charts, becoming the Diablos' biggest national hit. The group, now including Nolan Strong's brother Jimmy as well as George Scott (replacing Guiterriez and Eubanks, respectively), went on the road playing one-nighters in Ohio and Pennsylvania. They also signed for a tour on the northeastern theater circuit and appeared at New York's famed Apollo Theater. The group continued to record and tour into 1956. Although it wasn't a big hit, "You're the Only Girl, Delores" had some chart action in scattered markets, and the group shared a bill with Ray Charles at a big summer package show in Chicago. On Labor Day weekend they were back home and appearing at a holiday show across the Detroit River in Windsor with jazz great Stan Kenton and his orchestra.[19]

In November, just when things were rolling, Nolan Strong was drafted. Around the same time, in response to neighborhood complaints about "too much noise," the Browns relocated the Fortune operation to a small, long, and narrow brick building at 3942 Third Avenue.[20] As before, there was a record shop in the front, then a series of small offices and a storage room. At the very back, a tiny control room faced a primitive, cinder block studio, eighteen feet wide and forty feet long, that opened onto the alley.[21] The Brown's son Sheldon, who maintained the studio, purchased a modern but still one-track Ampex 350 recording deck. According to Devora, she did "most of the recording and engineering, especially on the important artists."[22] Her days were spent running back and forth from the control room to the studio, adjusting equipment. In the furnace room there was a hot plate where she would warm up coffee as well as the burgers she brought from home.[23]

Playing behind many of Fortune's artists were Joe Weaver and the Blue Notes. Weaver played piano, and Johnny Bassett handled lead guitar. The two had put their first band together while both were attending Northwestern High. Not long after, they formed the Blue Notes, with saxophonist Jesse Ulmer and drummer Calvin Andrews. Their afternoons were spent hanging around Joe Von Battle's record shop and studio, joined occasionally by schoolmate Aretha Franklin. After being given the opportunity to record, the band cut "15–40 Special," which Von Battle leased to DeLuxe Records. Unfortunately, the inexperienced musicians neglected to sign any sort of agreement and as a result earned not a penny on the recording.[24] The record did, however, give the Blue Notes a reputation, and soon they were backing artists such as Big Joe Turner, Dinah Washington, Ruth Brown, and Big Maybelle when they were performing in Detroit.[25]

After joining Fortune Records, Joe Weaver also scored a vocal hit in 1955 with "Baby, I Love You So." Background vocals were credited to the Don Juans, who were really the Five Dollars, a group that scored its own hits with "Doctor Baby" and "Hard Working Mama." When the Five Dollars performed as the Don Juans, they would come onstage wearing Mardi Gras masks. They also worked with Fortune's flamboyant "Mr. Rhythm," Andre Williams.

Born in Bessemer, Alabama, on November 1, 1936, Williams moved with his father to Chicago after his mother died when he was six. In Chicago Andre joined the church choir and grew interested in show business. After a stint in the military, he moved to Detroit, where his brother-in-law Eddie Hurt was a member of the Five Dollars.[26] Hurt's singing partners were Lonnie Heard, James Drayton, Charles Evans, and Richard Lawrence. Like the Diablos, the Five Dollars, originally called the Del-Torros, had been signed after showing up at Fortune for an audition.[27]

In 1955, Andre Williams entered the amateur talent contest held at the Warfield Theater, and his wild, over-the-top performances won him the twenty-five-dollar first prize eight weeks in a row. Mrs. Warfield called Devora Brown, recommending that she come down and see him, after which Devora offered Williams a recording contract at Fortune and invited him to join the Five Dollars, replacing Richard Lawrence, who had been drafted.[28]

Adept at self-promotion, Andre was soon out in front, dancing up a storm and performing some wild stage antics. At the Graystone Ballroom, he would let himself fall from the balcony railing, and once he'd landed, other group members would carry his limp body back to the center of the stage, where Williams would stun the audience by suddenly jumping up and dancing.[29] Along with the Five Dollars (billed as the Don Juans on Williams's recordings), he scored his first hit in late 1955 with the rockin' "Goin' Down to Tijuana." However, it was a recording called "Bacon Fat," released in 1956, that made Williams famous.

Aware that he was "no Clyde McPhatter or Nolan Strong," Williams claims to have said to himself: "Andre, you gon' have to come up with a gimmick."[30] That gimmick became talking in rhythm rather than singing. The idea came to him while driving down to Memphis for a gig. As he drove, he kept passing cotton pickers with sacks on their back: "I'm eatin' this bacon sandwich, I'm passin', I'm drivin', I'm hummin' to myself, 'Hey man, glad to see you back, we got a little thing called'—and I look in my lap and see the sandwich—'Bacon Fat!' So it hits me and I write the song."[31]

Back at the Fortune studio, Devora Brown was less than enthused when Williams started talking instead of singing over a funky, crude rhythm: "You're wasting my money! I can't sell this!" declared the label owner.[32] "Frantic" Ernie Durham, who had become Detroit's favorite R & B deejay on WJLB, happened to be in the record store that day, and listened in on the session. Ernie convinced Brown that the recording could work and advised that she should "press it up, try it."[33] Upon its release, Ernie played the record on the radio, and "Bacon Fat" became a local smash. The Browns leased the recording to Epic, and it quickly raced up the national R & B charts. Williams repeated the formula successfully in 1957 with an ode to the dangers of young love called "Jail Bait."

Other hits included "The Greasy Chicken" and "Mean Jean." The Browns, however, disliked splitting the potential profits, so these recordings were released only on Fortune, and sales suffered as a result of poor distribution. The background vocals on "Bacon Fat" had been sung by Andre's new group, which included Gino Parks, with whom he also cut a duet called "My Tears."[34]

Williams says that besides engineering all the sessions at Fortune, Devora also handled administrative duties: "Jack did all the field work. He took the records and sold them every week to different record stores. They had different distributors in different cities, but not in Detroit. Jack handled that himself."[35] Still, Williams felt that the Browns didn't know how to promote: "When Mrs. Brown got records in, she'd call and beg them [DJs] to play the records, send them a little payola. Not very much—they were very tight fisted."[36]

While Fortune had a regular family of R & B artists, they also did quite a few one-off recording sessions for blues artists such as early Detroit boogie pianist Big Maceo Merriweather ("Worried Life Blues #2"), and tenor sax player Choker Campbell ("Rockin' & Jumpin'"). Although under contract to Chicago's Vee Jay Records, John Lee Hooker stopped by to cut a few tracks ("Cry Baby," "Love You Baby").

Fortune was also a popular recording destination for Detroit-based rockabilly acts such as Dell Vaughn ("Rock the Universe"), Eddie Jackson ("Rock 'n' Roll Baby"), George Young ("Shakin' Shelly"), Don Rader ("Rock 'n' Roll Grandpap"), and Johnny Powers ("Honey Let's Go to a Rock 'n' Roll Show"). About his 1957 session at the studio, released on Fortune subsidiary HI-Q Records, Powers recalled, "I went to Fortune because it was about the only label that was active at the time and I wanted to get a record out. It cost me about a hundred dollars to record the session." Powers also recalled that part of the back room studio floor was dirt and there was an old lamp stand with a microphone draped over it: "One mike for the whole session! What you got was what you got!"[37]

Regarding her husband and their company, Devora Brown commented: "Jack loved the record business, but he didn't want to get big and have a whole staff running around the place."[38]

# 3. Freewheelin' in the Motor City

Detroit's rock music scene in the middle to late 1950s was in its infancy, spread out among a handful of local clubs; small recording studios; record, distribution, and management companies; and colorful radio, TV, and promotion personalities.

Radio deejays became the first real rock stars, repackaging rhythm and blues as rock 'n' roll for a hungry audience of white teenagers. Detroit's first superstar deejay had been Ed McKenzie, better known to the bobby-soxers of the late 1940s as "Jack the Bellboy." Starting in 1945, the former engineer and staff announcer had started to mix in some of the "boogie-woogie" music by "Negro artists" on his new afternoon pop show on WJBK radio. As a result, he took some heat from the establishment. More importantly, he won the hearts and minds of the white teenage audience who were tiring of Perry Como, Doris Day, and the Andrews Sisters. Kids were craving the beat music of Louie Jordan, Roy Brown, Wynonnie Harris, and other "Harlem Hit Parade" favorites. The "Bellboy," broadcasting from "Swoon Boulevard and Jive Alley," mixed them all together and embraced a "rock 'n' roll attitude" before there was rock 'n' roll. While the microphone was open he would take what he thought was a really terrible record and break it against the wall or send it flying into the trash can. Teenagers identified with the rebellious behavior of "J the BB," as many fans referred to him, and his popularity soared.[1]

Ed moved his afternoon show to WXYZ in February 1952, but six months later, a lawsuit filed by WJBK prevented him from using his "Jack the Bellboy nom d'air."[2] Despite the loss, McKenzie's popularity grew even greater. By 1954 he was also hosting a big two-hour music variety show called *Ed McKenzie's Saturday Party*, which aired from noon to two on channel 7. Ed would ask the teenage audience their opinions on new records and have them vote on a talent contest each week. Besides appearances by pop and rock artists, ranging from Eddie Fisher to Chuck Berry, McKenzie also featured many of the great names in jazz on this influential program.

On the radio dial, Ed was getting some competition from Robin Seymour's *Bobbin' with Robin* show each afternoon over WKMH. It was Seymour, who after seeing Johnnie Ray perform at the Flame Show Bar in April 1951, brought him to the attention of Columbia Records. The emotionally charged singer forged a link in the development of rock 'n' roll, starting with "Cry," released on Okeh, Columbia's "race" label. By 1956 kids were lining up for the deejay's big stage shows at the Riviera Theater, billed as "Robin Seymour's Original Rock 'n' Roll Revue." Chuck Berry along with Frankie Lyman and the Teenagers headlined the first show.[3]

Black rhyming deejay "Frantic" Ernie Durham was "your ace from inner space with the *swingingest* show on the ra-di-o," nightly on ethnic station WJLB. A former newsman who held a master's degree in journalism, Durham had gotten hooked on the music side of radio after filling in for a disc jockey in New York. Ernie picked up his "Frantic" tag when, while working for WBBC in Flint, he also started broadcasting at WJLB. As his closing theme was playing in Flint, Durham would frantically race to Detroit, arriving just as his opening theme began.[4]

Mickey Shorr was a larger-than-life personality hired to do the evening show at WJBK in June 1955. On a tip from a record plugger named Nat Tarnapol, Shorr was urged to "get with rock 'n' roll."[5] His hip delivery and code words, such as "pavolia" (be safe and be cool) and the "time tellin' mo-chine" (clock), quickly made him a favorite with Detroit teens. Shorr became the first deejay in town to play an Elvis Presley record, spinning the Sun recording of "Mystery Train" in September 1955.[6] On a newspaper promotion for his January 1956 "Rock 'n' Rollorama" stage show at the Fox Theater, the six-foot, four-inch Shorr was billed as "WJBK's Rock 'n' Roll Deejay." That show, featuring acts such as the Cadillacs, the Cleftones, and Detroit's Royal Jokers broke the house record for revenue at the Fox.[7] By April 1956, Shorr had become so identified with rock 'n' roll that WJBK fired him after receiving too many complaints from parents and advertisers about his corrupting influence. Shorr went out in a blaze of glory, going on the air on his last show and inviting listeners to a farewell party at his home. The next day thousands descended on his unsuspecting Palmer Park neighborhood in northwest Detroit, causing pandemonium and winning Shorr a million dollars worth of publicity. WXYZ radio, looking for ways to replace their dying ABC network programming, grabbed the deejay for an evening slot starting in August.[8]

In the mid-1950s, Detroit teens were crossing the border to Windsor each afternoon to appear on Channel 9's *Top Ten Dance Party,* aired from 5:00 to 6:00 P.M. and hosted by CKLW deejay Bud Davies. Bud was the emcee for Elvis Presley's first Detroit appearance at the Fox Theater in May of 1956, and remembers introducing Presley to a sea of "screaming fans." He also recalls the era: "It was a very exciting time. Everything was new, and there were no restrictions. We were picking the music. One minute you were playing Patty Page and then introducing Bill Haley and the Comets."[9] Along with his work in radio and TV, Davies pioneered another cultural teen phenomenon known as the "record hop." "It was 1954 and Denby High School asked me to come out and bring some records and recording acts for a school dance. It turned out to be a terrible rainy night, but when we arrived, the gym was packed and there were four hundred kids lined up waiting to get in." Bud brought along Detroit record artists Bunny Paul, and the Gaylords. "The hop was a huge success, and after that, Bobby Seymour, Don McLeod, and all the other deejays in town really started promoting hops," says Davies.[10]

The Gaylords were an Italian-American vocal group comprised of Burt (Banoldi) Holiday, Ronnie (Fredianelli) Gaylord, and Don Rea. The trio formed while students at the University of Detroit. After developing a reputation in Detroit nightclubs, they made a demo recording that came to the attention of Mercury Records, which signed them to a contract in late 1952.[11] Among their biggest national hits, all of which featured a verse sung in Italian, were "Tell Me You're Mine"(number 5/1952), "From the Vine Comes the Grape" (number 4/1953), and "The Little Shoemaker" (number 2/1954). To the melody of the latter, the Gaylords recorded a long running memorable commercial jingle for Roy O'Brien Ford, reminding everyone to "Stay on the right track to Nine-Mile and Mack . . . ."

It was an audition over the telephone in 1946 that took Detroit-born vocalist and songwriter Bunny Paul from a job in the mail room at Cadillac Motors to a singing career on stage, TV, and records. After singing with combos such as the Al Nalli Trio, Bunny caught the tail end of the big band era, spending two years as vocalist with the Detroit-based Don Pablo Orchestra, with whom she made her first recording, "Sentimental Rhapsody," in 1947 on the local Vargo label. The "attractive blonde" set out on a solo career playing clubs and hosting *Fifer Time,* an early television show on WWJ-TV, channel 4, sponsored by the Pheiffer Brewery.[12] In November 1953, Bunny had the number 1 record in Detroit with her own romantic composition, "Magic Guitar," released on Dot Records. The record also sold well in markets such as Cleveland, Pittsburgh, and Atlanta.

While the Gaylords performed strictly in the pop/standards mode, Bunny soon was making a transition to songs aimed at the emerging youth market, which was looking for music with a beat. After being signed to Essex Records out of Philadelphia (where Bill Haley first recorded), she scored in March 1954 with "Such a Night," an R & B hit for Clyde McPhatter & the Drifters, also in pop release by Johnnie Ray. Although extremely popular with teenagers, many adults felt the song, with its moaning "ooohs," was "too suggestive" and under pressure, Ed McKenzie was forced to remove all three versions from his WXYZ play list.[13] The local ban provided lots of publicity, and Bunny enjoyed great popularity in Detroit, where a loyal fan club had been established. But despite having her record named *Sleeper of the Week* in *Cashbox* on March 6, she says the ban "killed national momentum"[14] and "Such a Night" dropped off the charts after seven weeks, peaking at number 23 the week of May 1.

During this period when mainstream pop radio stations for the most part still refused to play so-called "race records," Bunny continued covering up tempo numbers from the R & B charts such as the Clovers' "Lovey Dovey" and the Drifters' "Honey Love." Both made the local top 10 during the spring and summer of 1954. The latter recording is notable for having background vocals by the Harptones, an East Coast R & B group (Sunday Kind of Love) on loan to Essex. The idea of a black male doo-wop group singing behind a white female vocalist was at the time considered a daring move. "Honey Love" spent nine weeks on the *Cashbox* charts where it topped off at number 21.

Bunny performed her hits in a big musical revue staged September 10 through 12 at the Michigan State Fairgrounds, sharing equal billing with artists such as the Four Aces, Billy Ward's Dominoes, the Treniers, and Nat "King" Cole.[15] She left Essex Records in early 1955 for a one-year contract with Capitol Records. Unfortunately her recordings there, such as "Please Have Mercy," failed to meet the label's sales expectations and her contract was not renewed.[16] In March 1956 she rebounded with the self-penned "Baby Sitter's Blues," released on the Detroit-based Dash label, where over an upbeat rhythm she sang "Gotta rock, rock the baby so I can't rock 'n' roll tonight." Next she wrote and recorded the rockabilly flavored "History," backed with "Sweet Talk" and released on the Point label. Although receiving local air play, these records failed to break out nationally. Most of Bunny's record deals were put together by her husband and manager, Saul "Star" Rapaport, who also worked as a promotions representative for several labels. Her songs were published by her own company, Paul Music.

During the last week of December 1956, Bunny played to huge crowds in a big Christmas package show at Detroit's Fox Theater, headlining pop singer Guy Mitchell ["Singing the Blues"]. Also appearing were Ivory Joe Hunter, the Chuckles, and other Motor City talent, such as Della Reese, Bobby Lewis, and the Royal Jokers. All the performers were backed by veteran Detroit band leader Maurice King and a full eighteen piece orchestra billed as his Rock 'n' Roll Wolverines.[17]

Teenagers and rock 'n' roll were making an impact. By 1956 the Federation of Teen Clubs was set up in communities around Detroit, and *Teen Life* became "the first newspaper written exclusively for, by, and about teens."[18] Both projects were created by adults hoping to capitalize on the new youth market. The *Teen Life* directors included Columbia promotions rep Lowell Worley, record shop owner Wilson Taylor, and realtor George Braxton. Record distributors provided talent to make the rounds of the different teen clubs. Marilyn Bond, who was involved in the music and promotion business in Detroit as a teenager, was in attendance at one such teen club dance. She recalled, "Right in the middle of everything, in walk Bill Haley, LaVern Baker, Johnny Ray, and Chuck Berry." Bond says that kids were allowed to "talk with the stars, take photos, and get autographs." The record label people figured it was a good way to get the kids into the record shops. Many of the photos that Marilyn took were featured in the pages of *Teen Life*.[19]

One of the artists making the rounds of the teen clubs, TV dance parties, and high school hops in 1957 was a local singer named Jack Scott. At the time, he was promoting "Baby, She's Gone," his first release on the ABC-Paramount label.

Jack Scott's real name was Giovanni Scafone Jr., and he was about to become the first national rock 'n' roll star identified with Detroit. Born in Windsor, Canada on January 24, 1936, Scott was given his first guitar at the age of eight by his father, an accomplished guitarist. Two years later, the family, which included seven boys and girls, moved across the river to the Detroit suburb of Hazel Park. When Jack wasn't helping out, working either as a gasoline attendant or truck driver, he was strumming his guitar and singing. His idol was country music star Hank Williams.[20]

Carl Thom, founder of the Harmony House record store in Hazel Park, was Jack's first manager. He introduced the singer to Jack Ihrie, a popular disc jockey who hosted a country music program called *Sagebrush Melodies* on WEXL. "Ihrie said my name might be too difficult to remember, so he suggested Jack Scott and I said 'ok,'" recalled the singer in a later interview.[21]

In 1954, at the age of eighteen, Scott formed his first band, the Southern Drifters, which also included his brother, Jerry. They started playing fifty-cent-admission Saturday night dances at Bill's Barn, located at Twenty-one Mile Road and Dequindre in Utica, Michigan. A year or so later, Scott became a regular attraction at the Dance Ranch, a huge venue on Rochester Road at Sixteen Mile Road in nearby Troy.[22] Although Scott's heart was still in country music, he was also increasingly influenced by the "styles of Chuck Berry, Carl Perkins, and Little Richard." But according to Scott, it wasn't "rock or rockabilly" that he sang, just "good music" that came from the "heart."[23]

At his own expense, he recorded an acetate demo of a couple of his songs and took them to a distributor. That in turn led to an audition with Bob Swartz, the Detroit rep for ABC-Paramount Records, who signed him to a recording contract.[24] Although missing the national charts, his first release, "Baby, She's Gone," with its rockabilly shuffle beat, scored high in Detroit, reaching number 11 on WJBK radio's *Hit Tunes Survey* in late May 1957. In April, Jack had performed the song onstage as part of Mickey Shorr's "Rock 'n' Rollorama Easter Edition" at the Broadway Capitol Theater. "My baby, she's gone and I don't know what to do—*what to do—what to do* . . ." Scott had pleaded to the audience. A follow-up called "Two-Timin' Woman" was somewhat less successful. Jack's backing band included Stan Getz on stand-up bass, David Rohiller on lead guitar, and Dominic Scafone on drums.

Scott's producer at ABC was Joe Carlton, and when Carlton left to form his own label in 1958, he bought out the singer's contract. Carlton decided to record two songs that Jack had been working on prior to his ABC-Paramount releases. The A-side was set to be "Greaseball," a fast rockabilly number Jack had written about a friend who keeps getting thrown in jail. A ballad was planned for the flip side. Besides Jack and Stan Getz, other musicians at the session at United Sound Systems were Al Allen on guitar and George Katsakis on saxophone. Impressed with the back-up vocals on Elvis Presley's records, done by the Jordanaires, Scott contacted a Windsor-based quartet known as the Chantones. "We were playing the Metropole Supper Club in Windsor when Jack called and invited us over to talk about recording together," recalls Jack Grenier, the group's lead singer. The other members included bass singer Roy Lesperance, tenor Larry Desjarlais, and baritone Jim Nantais. "We practiced in Jack's basement for quite a while before heading to the studio, and then we did quite a few takes," Grenier recalls.[25] Katsakis says the songs were recorded live, without overdubs: "Jack was at one mike, his group the Chantones were singing at another, and we were playing, all at the same time. That's just how they did it back then."[26]

At the session, a second version of "Greaseball" was recorded, with what was deemed to be the less offensive title, "LeRoy," and was released in May 1958. Despite fairly steady sales, Juggy Gales, the head promotion man for Carlton, had second thoughts, and after about three weeks, decided to ask all the deejays to flip the record over and start playing the B-side, titled "My True Love."[27] The intense slow-moving ballad showcased Jack's deep baritone and the strong backing from the Chantones. It raced quickly up the national charts, cresting at number 3 in July. In total, the record spent fifteen weeks in the Top 40, and earned Jack a gold record for sales of over a million copies. At the same time, "LeRoy" became a moderate hit, reaching number 25 on the national charts.

In August 1958, Jack went on the road for a grueling Dick Clark tour set up by the Gale Agency. He shared a bus with artists such as Jimmy Clanton ("Just A Dream"), Dale Hawkins ("Suzie Q"), Jody Reynolds ("Endless Sleep"), and Duane Eddy ("Rebel Rouser"), along with their backing musicians. Dale Hawkins recalled that "on the bus they had the acts lined up ready to perform," and it was only after the third night out that they got to "go into a hotel to sleep."[28]

In October, Carlton released the number 28 ballad hit, "With Your Love." In January 1959, Scott was back in the national top 10 with the gently rocking "Good-bye Baby," which peaked at number 8. His next release, the number 35 charting "The Way I Walk," had a honky-tonk beat and was loaded with attitude, fitting the somewhat tough, brooding image that Scott projected in photos, and through his rather stoic stage presence. "The Way I walk is . . . the way I walk." One writer commented, "Jack Scott sounded tough, like somebody you wouldn't want to meet in a dark alley unless he had a guitar in his hands."[29] A fan recalled hitchhiking across town to see Scott: "We went to see Jack, not because he was going to sing but because we had heard that he was going to fight some guy and we didn't want to miss that!"[30] Despite his somewhat intimidating image, when not on the road, Jack lived at home with his mom and dad.

On a 1959 "Cavalcade of Stars" tour, Jack appeared along with teenage favorites Bobby Rydell, Frankie Avalon, and Robin Luke. "We went and played the Hollywood Bowl in California, then a big rock show in Pittsburgh, and then we did the Michigan State Fair," the singer later recalled.[31]

His first album on Carleton was simply titled, *Jack Scott.* Jack had written ten of the album's twelve songs, including all his hits up to that point. At the time, it was highly uncommon for artists to be recording their own material, and unlike most rock 'n' roll acts, Scott used his own band and vocal backup group (the Chantones) on all sessions.[32]

George Katsakis, who played sax on Jack Scott's Carlton session for "LeRoy" and "My True Love," was a member of a band called the Paragons. The group hailed from the Detroit westside suburb of Dearborn. The other musicians included Jack Rainwater on lead guitar, Ken Anderson on saxophone, Bob Sanderson on guitar, and the twin brothers Mike and Greg Popoff, who played drums and keyboards respectively. The band had been performing one night at the Dance Ranch when Scott approached George about playing on his session. It wasn't long after that George and the Paragons would be making a record of their own.

While playing summer dances at Camp Dearborn in 1958, the band had visited the city's recreational offices upstairs at the Carman Towers Theater on Schaefer Road. There they met an usher who told them that there was a recording studio in the theater and set them up with an audition. The studio was operated by Stu Gorelick, the son of the building's owner. At the audition, the group played a song they had written called "Poor Boy." The instrumental had a catchy rhythm punctuated by Katsakis's honking saxophone. Gorelick decided to record the band in his dome-shaped studio. A local music promoter named Harry Nivins was present at the session and made some suggestions for improving the arrangement. "After the track was recorded, Gorelick really moved fast," recalls Katsakis. "He immediately left for New York to shop it around, and in just a few days he was back with a contract in hand. He had signed us to Jubilee Records. The only catch was that he had had to change our name because there was already an East Coast group called the Paragons. There had to be a name on the contract, so he decided that we would be the Royaltones. We had no say in the decision."[33]

Although guitarist Jack Rainwater chose to depart, the remaining members' unhappiness with their new name quickly faded. In just a few weeks, "Poor Boy" was being played on radio stations across the country. By November 1958, the record had reached number 17 in *Billboard*. "We just couldn't believe how fast things were happening," says Katsakis. "All of the sudden we're on Dick Clark's Saturday night show on ABC."[34] Katsakis also recalls appearing in some of the big package shows of the day. "We were doing a Thanksgiving show at the Brooklyn Paramount Theater in New York. Now at these shows you usually got to do your hit and that was about it. Well, although 'Poor Boy' was a smash, we didn't feel it was the right thing to fire up an audience, so without informing anyone we went on stage and played 'Johnny B. Goode.' The emcee was really upset."[35]

Back home in Detroit, the Royaltones were local heroes, appearing on TV shows such as Bud Davies's *Top Ten Dance Party* on channel 9. The celebratory mood soon soured. "It was the same old problem that lots of young artists had back then; we weren't getting paid. We figured Gorelick owed us something like thirty-five or forty-thousand dollars, but all we got were excuses."[36] Legal action ensued, and when the band returned to New York, expecting to discuss their future, Jubilee Records, not wishing to get involved in the dispute, opted to drop the Detroit band. "They were nice about it," says Katsakis, "but they just released us from our contract and dropped all promotion on our second release ('See-Saw' and 'Little Bo')."[37]

In early 1959, Harry Nivins had convinced Bob Sanderson to leave the Royaltones. "Bob did some singing for us, and Nivins told him he was going to make him famous as a solo act," says George Katsakis.[38] The only catch for Sanderson was that Nivins wanted to give him a flashier name, something in the mode of Conway Twitty. He decided to call his hot new pop sensation Melrose Baggy. Sanderson signed, and Nivins took his protégé into the studio in August 1959 to cut a 45 called "Beauty." Record in hand, Nivins then went to see Tom Clay about getting the new release played on Clay's top-rated seven-to-midnight show at WJBK.

After arriving in Detroit to replace Casey Kasem in November 1957, Tom Clay wowed listeners with his style and his stunts. Broadcasting from the top of a three-story-high sign at Jax Auto Car Wash at Six Mile and the Lodge Freeway, he danced to "Willie and the Hand Jive" as fans watched from below. After spinning a record he really liked, Tom was known to drop the needle back in the grooves of a catchy part of the song and play it again. On the air, he liked to refer to himself as "a guy by the name of Clay." His soft, dreamy approach when introducing ballads was popular on lovers lane.

Although WJBK had a Top 40–style survey, it was not an official playlist, and deejays "had the leeway to play a few new records" if they felt they had potential.[39] Many disc jockeys took pride in breaking a new hit record. Some, like Tom Clay, took pride as well as cash for the service. At the time, there were no laws on the books against accepting money or gifts in return for airplay. Clay was known even to have a rate card available for record promotion people.[40] He did, however, try to promote records he believed in, and saw no problem in taking a few bucks for helping what he thought was a worthy record move up the charts.[41]

Clay refused to play "Beauty," even for a two-hundred dollar payoff, saying he didn't think it was "a good record."[42] A vindictive Harry Nivins got hold of a midget tape recorder and a few days later secretly taped an incriminating conversation with Tom, sending it to WJBK. After local management showed little interest, Nivins contacted the Miami headquarters of Storer Broadcasting, WJBK's parent company.[43] By this time, the payola issue was starting to surface around the country. On November 18, 1959, the *Detroit Free Press* previewed an article by Ed McKenzie and scheduled for the November 23 issue of *Life* magazine. Titled "A Deejay's Expose," the article offered McKenzie's disdain for "formula radio," which had resulted in his departure from WXYZ earlier in the year. He described the ins and outs of payola, saying that several local deejays were on the take. McKenzie said that he had never accepted money to play records on his show because he thought it was "completely dishonest."[44]

The newspapers went on a feeding frenzy. On November 19, Jac LeGoff, Detroit's top-rated television news anchor, came to radio's defense, telling his audience that "payola in one form or another is a part of American business." Although he didn't "condone" the practice, LeGoff said "let him who is without sin cast the first stone."[45] The following day, WJBK-TV announced that LeGoff's employment had been terminated, not because of his beliefs but because he broke station policy of not editorializing on the air.[46]

A year earlier there had been similar charges about rigged television quiz shows. Now with attention turning to radio, Storer ordered an in-house investigation of all its stations. In Detroit, on November 21, 1959, Tom Clay was fired after admitting that he had accepted five thousand dollars in bribes over a two-year period. "Nobody's wrong, it's just business," said Clay at a hastily arranged news conference the morning after the firing.[47] The always dramatic deejay went on to say that his only regret was that "some of the guys and gals might think I had tried to fool them. I haven't. I have only tried to entertain them."[48] WJBK's afternoon personality Don McLeod quickly resigned with far less fanfare, saying only that his departure was the result of "a difference in principles."[49] Dale Young, the host of *Detroit Bandstand* on WJBK-TV, made a similar timely exit.

On November 26, when a story appeared in the *Detroit News* about the Royaltones' lawsuit against Harry Nivins for money that he owed them, WXYZ's Mickey Shorr found himself in the spotlight. In the story, the Royaltones' manager, Stu Gorelick, testified that 10 percent of the money had gone to "pay off a loan" from Shorr, who had loaned him money to promote the group. Gorelick went on to testify that a fifteen-hundred-dollar check sent to Shorr in January 1959 was partial repayment for that loan.[50] There was never any proof that the funds were "payola." WXYZ, worried about their upcoming license renewal, decided that Shorr was a liability and fired him. Shorr, claiming in the *Detroit News* that he was a "scapegoat," denied the charges: "I swear on my father's grave that I have never taken any payola."[51]

When their financial problems were finally settled, the members of the Royaltones wound up with, rather than forty-thousand dollars, about seven hundred bucks each.[52] Back in New York searching for a new label, the group, which had no management, passed up an opportunity to sign with Al Nevins and Don Kirshner, accepting a deal from George Goldner, who owned the End and Gone labels. "The Kirshner people wanted 20 percent, and a couple of the guys in the band thought that was too high," says Katsakis. "Goldner wanted 15 percent and offered a fifteen-hundred-dollar advance so we signed with him. In the long run I think we would have been better off with the other deal, but we went with George, who liked our song 'Short Line Hop' and released it on Gold Disc. It didn't do too well, but later on we had a pretty good hit with 'Flamingo Express' in 1961."[53]

After a brief stint in the army during late 1959, Jack Scott found himself in the middle of a dispute between Carlton, his record label, and Starfire, the company he was signed to for publishing and management. Starfire had objected when Joe Carlton wanted publishing as well as recording rights on a particular song. "Next thing I knew, they'd pulled me off Carlton," said Scott.[54] Starfire bought out Scott's contract with Carlton for fifty thousand dollars and placed the singer with a new label called Top Rank. There, he was rewarded with a huge hit right out of the gate. Jack's own composition of the mournful "What in the World's Come Over You" reached number 5 in *Billboard* in January 1960 and was certified a million seller. Scott made it back-to-back gold when the follow-up ballad "Burning Bridges" was released in April and climbed to number 3. That same year, in addition to doing the Dick Clark and Irving Feld tours, Jack's reputation was such that he went on the road headlining two of his own "Jack Scott Caravan of Stars" tours as well.[55] After his next release, "It Only Happened Yesterday," stalled at number 38, the hits began to fade. When Top Rank went out of business in 1961, Jack's contract was picked up by Capitol Records, but the singer was unable to produce any hits on that label or subsequently on RCA.

Other notable rockers on the local scene in the late fifties and early sixties included the Larados, a white doo-wop group from

Edsel Ford High School in Dearborn, founded in 1955 by Gary Banovetz. Between classes, the five members, who loved R & B, could be found practicing in the school's hallways, staircases, or bathrooms, all of which provided a much-sought-after echo effect. By 1957, the Larados were comprised of Tommy Hurst, Bernie Trumbull, Bob Broadrick, Ron Morris, and Don Davenport.[56] In 1958, they had a hit with the rousing "Bad Bad Guitar Man," written by Bernie Trumbull, who also sang the lead. It was released on the local Fox Records label that had been started by realtor George Braxton, who was also a director of *Teen Life* magazine. According to Don Davenport, Braxton was a guy who "wanted to get into the business," as well as "anything where he thought there was money."[57]

Prior to the Larados, Davenport had been the only white member of an R & B group called the Romeos. Lamont Dozier was the lead singer on their local hit "Fine, Fine Baby," also released on Fox in 1958.[58]

Sax player Danny Zella was a large and imposing figure onstage, fronting his band, Danny Zella and His Zell Rocks. Zella sang the lead vocal on "Wicked Ruby," which was also released on the Fox label, becoming a big local hit and charting nationally in the fall of 1958. The flip side was "Black Sax." As a promotional gimmick, he performed with a saxophone he'd painted black.[59] Zella shared label billing with the Larados on "You Made Me Blue," released on the Dial label in April 1959.

The Thunder Rocks were a unique instrumental band that featured two saxophones. Their recordings of "Rampage" and "Warpath," released on the band's own label, Sabre Records, received lots of local airplay. Bill Hennes, who managed the band, says they "got their distinctive sound by placing microphones directly into the saxophones."[60] The Thunder Rocks, along with the Zell Rocks, the Low Rocks, the Valiants, and the Five Invictas, were among the top bands performing at dances all over Detroit.

Johnny (Pavlik) Powers, who cut "Honey Let's Go" at Fortune and picked up a new last name from Devora Brown, had his greatest success with the regional rockabilly hit "Long Blond Hair," yet another Fox release in 1958. Due to the label's limited distribution, the single scored only in scattered markets, such as Seattle, where it reached number 3. Powers, who the following year became the last artist signed to the legendary Sun Records, recalls promoting his Detroit recordings by performing in restaurant parking lots along Eight Mile Road. "We'd set up a little stage and play—places like Luigi's, then we'd sell records right out of the trunk."[61]

Former WJBK radio personality Clark Reid recalls the era as a "gentle sunlit time. Freewheeling, friendly, funny, and fun."[62] This freewheeling atmosphere was about to give rise to a man who would take a more serious approach to the business of making hit records in the Motor City.

# 4. Motown and Other Sounds

In the spring of 1960 it seemed like everyone was turning up the radio to hear the pounding piano riffs that kicked off a huge R & B hit called "Money (That's What I Want)." Recorded by Barrett Strong, it was released locally on Tamla Records, a new Detroit label founded by a man named Berry Gordy.

There was a certain camaraderie in record and radio circles in the 1950s. On any given night, songwriters, record promotion men, and disc jockeys would gather at the Flame Show Bar at 4664 John R at Canfield. Built in 1949, the Flame was the leading "black and tan" nightclub, featuring mainly black entertainers performing for a racially mixed audience. Dinah Washington, Billie Holiday, Roy Hamilton, and Sarah Vaughan were among the national performers appearing on the club's unique stage, which had been built right into the bar. Maurice King led the seven-piece house band known as the Wolverines.[1] Berry Gordy was a hustling local songwriter who liked to hang out at the Flame, where his sisters Anna and Gwen had the photo concession downstairs. The Flame, along with the nearby Frolic Show Bar and the Chesterfield Lounge, had turned John R into a "Vegas"-like strip replacing Hastings Street and Paradise Valley. By the late fifties, that area had become run-down, home to hundreds of vacant businesses. In January 1959, bulldozers moved in, and construction began on the Chrysler Freeway, which would replace most of Hastings Street and destroy the once-vibrant neighborhood around it.[2]

The Flame was owned by businessman Morris Wasserman, and day-to-day operations were handled by Al Green, a music publisher who managed artists such as Johnny Ray and LaVern Baker, as well as Detroiters Della Reese and Jackie Wilson.

Born in Detroit in June 1934, Jackie Wilson started singing as a child, and by his teens he had formed a quartet called the Ever

Ready Gospel Singers Group, which performed in churches around town. Jackie himself was anything but religious, and he often used the money he earned from singing to purchase wine.[3] While growing up in Detroit's rough North End, Wilson had been a member of a street gang calling themselves the Shakers, and on two occasions did time at the Lansing Correctional Institute, where he learned to box. In 1950, at the age of sixteen, he dropped out of Highland Park High School to box full-time, eventually entering a Golden Gloves championship in Detroit, in which he lost.[4]

When he wasn't boxing, Wilson was singing. After King Records passed on Johnny Otis's signing recommendation in 1951, Wilson worked briefly with a local R & B quartet, the Thrillers, before recording a few tracks for Dizzy Gillespie's Detroit-based Dee Gee label under the name Sonny Wilson. He then auditioned for and won the spot Clyde McPhatter vacated when he departed Billy Ward and the Dominos. Wilson's first hit with the group was 1953's "You Can't Keep a Good Man Down." Later that year he sang lead on "Rags to Riches," which was also a pop hit for Tony Bennett. The Dominos' version hit number 2 on the R & B charts. In 1956, after a change in labels to Decca Records, Jackie sang lead on the group's first pop hit, "St. Theresa of the Roses."[5]

The following year, Wilson decided to pursue a solo career and signed a management deal with Al Green, who quickly secured a record contract with Decca's Brunswick label. On December 18, 1957, the day before the signing, Green collapsed and died in the lobby of his New York hotel. Wilson's career then fell into the hands of Green's assistant, Nat Tarnapol.[6]

Berry Gordy pitched Jackie Wilson a song originally called "She's So Fine," which he had written for the Five Jets, a local group he comanaged. His partner, Roquel "Billy" Davis, had once been a member of the group.[7] The song had never been a hit, but Gordy liked it and had made some adjustments, including a title change to "Reet Petite." Jackie Wilson recorded the track with a high-speed percolating rhythm and scored his first solo hit toward the end of 1957. The song hit number 11 on the R & B charts and number 62 pop. Gordy stayed close to Wilson, supplying even bigger national pop hits, including "To Be Loved" (number 22,

1958), "Lonely Teardrops" (number 7, 1958), "That's Why (I Love You So)" (number 13, 1959), and "I'll Be Satisfied" (number 20, 1959). The writing credits on all four songs went to the team of Berry Gordy and Tyran Carlo, a pseudonym for Berry's friend Billy Davis.

Berry Gordy Jr. was born at Detroit's Harper Hospital on November 28, 1929. His mother and father, Berry and Bertha Gordy, had moved to Detroit from Georgia in 1922, establishing a successful contracting business, and later his wife became a real estate and insurance agent. The seventh of eight siblings, Berry Jr. found plenty of competition in the high-achieving Gordy family. In his spare time he enjoyed writing songs, and even penned and performed a singing commercial for the family business, Gordy Printing.[8]

After graduating from Northeastern High School in 1948, Berry had a go at a boxing career, and then entered the army, serving in Korea from 1951 to 1953. Upon returning to civilian life, he went to work at the family print shop, hauling large rolls of paper to the printing press and doing an assortment of tasks that left him feeling miserable and dissatisfied. At night he made the rounds of hip Detroit jazz clubs, such as Baker's Keyboard Lounge and the Minor Key. In 1953, after obtaining a loan from his father, Berry opened his own record store, the 3-D Record Mart—House of Jazz. Unfortunately, he misjudged the public's interest in the music he loved, and the business failed.[9]

At twenty-four, Gordy married nineteen-year-old Thelma Coleman. She soon became pregnant with the first of three children. Gordy supported his family working on the assembly line at the Ford Lincoln-Mercury plant, where he earned $86.40 a week. That job didn't last long after he finally started having some success as a songwriter.[10]

Although Berry and his songwriting partners, his sister Gwen and his friend Roquel Davis, were having hits with Jackie Wilson, they were unhappy with the small amount of money coming in. They decided to ask Wilson's manager, Nat Tarnapol, to also give them the B-side of their A-releases for Jackie. But Tarnapol, the former tire salesman turned song plugger turned artist manager, had become a quick study in the fine art of making money in the record business, and had no intention of doing that. According to Berry Gordy, Tarnapol "would use songs written by others—usually his aunt—who would get a free ride, making the same amount of money" as the A-side writers.[11] "Jackie is a star. You need him—he doesn't need you," was Tarnapol's response.[12] When Gordy went to appeal directly to Jackie Wilson, the singer told him that although he "loved" him and his songs, he couldn't go against his manager.

In 1959 Gwen and Roquel decided to start their own label called Anna Records. Berry Gordy went his own way. He became manager for a group called the Matadors, whom he had previously met while they were auditioning for Al Green. The group's lead singer and principal songwriter was William "Smokey" Robinson. Born in Detroit on February 19, 1940, Robinson was raised by his sister Gerry after his mother died when he was ten. Gerry was a big jazz fan who influenced her younger brother's tastes along with the singing style of Nolan Strong. An uncle nicknamed him "Smokey Joe," in an effort to remind him that, despite being born with light skin and blue eyes, he was, indeed, black.[13]

Smokey attended Northern High School, where he and some friends soon formed a singing group called the Five Chimes, which in 1957 won the talent contest on Ed McKenzie's *Saturday Party* TV show.[14] Shortly after changing their name to the Matadors, they met up with Berry Gordy, who changed their name again, this time to the Miracles. Gordy had them cut a record that Smokey had written called "Got a Job," a clever response to the Silhouettes' big hit "Get a Job." Gordy released it through a deal with End Records out of New York. Gordy's frustrations over earnings not paid by his New York publisher pushed him to break new ground and establish his own publishing company, which he named Jobete, after his three children, Joy, Berry, and Terry. The first song he published was "I Need You," recorded by Herman Griffin and released on Carman Murphy's H.O.B. label, which was named for her popular House of Beauty salon.[15]

Both sides of the Miracles' next record, also released on End, were penned by Gordy and Robinson. The A-side, "I Cry," featured Smokey, while on the flip, "I Need Some Money," Smokey shared the lead with the group's female member, Claudette Rogers.

Ronnie White, Bobby Rogers, and Pete Moore filled out the group. After receiving a royalty check for $3.19, Berry decided he couldn't do any worse releasing a record himself.[16]

On January 12, 1959, using an eight-hundred-dollar loan from the Gordy family bank, Berry launched his own label, Tamla, and prepared for its first release, "Come To Me," by a local singer named Marv Johnson.[17] As was so often the case, the session took place at United Sound Systems. Joe Siracuse, who had engineered the John Lee Hooker sessions in 1948, was again at the controls. Gordy, unable to sit passively when he could not hear through the control room playback what he had heard in the studio moments before, convinced Siracuse to follow his instructions for making a better mix of all the voices and instruments.[18]

Gordy and pal Smokey Robinson drove fifty miles through a snowstorm to pick up the first copies of "Come to Me" from a pressing plant in Owosso.[19] Then they rushed promotional copies to Detroit's two R & B stations, WJLB and WCHB, where the dee-jays quickly put the new record on the air, and in no time Berry Gordy had a solid local hit in the black market. When Tom Clay played it on WJBK, it became a hit with the white audience, too. After splitting profits with distributors, though, Gordy found himself unable to take the record to the next level of promotion. But through the grapevine, he learned that United Artists was interested in distributing the record nationally. Larry Dixon, the velvet-voiced afternoon deejay at WCHB, placed a call to his friend at the label, Norm Ruben, and was able to arrange for them to pay for Gordy's airplane ticket to New York. Dixon recalls, "They really liked Marv and the song, and instead of just agreeing to distribute the record, they bought Marv's contract, and Berry Gordy came back to Detroit with twenty-five thousand dollars."[20]

In April 1959 "Come to Me," released on UA's Unart label, reached number 30 on the national charts. Later that year, Johnson's "You've Got What It Takes" made the top 10, as did its follow-up, "I Love the Way You Love." Berry used the earnings to put out another song by the Miracles called "Bad Girl." Again unable to afford a national release, he wound up leasing the tracks to Chess Records in Chicago. In the meantime, the Satintones became the first group actually signed to the Tamla label, releasing "The

Motor City" (with "Going to the Hop" on the flip side) in the spring of 1959. However, it was not destined to be the label's breakthrough recording.

Meanwhile, Gordy launched a second label he named Motown. Now divorced from Thelma, and remarried, he and his second wife, Raynoma, left their apartment at 1719 Gladstone Street and moved into a two-story house at 2648 West Grand Boulevard. The family's living quarters were upstairs. On the first floor Gordy built a control room and lobby and transformed the garage into a recording studio. The basement would soon house the engineering department. Barrett Strong was a local pianist and singer who had met Berry Gordy two years previously. Using a Volkswagen bus and help from Strong, Gordy hauled recording equipment from WJLB deejay Bristoe Bryant's little studio and set it up in the new building.[21]

One July afternoon, as Strong was working on a song, he overheard Berry Gordy playing piano and talking with receptionist Janie Bradford in the studio, and went to join them. After sitting down at the piano next to Gordy, Strong started to play a repetitive lick. He recalled, "I was playing that piano lick and Mr. Gordy said, 'What's that?' I said, 'I don't know.'"[22] Strong then started to sing the lyrics that Gordy and Bradford had been composing, and the result was "Money (That's What I Want)." The first recording session at 2648 West Grand Blvd. got under way, lasting for several days. Impressed by his improvised singing, Gordy chose Barrett Strong to record the vocal. Joe Hunter played the signature piano part, while engineer Brian Holland beat on the inside of a tambourine and drummer Benny Benjamin provided a tom-tom beat. Background vocals were done by Gordy's Raybear Voices.[23]

At the conclusion of the session, Berry Gordy grabbed the seven-and-a-half-inch tape of the song and raced over to see Larry Dixon at WCHB. When Dixon played the piano-driven song on the air, the phones lit up. Soon, the March 1960 release on the Tamla label was selling in the Detroit, Cleveland, Cincinnati, Baltimore, and Washington, D.C., areas, where Berry was shipping directly to distributors. Again pressed for funds, he then placed the record with his sister Gwen and Roquel Davis's label, Anna Records, which had national distribution through Chess. "Money (That's What I

Want)" went on to become another national hit for Berry Gordy, and the foundation of a new Detroit record company.[24]

Berry Gordy wasn't the only name on the list of movers and shakers in the music business in Detroit. There was also the team of Harry Balk and Irv Micahnik, two white businessmen who owned EmBee Productions. Although operating with far less fanfare, they actually preceded Berry Gordy by roughly six months or so in owning their own publishing company (Vicki Music), management company (Artists Inc.), and record label (Twirl).[25]

Harry Balk had owned movie theaters in black neighborhoods in Detroit, where he would show exploitation films such as *Reefer Madness*. To pick up business on slow nights, Balk hired promoter Homer Jones to produce amateur shows. When Little Willie John kept winning the talent show, Balk decided there might be some money to be made in music. "Kid, I'm gonna make you a star, just sign with me," he said to the fifteen-year-old singer.[26]

Little Willie John was born William Edgar John on November 15, 1937, and moved to Detroit shortly after his birth. The John family, including sister Mabel, performed in a gospel quartet known as the United Four.

In June 1955, Harry managed to get Little Willie John a recording contract with Syd Nathan's King Records. The label's management was already familiar with the singer by way of Johnny Otis's earlier recommendation. John's first release that year was "All Around the World," followed by the R & B smash "Fever" in 1956 and "Talk to Me" in 1958. According to Balk, managing the young singer—who liked to carry a gun—wasn't easy: "Willie was kind of a problem child on the road, always shooting up the hotel rooms."[27] After too many problems, Balk cut John loose despite three years remaining on his six-year contract.

Harry Balk also managed Kenny Martin, another Detroiter who recorded sides for King/Federal. Martin had a top 20 hit on the R & B charts in late 1958 with the pleading ballad "I'm Sorry."

During some of the sessions at King, Harry Balk had become interested in the recording process, and in a later interview recalled how he was able to make some suggestions to the engineer: "Why don't you use the sax here . . ." Back in Detroit he gained experience doing some sessions at Fortune Records, where, knowing "nothing about faders," he had directed the drummer on one early session to "keep hitting harder." The musician put a hole through the snare drum.[28]

Around 1958, Balk joined in a partnership with Irving Micahnik, a former furrier (Irv's Furs) with no musical background. The two formed a booking and management company called Artists Inc. While Harry focused on the talent, Irv kept track of the money. Described as "cool and upbeat, with a porkpie hat cocked on the back of his head and an ever-present long, thin cigar in his mouth," Balk fit the image of a "boppin'" fifties record man. Micahnik, on the other hand, came across to young artists like a "mean truant officer."[29]

Down the road in Toledo, the Orbits were a popular instrumental band at sock hops and local dances. They traveled to Detroit to be interviewed by Balk and Micahnik at their offices at 20 Alexandrine, just west of Woodward. The two men signed them to a long-term contract and renamed them Johnny and the Hurricanes. Johnny Paris's wailing saxophone over a rocking organ beat gave the group its trademark sound. For sixty dollars, Harry and Irv produced the group's first record, "Crossfire," in Stuart Gorelick's small studio inside the Carman Towers Theater. They took the track to New York in hopes of finding a buyer who "would pay them for the master and release the record." They found no takers. On the return trip they decided that they had nothing to lose in putting it out themselves. They pressed a thousand copies and then released the record on their own Twirl label. According to Balk, after the record took off, Warwick Records, Morty Craft's new label out of New York, leased it, and "Crossfire" became a national hit, reaching number 23 on the *Billboard* chart in June 1959. Balk and Micahnik then formed EmBee Productions.[30]

In no time, Balk had the group in the Bell Sound studios in New York to record a follow-up. During a break in the session, Balk heard the organ player fiddling around with a note. Harry called out to the musician, "Do it again, play that again." The notes came together and formed "Red River Rock," a revved up version of the western song "Red River Valley." Balk and Micahnik leased the master directly to Warwick, and it became a smash, going to number 5 in *Billboard* and making Johnny and the Hurricanes one of the best-known instrumental bands of the era.[31]

On the financial side, Balk and Micahnik took writing credits on "Red River Rock" as T. King and I. Mack. They continued to do so on other hits by Johnny and the Hurricanes culled from the public domain, such as "Reveille Rock" and "Beatnik Fly." According to Balk, musicians were receiving a 6 percent royalty rate on sales of their records.[32] At the same time, Johnny and the Hurricanes were paying 15 percent to their New York booking agent and 20 percent to Harry and Irv. In addition, hotel, transportation, and other expenses were deducted from their earnings.[33] There were some EmBee artists who complained about unfair contracts, low percentages, and missed royalty payments. Harry Balk says that many times he and Irv had their own problems when trying to collect money from distributors: "Most artists of the day were okay when they signed but after getting a hit, they want out."[34]

Balk and Micahnik's greatest success came with a singer from the Grand Rapids area named Del Shannon. Like Jack Scott, Shannon wrote most of his own material and had little in common with the typical teen idols of the times. His real name was Charles Westover, and he was born on December 30, 1934. He grew up in the western Michigan farming community of Coopersville. At fourteen he took up the guitar and started performing at local school shows. After graduating from high school in 1956, Westover was drafted into the U.S. Army, where he was able to gain performing experience playing with the Seventh Army's "Get Up and Go" program while stationed in Stuttgart, Germany.

Discharged from the service in 1958, he returned to Michigan and with his wife Shirley settled down in Battle Creek, where he worked during the day as a carpet salesman. At night, Westover was fronting a sort of country-rock band he called Charlie Johnson's Big Little Show, which played at the HiLo Club, a rather notorious Battle Creek nightspot.[35]

Westover, hoping for something better than the HiLo Club, decided on a flashier stage name and chose the last name of school friend, Mark Shannon, and a first name inspired by his boss's car, a Cadillac Coupe de Ville. The result: Del Shannon.

According to fellow band member Max Crook, the HiLo was "a rough club," especially on weekends, and the patrons would sometimes "tear the place apart, throwing bottles at each other, fist-fighting, and hurling each other over poor unsuspecting tables." Built long and narrow with booths on each side, under a dome-shaped ceiling, the stage was just six inches off the floor, so when a fight broke out, the band would make a hasty retreat.[36]

Crook and Shannon formed a partnership, writing and recording demos that Crook would audition for his music business friend Ollie McLaughlin, a black disc jockey at WHRV in Ann Arbor, whose *Ollie's Caravan* had been a nightly fixture on the station since 1952. McLaughlin took a tape he had recorded at the HiLo club and brought it to Balk and Micahnik in Detroit. Not only did they like Del Shannon, but Harry was intrigued by the sound Crook made on a high-pitched instrument he had created called a "Musitron," a custom-built, three-octave single-note-playing keyboard with a slide control.[37] Harry signed them both to contracts, and Del was flown to New York for a recording session. Unhappy with the outcome, Balk sent the singer back home to "write something a little more up tempo."

Back at the club a couple of months later, Crook caught Shannon's attention when he played an interesting chord change going between an A minor and a G. Shannon told him that he had "never heard such a great change."[38] The two kept playing around with the chords, with Shannon humming a melody and Max creating a bridge. The next day at the carpet store, Del wrote the lyrics to a song he first called "Little Runaway." Just before recording a demo of the song at the club, Shannon instructed Crook to do an instrumental break with his soaring "Musitron." After recording the song, they recorded other new demos on the same tape, inadvertently covering up all but a small portion of "Runaway." When Balk listened to the tape, he found none of the songs particularly compelling. Later, after noting their mistake, Shannon and Crook rerecorded "Runaway." Finally hearing the complete version, an excited Harry Balk quickly booked time at his studio of choice, Bell Sound in New York. This time Crook went along and wired his "Musitron" to a piano. Upon hearing the playback, some of the session musicians were coming to the control booth saying, "Oh man, I'll give you $15,000 for a piece of the thing." Harry just smiled and said, "No thanks, I don't need any more partners."[39]

Upon returning to Detroit, Balk again listened to the tape and decided that Shannon was "singing too flat." The same thing happened at a second session. With help from the studio owner, they were able to speed up the vocal part and get Del on key.[40] "Runaway" was finally released through an agreement with New York's Big Top Records in March 1961. According to Harry Balk, the record "broke everywhere, just exploded on the charts," going all the way to number 1 in *Billboard* and staying there for four weeks.[41]

Shannon's June follow-up, "Hats Off To Larry," reached number 5. "So Long Baby" and "Hey! Little Girl" also made the Top 40 during 1961. Although all were released on Big Top, Balk and Micahnik retained rights to the masters, becoming the first successful independent producers in rock. "Irv Micahnik was a genius at making deals," says Harry Balk. "He put this system together before anyone else."[42] After a certain period of time, the deal with Big Top returned the ownership of the masters and 100 percent of the publishing to EmBee Productions. According to Harry, the duo never tried to grow their Twirl label beyond the local market, simply because "it was too hard to do," and their system of leasing local hits to Big Top for national distribution was so successful.[43]

Harry and Irv kept busy in 1962 producing and releasing more local hits on Twirl. Harry discovered a pair of singing housepainters from Detroit named Roland Trone and Claude Johnson. Billed as Don and Juan, their recording of "What's Your Name," released nationally on Big Top in February 1962, went to number 7 on *Billboard's* Hot 100. "Casanova Brown," a great dance record by three Detroit area high school girls known as the Young Sisters, was released in September. The same girls sang backup on Del Shannon's number 12 hit, "Little Town Flirt," at the start of 1963. The Dynamics were yet another EmBee act from the Motor City who hit the charts that year with the cool and slinky "Misery," which went top 10 locally and reached number 44 on the national charts. Detroit deejays flipped the record over, and the infectious "I'm the Man" also became popular. The musicians playing backup on most EmBee Productions were the Royaltones. By then the band's lineup had changed dramatically. Saxophonist George

Katsakis was now playing with guitarist Dennis Coffey, bassist Bob Babbitt, drummer Marcus Terry, and singer Dave Sandy. According to Harry Balk, EmBee had no special method for finding talent: "Groups just showed up at our offices to audition. All we had to do was listen."[44]

Meanwhile, things had continued to hum over at 2648 West Grand Boulevard, the address of Hitsville USA. The Miracles' recording of "Shop Around" had gone to number 2 in *Billboard* in December 1960, becoming Motown's first million-seller. The Marvelettes had the distinction of scoring the label's first number 1 national hit, and second million-seller in October 1961, with the bouncy "Please Mr. Postman."

By applying methods learned from his days on the assembly line, Berry Gordy produced a steady stream of hits into 1962, hits such as "Playboy" by the Marvelettes, "You've Really Got a Hold on Me" by the Miracles, and "Do You Love Me," written by Gordy and performed by the Contours. There was also a trio of sexy songs that year written and produced by Smokey Robinson and performed by Mary Wells: "The One Who Really Loves You," "You Beat Me to the Punch," and "Two Lovers." All three reached the national top 10 and made Mary Wells Motown's first female star.

In the shadow of such towering success, tiny Fortune records managed to reclaim some chart space with two hard-rocking singles in 1962. The first, "Village of Love" by Nathaniel Mayer and the Fabulous Twilights, came blasting out of Detroit radio speakers in May. Detroit-born Mayer had grown up in a musical family, and by the time he was sixteen, in 1959, he was performing at a "Frantic" Ernie Durham record hop at the Graystone Ballroom.[45] It wasn't long before he cut his first side for Fortune, "My Last Dance With You." In 1962 he recorded his own composition, "Village of Love." It was the rawest of recordings and an instant Detroit classic. As Mayer shouted, screamed, and wailed, "The Village of Love" didn't sound like a very romantic place. Jay Johnson, bass singer for the Diablos since late 1956, was featured at the very beginning of the recording, delivering the deep-voiced invitation: "Why don't you come," which overlapped with the chorus, "Come to the village of love." Johnson's deep bass was again featured on the fadeout at the end of the song. While the other singers and instruments began to get softer, Johnson, singing "da, da-da daaa, da-da daa, da-da daaa," only seemed to get louder. Many listeners assumed the effect was the result of a bad recording technique, or possibly the singer getting too close to the microphone. According to Devora Brown, who engineered the session, neither was the case. "I liked what the bass man was doing and my instinct told me to pull up the volume at that point, so I just turned it up," Brown recalled. At first worried about the result, Brown said she was right because "people loved it."[46]

"Village of Love" was selling so fast in Detroit that the Browns decided to accept an offer to lease it to United Artists for better national distribution. The move paid off, with the record reaching number 22 in *Billboard*. As a result, Nathaniel Mayer played all the best spots in the Motor City, such as the Gay Haven on West Warren, and the 20 Grand, and then went on a national tour fronting his own revue, the high point being an appearance at New York's Apollo Theater.[47]

It was a one-two punch for Fortune when they released a new record by Nolan Strong in October. Strong, whom Devora Brown dubbed the "King of Fortune Records," had returned from a two-year hitch in the service in 1958. He had rejoined his group, now billed as Nolan Strong and the Diablos, but had been unable to score a hit. Brown claimed that while he was in the army, Strong had started using liquor and pills: "We didn't have it easy with him. He was sweet and nice, but he had his problems. Sometimes he wouldn't want to record when we wanted him to, or he'd not come around at all. Or he'd come in but he wouldn't be in the best shape to sing. You either had to go along with him or get rid of him."[48]

Devora Brown, who had real affection as well as respect for the singer, had no intention of sending him off. In 1962 she penned a song expressly for Nolan. Although only his name appeared on the label, the Diablos backed him up. "Mind Over Matter (I'm Going to Make You Mine)" was an irresistible midtempo dance record full of sudden stops, starts, and vocal acrobatics, as Nolan sang about putting a "hex" on a girl to win her love. The tough, raw guitar licks that seemed to dual with Nolan's vocal throughout the song were laid down by a white rock musician named Chuck Chittenden (Diablos' guitarist Bob Edwards had left to play jazz in New York).

"Mind Over Matter" shot to number 1 on the Detroit charts. Sheldon Brown, son of the label's owners, remembers that Berry Gordy was not pleased with Fortune suddenly having a number 1 record in his backyard: "Berry Gordy thought it was such a great record that he took the guys who later became the Temptations and they recorded 'Mind Over Matter' as the Pirates. Gordy tried to stop our version, but his wasn't nearly as good, and ours became the big hit."[49] Devora Brown was so confident about the release that she bought Nolan six hundred dollars' worth of clothes for a big appearance with WXYZ's Lee Alan, at his popular Walled Lake Casino record hop. Strong failed to show up for the heavily promoted appearance. Brown was upset but couldn't stay angry with the singer: "He always apologized. He'd look at me with those big eyes and say, 'I won't do it again.' It wasn't that he was so irresponsible, it was because of his drinking."[50] Despite Devora Brown's behind-the-scenes experiences, Nolan's problems did not seem to interfere with his performance once on stage. Jay Johnson only recalled Strong as a "true leader and a true person in what he believed in."[51]

As "Mind Over Matter" continued to sell locally, the Browns thought about the money they had been forced to split with United Artists on "Village of Love." This time they opted to try and take "Mind Over Matter" national themselves. Though it was a nearly perfect commercial recording, the Browns were only able to make it a hit in a few scattered markets such as Buffalo and Indianapolis. Although it reached number 82 in *Cashbox,* it failed to make the Hot 100 chart in *Billboard.*

There were always stories that an airtight contract kept Nolan Strong from moving to a bigger label. But Sheldon Brown says that "whenever Strong's contract lapsed, he would just sign up again. He felt it was home, and he didn't care to leave."[52] According to Devora Brown, Nolan had called her one day from Berry Gordy's office, where the Motown chief had offered him a thousand dollars to sign. Nolan had refused it, asking Brown to "come and take me home." Mrs. Brown said that Strong had even written her a note saying, "I'm going to stay with you forever."[53]

In addition to Fortune Records, there were other minuscule record labels in Detroit hoping to have hits. The LuPine and Flick labels were owned by Robert West, a black businessman who preceded Berry Gordy in record label ownership. In 1956 West launched his first label, Silhouette, with R & B releases from a Detroit group he discovered, known as the Falcons. (Surprisingly, the label also released two 45s by the Vo-Cals, a popular local white middle-of-the-road trio, one of whose members was guitarist and vocalist Howard Carson, father of the author of this book.) The Falcons' original lineup changed in 1957, with Joe Stubbs and Mack Rice joining established members Eddie Floyd (West's nephew) and Willie Schofield. The group's guitarist was Lance Finnie. The Falcons' blend of strong, gospel-influenced harmonies produced the hit single "You're So Fine," recorded in Bristoe Bryant's basement studio. Released locally on Flick in 1959, the record rose nationally to number 2 on the R & B charts and number 17 pop after being leased to United Artists. Stubbs also sang lead on "Just for Your Love" and "The Teacher," both of which made the R & B top 30 lists in 1959 and 1960 respectively.[54] In 1961, Stubbs departed, replaced by Wilson Pickett, who had been performing for four years with a Detroit gospel group known as the Violinaires. Pickett led the Falcons on 1962's soulful "I Found A Love," which went to number 6 R & B and number 75 pop. He didn't stay long before moving to a solo career on Atlantic Records. When the Falcons disbanded in 1963, Robert West, who owned the name, bestowed it on another of his groups, the Royal Playboys, who recorded and performed as the Falcons for a few more years.[55]

Chex Records, owned by producer Willie Ewing, was around for only a couple of years, and their one claim to fame was the 1962 recording of "I Love You," by yet another group of Detroit doo-woppers from Central High, the Volumes. Ed Union was the great lead singer on the record, although the performance by bass vocalist Ernest Newsom on the opening is also memorable: "Bum-ba-bum-bum-bum, bum-bum-bum-bum-bum, ba-bum-bum-bum, bum-bum da-daaa . . ." When the whole group falls in and Union in a high-pitched wail sings, "I—I—I Love You ooh ooh ooh ooh," it's R & B magic.[56]

After hitting the local top 5, Ewing worked out a deal for national distribution through the Jay-Gee Record Company. The arrangement kept the recording on the Chex label, where it climbed to number 22 on the *Billboard* charts in June. Although Ewing was unable to produce a successful follow-up, the Volumes managed to get back in the local top 10 in the spring of 1964, reaching number 8 with the similar-sounding but equally satisfying "Gotta Give Her Love," produced by Barney "Duke" Browner at United Sound. The backing musicians were the Royaltones. Released on American Arts, it missed the national charts.[57]

Karen Records was owned by Ann Arbor–based Ollie McLaughlin, the man who had brought Del Shannon to Harry Balk and Irv Micahnik. In 1962, McLaughlin decided to manage and produce his next talent find. Her name was Barbara Lewis, a small-town teenage girl from Salem, Michigan, just outside metro Detroit. She went to South Lyon High School and had been writing songs since the age of nine. Lewis not only wrote and sang but played guitar, harmonica, and keyboards, among other instruments. Ollie, always on the lookout for songs, found out about Barbara through a band leader friend of her father.[58]

McLaughlin saw potential in a peppy, upbeat tune Lewis called "My Heart Went Do Dat Da." Despite ties to Detroit, he booked a session at the Chess Studios in Chicago. "Because this was all new to me, Ollie took me to the studio a day earlier so I could get a feel for it," recalls Lewis. "Etta James was recording that day, and after hearing her I told him, 'I don't think I can do this!'"[59] McLaughlin encouraged Lewis, and the next day they cut her first single. He wasted no time in promoting the record to "Frantic" Ernie Durham of R & B station WJLB. "Ernie liked the record but told Ollie that they 'didn't play crossovers on JLB,' meaning he didn't think I sounded black," says Lewis. "Ollie told him, 'Ernie, she *is* black!'"[60]

McLaughlin drove Lewis to various record hops around the

Motor City to promote "Do Dat Da" and placed her with a mini-revue of up-and-coming Detroit artists. The lineup included the Spinners and Walter Jackson, both of whom recorded for Harvey Fuqua's Tri-Phi label, as well as Marvin Gaye, who had recently signed to Motown and was promoting his first Tamla release, a soulful version of "Mr. Sandman." "We played at a hop at Light Guard Armory on Eight Mile Road with Joel Sebastian. Then we did the Graystone Ballroom with Larry Dixon and of course 'Frantic Ernie's' show in the Gold Room at the 20 Grand. It went fast; you just got up there and pantomimed the record you were plugging," says Lewis.[61]

While Lewis performed her song at the 20 Grand that night, the crowd booed and threw pennies. "I was so naive, I didn't know what to think. I thought, 'Maybe they're showing that they like me,'" laughs Lewis. "Then Ollie comes up after and says, 'Barbara, you're such a trooper, the way you just kept going on, with all that booing!' That's when I found out what was really happening."[62] Despite the response of the crowd that night, "My Heart Went Do Dat Da" received considerable airplay on R & B and Top 40 stations in Detroit, becoming a mild regional hit in the spring.

For a follow-up, McLaughlin chose another song Barbara had written, called "Hello Stranger." Softly propelled by an organ and the chorus chanting, "Shoo Bop Shoo Bop my baby . . ." Lewis delivered a smooth, warm, achingly beautiful lead vocal. McLaughlin was so pleased with the outcome that he flew to New York and pitched the recording directly to Atlantic Records, the biggest independent label in the country. After taking the record, Atlantic then held it back for almost a year, deciding that "it was too different." According to Lewis, it wasn't until a competing label had a hit with "Our Day Will Come," by Ruby and the Romantics, that Atlantic decided to release her record.

A few weeks later, Lewis recalls being home one evening when the phone rang: "A friend called and said that 'Hello Stranger' was being played on the radio in a contest to pick the best new song of the week, or something like that. We all jumped in the car and drove into Detroit so we could call and vote without the long distance charges. By the time we got to some phones, the contest was over and my record had won."[63]

Winning the radio contest was just the beginning, as "Hello Stranger" quickly landed on the *Billboard* charts, going all the way to number 1 R & B and number 3 pop in April 1963. These were heady times for a young girl from a rural area on the far outskirts of Detroit. "Ollie McLaughlin took me first class all the way," says Lewis. "Ollie gave me the same treatment the artists were getting over at Motown. He put me through finishing school and had designer gowns made for me."[64]

One day, while "Hello Stranger" was at the top of the charts, Lewis went to the House of Beauty to get her hair done. In the chair next to her was Diana Ross, who sang with a struggling Motown group called the Supremes. Lewis recalls Ross leaning over and saying to her: "I sure wish we could get a hit record like you."[65]

In 1962, Jamie Coe and the Gigolos were about the most popular rock-oriented performing band in Detroit. Back in June 1959, Jamie, and his first band, then known as Georgie Cole and the Marquees, had been given the opportunity to perform one song at the "Cavalcade of Stars" show at the Michigan State Fairgrounds Coliseum.[66] Cole's real name was George Colovas, and he had attended Fordson High School in Dearborn. Although lacking a record contract, the singer had a burning ambition as well as the looks and talent to make himself believe he could be a star: "We got out there and I did a killer version of the Little Richard song 'Miss Ann,' and we just tore the place apart."[67] His manager at the time, Marilyn Bond, concurs, saying that "fifty thousand people rushed the stage" during his performance.[68]

Headliner Bobby Darin was duly impressed by the Detroit singer and the crowd's reaction to him. Interested in expanding his involvement in show business beyond performing, he invited Cole and his manager to come over to his hotel after the show. As Cole was showing off some songs he had written, Darin suggested a new name, Jamie Coe. After buying out Coe's contract from Bond, Darin flew his protégé to New York, and Coe was signed to Darin's own Addison record label.[69] In a few weeks, Jamie Coe had his first national release, "Summertime Symphony," penned by

Bobby Darin. Although barely denting the charts, the record put Jamie on *American Bandstand.*

After his second Addison release failed to chart, Darin sold Coe's contract to ABC-Paramount. His first release on the new label was "Good-bye My Love, Good-bye" in June 1960. The record received some airplay in Detroit and then faded.

That same year, Coe was appearing on a regular basis at a Detroit club called the Rose Bar on Verner Highway. In need of a new backup band for Coe, the club booked a group called the Motown Gigolos. Consisting of Jack Rainwater on guitar, Dave Kovarik on sax, Dennis Kovarik on bass, Jimmy Van on keyboards, and Lynn Bruce on drums, the band's versatile style of playing complimented Coe's. Lynn Bruce recalls Roses as being popular, but not so nice: "Roses was a dive. It was one of the few rock clubs for people over twenty-one, and these types of places were at the bottom in those days. Most adults were still into Patti Page and fancier nightclubs. We were playing Chuck Berry, Fats Domino, things like 'Peepin' and Hidin'."[70]

Dave Kovarik describes Roses as a "knife and gun" club: "One night right after we had finished a tune, a guy comes in through the back door and fires six shots from a .38 caliber pistol into the ceiling, turns around and leaves. That's the kind of place Roses was."[71] Nonetheless, the club was pulling in steady crowds. "We put on a really good show," says Kovarik. "Jamie could sing anything—Sinatra style or Chuck Berry. He was also very competitive, and sometimes if the place wasn't crowded enough, Jamie would drive by the parking lots of other clubs during the breaks, to see who had the business. He'd come back and push us to do better."[72] Kovarik also says that Coe was the "most honest person" he ever worked with in the music business: "People would come up and give him tips to sing a certain song, and even if it was a buck, he would always split it with the rest of the band."[73]

After a year or so, Harry Balk and Irv Micahnik dropped into Roses one evening and asked Lynn Bruce if he would like to join Johnny and the Hurricanes. Bo Savitch, the Hurricanes' drummer, had tired of the road and the constant one-nighters and was looking for something more steady. As for Lynn Bruce, the opportunity to go out with a name band seemed exciting, so a trade was arranged.[74]

In late 1961, it seemed like Jamie Coe's luck was about to take a turn for the better. His ABC-Paramount recording of "How Low Is Low" started climbing the local charts. Coe recalls, "That record was played twice on WXYZ, and the next day they had ten thousand requests for it. They were totally taken off guard, and the label dropped the ball and the record never made it out of Detroit."[75]

When their ABC-Paramount contract expired in 1962, Jamie Coe and the Gigolos signed a management and recording deal with EmBee Productions. As a writer, Jamie penned "Tell Her," a ballad recorded by another Detroiter, Mickey Denton. In May 1963 Jamie Coe scored a local hit with "The Fool." Despite the lack of national record success, Jamie Coe and the Gigolos' popularity remained high in Detroit, where they were a big draw at nightspots such as Club Gay Haven on West Warren. Former WJBK disc jockey Marc Avery worked with Coe a number of times in the early sixties and recalls that besides their popularity in nightclubs, "The kids would be more excited about seeing Jamie and the group than a lot of national artists" appearing at his record hops.[76]

In 1964, Balk and Micahnik released Jamie Coe from his contract. According to Coe, he had auditioned for the Jackie Gleason television show and was informed that he had been chosen. A few days later, he received another call, telling him that he was no longer on. Jamie blamed his managers for losing the deal, saying that they got "greedy and demanded more money. The Gleason people said 'forget it,' and that was it."[77]

After leaving EmBee Productions, Jamie recorded and released his next record on a small local label called Enterprise. Full of swagger and sounding like "Bobby Darin meets Dion on a Detroit street," Coe delivered a knockout, up-tempo version of the standard "Close Your Eyes," sometimes referred to as "Love's Holiday." Loaded with hooks, twists, and turns, and a blistering barrage of scatting, "Close Your Eyes" was a tour de force for Jamie Coe. Unfortunately, it went nowhere on the charts. While no one could deny Jamie's talent, perhaps "Close Your Eyes" would have been better suited for a nightclub audience than for the teenagers in a changing musical landscape.

Golden World Records had come along in 1963, posing the first real challenge to Berry Gordy's Motown dominance. By mid-1964, Golden World was on its way to becoming the most professionally run record company in town. Unlike the majority of small local labels, Golden World had its own recording studios, writers, and artists.[78] Originally located at 11801 Twelfth Street, the

expanded operation moved to 3246 West Davison. It was a black-owned and -operated company, founded by Ed Wingate, who had been successful in the hotel and restaurant business before deciding to try his hand at a record company. Early on, he had stopped in to observe the Motown operation. After visiting a number of other studios around Detroit, Wingate came away feeling that they were "lacking in professionalism." He decided that his company was going to have the best studio and equipment in town. He named the company Golden World because it had "a nice ring to it."[79]

Ed Wingate was color-blind when it came to talent, and he was impressed by a white five-man neo-doo-wop group from Livonia known as the Reflections. The group had met as teenagers and started singing together while hanging out at Daily Drive-in Restaurants on the West Side. By the late fifties they were performing at record hops and on local TV. Members included lead singer Tony Micale along with John Dean, Phil Castrodale, Dan Bennie, and Ray Steinberg.[80]

In 1963, the group recorded "You Said Goodbye" for Kayco Records, a tiny Detroit label. Although failing to become a hit, it did receive some airplay. When Ed Wingate heard the Reflections' slow, soulful performance on the radio, he contacted the group and asked them to come down to Golden World's new headquarters on West Davison. There they met songwriter Fred Gorman, who had defected from Motown to join the new label. He and partner Bob Hamilton had written a song called "(Just Like) Romeo and Juliet," which they thought would be perfect for the Reflections. "We thought it was tailor-made, because it had a pop feel, as opposed to the R&B thing that we were doing," recalled Gorman.[81] Tony Micale remembers that no one in the group liked the song: "We went into an upstairs rehearsal room, and Freddie Gorman sang this song he had written. It just didn't sound like much with him just playing a little piano backup, and we just didn't care for it."[82]

Several weeks later, the group was informed that the backing band tracks had been completed, and now they needed to add their vocals. Micale remembers, "At the time, a new recording studio was being built at Golden World, so the instrumental tracks had been cut at United Sound. They asked us to record the vocals at RCA in Chicago."[83] Although happy to have a record deal, the Reflections upon arriving at the studio were still less than enthused about the song that had been chosen for their initial release: "We went over the lyrics a few times, and then the engineer played the band tracks sent over from Detroit. When we heard it through the studio monitors, we were just blown away. They were on two-track and already mixed. Some of the Motown guys were playing on it and the sound was just amazing. Besides our vocals, the only thing added at that point were some a cappella doo-doo-doots that we had come up with and hand claps."[84]

In February 1964, "(Just Like) Romeo and Juliet" broke on Dave Shafer's afternoon show over CKLW. It also benefited from the station's powerful signal, which at night covered the East Coast. Locally, the Reflections really promoted the release, lip-synching the song at record hops. They also appeared on channel 7's *Club 1270* dance party show, hosted by Joel Sebastian and Lee Alan.

On February 29 "(Just Like) Romeo and Juliet" debuted on the WKNR *Music Guide* at number 29. The following week it moved up to number 18 and then jumped all the way to number 3. By March 19, "(Just Like) Romeo and Juliet" was the number 1 record in Detroit and held the position for two weeks. Tony Micale recalls the group huddling around the latest issues of *Billboard* and *Cashbox*, tracking their record as it "traveled up the national charts," where it topped out at number 6 in May, selling over a million copies.[85]

Record sales success won the Reflections a spot with Dick Clark's

"Caravan of Stars" 1964 summer tour. "There were seventeen acts crammed into two buses traveling through twenty-seven states," recalls Micale. "The Supremes, the Crystals, Gene Pitney, Bobby Freeman, and Major Lance were some of the other acts on the bill. After the Dick Clark tour, James Brown asked us to go on the road with his revue. James just loved our record, and we had a great time watching him perform," says Micale.[86] At the conclusion of the tour the group was invited to appear at the Apollo Theater in New York. "When we knocked on the back door, a guy opened it and asked who we were. We told him, 'We're the Reflections from Detroit.' He looked puzzled and said, 'Wait here.' He went and got someone else. They were expecting a black group," says Micale. "Anyhow, when we got on stage everything was cool, and the audience really liked us a lot."[87] Although distribution problems hurt future national sales, the Reflections had other local top 10 hits such as "Shabby Little Hut" and "Poor Man's Son."

As Berry Gordy had done, Ed Wingate decided to launch a second label. He called it Ric-Tic, named for the son of partner Joanne Bratten. The first artist signed to the new imprint was Gino Washington. Like a lot of black kids growing up in Detroit, Washington had dreams of becoming a recording star. He was thirteen when he started competing in the talent shows put on by "Frantic" Ernie Durham. Gino tried hard but kept losing. "Ernie was just a great guy," recalls Washington. "When he saw how upset I was, he said, 'Come back and watch the performances, that's what gets the attention.' I did, and after that I started doing the splits, and they would call me 'Jumpin' Gino Washington."[88]

Gino's first record, "Out of This World," had been originally released on a small local label called Amon, and then on Wand. According to Washington, after Tom Gelardi of Capitol was hired to do promotion, the record went to number 4 in Detroit. Another song Washington had written earlier was "I'm a Coward." After unsuccessful releases on Correc-Tone Records and SonBert, he brought it to Ed Wingate, who decided to rerecord it and make it the first release on Ric-Tic. Under the revised title of "Gino Is a Coward," the record became a huge Detroit hit in the summer of 1964.

To promote his records, Gino ran all over town, doing as many as four record hops in one evening. He also remembers "showing up at a lot of them with Stevie Wonder and some of the other Motown acts."[89]

Although Golden World was finding some early success, Motown with its "Sound of Young America" was moving into the stratosphere of the record business. By the end of the year, the Miracles, Marvelettes, Marvin Gaye, Mary Wells, Martha and the Vandellas, and "Little Stevie Wonder" were sharing the Top 40 charts with the Supremes ("Where Did Our Love Go"), the Temptations ("The Way You Do the Things You Do"), and the Four Tops ("Baby, I Need Your Lovin'"). Berry Gordy had fostered an atmosphere of teamwork, while at the same time encouraging competition. As a result, he had brought out the best in not only the writers, producers, performers, and musicians, but also those involved in behind-the-scenes activities such as sales, marketing, and artist development. By 1964, with an estimated ten million dollars in gross sales, Motown could no longer be regarded as a "local label."[90]

# 5. The Village Is on Fire

In the spring of 1964, Billy Lee and the Rivieras, a white rock band, were bringing down the house amid a roster of Detroit R & B talent on stage at the Village. Realtor brothers Gabe and Leo Glantz managed the club, and Gabe booked the talent.[1] Located at 3929 Woodward Avenue, between Alexandrine and Selden, the venue was originally known as the Garden Theater, and later the 509 Club, before transforming into the Village at the start of 1962.[2] Although often portrayed as either a shabby, dangerous bar or a run-down coffeehouse, the truth was somewhere in between. Entering the building from Woodward Avenue, patrons passed through a long hallway that opened into a room with theater-style seating and a dance floor right in front of the stage. The place held two to three hundred people paying a $1.50 admission. No alcohol was served, but food, coffee, and soft drinks were available at a concession stand. Local blues and R & B artists performed for an audience made up of black and white high school and college students, along with anyone else who drifted in.[3]

"The Village was all about fighting for territory," says William Levise Jr. in recalling his early days as Billy Lee. "Everybody down there was always plotting how to move up on the bill, how to get your first shot as a headliner."[4]

The Rivieras' lead singer was born in the Detroit enclave of Hamtramck on February 26, 1945, later moving with his family to the northern Detroit suburb of Warren, where he grew up to be a fan of black music, sampled locally on WJLB.[5] Late at night he would tune in the huge skywave beaming in WLAC from Nashville, Tennessee, where disc jockey John R would play the newest and hottest R & B releases. After hearing the deep, gravel-voiced announcer spin "Tutti-Frutti" by Little Richard, Billy ran out to the store and bought a copy.[6] Aside from music, Levise had an empathy for black culture in general, possibly derived from time spent singing with his father in gospel churches around town. William Levise Sr. had been a singer performing professionally on Detroit radio in the mid 1940s.[7]

In high school, Billy Levise Jr. was part of a wedding and party band called Tempest. When that band broke up, he started hanging around jazz and blues clubs such as the Minor Key on Dexter, and the Tantrum on Haller near Joy and Middlebelt. Through his father, he met the Reverend James Hendrix, who owned the local gospel label Carrie Records. In 1962, Billy cut his first record there, as well as the label's first secular release, an R & B effort titled "That's the Way It's Going to Be," coupled with "Fool For You" on the flip side. The recording session took place in a garage, and according to Billy, "Nothing much happened with the record."[8]

At about the same time, Levise had started bugging Gabe Glantz to let him sing at the Village.[9] Once in, he hooked up with a black vocal group called the Peps, one of the most popular up-and-coming acts at the club. The trio was made up of former Northeastern High students Thomas Hester and Joe Harris, along with Ronnie Abner, who graduated from Miller High School. "Billy Levise was always hanging around, getting on stage whenever possible," says Abner. "Billy was a fun guy. He was the type of person you just liked being around. He had lots of ambition. One night we were doing a number, and he was nearby and we said, 'Come on, we gonna do this one together.' And that's how Billy started singing with us. It was never a real formal association."[10]

Thomas Hester, who also recorded under the name Tom Storm, recalls that the entertainment at the Village was presented vaudeville style, with something like twelve to fifteen acts appearing on stage on any given evening. "Musicians from all over the city would play," says Hester. "Everybody knew each other's styles and material, so it really didn't matter who was playing backup, it always sounded good. You'd have some of the older established performers like Nolan Strong onstage along with new artists such as Richard Street and his group the Distants. We worked with Emmanuel Laskey and David Ruffin, who was doing a solo act in those days. There was also a lot of comedy and dancing on the bill.

People would be clappin' and shoutin,' and it was always a full house at the Village."[11]

Fellow Peps member Ronnie Abner recalls that no one was getting rich playing there: "Gabe Glantz was nice—cheap but nice. On an average night I think we made enough to pay for three White Castles and a milk shake, which we split three ways. But it was great training, and it gave everyone the chance to develop a name and skills. We became known for putting on an all-around great show with choreography and comedy along with the music."[12]

Aside from shows at the Village, the Peps with Billy also performed for mainly black audiences at private parties, banquets, Moose lodges, and at the 20 Grand club. "They'd say things like, 'My you sing nice . . . and so white too,'" Levise recalled.[13] Of all their gigs together, Billy says that "singing a cappella with the Peps on the Bob-Lo boat," as it made its way down the Detroit River to the island amusement park, remains one of his "most treasured memories."[14]

Later the Peps auditioned for Thelma Records, a small label founded by Robert and Hazel Coleman, the parents of Berry Gordy's former wife. But before anything could happen, Billy stopped working with them. "There was no big reason for the split," says Tom Hester. "I think it just had to do with individual contracts and everybody wanting to do what was best for their own career."[15] Sans Billy, the trio went on to release several singles, including "Detroit, Michigan" on the D-Town label owned by singer-producer Mike Hanks. They also continued as a popular club act, appearing regularly as the Fabulous Peps at the Webwood Inn as well as the 20 Grand's Driftwood Lounge.[16]

Meanwhile, with financial help from his parents, sixteen-year-old Billy Levise decided to go for the big time. He made a solo trip to Los Angeles. The only address he carried with him was that of RCA Victor. After arriving at the record company's door without an appointment, and with not even a tape recording of himself to present, he was turned away. Unsure of what to do next, Billy spent the rest of the week in his hotel room, afraid of getting lost in L.A., and too embarrassed to go home.[17]

Once back in Detroit, he returned to the stage at the Village, where he began appearing as a solo act and soon was headlining. The star attraction at the time was Fortune Records artist Nathaniel Mayer, of "Village of Love" fame. Mayer remembered Billy as "a *baaad* dude," right from the beginning. "It was amazin' because, you know, usually when guys sing with all that soul, first thing you think, 'it's a black dude,' then you look up and there's a white dude doin' it. So all of us were shocked," he recalled.[18]

It was at the Village that Billy first connected with three young musicians calling themselves the Rivieras. "The management would bring in new bands under the guise of auditioning," says Levise. "In other words, the bands would audition while playing behind the acts. They [the owners] saved a lot of money that way."[19]

The Rivieras all grew up on Detroit's Eastside. They included guitarist Jim McCarty, bass player Earl Elliott, and drummer Johnny "Bee" Badanjek, who at just fourteen was the baby of the group. Earlier, Bee had performed as "Little Johnny" in a local television talent show. "I met Jim McCarty through my father, who had become acquainted with his dad," he recalls. "At the time, McCarty was also playing drums and just getting started on guitar. Earl Elliott lived nearby, and joined on bass and we started jamming together. We really weren't much of a band at the time. We just practiced a lot and played at parties until a guy named George Williams saw us play at the Teen Fair section at the Michigan State Fair in the summer of '63. He really liked how we sounded and asked if he could manage us."[20]

According to Jim McCarty, what the band members had in common was the "R&B thing as opposed to pop Top 40." Blues guitarist B. B. King had been McCarty's inspiration.[21] Johnny Bee attended Detroit's Pershing High, an integrated school, and he had a lot of black friends, including some with whom he played music. When their new manager took them into the Village, the three teenagers were overwhelmed by the strange, somewhat seedy, quasi beatnik, R & B environment. "It was such a great experience at the Village 'cause we were exposed to all this great Detroit talent," says Bee. "Lee Rogers would be down there, LeRoy Belcher, Nolan Strong, and Nathaniel Mayer. We'd play behind 'em, and I remember these guys tellin' me things like, 'Hit them drums hard, white boy!' They gave us a lot of encouragement."[22]

On any given night, the Village was a wild, "anything goes" scene. Bee remembers, "Oh man, I remember a real character who used to hang out there, a guy named Darryl. He'd dance around the club, goin' up and down the aisles while he was playing a Congo drum, and wearing some outrageous women's clothing. When we first saw Billy, he was singing with this black group, the Peps, and we thought he was such a great R & B singer, for a white guy!" Levise was also impressed with the Rivieras, accepting an invitation to a band practice session at Johnny's house. Billy brought along his friend Joe Kubert, who played guitar. Bee says, "After an all-afternoon jam session, Billy asked if we wanted to form a band, and we said 'Yeah, that sounds cool.'"[23] There turned out to be great chemistry between the musicians, and suddenly word was out that the Motor City had a hot new band called Billy Lee and the Rivieras. Billy's father helped them get a recording session at the Special Recordings studios on Duffield at Cass. "You Know," paired with "Won't You Dance With Me?" on the flip side, was released on Highland Records and received some local airplay.[24]

By the summer of 1964, the band's reputation won them a gig at the biggest rock venue in the Detroit area: Walled Lake Casino. Located at Thirteen Mile and Novi Roads in the western suburb of Novi, the former big band ballroom had closed its doors in 1960 and had been sitting vacant until Red and Cleo Kramer purchased it in 1962.[25] The Kramers had then hired Lee Alan, the popular evening disc jockey on WXYZ, to host record hops and originate his show from the Casino three nights a week: "This is Lee Alan *on the horn!* We're broadcasting *live* from the stage of *beautiful* Walled Lake Casino on the shores of Walled Lake in Novi, Michigan— *come on out!*"[26]

The music and crowd noise heard on the radio between songs turned out to be something teenagers found hard to resist. Along with records, major recording artists such as Chuck Berry and Roy Orbison appeared. Alan had also showcased new talent, including a memorable night when he introduced "Little Stevie Wonder." However, by the summer of 1964, following a dispute with his station, Alan and the remote broadcasts were gone.[27] Now, it was Billy Lee and the Rivieras, playing their brand of supercharged, high-energy rock 'n' roll flavored with R & B, that were bringing the kids through the door.

The band had been booked by Dave Prince, another WXYZ personality, who had continued to host dances at the Casino following the departure of Lee Alan. As they had done at the Village, Billy Lee and the Rivieras poured on a combination of hard rock and wild theatrics that quickly moved them from opening act to headliners. The band members would trade instruments while running and jumping around the stage, doing splits and flips. Out in front, Billy was driving the girls to a frenzy with James Brown–styled knee drops. "I studied James Brown shows so intently it was almost a crime," said Levise, looking back. "We'd get so hot we'd have to take our shirts off and the girls went crazy and the next thing you know you'd be opening your belt buckle and throwing all your clothes into the audience. We couldn't afford to keep doing that."[28]

Although having no hits, the band was packing the place solely on reputation. Smokey Robinson and the Miracles reportedly walked out one night after disputing the equal billing Billy and the Rivieras had been given on a card circulated to promote the show. "It got to the point that our popularity was so massive that we started drawing two and three thousand kids every night we appeared," Levise recounted a few years later.[29]

After witnessing the group's incendiary show night after night, Dave Prince suggested that they make a new audition tape. He sent over a van from WXYZ with recording equipment, and the band set up in the basement of Johnny Bee's home and recorded six songs on a two-track Walenzak tape machine. Prince then sent the tape, along with his enthusiastic recommendation, to New York producer Bob Crewe, a former Detroiter famous for producing hits for the Four Seasons. Impressed, Crewe traveled to the Motor City to check out the band as they opened for the Dave Clark Five at Cobo Hall. That night, Billy and the Rivieras were third on a three-act bill, slated to perform only a few songs. But to the surprise of the other bands, the hometown audience wouldn't let them off the stage for close to an hour and a half.[30] According to Billy Lee, Detroit was "so competitive" at the time that his band didn't realize they were "over achieving" until the night of the concert: "All they had to do was stand there and look British, which a cornstalk could do. Our show never stopped."[31]

A few days later, Dave Prince got in touch with the band members and asked them to meet with him that afternoon. According to Earl Elliott, Prince sat them down and said, "I don't know if you guys are ready for this, but I've got some pretty incredible news. Bob Crewe would like to see you in his office (in New York) along with all of your instruments and everything else, next Wednesday."[32]

Arriving by train at Grand Central Station in February 1965, the band needed five cabs to carry their instruments and clothes to a not-so-nice Upper West Side residence hotel at Seventy-first and Broadway. It was during this trip that Levise learned of Bob Crewe's dislike for his name. He felt that "Billy Lee sounded too much like a hillbilly."[33] Crewe picked up the Manhattan phone book and scanned for possibilities. His first choice was Michael Rothschild, which everyone thought was a little "unbelievable." Then his finger stopped at the entry "Ryder, Mitch." "There were five Mitch Ryders in the phone book at that time," Billy recalled. "I tried to call them all to apologize for any inconvenience. One guy hung up on me, and I never got through to any of the others."[34] As there was already a group called the Rivieras, known for their hit "California Sun," Billy's Rivieras were rechristened the Detroit Wheels.

After a slow start, Mitch Ryder and the Detroit Wheels began to pick up better gigs. Bob Crewe appointed Alan Stroh as their manager, and he made sure the band "stayed busy and earned money" by playing at Greenwich Village clubs such as the Rolling Stone and Ungano's, while waiting for the call to record. Johnny Bee recalls, "It didn't take them long to get us into some very good New York clubs such as the Metropole, Trude Heller's, Odines, and the Eighth Wonder. At the Metropole, we alternated sets with Gene Krupa, who was one of my drumming heroes. We worked with Gene for three weeks, and then we did the same sort of arrangement with Dizzy Gillespie."[35]

As to why it took so long getting into a studio, Mitch Ryder says that "Crewe had a lot going on in those days, and he just wanted us there so we'd be ready when an opening occurred."[36]

Six months had gone by when Bob Crewe was finally ready to record the Detroit band. Their first release on New Voice Records, "I Need Help," written by Crewe, utilized only Mitch and Jimmy, augmented by studio musicians. The record bombed. Their second attempt did much better, with the whole band in the studio recording a hot medley combining Chuck Willis's "C. C. Rider" and Little Richard's "Jenny Jenny." Although it was Bob Crewe's decision to record those particular songs, the concept of putting tunes together was nothing new where the band was concerned. Mitch Ryder recalled, "We had done that in our club acts. We had a lot of energy and once we started playing we didn't want to stop. And so we figured out ways to make the songs run together. It was like a little game."[37] The group recorded the medley live in the studio: "We sang and played at the same time, recorded it in stereo and mixed it on a two-track," Ryder recalled.[38] Jim McCarty played his amazing rockin' guitar lead on a Gretch Chet Atkins Country Gentleman.[39]

Johnny Bee also recalls that session: "We were recording in the Stei-Philips Studios, which were in the Hotel Victoria on Seventh Avenue at 51st Street in New York. In the middle of the session, in walk Keith Richards and Brian Jones of the Rolling Stones, checking the place out. We were all excited and trying to talk to these guys, but Crewe was in the control booth shouting at us, 'Get *back* in the studio!' You got, like, three hours to do everything back then."[40] Although Bob Crewe is credited as producer, his involvement did not go much beyond overdubbing a tambourine onto the already completed tracks and releasing the record.[41]

"Jenny Take a Ride," showcasing Ryder's impassioned vocals, McCarty's stinging guitar, and Johnny Bee's propulsive drumming, was released right after Thanksgiving in 1965. It quickly charged up to number 10 on *Billboard*'s Hot 100. In Detroit, it made number 1.

The group was performing in Macena, New York, when they received word that they had a hit record. "Up to that point we were busting our asses," says Mitch Ryder. "At the gig in Macena, we were doing like five or six forty-five minute sets a day, and making like $350 a week. A couple of weeks after 'Jenny' came out we did one fifteen-minute show for $1,000."[42] The record broke first in Philadelphia, followed by San Francisco and then Detroit. After driving back to the Motor City, Ryder recalls waking up one morning to the clock radio blaring his new record: "I'm waking up and hearing us on the radio, and I'm thinking, how foreign and strange it all sounded. I remember turning to my wife and saying, 'Wow!'"[43]

"Jenny Take a Ride" was followed into the charts by "Little Latin Lupe Lu," a number 17 hit in March 1966. Before long Mitch Ryder and the Detroit Wheels were out on a Dick Clark "Caravan of Stars" tour and making national television appearances on *American Bandstand, Where the Action Is,* and *Shindig.* The Detroit band had come a long way from the stage at the Village: "We were doing good music, exciting music, we had fans, we had fame, we were just young men and it was like a dream come true."[44]

When Billy Lee and the Rivieras moved out of the Village, a band called the Lourds moved in. Wearing pointy sharkskin boots known as "Puerto Rican roach slammers," and sporting pompadours, they played songs by Elvis, James Brown, Chuck Berry, and Little Richard, along with Dick Dale and Lonnie Mack style instrumentals. "We won a Battle of the Bands in '63 with a dangerous, guaranteed-to-scare-white-people version of 'High Heeled Sneakers,'" lead guitarist Ted Nugent told writer James Thompson, adding, "I did the guitar solo flying across the judge's table."[45]

Ted Nugent was born in Detroit on December 13, 1948. He showed an interest in playing guitar as early as age seven. When he asked his dad for an electric guitar, he was told to "earn the cash himself."[46] Ted "started selling night crawlers, washing windows, and shoveling snow" to help pay for his first Epiphone. He described the instrument as "real fat and difficult to play" with strings that were "far off the neck."[47] Ted's father, who was a drill sergeant in the United States Riding Cavalry, "brought his horse-breaking riding crop home with him and he wasn't afraid to use it."[48] When his parents insisted that he practice everyday, Ted obeyed.

In the summer of 1958, at age nine, Nugent performed in public for the first time, at a Polish Arts Festival at the State Fairgrounds. He played "boogie-woogie and honky-tonk" songs.[49] It wasn't long before he became caught up in the sounds emanating from the guitar of Chuck Berry. "It was a possession," said Nugent, recalling Berry's music. "I was possessed by the electricity, the sounds of those guitars."[50]

Nugent was barely a teenager when he and drummer Tom Noel started jamming together around 1960. Ted was now playing a white Fender Duo-Sonic with a Tortoise pick guard through a Magnavox amp.[51] The young musicians were inspired by "Walk Don't Run," the big instrumental hit that year by the Ventures. According to Ted, that record "established the quintessential Fender guitar-amp combo sound of all time."[52] Soon Nugent and his buddies were calling their new group the Royal High-Boys, after some high-collar shirts sold at Todd's Menswear in the Northland Mall. "There was a shirt back then called a 'High Boy' that all the greasers wore," recalled Nugent. "We wore them because they were cool."[53] Nugent and Noel were joined by John Finley on guitar, and they added John Drake on vocals and Pete Primm on bass, and the group evolved into the Lourds.

After the British invasion, the Lourds really got into the Rolling Stones, and Ted "studied" the technique of each member. His favorite Stones songs were their version's of "Route 66" and "The Last Time."[54] Nugent cites Dale Hawkins and Lonnie Mack as other major influences on his style.[55] Above all else though, his band had learned a lot from watching Billy Lee and the Rivieras perform: "Their tightness, R&B-soul feel and sheer energy abandon, set my benchmark for performance and musical vision forevermore."[56]

As the Lourds' local reputation grew, they were soon opening for the Supremes and the Beau Brummels at a big Cobo Hall show. "We played black music, that was our inspiration. All my musicians; we adored, we revered, James Brown, and Bo Diddley and Chuck Berry. You had to know every lyric, every bass line, you had to know all the black stuff because it was just more moving than the white shit."[57] Nugent felt honored when he received a compliment on his playing from a member of Choker Campbell's big Motown Orchestra, who were backing the Supremes at the Cobo Hall show.[58]

Although they had no record deal, the Lourds were working steadily and gaining in popularity, when midway through 1965, Ted Nugent's father announced that he was being transferred to Chicago.[59] Only sixteen, Ted had no choice but to go along. For his parents, the move presented an opportunity to wrest their son away from the Village and the rock 'n' roll world of which they did not approve. "My dad took me to the barber shop and made me get a G.I. haircut," Nugent explained. "He threatened to get rid of my guitars, but he knew it was hard on me and let it slide."[60]

# 6. On to the Hideout

The year 1964 was a time of transition. The emergence of the Beatles and other new British groups gave a definite feeling that a lingering era was beginning to pass. Besides the big dances at Notre Dame High School and Walled Lake Casino, still open prior to being destroyed in a fire, a new midsixties scene began to evolve when a new teen venue opened for business in May of that year. Known as the Hideout, the club was a radical change from the chaperoned sock hops kids had been attending for years at schools, churches, and roller rinks. At most of these functions, a disc jockey played records and gave away free merchandise. Occasionally, they brought along recording artists to lip-synch their current hits, as teachers or uniformed security guards looked on.

Dave Leone had been one of those sock hop kids, and he had become bored with the scene.[1] Born in Detroit, he grew up with a passion for rock 'n' roll, and according to his son, "He would have loved to be a lead singer in a band, but he didn't have the voice for it."[2] Leone was in college at the University of Cincinnati when his father died and left him a thousand dollars. He and high school buddy Ed "Punch" Andrews quickly put the money to use, renting out a VFW hall on Detroit's east side. Located at 20542 Harper Road, near Eight Mile in Harper Woods, it was normally the scene of wedding receptions and bingo games. Leone had an entirely different thing in mind. Each Friday night, they would hang a sign outside, and this rather plain, rectangular structure would be transformed into a cool "teen club," open only to kids sixteen and up. Instead of records, there would be live music from local bands.[3]

Surprisingly, there were not many rock bands around equal to the caliber of Billy Lee and the Rivieras or the Lourds. Most still tended to play in the style of instrumental groups such as the Ventures or Johnny and the Hurricanes. But there was one band that grabbed the attention of Leone and Andrews. They called themselves the Tremelos. "We were the first band in Birmingham to get a good singer," recalls Gary Quackenbush, who at fourteen was the Tremelos' lead guitarist and youngest member. "It was a big deal because it was all instrumentals before then. John Boyles joined our band, and it really made the difference."[4] By late 1963, the Tremelos were playing high school hops and weddings as well as fraternity parties at the University of Michigan. At one such party they met college student Punch Andrews, who hired the band to play at a New Year's Eve party at a home in Grosse Pointe. Dave Leone was also in attendance that night.[5]

Already dreaming of being big-time record moguls, the two convinced the band that they should be recording. A fan of the TV show *The Fugitive*, Dave Leone wrote a song with the same title, and then convinced the Tremelos to record it and change their name to the Fugitives.[6] Gary Quackenbush recalls that "Dave contacted Quinn Martin, the producer of the TV show, to get his permission, but Martin shut him down as far as rights and usage [of the show's name], so Dave decided to put the record out as 'A Fugitive.'"[7]

In early 1964, the band recorded the single at United Sound Systems, and Dave Leone managed to get it released on D-Town Records, which normally served as a local outlet for R & B.[8] Gary Quackenbush recalls "staying up late at night" to hear Don Zee play the record on WXYZ.[9] Although "A Fugitive" faded fast, the record did provide some publicity. The Fugitives were hired as the house band at Dave Leone's new Hideout club when it opened in May.[10]

There was no real promotion or advertising beyond a few handbills for the club, which rocked from eight to midnight each Friday night. Kids heard about the Hideout strictly by word of mouth. The first night, eighty people showed up and heard the Fugitives do an ultradirty version of "Louie, Louie," a recent smash by the Kingsmen.[11] As word of their performance spread and kids realized there were no chaperones, the building filled to its capacity, 550 persons.

The Hideout was just as nondescript inside as out. There was a ticket booth as you entered, then a bar along one wall to the right, and a small four-foot stage against the wall. The ceiling was low, and once the place filled up and the music kicked in, the Hideout felt like a basement party minus the parents upstairs. It was a wild scene, with tightly packed bodies dancing feverishly to bands playing cover versions of hits by the Rolling Stones, the Animals, and the Kinks.[12]

To promote the Fugitives, Leone decided to release a record album. Recalling his previous experience with D-Town Records, especially the low royalty rate, Dave decided to release the album on his own "Hideout" label, which became the first local record label to emerge from the new midsixties rock scene. "It was a 'thank you' live album of sorts," he recalled many years later.[13] The album's ten songs were recorded on two tracks into a portable tape machine at the home of Glenn and Gary Quackenbush. "On one track we had already recorded the songs, and then we put a crowd of kids together and recorded them making the live sounds," related Leone.[14] The night before the album went on sale, Dave gathered a bunch of the regulars and had a party, with everyone helping to put the covers together with mask tape. The record sold for three dollars. "I pressed three hundred copies of 'The Fugitives Live at Dave's Hideout' and we sold out in one night," claimed Leone.[15]

"Dave Leone was a visionary dude," says Gary Quackenbush. "He had ideas. He started the sixties rock 'n' roll scene in Detroit. Mitch Ryder really came up through the black part of the stuff and was ahead of it, and boy, weren't they just the best band, but Dave Leone should really get credit for launching the big white Detroit rock 'n' roll scene."[16]

Within a few months, Dave Leone's Hideout in Harper Woods had become a huge success. He decided to open a second location in a Knights of Columbus hall at the corner of Southfield and Thirteen Mile Roads in the northwest suburb of Southfield. Punch Andrews, just back from college, was managing the new club. The Fugitives moved to the Southfield location, and Leone hired a Grosse Pointe band called the Underdogs to replace them at the original site.[17] By late 1965, the Hideouts number one and number two were among the most popular teen destinations in town. "The kids we drew wanted to dance," recalled Punch Andrews.

"We didn't even have any tables or chairs in the place. They'd just dance for hours nonstop."[18] Andrews went on to open Hideout number three in Clawson, about four blocks north of Fourteen Mile on Main Street.

According to Gary Quackenbush, Punch Andrews was "just a different guy" from Dave Leone: "Dave was mellower, Dave was much more visionary and artistic; Punch was pretty much business."[19] In the spring of 1966, Dave Leone got the idea to sell membership cards good for one year. The cards cost one dollar, and kids flashing them at the door were allowed in first. They paid a buck for admission. Those without the card paid $1.50. The membership club soon numbered four thousand.[20]

Meanwhile, at the first Hideout, the Underdogs were proving themselves as popular as the Fugitives. Before being approached by Dave Leone about recording for Hideout Records, the Underdogs had been playing mainly at parties and church dances.[21] When they started out, it was a six-man lineup featuring Dave Whitehouse on lead vocals and bass, Chuck Schimento on lead guitar (replaced in late 1965 by Tony Roumell), Chris Lena on second lead guitar, and Steve Perrin on rhythm guitar. Jack Louisell played keyboards and Michael Morgan played drums.[22]

The Hideout had no real sound system. Instead, the Underdogs played through their own amps, until they received permission from the building's owner to run wires for speakers in the rear of the club.[23] According to founding member Chris Lena, one band would usually be booked to play the whole evening, but occasionally there would be three, for a kind of "battle of the bands" night. While there "may have been some beer consumed in the parking lot," Lena says, there was "no noticeable drug scene at the Hideout, at least in the early days": "I just remember the place always being packed, and how hot it was in there, kids sweatin' and dancin' all night."[24]

Tony Roumell recalls how "all the body heat would cause the wax to melt into a gooey film on the linoleum floor."[25] A writer in a high school paper at the time quoted one attendee as commenting that "the place is so fast and hot they should maybe change the name to 'Abdul's Sin Bin.'"[26] In the summer, Dave Leone would be forced to open the doors for fresh air. As the air came in, the music went out into the surrounding neighborhood, and residents would call the police to complain.[27]

Although starting out as the house band at Hideout number one, the Underdogs began rotating through the other locations. In the beginning they had booked their own gigs, but eventually they turned that responsibility over to Leone and Andrews, who had formed a regular booking agency. "They would have us out on minitours to towns like Traverse City, Saginaw, and Ft. Wayne, then it was back to the Hideout," recalls Chris Lena.[28] Fellow Underdog Tony Roumell says that at a time when many bands complained of dishonest management, Dave Leone was a "good guy" and a "very straight business guy": "Dave was like a big brother to us. He still lived with his mother, and he would have us and the other Hideout musicians over to his house from time to time."[29] Most of the bands playing at the Hideout clubs were getting paid fifty or seventy-five dollars per night.[30]

The Underdogs became the first group to record and release a 45 on the Hideout label. Their recording of "The Man in the Glass," produced by Leone and recorded at United Sound Systems, was released in mid-October 1965. It sold so fast that radio station WXYZ added it to their playlist as a "hot prospect." The group performed the song on channel 7's *Club 1270*, now hosted by Dave Prince.[31]

Within a few weeks, "The Man in the Glass" was a top 10 hit on WXYZ, as well as WKNR. The Underdogs became an "added attraction" to the bill opening for the Dave Clark Five at Cobo Hall on December 10, along with Terry Knight and the Pack, and another group who played often on the record hop circuit, the MC5. Neither of those groups had a hit record. Tickets for the show were priced at two dollars, three dollars, and four dollars.[32]

Having played in front of audiences of no larger than a few hundred, Chris Lena remembers being terrified when they stepped on stage before thousands of kids at the huge Cobo Hall arena: "We did just two or three songs, and I played in a daze the whole time."[33] Tony Roumell also remembers that show: "There was no sound check, so we couldn't hear each other, but there was so much screaming, it hardly mattered."[34]

Sales of "The Man in the Glass" were strong enough that Dave

Leone was able to make a deal for national distribution with Reprise records. But after finding out that the song's composer, Buzz Van Houten, had lifted the lyrics from the pledge given by members of Alcoholics Anonymous, all promotion was called off.[35]

The Underdogs also recorded the Dave Leone penned "Little Girl," and a song with a much harder edge titled "Get Down on Your Knees," a collaboration between Leone, Dave Whitehouse, Doug Brown, and a member of his band named Bob Seger.[36]

The Hideout's stable of bands also included the Birmingham-based band the Four of Us. Formed in 1965, the band displayed a more harmony-driven, folk-rock sound than the other Hideout bands at the time.[37] According to Gary Burrows, the group's leader, they had shown up at the Hideout one late afternoon to audition for Punch Andrews. As they were waiting in the parking lot with all their equipment, a member of another band drove up and yelled out: "Tell Punch we can't make it tonight," and then sped off. When Andrews arrived and was told the news, he realized what a bind he was in, and suddenly the audition turned into a first-time gig for the Four of Us.[38]

Punch continued to manage the band, booking them into the Hideout every other weekend, and into plenty of University of Michigan frat parties. For their first Hideout Records release they recorded "Gonna Be Mine," written by Dave Leone. Their second single was Gene Clark's "I'll Feel a Whole Lot Better," from the Byrds' *Turn, Turn, Turn* album. To promote the records, Punch booked the group into some unfamiliar areas: "One time we played in the sticks in front of a total greaser crowd. There were these guys there that didn't like our long hair," recalled the group's bassist, Jeff Alborell. "They threatened us and forced us to play James Brown songs, which we'd never done before. We learned real fast."[39]

Suzi Quatro was fourteen in 1964 when she started hanging out at the Hideout in Harper Woods. Dave Leone eventually gave her a job selling Cokes at the bar.[40] She was the daughter of Art Quatro, a Detroit jazz musician, and grew up in the upscale suburb of

Grosse Pointe, the second youngest of three sisters and a brother. As a child she played bongos in her father's band. Despite being trained on classical piano, her interests rapidly turned to rock 'n' roll.[41] One night after complaining to Leone about the performance of the band onstage, she and her sister Patti decided to form their own group. Dave Leone helped them obtain instruments and get started.[42]

They called themselves the Pleasure Seekers, after a recent motion picture of the same name. Patti was featured on lead guitar, and the third sister, Arlene, joined on keyboards (replacing Diane Baker). Completing the lineup were the Ball sisters, Nancy on drums and Mary-Lou on rhythm guitar. "All the girls had chosen their instruments and the bass was left over, so it came to me," recalled Suzi, who played her father's 1957 Fender Precision, "the best bass of its time."[43]

At first, looked on as a novelty, the Pleasure Seekers soon proved they could hold their own on the bandstand. They developed a tough sound that made the Shangri-las sound like the Lennon Sisters, in comparison. One night when they were playing on the floor of a gymnasium at a high school dance, "Someone yelled out that they couldn't see me," says Suzi Quatro. "So they put me on top of a table and I sang 'Do You Love Me.' The audience was going nuts, so I just screamed 'Whew!' Everyone was going nuts. I thought: 'I'll keep that in the show!' I guess it was my primal scream."[44]

By 1966, the band recorded the Dave Leone–written and -produced "Never Thought You'd Leave Me," an up-tempo, electric-piano-driven number that received some local airplay. The flip side, also written by Leone, was a wild tribute to underage drinking titled "What a Way to Die."[45] The Pleasure Seekers' reputation, however, was being made mainly through their live performances. Their notoriety as a kick-ass, all-girl rock band eventually landed them a gig on a USO tour of Vietnam.[46]

# 7. So You Wanna Be a Rock 'n' Roll Star?

Venues similar to the popular Hideout were soon popping up all over the Detroit metropolitan area. The Chatterbox, with locations in Warren and Allen Park; the Hullabaloo clubs in Dearborn and Roseville; the Pumpkin in Wayne; the Drumbeat in Dearborn; and the Crow's Nest with locations at John R and Gardenia in Madison Heights and at Joy Road near Middlebelt in Dearborn were among the most popular.

While the Hideout was limited to one stage, the cavern-styled Crow's Nest had two and was able to keep the live music going non-stop. There were also two rooms at the Crow's Nest, one for dancing, and one for eating and hanging out.[1] To the south in Monroe, kids lined up to get into a place called the Club. In Clarkston, kids flocked to the Platter Box. Each of these dance clubs varied in size and clientele, some, like the Hideout, appealing to the white Levis and madras shirt crowd, while others drew the "greasers," who favored pegged pants and Spanish boots with Cuban heels. All the clubs featured undersized dance floors and very loud bands.

As new clubs opened, there was a growing demand for more live entertainment, and with the popularity of the new British bands, kids were purchasing guitars and drum sets in record numbers. Soon bands were forming in basements and garages all over the Motor City. The Human Equations, the Ruins, the Warlocks, the Henchmen, the Wha?, the Gang, the Fallen Angels, the Opposing Forces, the Yorkshires, and the Rainy Days were just a few.

Some forty miles to the west of Detroit lay the college town of Ann Arbor, far enough away to have its own identity, yet close enough to bond with the emerging Detroit rock scene. Favorite hangouts there included Mother's, the Mump, and the Fifth Dimension. Hugh Henry Holland, who went by the nickname "Jeep," was a young entrepreneur who had been a National Merit Scholar at the University of Michigan before dropping out to pursue the life of a bohemian. For a time he managed the city's popular Discount Records store and several local bands.[2] Like Dave Leone, Holland had also formed his own record label to promote the bands he managed. He named the label A-Square, the algebraic expression used for Ann Arbor. Holland felt that having a record out made it easier for his bands to get bookings. He operated out of a one-bedroom apartment at 521 North Division that was cluttered with stacks of records, tapes, magazines, soda pop cans and other debris. A steady stream of visitors were always waiting to talk to Holland when he would occasionally put down the telephone.[3]

Holland's first shot at managing a rock band came by way of an Ann Arbor–based group known as the Rationals. In the beginning, guitarists Scott Morgan and Steve Correll jammed together as a duo. After Correll's parents sent him off to military school, Morgan hooked up with a guitar player named Terry Trabandt and drummer Bill Figg. When Correll returned, Trabandt moved to bass.[4]

Like many other bands, the Rationals played mostly instrumentals when they were starting out, tunes by the Ventures, Lonnie Mack, and Link Wray.[5] One of their earliest gigs was with WXYZ Detroit deejay Don Zee, who was hosting a regular record hop at the Imperial Roller Rink in Ypsilanti.[6] A year or so later, they were performing at a YMCA dance run by Jeep Holland. Soon after, Holland became their manager and encouraged the band to add more vocals to their repertoire. Scott Morgan sang lead on songs such as "Money" and "High-Heeled Sneakers."[7]

Heavily influenced by the British invasion bands, Morgan wrote the group's first record release, "Look What You're Doing To Me," a garage rock prototype with a Morgan-Correll penned ballad on the flip side called "Gave My Love." The two songs, featuring lots of harmonies and complex chord changes, were recorded at a small two-track studio, with Jeep Holland producing the session.[8] Morgan wrote the lyrics and Steve Correll the music on another British-sounding single that followed called "Feelin' Lost," on which Correll sang lead. Recorded at Detroit's United Sound Systems studio, the session was again was produced by Jeep Holland. "We didn't get very far with that record," recalled Scott Morgan. "The Detroit radio stations wouldn't play it because it sounded too much like the Beatles."[9] The record did top the charts at WPAG in Ann Arbor.

Jeep Holland's father had been an army ordinance man in charge of "tanks, alligators, jeeps—anything that moved." When his son was born, his friends kidded him, asking, "Has the Jeep come yet?" The nickname stuck.[10] In high school, Holland was a member of the football and wrestling teams and played violin in the orchestra.[11] At twenty-two, he was five or six years older than the guys in the band and was, according to Scott Morgan, something of a "megalomaniac."[12] "He wanted to be the manager, producer, booking agent, take us to all the gigs and write the sets and do it all. He had a little trouble giving any of that up to anybody else." Morgan did admit that Holland was "good at it all."[13] Rationals drummer Bill Figg describes Jeep as a guy who was fun to be around: "Jeep was a real people person and the only person who could control the band. He knew how to get what he wanted out of each member."[14]

Holland quickly moved the band beyond local frat house gigs to more high-profile appearances, including the big dances at the Mt. Holly Ski Lodge on Dixie Highway, promoted by Bob Dell of WTAC in Flint. He also booked the group into the Lakeland Castle up in Michigan's Lower Peninsula resort area.[15] More importantly, he brought the Rationals to the attention of Robin Seymour of CKLW-TV, Channel 9.

Following years of radio success on Detroit station WKMH, and its successor WKNR, by 1964 Seymour had branched out into TV with a weekly show called *Teen Town*. Now in the summer of 1965 he was hosting a new Monday-through-Friday afternoon dance party show, *Swingin' Summertime*. Robin booked the Rationals to appear on four shows to be broadcast remote from Bob-Lo Island, the Detroit River home of a popular amusement park.[16] Bill Figg recalls appearing on those Bob-Lo Island shows with other Detroit acts, such as Martha and the Vandellas, Deon Jackson ("Love Makes the World Go 'Round"), Barbara Lewis ("Baby I'm Yours"), and Tony Clarke ("The Entertainer"): "We were pretty nervous being on live TV. We lip-synched all our stuff on those shows, and for some reason they even had us lip-synch 'Satisfaction' by the Stones, which seemed pretty crazy."[17]

At about the same time, the Rationals had the opportunity to perform at a concert held at Detroit's Masonic Temple, where they played behind Sonny and Cher, who, following their huge hit "I Got You Babe," were at their peak of popularity. "We opened the show with a short set and then we played backup for Sonny and Cher," recalls Bill Figg. "We had just an overwhelming response from the crowd, and I remember looking out and seeing some kids holding a huge banner with our name across it. I also recall Sonny looking out from the wings with sort of a perplexed look on his face just before they went on."[18] Looking back, Terry Trabandt recalled the same concert: "That probably got us a lot of publicity. There were about five or six thousand people there. It was the first big thing we ever did."[19] Although their early releases were stalling, the Rationals were building a big local following.

One of the advantages of being associated with Jeep Holland was gaining access to his extensive record collection, which leaned heavily on rhythm and blues.[20] As they had had very little luck imitating the lighter British sound, Jeep turned the Rationals on to a song called "Respect." It had been written and recorded by the increasingly influential soul artist Otis Redding the previous year. Earlier in their career, the Rationals, like most other local bands, had played their share of R & B tunes in the style of Chuck Berry and Little Richard. Their recording of "Respect" was different in that it was a contemporary rock arrangement, less funky than the original. Scott Morgan's spirited performance showed him to be one of the strongest lead vocalists on the local scene, and a very capable harmonica player as well.

The recording session for "Respect" was a pretty stripped-down affair, with Steve Correll and Terry Trabandt singing what had been the horn parts in the Redding version as backup vocal parts.[21] The Rationals' interpretation stood on its own, and was strong enough to make the Detroit charts of WXYZ, CKLW, and WKNR where it climbed to number 6 in October 1966.

Although it never became a solid national hit, the song did do well in markets such as Cleveland and Chicago, where the band had promoted it during its original release on A-Square. Then Cameo-Parkway picked it up for national distribution and had some scattered regional success.[22] The flip side was a rock interpretation of an R & B number titled "Leaving Here," which had been a minor Motown hit for its composer, Eddie Holland. In fact, "Leaving Here" had been the original A-side of the release, favored by Jeep Holland, before Detroit deejays flipped the record over and made "Respect" the hit.[23] The Rationals' stage performance was also changing around this time. Up until "Respect," Scott Morgan had played guitar onstage, but the group decided it would be better if Morgan just sang and fronted the band. Now that he didn't have to stand and hold on to an instrument, Morgan was free to move around and be more expressive.[24]

Top 10 success with "Respect," gigs at the big teen clubs, continued television exposure, and Jeep Holland's inventive promotions kept the group out in front of the pack. Their fan club received newsletters with exclusive information on each member, and Jeep made sure to bring along plenty of "Think Rational" buttons to throw out to audiences at their many appearances.[25]

At a big benefit show at Cobo Hall, the group realized just how popular they had become. Every year, WKNR, which had become Detroit's Top 40 powerhouse, would organize an "Alsac Teenager's March" to raise funds on behalf of St. Jude's Children's Hospital in Memphis, which specialized in treating children with leukemia. At the conclusion of the drive, "Keener" would put on a big "thank-you" show for the kids participating in the march. "We were only expecting a couple of hundred people, and there were like twelve-thousand," recalled Scott Morgan in a later interview.[26] The scene in Cobo Hall was chaotic, with thousands of screaming girls, many of whom were running up the aisles, knocking over barricades, and attempting to jump onto the stage. The show had to be stopped momentarily and then started again, only to have the lights come on and the plug pulled yet again.[27] As the screaming continued in the background, the police escorted the Rationals to a small room backstage and explained to them that they would have to go back out and tell the fans to stay in their seats or the show would be called off. Terry Trabandt recalled the group's immediate response: "We all just started hugging each other, just jumping up and down because it was so exciting."[28]

Upon returning to the stage, with the lights still on, Scott Morgan delivered the ultimatum. As the lights dimmed, the band cranked up "Respect," all hell broke loose, and the show was shut down. After fleeing Cobo Hall, the band ducked into the Pontchartrain Hotel across the street, where other performers from out of town were staying. In a scene reminiscent of Beatlemania, members of the Rationals hung out the window, throwing notes to the girls crowding around the base of the hotel. Bill Figg, says, "They had us way up there at the Ponch and we were looking down on this huge crowd of screaming girls and I'm thinking, 'We're famous!' Then we had to leave so we could get to this little gig at a club called the Pumpkin in Lincoln Park. Here we had just been playing before thousands and receiving all this attention and now we're in this little place that held maybe two hundred people."[29]

On the momentum created from "Respect," the jobs got better and the Rationals hit the road, performing all over the Midwest, the East Coast, and in Florida, where they played on a package tour with the Young Rascals. "The Rascals thought we were great," recalled Steve Terrell, "but we were just in awe because we're about sixteen or seventeen and they're twenty."[30]

Meanwhile, back in Detroit, WKNR listeners voted the Rationals the city's most popular band in 1966.

The Tidal Waves were a quintet with two members still in junior high when the they started out in 1965. "We were a pretty typical band, I guess," recalls drummer Tom Wearing. "We played block parties and garage parties and then moved on to some of the teen clubs."[31] The other members included Tom Wearing's brother John, along with Bob Slap, lead guitarist Bill Long, and Mark Karpinski. The Wearings' cousin was a local record producer named Jack Checkaway, and at the urging of the other band members, Tom Wearing contacted him about making a record.[32] The song the band wanted to record was a rousing party number called "Farmer John" that had previously been a mild hit for a Los Angeles group. Tom Wearing: "Although we had been performing the song at parties, we were really unaware of the version done by the Premiers two years earlier."[33]

"Farmer John," recorded by the Tidal Waves at United Sound, and released on SVR, landed on the "WKNR *Music Guide*" at number 30 on May 2, and in four weeks climbed to number 6. The record did even better to the north in Flint, where it reached number 1 at WTAC. Tom Wearing remembers the first time he heard their record played on the radio: "I was driving down Lakeshore Drive in Grosse Pointe in a powder blue 1960 Ford convertible listening to Keener [WKNR], and all of the sudden our record comes on and it was quite a thrilling moment!"[34]

The group scored a mild follow-up hit with "I Don't Need Love," which went to number 18 in Detroit. Also in 1966, the Tidal Waves were among the opening acts for the Dave Clark Five at Ford Auditorium, and for the Animals when they played at Olympia.

A band from Oak Park known as the Shy Guys also kept busy on the teen club circuit. Ron Lefko and Stu Howard both played guitar and sang, Marty Lewis played bass, and Mark Finn played drums. In May 1966, when they were not yet old enough to drive, they had a top 20 Detroit hit called "We Gotta Go."[35] It was a simple but catchy song about how most people are thinking that their lives are okay, when in reality they're too busy, always saying, "We gotta go, we gotta go." The record was released locally on Panik records, and then on Detroit's Palmer label.

Scott Regen, the early evening deejay on WKNR—at the time, Detroit's top station—really got behind the record, and it climbed as high as number 15. Regen, whose real name is Bob Bernstein, was a big booster of Detroit music, rock, and R & B. Some of his on-air shtick had to do with cool kids being referred to as "burgers." Scott had a "burger club" numbering over twenty thousand card-carrying members, and he aired a nonsensical skit about the "Lone Burger." Daily Drive-ins, popular Westside teenage food hangouts, even listed a "Regen Burger" on the menu. Using the same instrumental track from "We Gotta Go," the Shy Guys recorded "The Burger Song," which of course received a lot of airplay on WKNR.[36]

"Keener 13" was the first button kids pushed when they got behind the wheel to cruise up and down the northern suburban stretch of Woodward Avenue. Lined with colorful drive-in restaurants such as the Big Boy, Totem Pole, Big Town, Mavericks, and Ted's, Woodward was the most popular of the "unofficial" dragways in town, of which also included Gratiot, Eight Mile Road, and Telegraph Road. Aside from Scott Regen, WKNR also had irreverent tongue-in-cheek morning guy Dick Purtan, and upbeat afternoon drive man Bob Green, playing hits that blasted out of the radio drenched in Keener's unique "springy" reverb sound.

Palmer Records, owned by John Kaplan and Tom Schlesinger, scored a hit early in 1966 with Tim Tam and the Turn-Ons' recording of "Wait a Minute." Tim Tam (Rick Wiesand) and company were a six-man vocal group from Allen Park. Wiesand, the group's lead singer, had an awesome, high falsetto that sent the record, despite its somewhat retro sound, up to number 6 in the Motor City. The Satellites, a band from Allen Park High School, played the backing track. A customized intro was also recorded especially for Scott Regen's show.

Tim Tam and the Turn-Ons had follow-up hits with "Cheryl Ann" and "Kimberly." The sessions were done at Detroit's Tera Shirma studios, owned by Ralph Terrana, a musician who had formerly played with the popular club band the Sunliners.[37]

As the automotive business stretched up I-75 through Flint and Saginaw, the area came to seem like an extension of the Motor City in lifestyle and attitudes. Records and artists from the area contributed to the Michigan rock movement with Detroit at the core. In the fall of 1966, after having scored several regional hits, Flint's Terry Knight and the Pack made the national charts, with "I (Who Have Nothing)."

Terry Knight was born Richard Terrance Knapp on April 9, 1943, and grew up in Lapeer, Michigan, just outside of Flint. His father owned a milk delivery route, and after school Terry would help out. Nights he spent tuned to the radio. Although Terry enjoyed the music of Buddy Holly, Ritchie Valens, and other fifties rock legends, it was the disc jockeys that he was originally drawn to.

Locally, he listened to "Big 600," WTAC from Flint. His idol though, was loudmouthed, attention-getting Dick Biondi, the "Supersonic Spaghetti Slurper," broadcasting nightly over powerful WLS from Chicago.[38]

Terry practiced his deejay patter, recording into a little home tape deck. By tenth grade, he felt ready to be a radio pro. After making an audition tape on a three-inch reel, he decided to bypass the small stations, and without the slightest reservation, drove directly to WLS, one of the biggest stations in the country. There, the program director listened to his tape and recommended that Terry go home, finish school, and contact him again when he was done. Terry followed his advice to "keep practicing," and soon he was on the air at a little station in Alma, Michigan, after which he was hired by Flint's WTAC, where he developed a reputation for breaking hits.[39]

An already fast-moving career moved even faster, when, in May 1963, Terry was offered a position at WJBK in Detroit, the seven-to-midnight, "Jack the Bellboy Show," named after the popular record program begun by Ed McKenzie back in the forties. The station was not fond of the name Knapp, so Terry suggested he use "Knight," as he was on the air in the evening: "This is 'Jack the Bellboy,' Terry Knight, and here's another hit from the 'Radio 15 Record Review,'" he could be heard to say.[40]

A short nine months later, two record promotion men who had loaned Terry two hundred dollars to buy furniture when he first arrived were urging him to go into the station's weekly record meeting and push a single they were promoting. "The record was stinko," said Knight. "I wouldn't do it."[41] After Knight resisted a threat, the record guys went to his boss claiming that the two hundred dollar loan had been a payoff. Shortly he was called in the manager's office and confronted with sworn affidavits stating that the money had been an under-the-table bribe to play records. Unaware of 1959's huge payola scandals that had resulted in three WJBK announcers being fired or forced to resign, Knight thought he could talk his way out of the accusations. The manager would hear none of it, and after being told that he had "disgraced Jack the Bellboy," Knight was canned on the spot.[42]

Terry returned to Flint in February 1964, only to be brought back to Detroit radio in June as the new evening deejay on CKLW, the powerful station located across the river in Windsor. While it seemed that disc jockeys everywhere were doing everything possible to link themselves with the Beatles, Terry was instantly attracted to the Rolling Stones. After receiving an advance copy of the group's first release, "Tell Me," he went on the air and played the record over and over for an entire evening.[43] At the same time, he was becoming less enchanted with broadcasting and more interested in becoming a performer and writer. While working at WJBK a year earlier, he had started to play guitar, and would usually have the instrument slung over his shoulder wherever he went.[44] By the fall of 1964, he was performing around Detroit, and by the middle of December, he had made a firm decision to quit radio at the ripe old age of twenty-one.

During his emotional, final sign-off at CKLW, on December 18, Knight indicated that he would be moving to England to share digs with Brian Jones of the Stones, whom he had befriended when the group had visited America.[45] The trip to England was scuttled, and Terry wound up playing his guitar in a coffeehouse in Buffalo for twenty dollars a night.[46]

Several months later, he was back behind a radio microphone at WTRX in Flint. At a record hop he met up with a band calling themselves the Jazz Masters. The original members included Don Brewer on drums, Al Pippens on guitar (replaced by Curt Johnson), Bob Caldwell on keyboards, and Herm Jackson on bass. Terry approached the group about becoming their lead singer. Impressed with Knight's contacts, they welcomed him into the band. Several years older than the other members, Terry quickly took control, changing the group's name to the Pack.[47]

Before long, the band made their first recording, "The Tears Come Rollin' Down," produced by John Rhys and released on the Golden World subsidiary label Wingate Records, named for owner Ed Wingate. The record bombed, but Terry rebounded, using his past radio connections to arrange for the band to open for the Rolling Stones and the Yardbirds on Michigan tours.

In late 1965, Herm Jackson left for the army, and Mark Farner, a guitarist in another Flint band, replaced him on bass. The Pack then covered a Yardbirds song called "Better Man Than I" and were rewarded with a top 10 hit in Detroit and Cleveland.[48] They recorded the song on the Lucky Eleven label, owned by Flint businessman Otis Ellis. When the record was released, the label read "Terry Knight and the Pack."

The group's next release was a socially relevant song titled, "A Change on the Way," and it reached number 14 on the Detroit charts. After "I've Been Told," written by Terry, failed to ignite, they decided to record "I (Who Have Nothing)." A hit for Ben E. King in 1963, Terry altered the recording to include a dramatic spoken word segment. Again released on Lucky Eleven, the record took off and hit the top 5 in Detroit. After being leased to Cameo Records, the record climbed the national charts, eventually stopping at number 46. The group even made an appearance on Dick Clark's *Where the Action Is*.

Another band from north of Detroit was Question Mark and the Mysterians, a five-piece outfit from Saginaw. They were Mexican-Americans, most of whom were born in Texas and had moved north with their families.[49] In September 1966, Question Mark (real name, Rudy Martinez) and the Mysterians, whose name derived from a 1957 Japanese sci-fi movie, scored a huge national hit with a song Rudy had written called "96 Tears." During the four years that preceded that release, the group had been local favorites in the Saginaw Valley, mixing James Brown–style soul with more melodic Tex-Mex rhythms familiar to the many resident and migrant farmworkers in the area.[50] Question Mark was the centerpiece, looking mysterious behind his ever present dark sunglasses. The group also included lead guitarist Bobby Balderrama, keyboard player Frank Rodriguez, drummer Robert Martinez (replaced by Eddie Serrato), and guitarist Larry Borjas (replaced by bass player Frank Lugo).

The band went to see about making a record for a tiny label in the area called Pa-Go-Go, owned by a woman named Lilly Gonzales, who subsequently became their manager. Gonzales scheduled a recording session at Art Shield's studio at 405 Raymond Street in Bay City.[51] According to Question Mark, the "studio" was actually a closed-in patio with storm windows, and no acoustics. There were also no headphones, no separation, and not even a bass drum.[52]

The plan was to record another song written by Rudy called "Midnight Hour," as the A-side with "96 Tears" on the flip. On April 14, they cut their record, and having pressed 750 copies, went about trying to get it played on the radio.[53] Finally, Saginaw's WSAM agreed to feature "Midnight Hour" on a program spotlighting new talent. The band was happy but Question Mark felt strongly that the B-side had the greatest potential. He went back to the station the next day and convinced the deejay to flip the record over. The next time the band heard themselves on the airwaves, it was "96 Tears" with its chugging little Vox organ, and vengeful lyrics sung by a surly Rudy Martinez, that the deejay was playing.[54]

Within days, Bob Dell debuted the record on the dominant station in the area, WTAC in Flint. Soon Detroit disc jockey Tommy Shannon was playing it on his evening show on fifty-thousand-watt CKLW: "I heard this thing and it had that great grunge rock sound and I knew it could be a smash," Shannon recalls. "I leaned on it a little, which wasn't hard to do in those days, and we were really getting a good reaction. I pitched it to Neal Bogart, who was running Cameo-Parkway records out of Philadelphia, and he took it national. It sold a million and they gave me a gold record for it."[55]

Despite its ramshackle beginnings at a home studio in Bay City, Michigan, "96 Tears" had done what many other local acts had failed to do: get picked up nationally and go all the way to number 1 in the United States. It even made the charts in the United Kingdom, where it reached number 37. They followed it up with "I Need Somebody," which charted at number 22.

As new groups were drawing more and more attention, existing bands were changing their styles to look and sound more contemporary. Out were the matching jackets, ties, and pompadours; in were jeans, vests, and longer hair combed down in the style of the Beatles.

One of the better-established bands was Doug Brown and the Omens, a regular attraction on Detroit's suburban bar circuit, performing at places such as the Red Carpet, the Norwest Lounge, and the 300 Bowl, a Pontiac bowling alley.[56] Their initial 1965 release for Hideout subsidiary Punch Records was a party foot stomper called, "TGIF (Thank Goodness It's Friday)".

Along the way, Doug Brown had become impressed with the talent displayed by his current keyboard player, Bob Seger. As a member of Doug Brown's Omens, Seger had written a novelty tune called "The Ballad of the Yellow Beret." Released on the Are You Kidding Me label, the writing credit went to "D. Dodger," and artist credits reflected "The Beach Bums." An obvious takeoff on Sgt. Barry Sadler's "Ballad of the Green Beret," the record was quickly shut down when the producers of the original issued a cease-and-desist order.57

Meanwhile, Doug Brown had become a mentor of sorts to Seger, singing his praises to Dave Leone: "Hey, look. The organ player in my band—he writes great songs. I think we should record him separately. I think he's got some hits."58 A few days later, Brown, with Bob Seger in tow, showed up at Leone's small storefront office on Mack Avenue. As he and Leone sat back on an old sofa, Bob Seger picked up his acoustic guitar and played a song that he had recently written, "East Side Story."59

Bob Seger was born the younger of two sons in the Detroit suburb of Dearborn on May 6, 1945. His father was a part-time bandleader and musician whose regular job as an in-house medic at the Ford River Rouge plant supported his wife and two children. By the time Bob was ten, his father was gone, chasing his musical dreams to California.60 The family moved into a one-bedroom apartment in a black and predominately poor area of Ann Arbor. "The neighbors would be out washing their cars in the summer, and I'd hear R & B. It just permeated the neighborhood," Seger recalled.61 As Mitch Ryder had done, Bob would spend his nights listening to a transistor radio, bringing in the sounds of James Brown, Little Richard, and other influential soul artists such as Solomon Burke, Otis Redding, and the Falcons with Wilson Pickett. When he went to the local record shop, the records he purchased were most often the ones by black artists.62

Before deserting his family, Stewart Seger had taught his shy son how to play the four-string bass ukulele. In high school, after starting out as an honor student and track star, Bob moved on to the guitar and started dressing like a greaser: slicked-back hair, pointy shoes, and pegged pants.[63] He formed a three-piece band called the Decibels, who were booked at fraternity parties around the University of Michigan. Bob also played at his junior prom, where the applause made him feel that he had found his calling in life.[64] In 1961, at the age of sixteen, he wrote and recorded his first song, called "The Lonely One." He cut the acetate demo of it in the basement of Del Shannon's keyboard player, Max Crook, who lived in Ann Arbor.[65]

Following graduation, Seger quit music for a year while his brother went into the service; he and his mom just couldn't live off the money he made from playing. To make ends meet, he worked at a clothing store during the day and in a pizza place at night.[66] As soon as his brother got out of the service, Bob got right back into rock 'n' roll, joining a band called the Town Cryers. Seger really liked rockin' R & B, and he found that audiences appreciated him best when he "sang real hard": "Those guys—Wilson (Pickett) and James (Brown) and guys like that—sang their brains out. Those were the guys who got me going."[67] It's no surprise that the album *James Brown Live at the Apollo Vol. 1*, topped his list of all-time favorites. Seger told writer Chris Cioe that the guys in his early bands would say, "Seger, you sing the black songs and we'll sing the white ones." It wasn't long before he was being encouraged to "sing them all."[68]

The Town Cryers worked steadily in local cocktail lounges and teen clubs, where they would play "three forty-fives," referring to the length of each set. Next came a nine-week stand at the Rose-land Inn, a strip club in Jackson, Michigan. "We'd back up the strippers for three fifteen minute shows a night. But these were also the gigs where I learned to go out and meet the audience between shows, so they'd get to know us and come back," recalled Seger.[69] Rationals drummer Bill Figg went to school with Bob in Ann Arbor, and recalls that he was "just a regular guy who loved to play." They remained close as their music careers progressed. "We would see each other all the time, and Bob would come by and play or sing a part on a couple of our records, and we played at a lot of frat parties together. They were fun times."[70]

Bob Seger had originally written "East Side Story" for the Underdogs.[71] Dave Leone's partner, Punch Andrews, recommended that Bob record it himself. So in August 1966, the song became his initial release on the Hideout label. Produced by Doug Brown, the record cost eighty-five dollars to make and, like many other local recordings, was cut at the popular United Sound Systems studio in Detroit. On the Hideout 45, the song is credited only to Bob Seger, but the backing band consisted of Brown on guitar and organ, along with various members of the Town Cryers and the Omens, including Dan Honaker on bass, Bob Evans on drums, and Pep Perrine playing bongos.[72] When the record was picked up for national distribution on Cameo, the credit was changed to read, "Bob Seger and the Last Heard." A tale of urban despair and heartbreak set to a pulsating beat with tom-toms and fuzz guitar, "East Side Story" became a bona fide smash in the Motor City, climbing the local charts as high as number 3.

Despite the song's social message, Seger did not get into music as a form of rebellion or to pursue social change. "I found my recognition in music," he related, "but more than that, I just really enjoyed it."[73] Because he had not written "East Side Story" for himself, Seger thought it might have been a little "derivative" and remembers "losing some sleep over the fact that it sounded an awful lot like 'Gloria.'" At the same time he believed that his song had "a lot more chords" than the other.[74] As sales of "East Side Story" topped fifty thousand in the Detroit area, Bob Seger, who had become a top draw at the Hideout clubs, was poised for regional stardom.

# 8. A Whole Lotta Soul, a Whole Lotta Funk

As the rock music scene continued to mature, R & B had been evolving into what audiences were now referring to as "soul music." Many critics felt that records being produced by Stax Records in Memphis by artists such as Wilson Pickett, Otis Redding, and Sam and Dave were truer to the gospel-inspired definition of "soul" than Motown's more pop-oriented approach. Most audiences, however, both black and white, were associating "soul" with black music and lifestyle in general. Detroit's WCHB, a black-owned and -programmed station, promoted itself as "Soul Radio." Despite the strong competition from Stax releases distributed by Atlantic Records, Motown was still the leader.

The statistics were impressive. During the period from 1964 to 1967, Motown racked up fourteen number 1 pop singles, twenty number 1 soul singles, forty-six more top 15 pop singles, and seventy-four other top 15 soul singles.[1] Although operating in a parallel universe, Detroit rock bands couldn't help but be influenced by the writing and musicianship displayed on hit after hit from the studio on West Grand Boulevard. "Motown was God," says veteran Detroit rocker Gary Quackenbush. "We were just little white punks from the suburbs. We were trash compared to Motown. I think that's why it got so intense. I remember really trying harder because of the superior musicianship there. Motown was just such a monolith."[2] Bob Seger felt that Motown's bass players and drummers "just hammered it," saying that "if you came out of Detroit, you had to have some of that in your sound."[3]

Motown writer and producer Lamont Dozier has named the label's house musicians as being "at least fifty-percent responsible" for the success of the company's many hit records.[4] The core group of players consisted of designated leader Earl "Chunk of Funk" Van Dyke on piano (who joined in 1962, taking over as band leader when Joe Hunter left in late 1963), Robert White (guitar), James Jamerson (bass), and Benny Benjamin (drums). There was also Joe Messina and Eddie Willis (guitars), and Richard "Pistol" Allen and Uriel Jones (drums). Other members continually rotating in and out of Studio A, better known as the "Snakepit," included Jack Ashford (vibes and tambourines), Eddie "Bongo" Brown (bongos and congas), and Johnny Griffith (keyboards). Most of these players had backgrounds in jazz, and some, such as Jamerson, had been on the road backing artists such as Jackie Wilson and the Miracles. Jack Ashford had played behind Marvin Gaye.[5] They were all exceptional musicians, and each was considered to have a unique style that was called upon at various sessions.

With so many producers telling them to "play it funky," the house band started referring to themselves as the Funk Brothers, a name coined by Benny Benjamin. "It was incredible how they knew each producer," recalled Lamont Dozier. "They locked right into what we were about as producers and songwriters, which made our job very easy."[6]

The team of Holland-Dozier-Holland had become the most successful writing and production unit at Motown. Although often overlapping, each member of H-D-H had his primary responsibilities: Brian Holland was the engineer, responsible for the sound and structure of their songs, as well as some melodies. Dozier, who had soloed as Lamont Anthony after leaving the Romeos, came up with basic ideas and also provided melodies, lyrics, and titles. Eddie Holland was the main lyricist and was in charge of teaching new songs to the artists, making them understand the feeling that the writers wanted to get across to the listener.[7] As a recording artist, Eddie had scored minor but impressive Motown hits such as "Jamie" and "Leaving Here."

Holland-Dozier-Holland experienced their first big success in May 1963 with Martha and the Vandellas' debut hit, "Come and Get These Memories." According to Lamont Dozier, that record was the "catalyst that opened everybody's ears up to reach out for heavier chords and to mix those chords with country-type feelings and jazz and gospel."[8] Hits such as "Heatwave" and "Quicksand" quickly followed.

Many H-D-H songs started out as jam session collaborations. Lamont Dozier recalled that he was just "killing time" at the studio piano when he came up with the line: "Baby, baby, where did our love go? Don't you want me no more?" Soon Brian Holland joined him and they worked out where the chorus, verse, and bridge should go.[9] They first offered "Where Did Our Love Go?" to the Marvelettes, but they turned it down. Then it went to the Supremes and became their first chart-topping hit. "Baby Love," "Come See About Me," "Stop! In the Name of Love," and "Back in My Arms" completed the initial run of five consecutive number 1 hits. There would be many more.

As there was limited space in the Motown studio, recordings were always overdubbed. Chief engineer Mike McClean designed the studio's original three-track recorder used on everything up to and including "Where Did Our Love Go." After that, all recordings were made on Motown's new eight-track system, also designed by McClean.[10] Lamont Dozier: "The rhythm track was first. Everybody was together on that. After the rhythm we'd put the vocals on. After the vocals some extra added percussion—congas, tambourines, guys foot-stomping on a piece of plywood, and what have you. Then the horns and then the strings, which would always come last."[11]

Dozier also recalled that as producers they would often "fatten the tracks" by bringing in separate session singers. The group most utilized were Motown's in-house female recording group, the Andantes—Marlene Barrow, Jackie Hicks, and Louvain Demps. Their smooth vocals were blended in on records by the Marvelettes, the Four Tops, and on countless other recording sessions. Extra male vocals were often provided by the Originals.[12] Motown's trademark saxophone breaks were usually handled by Mike Terry and Thomas "Beans" Bowles on baritone sax, Hank Cosby on tenor, or Teddy Buckner on alto.

According to Earl Van Dyke, "The basis for the whole Motown sound was the way Benny's foot (the one playing the bass drum) and James' bass functioned as a unit," resulting in a "tiny space between the beat and the accents James and Benny actually played."[13] In a later interview, James Jamerson described how the sessions were structured: "I started to play. Benny started the beat. We'd look at each other and know whether we needed a triplet, quarter triplet, double time, or whatever. We didn't need sheet music. We could feel the groove together."[14] Bahamian-born Benny Benjamin, nicknamed "Papa Zita," started playing for Berry Gordy in 1958 and was best known for having incredible speed and accuracy with his sticks. Benny laid down the beat to Motown classics such as "Shop Around," "Get Ready," and "Going To A Go-Go." "They used to call him Mr. Motown," recalled fellow drummer Uriel Jones. "He was definitely the founder of the Motown sound. . . . It was just a touch that he had, a feeling for what we were doing. We all learned from Benny."[15] Earl Van Dyke recalled that when Benjamin "got sick, Motown had to bring in *two* drummers to replace him! And that's God's truth!"[16]

Prior to his work at Motown, South Carolina–born James Jamerson could be found playing stand-up bass in any number of Detroit's night spots. His mixing of jazz-inspired improvisation with the backbeat requirements of the Motown sound were spectacular. As songwriter Dan Forte said, "Sure, there were instances where he was asked to repeat a certain pattern throughout a song, but more often, even if he started with a set bass line, he would continually embellish it, depart from it, reinvent it throughout the tune."[17] Producer Don Was commented, "You have to be absolutely fearless to play those notes in that place and yet be responsible for the bottom of the groove like that."[18]

"We always listened to the bass playing on those records," says Gary Quackenbush, looking back to his days in the Fugitives. "It was much later before we knew who was playing, but we were very aware of it."[19] Suzi Quatro, who played bass for the all-girl group Pleasure Seekers, recalled the time she slipped into the Motown studio and did a couple of runs on Jamerson's bass. According to Quatro, Jamerson shook his head, unimpressed. "It's not about what you can play, it's what you leave out that counts," he had advised.[20] Quatro went home and "totally changed" her approach, paring her bass lines down to the bare essentials.

An important part of Motown's incredibly strong backbeat was the sound of two or three guitars playing at the same time. "Somebody came in and said, 'I want three guitars to play the backbeat,'" recounted Joe Messina, who earlier in his career had played in the band on Soupy Sales's nighttime show on channel 7. "So we'd all be playing the backbeats, but in different registers."[21]

Motown had a special black box that enabled the guitars and bass to be recorded directly into the console. According to Joe Messina, it was done that way "so they could do whatever they wanted to in the control room—mix us, take us out."[22] While Joe Messina was the master of the backbeat, such as displayed on "Dancing in the Street," by Martha and the Vandellas, Eddie Willis's country and blues background enabled him to lay down the funkiest rhythms on tracks such as the Temptation's "The Way You Do the Things You Do." Robert White, who played with his thumbnail, crafted clean lead guitar lines such as the opening notes to "My Girl" by the Temptations, and "Something About You" by the Four Tops.

Eddie Willis recalled that a lot of times the producers "would hum something, and they really didn't know what the hell they were humming. A lot of times it wouldn't fit, but they would leave it up to the individual how to make it fit." Willis said that the Funks "did so much stuff with Holland-Dozier-Holland that they just started letting us do what we wanted . . . and it worked."[23]

The Detroit Vibrations were a pretty typical white cover band, specializing in playing Motown hits. "We didn't have the horns and the strings and stuff like that, but for being just a four-piece band beltin' those songs out, we did pretty good," says drummer Richard Stevers. "That's what was on the radio. If you wanted to play, you stayed up with what was hot, and that was what was hot. We listened to the songs, everybody picked out their own parts and made it sound as close to the original as possible, which is how they wanted to hear them. I paid close attention to the drum part."[24]

While fellow musicians learned to respect their talents, the Funk Brothers were invisible to the record-buying public. They were never credited on records and, with a rare exception, never went on the road with the artists. Berry Gordy didn't want anyone stealing his hottest musicians, the guys responsible for the "Motown Sound."[25]

To augment their studio incomes, at night the Funks played at clubs such as the Chit Chat Lounge on Twelfth Street and the 20 Grand at Fourteenth and West Warren, where they were billed as Earl Van Dyke and the Famous Motown Recording Band, or just the Earl Van Dyke Band. Another source of income were clandestine recording sessions for other labels, which Gordy strictly forbade. They played at studios such as Golden World, United Sound, D-Town or at Artie Fields, where they even cut commercial jingles. Many of these sessions took place at three in the morning so the guys could finish up their nightclub gigs.[26]

Following early successes by the Reflections and Gino Washington, Golden World had continued to improve its overall operation, and chief engineer Bob D'Orleans had built what was arguably the most advanced studio in town.[27] To keep up with the increasing work load, D'Orleans eventually hired Motown engineer Ed Wolfrum and musician-turned-engineer Russ Terrana. In the summer of 1965, some of the Funk Brothers showed up at Golden World to record a song called "Agent Double-O Soul," which became a hit for Edwin Starr on Wingate's Ric-Tic label. A white bass player named Bob Babbitt had been booked for the session.

Babbitt had been a latter-day member of the veteran Detroit band the Royaltones, along with drummer Marcus Terry, guitarist Dennis Coffey, singer Dave Sandy, and founding member George Katsakis on saxophone. Besides cutting some hits of their own, such as "Our Faded Love," which went to number 8 in Detroit in 1964, the Royaltones did a lot of session work, especially for Harry Balk, with whom they were signed. Harry was still producing Del Shannon, and he used the Royaltones to play backup on Del's second wave of hits, such as "Handy Man," "Do You Wanna Dance," "Keep Searching," and "Stranger in Town." Some of Del's recordings had been cut at United Sound. Bob Babbitt recalls, "Then, all of a sudden, there was kind of a buzz going around town about a new studio, which was the Golden World studio. Harry Balk decided to try the studio out, so I started goin' in there along with some other people. That was the thing . . . you couldn't get into the Motown studio, and this was like the closest to it. For those days it was a modern, state-of-the-art studio."[28]

After his first Del Shannon session at Golden World, Babbitt recalls wandering into a rehearsal room and seeing a bulletin board with all the phone numbers and musicians: "I saw about eight bass players, it seemed like. I remember [James] Jamerson's name was up at the top. I thought to myself, 'Well, I'm never gonna work here, you know.' "[29] But during a freelance session, Ed Wingate approached Babbitt and offered him the chance to go to work regularly at his studio, and he readily accepted.

"Agent Double-O Soul" became Bob Babbitt's first official session. The fact that he was a classically trained musician came in handy when he was asked to read the introduction, which had been written out note for note by the arranger, Sonny Sanders. "If I hadn't been able to read that, I don't think they would have called me back," says Babbitt.[30] "All of the sudden they were calling me for about everything over there." With its distinctive bass line the finished product reached number 21 on the national charts.

Babbitt recalls being asked to recommend a guitar player for another session: "His name was Roy Nievelt, and he was the buzz of the town, by the way. He worked with Jamie Coe. Everybody just fell over this guy when he played. At the session, we set up, and then they were passing music around and Roy was sitting next to me, and I noticed that he was kind of restless and moving around in his chair. Finally he leaned over and said, 'Bob, I don't know how to read music.' It was one of those three A.M. sessions, and I had to tell the arranger. I said, 'There's one other guy I know,' and I called Dennis Coffey. They didn't expect you to read all the time, but you had to be ready."[31]

The Funk Brothers slipped in and out of Golden World and also played on Edwin Starr's follow-up hit, "(SOS) Stop Her On Sight," with James Jamerson handling bass. That GW release is regarded by many as being as great a production as ever came out of Motown.

The Golden World studio was rated as the best in Detroit for recording strings. Members of the Detroit Symphony, moonlighting as the San Remo Golden Strings, cut a soulful top 20 instrumental hit there in late 1965 titled "Hungry For Love." Earl Van Dyke played the featured piano part on the Ric-Tic release.

Ann Arbor–based producer Ollie McLaughlin, whose labels included Karen and Carla Records, also recorded some of his artists at the Golden World studio. Deon Jackson's "Love Makes the World Go 'Round" was cut there, along with "Cool Jerk" by the Capitols. Funk Brothers Eddie Willis played guitar and Johnny Griffith piano on those recordings, along with Bob Babbitt on bass. Ray Monette, another white rock musician, also played guitar on the "Cool Jerk" session engineered by Ed Wolfrum. The two records reached number 12 and number 7 respectively on *Billboard*'s pop charts. Along with the Royaltones, Babbitt also played on Harry Balk's Impact label production of "Oh How Happy" at Golden World, a hit for the Shades of Blue, a white mixed-gender group from the Detroit suburb of Livonia. That song had gone to number 12 on the national charts in May 1966.

At night, Babbitt found himself playing with many of the Motown musicians at clubs around town. After he played in Stevie Wonder's live band, Wonder eventually invited him to play on Motown recording sessions.[32]

# 9. Birth of the Noise

Russ Gibb seemed an unlikely rock 'n' roll hero in the fall of 1966. Already in his midthirties with short hair and glasses, he was employed as an English teacher at Allen Park Junior High School North. A closer look, though, revealed a man who liked to ride motorcycles, take chances, and make money. Away from school, Gibb had been successful promoting dances at a rented union hall he called the Pink Pussycat, fronted by WKNR disc jockey Gary Stevens.[1]

Born in the Detroit suburb of Dearborn in 1932, Gibb graduated from Michigan State University in 1953 with a degree in educational radio and television administration. While teaching in Howell, Michigan, he also worked weekends as a floor manager at WWJ-TV in Detroit, as well as handling production duties and some weekend deejay work for radio station WBRB in Mt. Clemens and then WKMH, a larger Detroit area station, licensed to Dearborn.[2] His best friend was former classmate Jim Dunbar, who worked as an announcer for Detroit's WXYZ in 1956, and went on to greater fame at WLS in Chicago. By 1965 Dunbar was a popular personality in San Francisco at KGO, a middle-of-the-road station programmed for adults.[3]

It was during a trip to visit Dunbar early in 1966 that Russ Gibb's life was altered dramatically. West Coast concert promoter Bill Graham had just opened a new music venue at the Fillmore Auditorium, and Dunbar, who had passes, took Gibb along when he was invited to check it out.[4] What they witnessed was a performance by the Byrds amid a light show that Gibb likened to "amoebas on a ceiling."[5] Russ soaked up the psychedelic culture that was all around: "I had never seen a strobe light before, and I thought, 'Wow, this would be terrific in Detroit,'" he related. "I met with Graham in his office, found out who made the strobe light and obtained the numbers of some of the bands."[6]

After returning to the Motor City, Gibb set out to find a suitable facility similar to Bill Graham's Fillmore. He found it in an abandoned old big-band ballroom located at 8592 Grand River Avenue, one block south of Joy Road. "I liked the Grande, but when I told a friend where it was located, he told me that it was a really tough neighborhood," recalls Gibb.7

Built in 1930 as a classic-style ballroom, the Grande was long past its prime. In recent years, the gothic structure had served as home to a roller rink and mattress warehouse.8 Russ Gibb signed a rent-to-buy deal with real estate agent Gabe Glantz, who represented the building's owner, a Mr. Kleinman, who also happened to be Glantz's father-in-law.9 The deal in place, Gibb immediately made plans for the opening of his new rock emporium. Searching for local talent to play at the Grande, he sought advice from Harvey Ovshinsky, publisher of the counterculture newspaper the *Fifth Estate*. Harvey introduced Russ to John Sinclair, the paper's music columnist. Recently, Sinclair had become a big fan and friend of the local hard rock band known as the MC5. Sinclair recommended the group to Gibb.10

As he wished to emulate the San Francisco scene, Russ Gibb asked MC5 lead singer Rob Tyner if he knew anyone who would be able to produce colorful poster-style promotions, such as the ones done for the Fillmore. It so happened that just such a person was close at hand. Tyner's friend from high school Gary Grimshaw was back from the service, and at that moment sleeping on Tyner's couch.11

While growing up in the downriver blue-collar community of Lincoln Park, Gary Grimshaw had been part of a group of friends that thought of themselves as a sort of "art gang." Being the only member with a car, Gary became the official driver as they cruised around town in his 1953 Ford two-door sedan. A favorite hangout was the parking lot of White Castle Hamburgers on Fort Street near Southfield, where the radio was usually tuned to WCHB. Deejay Larry "The Ugly Duckling" Dixon played some jazz during the last hour of his R & B show each afternoon and quite often featured recordings by John Coltrane. Grimshaw's friend Bob Derminer was such a fan of Coltrane's piano player, McCoy Tyner, that he opted to change his own name to Rob Tyner.12

Grimshaw along with buddies Tyner, Kelly Martensen and Carl Schigelone started making regular runs between Lincoln Park and the Cass Corridor, the "artists community" around Wayne State University. There they would drive around looking for "beatnik parties" to crash. According to Grimshaw, growing up in the white, mostly Polish Catholic community of Lincoln Park, he'd had no exposure to different cultures, saying there was "no hipness." Trips into the Cass Corridor were a life-changing experience. Gary Grimshaw: "Suddenly you are confronted with people from many different backgrounds who share a common understanding, something that you don't get right away."[13]

Following graduation from Lincoln Park High in 1963, Gary was accepted at Wayne State University and moved to an apartment nearby at 633 Prentiss. Down the street, he found a market that would sell him beer and wine without checking his ID, and partying took precedent over studying. In no time he managed to flunk out of school. Fearing the draft, he joined the navy, and wound up in boot camp in San Diego. Later, while stationed in San Francisco, Grimshaw, like Russ Gibb, attended a show at the Fillmore. Already trained as a graphic artist, he was impressed with the style of the Fillmore posters, created to promote upcoming shows.[14] Now, sitting at Rob and Becky Tyner's kitchen table, Gary was producing the first of his own promoting the MC5's first show at the Grande Ballroom.

The MC5 had its origins in 1963, when Wayne Kames moved into a Lincoln Park neighborhood. Born the son of Stanley Kames in 1948, Wayne later changed his last name to Kramer, to "distance" himself from a father who he felt had "abandoned" him when his parents divorced.[15] He started playing guitar after being impressed by a guy his mother had dated who played and "sang like Elvis." It was, however, the electric guitar of Chuck Berry that most influenced Kramer's musical direction: "When I heard that sound when I was nine years old, that was it," Wayne confided. "When I was a teenager, the fiercest competition was who could play Chuck Berry solos note-for-note." Kramer mastered the solos by playing along with each of Berry's records "a thousand times."[16]

In Lincoln Park, he met another kid who dabbled with bongos

as well as a little guitar. He was named Fred Smith, and his father had come to the Detroit area from Kentucky and worked in a factory. They were both the same age and still in junior high school. Wayne would take his new solid-body Sears Silvertone electric guitar over to Fred's house every day during the summer and teach Fred to play chords. Smith soon became adept as a rhythm guitarist and joined a band known as the Vibratones. Meanwhile, Wayne played in a competing group called the Bounty Hunters, named for racing star Connie Kalitta's famous dragster. Eventually, Wayne and Fred decided to take the best players from both bands and merge into one new group, keeping the name of Wayne's band.[17]

Wayne Kramer met Rob Tyner through Rob's younger brother, Rick. "Rob was a real non-conformist beatnik type, an intellectual," Kramer recalled years later. "I tried to turn him on to how much fun it was being in a band with electric guitars, lights, sweat, noise and energy. He would tell me, none of that was hip, it was all 'passe.' Jazz is really where it's at. You need to listen to Gene Ammons, Sonny Rollins, John Coltrane."[18]

It was sometime later, after Rob had become a fan of the Rolling Stones' electrified versions of blues and R & B, that the two again crossed paths. Not long after, Wayne, Fred, and Rob were making plans to start a new group. At first, Rob wanted to act as manager, but they convinced him to join as the bass player.[19] Bob Gaspar was recruited to play drums. Although there were only four members, they decided to call themselves the Motor City Five, because they thought "five sounded better than four."[20] Rob tried to play bass, unsuccessfully, then left the group for a while, replaced by Pat Burrows. After a couple of months, Tyner returned as lead singer, becoming the fifth member of the Motor City Five.

Wayne Kramer credits his mother as a driving force in the development of the band, remembering how she would allow them to rehearse as well as hang out at the house. Although providing a lot of encouragement, and even managing them for a while, Wayne's mother also warned him that "music was a career full of hardship."[21] Despite the advice, the band soon moved on to the record hop circuit, decked out in matching green corduroy jackets, black pants, vests, and bowl haircuts. Wayne Kramer felt that playing in a rock 'n' roll band could be "a way out, out of the factory, out of the hum-drum and out of the possibility of winding up in the penitentiary."[22]

Though displaying a bit more blues influence, their repertoire at the time consisted of James Brown, Chuck Berry, and the Rolling Stones, mixed in with some blues and Motown. Midway through 1965, at the urging of Rob Tyner, the band decided to modify their name, opting for "MC5." Wayne Kramer said that "the name had that industrial, anonymous car factory sound to it, which was cool in the teen-age car culture and drag racing world that we were into."[23]

An important step in defining the band was the acquisition of three-thousand-dollar Vox Super Beatle amplifiers from England, which gave the MC5 the ability to play at an ear-splitting volume. Up until this point, the biggest amps in America had been Fender Dual Showmans, which were powered with sixty-five watts and held two fifteen-inch speakers. The Vox Super Beatles were one hundred watts, with four twelve-inch speakers and two high-frequency horns mounted in a tubed frame cabinet that could be tilted back. According to Wayne Kramer, it was a "huge piece of machinery, and very intimidating because it was black."[24] The band's two units included a transistor bass amplifier called a T60, which featured a fifteen-inch and a twelve-inch speaker, and two Vox columns for their "state-of-the-art PA system" that held six or eight ten-inch speakers mounted on chrome stands placed on each side of the stage. Kramer recalls that "there was one guy in town that owned one Super Beatle amp—we had a whole set!"[25]

It was the band's new manager, Bruce Burnish, who had taken out a bank loan to pay for the new equipment. "Bruce was just a nice guy in the neighborhood," recalls Kramer. "He was only a few years older than the rest of us, but he had a good job, and I guess we sort of manipulated him into helping us finance the new equipment. We told him about all the beautiful girls he would meet through us, and all the great restaurants where he would be dining, and I guess it sounded pretty good."[26]

Kramer traded in his Silvertone for a Fender Esquire, and Fred Smith played a Mosrite, made famous by the Ventures. Before purchasing the Mosrite, Fred had tried out a Fender Duo-Sonic guitar.

He didn't care for the instrument but loved the name. From then on he liked to refer to himself as Fred "Sonic" Smith.[27]

The band stayed busy playing record hops with the disc jockeys from WKNR at high schools and at venues such as the Ambassador Roller Rink in suburban Clawson. Although the MC5 played mainly cover versions of hits, they had also started to include an original piece of improvisational noise they came to call, "Black To Comm," named for wire connections on their amplifiers: *Comm* the negative ground, and *Black* the wire from the power source.[28]

WKNR deejay Jerry Goodwin had the MC5 with him for a Saturday night dance at Plymouth High School around May 1965 and recalled how "both Wayne and Freddie hit an off-key chord and then moved toward the speakers, creating a cacophonous feedback." After Rob Tyner stepped up to the mike and started screaming at top volume, Goodwin said, the two thousand kids in attendance stood "frozen" staring at the stage as the MC5 just kept jamming for the rest of the twenty-minute set, while he kept the security guard from "pulling the plug."[29]

According to Wayne Kramer, the band had been coming to the realization that the way for them to be successful was not to try to sound like an average teen band reaching for the top 10, but instead to "turn the amps up and jam!" Kramer sensed that people in Detroit "worked hard and wanted to see their bands play hard." Using energy, feedback, and distortion, the MC5 strove to "unleash the power of the electric guitar."[30]

While Rob, Wayne, and Fred were anxious to move their loud, "high energy" sound in a new jazz-influenced, improvisational direction, members Pat Burrows and Bob Gaspar were not so inclined. Burrows left in late 1965, followed by Gaspar in February 1966.[31] They were replaced by Michael Davis on bass and Dennis Thompson on drums.

Following art school, Michael Davis had enrolled at Wayne State, where he was studying to be a painter. It was after attending a Bob Dylan concert at Masonic Temple in 1963 that he started playing acoustic guitar and harmonica. Davis moved with his wife into a "rather infamous" building at 633 Prentiss, the same place where

Gary Grimshaw had been living. "Becky, Rob Tyner's girlfriend, lived across the hall from us, and she was friends with my wife," Davis recalls. "Rob came by a couple of times and was telling me that he played in a rock band, and why don't I come down and check 'em out sometime. So eventually I went to hear them at a little bar on John R." During a break, Rob Tyner introduced Davis to Wayne Kramer and Fred Smith. "I had on these brown Beatle boots that I had bought at Sibley's Florsheim down on Woodward Avenue," says Davis. "Wayne saw my boots and went, 'Whoa, where did you get those!' He thought I was the coolest guy in town."[32] The two soon started hanging out together, and when Kramer wasn't busy playing with the MC5, he and Davis strummed their acoustic guitars and developed a good friendship. The fact that Davis was older, well traveled and had even lived on New York's Lower East Side was attractive to both Kramer and Tyner.[33] Soon the two agreed that Davis would be a good fit for the MC5. When bassist Pat Burrows left to join the marines, Davis joined the band.

At the time, Michael Davis was "deeply" into R & B music, but he did not consider himself a musician. "Folk music . . . like Joan Baez, the Kingston Trio, Dave Van Ronk and of course Bob Dylan. That's what I started out playing or imitating," says Davis. "I thought of myself as being an artist and a beatnik."[34] Despite having never played the instrument, he jumped right in, going out and purchasing a new white Fender Precision Bass. He quickly mastered the twenty cover songs the band performed.

Davis's first gig with the MC5 took place at the student union at Wayne State University, where the band opened for the Elgins, a Motown vocal group. On another early gig, the MC5 was booked to play for a "Teen Fair" on Bob-Lo Island. The weather was not as warm as the promoters had hoped for, and the band was freezing as they played in the cold cement band shell. However, on the return trip, for some reason it felt a bit warmer on the boat, so the band plugged in their instruments and started an impromptu performance, and soon everyone on board was dancing.[35]

Davis thought the MC5's two guitarists were "the most outstanding guitar players" he had ever heard, saying, that, to him, "they were every bit as good as Jeff Beck or Keith Richard."[36] As for his own bass playing, Davis recalls Wayne Kramer trying to "influence him" by drawing his attention to bassist James Jamerson's parts on Motown hits. "Wayne called him Jameson back then," laughs Davis. "He'd say, 'Jameson, man, listen to Jameson play that part!' He was great and I would try to copy some of that stuff, but we were also watchin' the Who and the Yardbirds. When I joined the MC5 I was a young guy, and I thought there was no better time to try something out. If I was going to be in a band that I didn't think would be anything but successful, then these were some good guys to be in a band with."[37]

Although only in tenth grade at Lincoln Park High, Dennis Thompson had been playing drums since the age of six. His older brother had been in a band that practiced in their basement, and whenever they took a break, Dennis would jump on the drums. By age twelve, he was playing weddings, and at fourteen had joined his brother on club dates. For a while he played with Wayne Kramer in the Bounty Hunters, before going off in another direction. Then, when Dennis was in the latter half of his junior year in high school, Kramer reappeared. "Wayne had already formed the Motor City Five and they were playing in a little club called the Crystal Bar, which is a shot and a beer bar, over off of Springwell. Wayne came by my house on his motorcycle one night and asked me to play in this bar and I did. I joined, and from that point on I was in the band. We had about three toothless bums just sittin' there that first night and we're onstage playing 'My Generation.' I also have a memory of us playing at my all-night party at Lincoln Park High later on."[38]

Davis and Thompson quickly adapted to the more "free" sound the other band members were trying to produce. Davis recalls, "We had some blues, we had a few Stones songs, Kinks songs, you know, things like, 'You Really Got Me,' and we did 'We Gotta Get Out of This Place.' We'd also play some James Brown things, like 'Please, Please, Please,' because Wayne always had it for James Brown. Then we'd do some improvisational stuff in the middle of some of these tunes."[39]

According to Wayne Kramer, the MC5 sound was unique in that neither Dennis Thompson on drums nor Michael Davis on bass, held the bottom down: "They both were raging around the beat, through the beat, above the beat, beyond the beat. Even in The Who, John Entwhistle held the bottom down. In the MC5, nobody did. The closest we came was Fred Smith and he held it down with rhythm guitars, but the rest of it was just raging."[40]

For Dennis Thompson, a lot of the rage came in the form of hitting the drums really hard: "In the early days, we weren't miked. There weren't enough microphones to go 'round, and there wasn't enough PA equipment to go around, so we had to cut through Marshall stacks [amps]. So we developed the match grip style as opposed to the traditional style of drumming and started playing as hard as we could."[41] Thompson was most influenced by rock drummers such as John Bonham and Charlie Watts, but also credits pioneers Buddy Rich and Gene Krupa: "That was when drumming was all about the wrists," he commented. "And then what happened was, probably because of rock'n'roll, you had to pretty much scrap the wrists and get into the arm."[42]

Their new lineup firmly in place, its members invigorated with a common determination to be a truly great rock 'n' roll band, the MC5 powered their way into 1966.

# 10. A Mythical Figure

John Alexander Sinclair, who had recommended the MC5 to Russ Gibb, was a Renaissance man of sorts whose music column in the *Fifth Estate* represented just one of many facets of his involvement in Detroit's arts community.

He was born in Davison, Michigan, on October 2, 1941, the son of a career employee at Flint's Buick Assembly Plant. Following graduation from high school in 1959, Sinclair attended Albion College before dropping out in favor of hanging out on Flint's north side, attracted to the black culture that dominated that part of town. He returned to school at the University of Michigan, Flint College, and received a B.A. in American literature. By April 1964, Sinclair had moved to Detroit and enrolled in graduate school at Wayne State University, where he completed course work for his M.A. He wrote his thesis on William Burroughs's *Naked Lunch*.[1]

Growing up in the 1950s, Sinclair became a big fan of blues and R & B while listening to the radio. "Man, I used to listen to 'Frantic' Ernie Durham every night on WBBC from Flint," he recalls. "He was my idol. He played Muddy Waters, Little Walter, Sonnyboy, and Howlin' Wolf, and he would rhyme everything he said, like 'Great Googa Mooga Shooga Wooga!' or 'We've got the jive that's truly alive.' I thought he was the greatest." Such a fan was Sinclair that he had even billed himself "Frantic John" while playing records at a high school dance.[2]

In college, Sinclair's musical tastes expanded to include the "free jazz" movement represented by artists such as John Coltrane, Ornette Coleman, and Pharaoh Sanders. He also pursued the Beatnik scene by way of poetry readings at clubs such as the Purple Onion near Brush and John R, and at Verne's Bar on Forest between Cass and Woodward. In the fall of 1964, he met and began a relationship with fellow student Magdalene "Leni" Arndt, who shared his interests in the arts. Arndt had emigrated from East Germany in 1959 and was living with relatives in the Detroit area while putting herself through school at Wayne State.[3] It couldn't have been a better match. Leni loved jazz and "wanted to be a beatnik real bad."[4] After meeting John, she started to tag along when he visited the jazz clubs on writing assignments. Leni recalls that at the time, she and John were living together in a big house on Hancock Street: "There was no heat, the furnace was broken, and the owner wouldn't fix it, so John and I would put our feet in the oven to stay warm."[5]

On November 1, 1964, the couple, along with fourteen friends, including poet-filmmaker Robin Eichele, jazz trumpeter Charles Moore, and political activist Martina Algire, founded a small bohemian artist colony and social collective they named the Detroit Artists Workshop. "Back when I first arrived in the area, Leni, George Tysh and some of the others, had been members of a similar group that had a place called the Red Door Gallery over on Second and Willis," says Sinclair. "It closed in the summer of 1964. We took what they'd been doing and expanded on it."[6]

At its outset, the Detroit Artists Workshop issued a communal manifesto calling for a community of artists to support each other. The members of the DAW made a point of avoiding mainstream life, which John Sinclair liked to refer to as the "death system."[7]

The sixteen original members each contributed five dollars to pay the first month's rent on a two-story house at 1252 West Forest, in the Warren-Forest neighborhood, adjacent to Wayne State. It was an inner-city neighborhood populated by beatniks, students, and lower-class whites and blacks, many of whom had originally migrated from the South. Within a year, they were renting six other houses and two storefronts, providing space for a print shop, a performance and meeting center, and more living area for members and for anyone else who wanted to hang around.[8] At the Workshop, Sinclair stayed busy producing jazz concerts and poetry readings, as well as photography and painting exhibitions by local talent. There was an "Open House" on Sunday afternoons.

Leni started taking photos chronicling the jazz and art world that they lived in, and the Artist Workshop journals published many of them, including photos of John Coltrane, Yusef Lateef,

Thelonious Monk, and Miles Davis. John helped create and compose original music for the Workshop Arts Quartet and Music Ensemble, and with Eichele, George Tysh, and Jim Semark founded the Artists' Workshop Press.[9] Aside from the DAW and his column at the *Fifth Estate,* Sinclair served as local correspondent for the jazz magazine *Downbeat,* and his articles, poetry, and reviews were published in a wide range of regional and national publications. For a time, he published a small counterculture paper called *Guerilla.*[10] John Sinclair had one other passion that caused him some inconvenience from time to time: smoking marijuana. On November 1, 1964, he was arrested for the first time and charged with "sale and possession." It had been a setup. A friend who was facing jail time for drug dealing cut another deal to purchase marijuana from Sinclair as part of a sting operation by Detroit police. Sinclair received two years' probation and a $250 fine. At the time, a trace of marijuana was a felony in Michigan.[11]

Since arriving at Wayne State, John Sinclair had become acquainted with most of his friends through the marijuana underground. "I had connections with some brothers on the west side, dudes I knew through the black jazz scene, and I had like the only steady reefer supply in the campus area, so my apartment got to be like the meeting place for all different kinds of heads, musicians, poets, and other incipient freaks," Sinclair recalled in an interview with Peter Steinberger.[12]

After returning from the Berkeley Poetry Conference in California, where he and Leni had been able to meet some of their countercultural heroes such as publisher Ed Sanders and poet Allen Ginsberg, Sinclair was arrested for the second time.[13] An undercover narcotics cop named Vahan Kapagian had managed to infiltrate the Detroit Artists Workshop. Kapagian, going by the name Eddie, always seemed to be asking where he could buy some pot. After a few months, Sinclair, who had stopped dealing after his first arrest, relented, and one afternoon in October 1965, drove Eddie over to the house of a friend to score some grass. According to Sinclair, he thought the best way to get rid of Eddie was to "cop him some worthless weed" and overcharge him.[14]

Five minutes after returning from the buy, twenty-five cops descended on the DAW headquarters at 4825 John Lodge. Sinclair recalled that "the raiding team started climbing through the windows and busting down the doors, guns in hand, handcuffing everybody in sight and tearing the house apart."[15] Sinclair and five others were arrested and taken to police headquarters. In covering the events, both Detroit newspapers described Sinclair as "the leader of a campus drug ring."[16] On February 24, 1966, to avoid a more serious conviction for sales, Sinclair pled guilty to a charge of possession. Although told by his lawyer to expect probation, Sinclair was sentenced to six months in the Detroit House of Corrections.

Upon his release on August 6, John's wife Leni organized a welcome back party called "Festival of People." A late and unexpected addition to the talent set to perform was the MC5. "At the end of the evening, this band showed up. I really didn't know anything about them or who said they could play here," recalls Leni Sinclair.[17]

John Sinclair was already a "mythical figure" to the MC5's Wayne Kramer and Rob Tyner, who had both been reading his poetry and writings, and had been closely following his run-ins with the police.[18] By this time, all the band members had departed their Lincoln Park homes and were renting an apartment in the same building where Rob Tyner and his girlfriend Becky had moved to 659 West Canfield in the Cass Corridor area. The band enjoyed playing for "beatnik" audiences and had decided they would try and join in the celebration. Wayne Kramer recalled, "All these jazz groups played, poets read, dancers danced and Sinclair was holding court."[19] It was three in the morning when the MC5 finally got the opportunity to plug in their gear and start jamming. According to Leni Sinclair, the band was playing so loud that a "redneck" neighbor threatened them with a shotgun: "If you don't stop this, we'll have to do something." Worried that an altercation might cause John to be sent back to jail, Leni pulled the plug.[20]

A few weeks later, Sinclair wrote a column in the *Fifth Estate*, putting down rock and roll and the people who played it. The MC5 responded by letter, and an ongoing argument began. Sinclair stated that Coltrane and Miles Davis were "where it was at" and that the MC5 didn't know what was happening. "We wrote a letter back, recalls Kramer, "sayin' 'hey man, we know all about John Coltrane'; 'cause Tyner had turned us on to him.'"[21]

One day, while searching for a new place for the band to rehearse, Wayne knocked on the door of the Artist's Workshop, which was always making it known that they had space available for artists and musicians to rehearse. Kramer recalls, "I said to John, 'What's up with this rehearsal space? Can our band rehearse here?' He said, 'Come on in and let's smoke a joint.' We found we had a lot in common, and he said we could practice during the day if we didn't cause noise problems with the neighbors or police. So we were cool."[22]

Once John Sinclair finally sat down to listen to the band play, his opinion of them quickly changed: "I saw where they were doing the same sorts of things as Coltrane and the other free jazz artists. Yeah, they were playing rock 'n' roll, but with more creativity and improvisation."[23] Sinclair began attending all their gigs, starting with an appearance at the Cavern in Northville, where the MC5 participated in a "battle of the bands."

In the fall of 1966, when Russ Gibb made the call, asking Sinclair if he knew of a good band with its own sound, John invited him over. According to Kramer, "Russ was looking for a band that played their own music as well as some cover versions. There just weren't any bands like that around back then. Everybody played only covers of top 10 hits. We had done record hops with Jerry Goodwin, and he also advised Russ that 'there's only one band in town that does originals, and that's the MC5.'"[24]

"We were working on this really loud new song when Russ arrived," says Michael Davis. "I think we were calling it 'You Got Me Freakin' Out.' When we finished playing, I remember Russ saying, 'Yeah, *yeah,* that's exactly what I'm lookin' for!'"[25] Gibb asked the MC5 if they would be interested in being the house band at the Grande Ballroom, although he would be unable to pay them for a while. The band accepted the offer. "For us to be able to rehearse in the same place we were going to be performing and at the same sound levels was just a very attractive situation," recalls Kramer. "We could see that it would really give us the chance to develop and grow."[26] During their first few months at the Grande, the MC5 spent the afternoons practicing there with their coats on, because

Russ Gibb couldn't afford to turn on the heat during the day.[27] "We knew that exposure was the name of the game," says Dennis Thompson. "To break in, back in those days, you had to make your own noise, you had to establish your own identity. We didn't make a lot of money at the Grande, but we got exposure and we started to build a fan base, which is what we wanted to do."[28]

According to Kramer, while Russ Gibb signed the band, John Sinclair went into a sales pitch for his entire range of services: "Yeah Russ, we've got a band, we've got a light show . . ."[29] That night, the MC5 made a critical move forward in their career, and John Sinclair locked up several lucrative concessions at the Grande Ballroom for his evolving organization, still operating as the Detroit Artists Workshop.

At nine o'clock on the evening of October 7, 1966, the Grande Ballroom opened for business. After all of Russ Gibb's promotion, just sixty people showed up that first night to hear a Birmingham band called the Chosen Few warm things up for the "avant rock" of the MC5. Aside from the music, the audience was treated to psychedelic light beams and the aroma of incense in the air. The following night, the crowd doubled, but there was still ample empty space for kids to move around in.

In mid-January, 1967, posters appeared along the streets of Detroit promoting an upcoming event scheduled to take place at the Grande Ballroom on January 29. "Guerrilla Lovefare" was to be the "most explosive gathering of 'freeks' in Detroit's history."[30] Poets, rock bands, jazz groups, light shows, and plenty of "weed and acid" were to be on hand that night. It never happened. On January 24, thirty-four law enforcement officers staged a series of raids around the Wayne State area, including the headquarters of the Detroit Artists Workshop. John and Leni Sinclair, along with fifty-four others, described to the press as "the long haired type with beards and mod clothes," were once again hauled off to jail.[31] Although claiming that it had been "one of the largest raids in Detroit in recent years, in number of arrests," the six-hour operation had netted the police only small quantities of marijuana and possibly a little LSD. To accomplish all of this, the Detroit police had been assisted by seven federal narcotics agents, five customs agents, three members of the Michigan State Police, and a federal Food and Drug Administration agent.[32]

While the other arrestees were quickly released on bond and forty-three were not even charged, the police held on to John Sinclair. The Special Investigative Bureau of the Detroit Police Department had opened a file on Sinclair and the "hippie community" around Wayne State, following his first arrest in November 1964.[33] In the meantime, Sinclair had attracted further attention after starting a Detroit chapter of LEMAR, an organization whose name stood for Legalize Marijuana.[34]

The latest raid had been ordered at the end of a four-month-long sting operation by the Detroit Police Narcotics Division. Once again, it was Detective Vahan Kapagian, now sporting a beard, who had managed to get inside the DAW, this time disguised as a "hip candle maker" going by the name Louie. Another narcotics cop named Jane Mumford also made it in, posed as a hippie chick named Pat. After several months had gone by with no major drug transaction in site, the cops were losing patience, so when Sinclair, according to the police, casually passed Mumford two marijuana joints for free at Christmas, the raid was ordered. As this was his third arrest on drug charges, Michigan law at the time called for an automatic ten-year sentence. Sinclair's lawyers managed to keep him out of prison by arguing against the constitutionality of the state's marijuana statutes.[35]

Despite the inconvenience, Sinclair wasted no time in getting back to his counterculture interests. By February, shortly after forming a steering committee for 1967, Sinclair, Leni, and new friend Gary Grimshaw were transforming the Detroit Artists Workshop into a "new total cooperative tribal living and working commune," which they decided to call Trans-Love Energies Unlimited.[36] The name was inspired by the lyric "Fly Translove Airlines" from a song by British folk artist Donovan.

The new identity would align the group more with the developing rock scene and youth movement in Detroit. According to their own doctrine, Trans-Love Energies existed "to promote self-reliance and tribal responsibility among the artists, craftsmen, and other lovers" in the commune.[37] The "hippie cooperative" was incorporated as a nonprofit organization, not having to answer to any special interest group. To support its efforts and feed its members, TLE would generate money producing rock 'n' roll concerts, light shows through its Magic Veil Light Company, books, pamphlets, and posters from the holdover Artist Workshop Press. They would also publish the *Warren-Forest Sun* newspaper. Among the other notable services provided by TLE was an inner-space travel agency, providing helpful information for those wishing to take a mind-expanding trip via LSD.[38]

John Sinclair described their new communal culture as a "revolutionary culture," saying "the commune is the life-form of the future."[39] He also viewed this new culture as a "political force."[40] In addition to the Sinclairs and Grimshaw, the board of directors for Trans-Love Energies included Emil Bacilla, Judy Janis, Linda Carlson, Danny Bellinger, Tom and Grace Mitchell, and a new arrival, activist and sandal maker Lawrence Robert "Pun" Plamondon. A native of Traverse City, Michigan, Plamondon arrived in Detroit after working with migrant farm laborers in California.[41]

The creation of Trans-Love Energies moved Sinclair from the "underground beatnik life" to the forefront of a movement that believed they could effect political and social change in the country. According to Sinclair, the war in Vietnam "created the context" for change, as did the civil rights movement, but he also points to the changing drug culture: "Don't forget, we were on acid. That was what made all the difference. Before acid we didn't want to turn anybody on."[42]

On Sunday, April 30, 1967, Trans-Love Energies Unlimited produced its first major event, promoted as a "love-in" to be held on Belle Isle. The six-hundred-acre island park sits in the Detroit River, with a small bridge connecting it to East Jefferson Avenue and East Grand, a short distance to the east of downtown. The MC5, Southbound Freeway, the Up, Seventh Seal, and Billy C. and the Sunshine, were set to perform. This was to be an afternoon of peace, love, and music, and John Sinclair had assured authorities that there would be no problems. In fact, he promised that the "Trans Love Psychedelic Ranger Patrol" would be on hand to keep everybody cool. The Detroit police relaxed and assigned just a few mounted officers to the event.[43]

Things got underway around eleven in the morning with people gathering around the Remick Music Shell. At about twelve-thirty, Trans-Love guru John Sinclair arrived on the scene. Attired in a ground-length pink print gown designed by Leni and wearing love beads, he held court in a picnic pavilion close by. Surrounded by followers paying homage, Sinclair announced that the gathering was "an opportunity to love one another."[44]

By midafternoon, the peaceful crowd grew to six thousand, with attendees singing and dancing as the bands rocked on stage. MC5 bass player Michael Davis recalls that the band was "really on a roll" that day. "It was a really open atmosphere, and the people there were not necessarily rock and roll people but more like the curious, and we hit the stage feeling like we could really blow some vibes with our style. We knew we had certain songs that just excited any crowd, like 'Gloria,' for instance. We particularly drove that one home. So we'd get on some of these things like 'Can't Explain' and 'Gloria' and get on a roll, and when you start playin' those songs back to back and a bunch of people start dancing, you're really messing with some euphoria there."[45]

But as the day wore on, a mix of flower children and curious onlookers was joined by leather-jacketed motorcycle gang members. Colorful balloons, candy, and good karma began to be replaced by beer, wine, and bad vibes. When a bystander objected to a member of the Outlaws motorcycle gang making moves on his girlfriend, the man was surrounded and savagely beaten by the gang as a dumbstruck crowd stood by and watched.[46] By dusk, the band Seventh Seal was being asked to quit playing in hopes that the crowd would disperse. They refused, and things grew uglier. People lit smelly bonfires from all the trash and garbage piling up. When the police arrested a gang member for driving his motorcycle dangerously through the crowd, someone responded by tossing a firecracker near the police horses.[47] Others in the crowd began throwing rocks and bottles. Soon a full-blown riot was taking place, and the police brought in 150 reinforcements to restore order. According to Wayne Kramer, the police response was "ridiculously out of proportion to the danger they faced," as if the cops were "really enjoying their overpowering dominance."[48]

After jumping on an open-bed truck with some of the band

gear, Kramer and the others headed in the direction of the MacArthur Bridge, only to be stopped by a police roadblock and then the sound of approaching hoof beats. According to Kramer, "The mounted cops galloped toward the running people and clubbed them like they were playing polo."[49]

A pregnant Leni Sinclair was holding tight to her husband and recalls the scene: "We saw the police charge into the crowd just as we escaped to some friend's house. We were scared that they were going to arrest us because the police really started the trouble and were blaming us."[50] An eerie scene played out in the darkness as the beams from police headlights and flashlights shown through the trees. It was pandemonium, with heads cracking, blood spurting, and voices screaming. Finally, the crowd was forced out onto the bridge and off the island. A number of people smashed windows along Jefferson Avenue before scattering in different directions and disappearing into the night.

John Sinclair's take on the days events had been to say that the real hippies didn't cause any trouble and had left earlier, and it had been the "straights" and "weekend hippies" who were responsible for all the chaos.[51] It was however, Sinclair and his Trans-Love Energies who took the blame for the whole mess and caused the police to focus even more closely on their activities.

In a later conversation between Sinclair and MC5 vocalist Rob Tyner, Sinclair commented on the event: "At the Love-In, you saw that the people who didn't have any trouble at all were the ones who were right there where the music was. The music was so out-of-sight that day."[52] Recalling the concert, MC5 drummer Dennis Thompson commented: "I'd have to call the 'Love-In' . . . really the best show. That's when we were perfectly in tune."[53]

The MC5 had finally gotten the opportunity to record in March 1967, but according to Wayne Kramer it was a less than ideal situation: "We had hooked up with three guys who had come to see us play a couple of times, and they had big plans for us. Arnold Mark Geller, Larry Benjamin, and a third guy named Cliff Goroff. They had this little operation and managed us for a while. We would go over to their office and they would act like big shots. At the same time the building's landlord was chasing them to pay the rent."54 The band, which had no studio experience, was now being recorded by inexperienced producers. "They were just some guys who were young music-business entrepreneurs trying to cash in on us," says Kramer, adding, "They weren't artists; they certainly weren't creative."55 The band was given the standard three-hour session at United Sound to set up and try to complete two songs—not only the basic track but also the overdub and the mix.

The MC5 had chosen a Van Morrison–Them song called "I Can Only Give You Everything" as the A-side. They liked it because it was similar to "Gloria," which had been successfully covered by a Chicago group called Shadows of Night. The recording session was done under a lot of pressure, said Kramer: "I'd start working on my guitar tone, and the engineer would say, 'Turn that down. It's distorted.' I said, 'that's what I want.'"56 At the end of three hours, they'd completed only one song.

The band moved to Tera Shirma Studios for the second session, and it was another three-hour rush job. The B-side of the record, "One Of The Guys," was an original, written by Rob Tyner. The AMG label released the record, which failed to receive airplay or generate sales.

In live performances, the MC5 continued to blast away at top volume as they delivered their high-energy rock 'n' roll. The group was set to perform at a "Teen Fair" show at Cobo Hall in 1967 when they faced resistance to their noise. Musician Marshall Crenshaw recalled being there as a teenager and waiting for the band to start their set. "I was wandering around and got right up close and the guys were just standing there waiting and waiting, and the crowd just stood there watching and waiting." Crenshaw felt that the band had a certain "aura" about them and that they really gave off a "vibe" just standing there. "After maybe ten minutes of this heavy anticipation," says Crenshaw, "the lead singer [Rob Tyner] walks back out to the microphone and politely announces to the crowd: 'Well, I'm sorry folks, but the people in charge of the amplifiers won't let us turn them up past 5. If we can't turn them up all the way, then we can't play our music the way it's supposed to be played, so we'll see you some other time.' And they walked off and that was it."57

John Sinclair's ties to the MC5 continued to strengthen, especially the relationship with Rob Tyner, the group's resident beatnik. "John was Rob's idol," Wayne Kramer related to writer Ken Kelly. "He was a beatnik, and John was even more of a beatnik, shit, he was the embodiment of a beatnik. A poet who did spoken-word gigs, heavy into far-out jazz, and smoked marijuana continuously."[58]

At six foot three, and now wearing his hair in long flowing curly locks, with a Fu Manchu mustache, goatee, and wire rim glasses, John Sinclair was an imposing figure. A deep, somewhat gruff voice only added to his increasing role as an authority figure to the band. Wayne Kramer felt that Sinclair "could articulate eloquently things that he felt on a gut level, but was unable to express."[59] Sinclair had also begun to contribute philosophical advice to the band regarding their performance and the direction they were taking.

Soon the band moved to the DAW building on the corner where East Warren Avenue meets the John C. Lodge Expressway. Along the Lodge service drive there was a long block of apartments with a sandstone facade that people called "The Castle." It was here that John Sinclair and other members of the Detroit Artists Workshop resided. To the north, on the corner, was a series of two-story commercial structures with storefronts along the street. The Detroit Office of the Committee To End the War in Vietnam was located there, as well as the *Fifth Estate* newspaper and the band's rehearsal space at the Artists Workshop.[60]

The corner of Warren and Forest became the "center of the universe" to Wayne Kramer, whose late nights were spent "tripping out on acid, smoking the best Mexican herb to be found," and listening to influential free jazz musicians such as Sun Ra, John Coltrane, and Albert Ayler while "plotting the future."[61]

At the Grande Ballroom, the MC5 was developing a reputation that enabled them to pick up more paying gigs around the area. Some of the other local bands taking the stage at the Grande in the spring of 1967 included Southbound Freeway, Thyme, the Rationals, the Scott Richard Case, Jagged Edge, Seventh Seal, the Apostles, Früt of the Loom, and southern blues rockers Billy C. and the Sunshine.

Billy C. Farlow had grown up in Alabama, Indiana, and Texas, inspired by both black and white musicians. After learning how to play both guitar and harmonica, he started to perform the same songs made popular by blues legends and covered by other aspiring artists like himself. Following his family's move to Detroit in the early 1960s, Farlow started to perform in various coffeehouses and blues clubs. By the fall of 1966, he formed his first band, Billy C. and the Sunshine, which included Larry Welker and pianist Boot Hamilton. By April 1967, they brought their unique sound to the stage at the Grande Ballroom, opening for the MC5. Although a record contract was still the goal of any up-and-coming group, the expanding club scene, including the addition of the Grande, gave groups such as Billy C. and the Sunshine the opportunity to build a reputation and a loyal following without the support of a hit record.[62]

# 11. Summer in the City

On Sunday afternoon, July 23, 1967, two teenagers (one of whom was this book's author) were on their way back home to suburban Royal Oak, after a day of joyriding to downtown Detroit. Heading north on Woodward Avenue, they spotted several police and fire vehicles with sirens wailing, turning west on Clairmount Avenue. Curious, they swung a sharp left and proceeded down the same street where they soon encountered the unusual sight of policemen armed with rifles, standing along the curb. Just before arriving at Twelfth Street, auto and pedestrian congestion forced their car to slow down to a crawl and then a cop yelled out to them: "You better get the hell out of here, now!" As the two scanned the intersection, they witnessed a chaotic scene. There were stores with broken windows and black people running out of them with arm loads of merchandise. Sensing a definite air of danger, the driver jaggedly pulled around a parked car, turned a corner and sped out of the area.[1]

The trouble had started the night before, when police had raided an illegal "blind pig," operating at 9125 Twelfth Street, at the corner of Clairmount Avenue. Originally established as the United Community League for Civic Action, the action now revolved around drinking and gambling, especially after Detroit's 2:00 A.M. curfew. One of many such illegal establishments in the area, there had been two successful raids there during the preceding nine months.[2]

It was at 3:45 A.M. on July 23, a very hot and muggy Sunday morning, when the police made their move. The raid was led by Tenth Precinct sergeant Arthur Howison, and seventy-three black customers and the bartender were quickly taken into custody. Since the rear door was locked, the police and their prisoners exited through the front door facing onto Twelfth Street. Outside a small group of people was hanging out, described as a "few drunks, some drifters, prostitutes and petty gamblers."[3] As the police loaded the arrestees into squad cars and a paddy wagon, the onlookers jeered and taunted them, angry at the way the police were pushing their prisoners around. The crowd in this twenty-four-hour-a-day neighborhood got larger. As Howison's squad car finally pulled out, a bottle came smashing through the rear window. Suddenly, store windows were breaking and people were helping themselves to whatever was inside. A young man who was working in a nearby shoe store said later that the crowd had gotten mad, "not because of busting the blind pig, but because of the way they [the police] were treating everybody."[4] What had begun as an isolated incident was now developing into a major urban uprising. In addition to looting, the rioters were setting fire to the stores, and the flames were spreading to homes and apartments. By early Sunday afternoon, a mile of Twelfth Street was in flames and bands of roving looters were crossing Woodward Avenue and moving through the east side. Many black merchants quickly scrawled "Soul Brother" across their windows in hopes of avoiding trouble, most to no avail. The situation became more grave by the minute, with reports of sniper fire.[5]

Not far away on Woodward Avenue, Martha Reeves and the Vandellas were onstage at the Fox Theater, headlining the "Swingin' Time Revue," staged by Robin Seymour of CKLW-TV. Also on the bill of Detroit talent were J. J. Barnes ("Poor Unfortunate Me"), Deon Jackson ("Love Makes the World Go 'Round"), and the Parliaments, led by George Clinton ("(I Wanna) Testify").

"It was a Sunday matinee and I will never forget it," recalls Seymour. "We had been getting huge crowds, but this particular Sunday we only had about five hundred people and wondered what was going on. Well, we found out when the police arrived to warn us about the riots that were breaking out all around us."[6] After the Vandellas concluded their set with their signature song, "Dancing in the Street," Martha Reeves stepped out of the spotlight and was briefed about the situation. She then went back out on the stage and explained to the audience what was happening outside. She told the crowd to be calm, and for the kids not to worry, they would get them to their parents.[7]

Like many other people around the metropolitan area that day,

Russ Gibb was unaware of what was going on in the heart of the city. Folk artist Tim Buckley had performed at the Grande Ballroom on Friday and Saturday nights and had agreed to add a Sunday night show. Gibb recalls, "After we wrapped things up on Saturday night, Tim Buckley and I were standing on the roof of the Grande. It was around two-thirty, a real hot night, and we were just getting some air. We decided to go out to Kensington State Park on Sunday for a picnic."[8]

Later on Sunday afternoon, as Gibb, Buckley, and his percussionist Carter C. C. Collins drove back into town, they sensed that something wasn't right. "When we got to the light at Greenfield and Grand River we saw smoke floating over much of the surrounding area," recalls Gibb. "We had been listening to tapes on the eight-track player, so we hadn't heard any radio news. We drove back to my place, where Tim and Carter were staying, and after seeing what was happening on TV, decided that we better get over to the Grande as fast as possible. They were worried about their equipment, and I had a whole lot more on the line."[9]

Russ slid behind the wheel of his Thunderbird as the trio roared out of Dearborn, with Buckley in the passenger seat and Collins, who was black, lying on the floor behind. "When we got to Joy Road," says Gibb, " we thought it was a good idea to let Carter drive while Buckley and I crouched as low as we could in the backseat."[10] Grand River was already being looted and trashed, and not far up the road buildings were on fire, but when they pulled up next to the Grande Ballroom, they were amazed to find it intact, "not even a broken window." Gibb remembers Carter Collins coming out of the Grande and asking some kids standing around why the ballroom had been spared. "The kid shot back one of those really classic lines," says Gibb: "'Cause, you got the music, man."[11]

The MC5's Wayne Kramer had also attended the Kensington Park party on Sunday. Later, from his apartment window in the Warren-Forest area, he had been looking into his telescope to get a better view of the police and military activity taking place nearby. Wednesday morning, several days into the riot, Wayne and a few other friends staying at the apartment were awakened by the sound of police breaking down their door: "Everybody get up because you're gonna get shot!" Kramer recalls the greeting.[12] The cops, shotguns drawn, ran from room to room looking for guns. They were accusing Kramer of using the telescope to sight cops so they could be shot by snipers. Incredulous, Kramer responded: "Look at all the guitars lyin' around here! We're musicians!"[13] The explanation fell on deaf ears, and after finding a bag of reefer seeds, the police arrested everybody and transported them to the main lockup in the downtown jail. Kramer heard someone say, "Yeah, put those white boys in here with us," as they were marched through a cellblock full of recently jailed inmates.[14] That evening, Kramer and his friends were released, and returned home to find tanks patrolling the neighborhood.

Following similar riots in other cities, such as Newark, New Jersey, and, most notably, L.A.'s Watts area in 1965, Detroit Mayor Jerome Cavanagh and other city leaders had proudly proclaimed: "That sort of thing can't happen here."[15] Cavanagh, a liberal Democrat, had been making inroads in race relations, launching a major war on poverty. His plans for the summer had included a new Head Start educational program and various recreational activities for the inner city. But none of these efforts would immediately change the fact that the unemployment rate for black Detroiters between the ages of eighteen and twenty-four was close to 30 percent.[16] Something else slow to change was the relationship between the black community and the Detroit Police Department. Despite a pledge to hire more black officers, African Americans still accounted for only 5 percent of the force in July 1967. There were many residents who felt that Detroit was "long overdue" for a riot.[17]

Despite the frequency of reports of police brutality, there never seemed to be a strong response from officials. Police commissioner Ray Girardin was quoted as saying, "It's a son of a bitch to stop. These guys [police officers] are hard to handle, and they can screw you in ninety ways."[18]

It was the Cavanagh-Girardin decision to have Detroit's undermanned police force hold their fire in the hopes that the crowds would disperse that people blamed for the rapid escalation of violence and destruction. Eventually, they abandoned it, and with the arrival of seventy-three hundred National Guard troops and forty-seven hundred paratroopers from Ft. Bragg, Kentucky, the looting and sniping finally wound down. After five days, forty-three persons were known dead, 347 injured, and thirty-eight hundred arrested. Estimates of damage hovered around $500 million. Thirteen hundred buildings had been destroyed, and twenty-seven hundred businesses had been sacked.[19] Mayor Cavanagh commented, "It looks like Berlin in 1945."[20]

In his "Coatpuller" column in the *Fifth Estate,* John Sinclair had a different take on the summer event: "No, baby, it's not a 'race riot' or anything as simple as that. People just got tired of being hassled by police and cheated by businessmen and got out their equalizers and went to town. . . . Oh it was Robin Hood Day in merry olde Detroit, the first annual city-wide all-free fire sale, and the people without got their hands on the goodies."[21] Sinclair and Trans-Love Energies provided food and clothing for many of the five thousand people left homeless.

Following the riots, the police became even more oppressive. According to Leni Sinclair, Detroit cop Warner Stringfellow, who had directed the earlier raids on the DAW, had become an archenemy of Trans-Love Energies. He believed that John Sinclair, now being called Detroit's "King of the Hippies," was "the number one enemy of the people and was turning millions of teenagers into hippies." Since his own daughter had embraced the lifestyle espoused by Sinclair, Stringfellow had developed a personal vendetta against him.[22]

In August 1967, the members of the MC5 asked John Sinclair to become their manager. Although he had been providing spiritual advice to the band, Sinclair thought of himself as a "music lover and cultural activist." He did, however, believe that the band "desperately needed management," and that its members were serious about becoming the "biggest rock 'n' roll band in the world."[23]

During the Grateful Dead's recent visit to Detroit, John had been able to spend some time with their managers, Rick Skully and Danny Rifkin. Afterward, he had thought to himself: "These guys are as nuts as I am. It must be possible to do this." Sinclair came to the realization that being a manager "was just a matter of applying yourself to the situation, making things happen and dealing with squares on behalf of the band members."[24] "He was the only guy everybody in the band would listen to," Wayne Kramer told writer Ken Kelly. "Everybody respected him, because he was smarter than everybody else. You couldn't out-argue him."[25] At the time, Sinclair couldn't believe how "untogether" the band's business operation was. All their equipment, save for Dennis Thompson's drums, had recently been repossessed. They hadn't made a payment for eight months. Wayne Kramer: "We were playing a really big gig at Ford Auditorium with the Jefferson Airplane, and just before we go on, our old manager Bruce Burnish shows up with the cops and wants all the equipment back. Russ Gibb paid them two hundred bucks to let us finish the show. As soon as it was over, Burnish had the cops load up all the gear, and they drove off."[26]

Sinclair quickly made arrangements for Russ Gibb to sign for two sets of equipment for Fred and Rob. Wayne got his mother to sign for his, and Michael Davis received help from his father. John made sure that payments to a finance company were made on time each month. They purchased new equipment at Joe Massimino's Music Store: three Sunn 100 series amps, and a PA system. Their friend, Emil Bacilla, loaned the group a van.[27]

Wayne Kramer also appreciated the fact that Sinclair related to the music. "John was the first to say that he wasn't in the business world. He was into us because he loved music, and he thought we were a great band," said Kramer.[28] In a more recent interview, Kramer described Sinclair as an "interface between the band and the outside world," adding that even though he was "as crazy as we were, he at least had the ability to talk and explain what we were trying to do in a way you could understand, to people in the music biz."[29]

Early on, Dennis Thompson had positive feelings about Sinclair: "From the very beginning, I found him as a very colorful guy. He had a lot of energy, he was smart, he was articulate. I really liked him."[30] The group's bass player, Michael Davis, felt that Sinclair brought the band together and made them "feel important."[31] John Sinclair handled all finances and all the business, with the band's advice and consent. There was never much in the way of spending money around, with most of the earnings going to pay for more equipment and to fill the coffers of Trans-Love Energies.[32]

By this time, Sinclair and the member [    ] and were also coming together through drugs: "We th[    ]get high were on the other side," claime[    ]dope was the link between the neob[    ]involved with prior to 1966 and [    ]evolved out of it.[33]

# 12. Hippies and Head Shops

To experience the "hippie scene" in Detroit in 1967, one needed only to visit Plum Street, in the Elton Park neighborhood, located between Michigan Avenue and the Lodge and Fisher Freeways downtown. The media was likening Plum Street to San Francisco's Haight-Ashbury district, which had recently gained notoriety as home to the flower children during 1967's so-called Summer of Love.

The revitalized Plum Street was a brand new addition to the city, but it had already become something other than what its designers had intended. Robert Cobb, one of the developers, was a twenty-four-year-old high school history teacher, who envisioned the area as a throwback to the Gay Nineties and the Roaring Twenties. Prior to its facelift, Plum Street was lined with little wooden buildings that Cobb thought would lend themselves nicely to quaint shops, theaters, and restaurants, and attract customers from all over the metropolitan area. He and his partner, Sherman Shapiro, purchased most of the buildings on Plum between Fourth and Fifth. Mayor Cavanagh got behind the project and was on hand for the grand opening in September 1966.[1]

By the fall of 1967, gaslights and trash cans had been installed, and the bustling little area was home to around forty businesses. It also became home to hippie wannabes and motorcycle gangs. Antique dealers and pottery shops were joined by the House of Mystical Incense. There were head shops, hippie clothing boutiques, and the Hai-Ku and Red Roach coffeehouses. The *Fifth Estate* had moved its offices there, as well as opening its own bookstore, stocked with radical newspapers such as the *San Francisco Oracle*, the *Chicago Seed*, and the *East Village Other*, and books by Burroughs, Kerouac, and the like.[2]

The *Fifth Estate* had come to life in November 1965, when Harvey Ovshinsky, a seventeen-year-old graduate of Mumford High School, decided to publish a small newspaper providing an alternative to the mainstream media. Earlier in the year, Harvey's mother had insisted that he accompany her on a visit to Los Angeles. While there, Ovshinsky landed a job at the *LA Free Press,* an established alternative paper that opened his eyes to a whole new subculture. The paper's offices were located in the basement of a coffeehouse called the Fifth Estate.[3]

At the end of the summer, Harvey returned to Michigan, and from the bedroom of his father's home in Bloomfield Hills launched his own "underground newspaper." "I had absolutely no journalistic experience," he recalls. "I had only done a little work for the *Idiom,* a small school paper, but because I had no idea about how a tabloid was put together, we wound up with two blank pages in the first issue. It was really embarrassing."[4] The issue itself almost didn't make it to press: "The printer we were going to use got offended by a cartoon, depicting an American flag with bayonets as stripes, and refused to do the print job." Harvey grabbed the plates and took them to the *Star of the Black Madonna,* a black newspaper in the area. They agreed to print the issue, which went on sale for a dime.[5] Inside was a Jules Feiffer cartoon lifted from another source, and a negative review of a Bob Dylan concert. "We said he'd never make it, we were such visionaries," said Ovshinsky.[6]

Always looking for ways to improve the paper's content, Harvey was told by friends that he "had to meet John Sinclair," a local freelance writer. "I went over to their place, I think it was on Hancock, and I was so impressed," remembers Ovshinsky. "There were books all over, Coltrane was on the stereo, and you could smell Leni's home cooking. It was a real intellectual scene. I was just a kid, and John was like an 'older guy.' However, when I explained what I was trying to do, he was not at all patronizing, and he understood. Both he and Leni were very supportive, and I was more than happy when John agreed to do a regular column in the paper."[7] Sinclair named the column "The Coatpuller."

Despite a shaky beginning, the paper started to find an audience, especially around the Wayne State campus. Overloaded with work, Harvey invited Peter Werbe to come on board as coeditor.

The *Fifth Estate* was soon being described by one reviewer as an "organ for hippies, liberals, and anarchists."[8] The paper's content included stories protesting the Vietnam War, Dow Chemical Company, and religious Christmas stamps. There was a column by Timothy Leary, and the back cover of one issue featured a mock wanted poster for infamous undercover narcotics cop Vahan Kapagian. The poster promised a reward of "one pound of U.S. grass to anyone who can drop 1000 micrograms of LSD into this man's misdirected body."[9] Together with five other publications around the country, the *Fifth Estate* became a founding member of the Underground Press Syndicate. Each member had the opportunity to share stories and features from the other papers at no charge, beyond the annual twenty-five-dollar fee. The syndicate soon grew to twenty-six publications.[10]

The *Fifth Estate* regularly criticized "the pigs" in the Detroit Police Department for harassment. One such issue headlined: "Pot Heads Bust Fuzz Heads!"[11] National political coverage tended to lean left, knocking Lyndon Johnson and praising Ho Chi Minh. Readers could also catch up on the latest happening at the Grande Ballroom. Distribution, however, remained a problem: "A lot of the kids selling it around their schools would get busted, because the paper had such a radical reputation," says Ovshinsky, adding, "Russ Gibb helped a lot by letting us sell the paper at the Grande Ballroom."[12]

When Robert Cobb approached Harvey about moving the paper to a location on Plum Street, and expanding the concept to include a bookstore, it seemed a good idea: "The paper was barely hanging on, and while Peter [Werbe], being more political than I, was sort of opposed to it, I saw how we could make more money by also selling counterculture stuff like radical bumper stickers, records by the Fugs, along with books and magazines, and it worked."[13]

While the headquarters of Trans-Love Energies remained in the Warren-Forest neighborhood, John and Leni Sinclair decided to move to Plum Street in the fall of 1967. They wanted to "keep a close check on what was happening there," and to be closer to the *Fifth Estate*. In fact, the Sinclairs lived in the same building that housed the paper's bookstore. Gary Grimshaw, usually hard at work producing posters and handbills for the Grande Ballroom, lived across the hall.[14]

Although the Plum Street neighborhood appeared to be healthy, the summer riots had caused most suburbanites to avoid the inner city, and many of the kids hanging around the street didn't have any money to spend. Despite the hippie aura, a very capitalistic Plum Street Merchant's Association was formed to pool advertising funds to attract Christmas shoppers.[15]

# 13. Hits and Misses

In 1967, while the MC5 toiled away at the Grande Ballroom, Detroit-area rock bands produced a bumper crop of hits.

The Underdogs were now performing with a four-man lineup after Steve Perrin and Jack Louisell left to attend college. According to lead guitarist Tony Roumell, the band stopped playing regularly at the Hideout toward the end of 1966 because "so many fights had been developing, as kids from the different locations didn't mix well." Dave Leone had joined the Air Force National Guard for six months and left Hideout number one to be run by Punch Andrews, who was managing the other two locations as well.[1]

Roumell's father owned a large catering company and the Latin Quarter, a famous Detroit nightclub. He was well connected politically in the city and a close acquaintance of State Representative George Edwards, whose wife, Ester, was the sister of Berry Gordy. "One day, Dad said, 'If you guys think you're going somewhere, call Ester for an audition,'" recalls Roumell.[2] Heeding his father's advice, the band made the phone call and was asked to come down and audition: "They had us set up in a building across the street from the main Hitsville location on West Grand Boulevard. It was in an old ballet studio, with wood floors and mirrors all around. We played so loud that the light fixtures fell from the ceiling. I thought we had really blown it, but they were so impressed that someone ran over to the other building and brought back half the company to listen to us."[3]

After two or three weeks, the label asked them to return and sign a contract. Prior to the Underdogs, there had been two other white groups at Motown. The first, the Valadiers, had been a vocal group, and the second, the Headliners, more of a nightclub show band. There had also been a Canadian rock band called the

Minah Birds, which included a black singer named Rick James, and guitarist Neil Young. But their recordings were shelved.[4] The Underdogs were the first true rock band of the late sixties scene signed, recorded, and released by Motown.

The group's producer, Clarence Paul, chose a song written and originally recorded by the label's Chris Clark to be the Underdogs' first single. "Love's Gone Bad" was released on the Motown subsidiary label, VIP, in late December, and by mid-January 1967 it had become a smash in Detroit, reaching number 3 on the charts. The flip side was "Mojo Hanna." Tony Roumell recalls the recording session: "They wanted that Motown energy on the record, so Earl Van Dyke played the Hammond B3 and James Jamerson played bass. When we started to record, I just couldn't believe how great these guys were. They elevated my level of playing."[5]

Roumell remembers playing on many of the "Motortown Revue" shows with all the greats, like Stevie Wonder, Martha Reeves and the Vandellas, Gladys Knight and the Pips, and Marvin Gaye. "I must say that sometimes the reception we received from the black audiences at those shows wasn't the greatest. I guess we didn't really fit in, but they kept booking us."[6]

The Unrelated Segments was a band whose members all came from Detroit's downriver suburbs. Lead vocalist Ron Stults and lead guitarist Rory Mack were from Taylor, bass player Barry Van Engelen, from Lincoln Park, drummer Andy Angellotti from Melvindale, and rhythm guitarist John Torock from Allen Park. Torock was the band's oldest member, and it was while taking a course in microeconomics at business college that he took part in a discussion about "unrelated segments." Later it seemed like a good name for a band.[7] Although the members had several years experience in various groups, they had been playing together in Torock's basement and garage for only a few practice sessions before coming up with some strong original material. John's father, Louis Torock, who served as the band's manager, liked what they were doing, and contacted Jack Checkaway, owner and primary producer of the SVR and HBR labels. After hearing their songs, Checkaway booked studio time at United Sound, where he had recorded the Tidal Waves' "Farmer John" earlier in the year.

Checkaway took pride in the "studio professionalism" of his recordings, most done on United's Scully 280 four-track. He credited engineer Les Cooley with helping to achieve a distinctive, clean sound.[8] On November 26, 1966, the Unrelated Segments cut their first single, "The Story of My Life," paired with "It's Unfair" on the flip side.

The session lasted only three and a half hours, after which the band packed up their equipment and left to play a dance at Lincoln Park High.[9] In February 1967, as Ron and Rory were about to drive off in Ron's car, Rory turned on the radio and they heard "Story of My Life" on WKNR. "It's a weird feeling when you first hear it," recalled Ron Stults. " You say to yourself that I wish I could have done it this way or mixed it another way."[10] Regardless of how it was mixed, "Story of My Life," with its driving bass riffs, climbed to number 9 on the Keener *Music Guide*, and was a top 10 hit in nearby Toledo. However professional his recordings, Jack Checkaway, like other small independent labels, still faced the obstacles of inadequate promotion and distribution, and as a result, "Story of My Life" would fail to chart nationally.

A Detroit area blues-rock band known as the Woolies scored a big hit in February with a revved-up, high-speed, high-powered version of Bo Diddley's "Who Do You Love." Formed in 1964, the band was composed of members from Dearborn, on Detroit's westside. Bob Baldori played bass as well as keyboards and harmonica. Stormy Rice was the lead vocalist, Jeff Baldori played lead guitar, Ron English played rhythm guitar, and Bee Metros was the drummer. The Woolies opened for the MC5 at the Grande Ballroom on October 14 and 15, 1966, its second weekend in operation.

Earlier in the year, the Woolies had won a "Best Band in the Land" contest sponsored by Vox amps. First prize was a trip to Hollywood and a recording contract. "It turned out to be a big fraud," recalls Bob Baldori. "There was no trip or contract, just some equipment."[11]

Undeterred, the band members talked the promoters into at least coming up with plane tickets to Los Angeles. "Before we left Michigan, we recorded five demo songs to take with us," says Baldori. "When we got to L.A., we just hit the streets, and we managed to get in to see people at several labels. Capitol Records and ABC-Dunhill were both interested, but we accepted an offer from Lou Adler at Dunhill because he said he 'could get us right into the studio.' Now this was important because I had to get my little brother Jeff back to school. He was only fourteen at the time."[12]

The Woolies cut "Who Do You Love" at the Western Sound Studios in Los Angeles. The record took off immediately with their hometown audience in Detroit and peaked at number 3 on WKNR's *Music Guide*. A month or so after hitting in Detroit, it became a hit in Boston. According to Baldori, it sold a lot of records, but not enough in one week to move up the national charts.

The band was back playing a gig at the Dells, a club on Lake Lansing, when they were offered the chance to play behind Chuck Berry. The musicians clicked so well that from that time on Berry would always use the Woolies as his backup band when he played in the Midwest.[13]

A local Detroit band called the Wanted scored a number one record in the Motor City in February 1967 with a hard-rockin' version of Wilson Pickett's "In the Midnight Hour." The members of the band were Arnie DeClark on guitar, Dave Fernstrom on keyboards, Bill Montgomery on bass, Tim Shea on lead guitar, and Chip Steiner on drums. The record was produced by Doug Brown and released on a small local label called Detroit Sound Records, which happened to be owned by Chip Steiner's father.

Originally "Here to Stay," a teen ballad written by the band, had been the A-side before deejays went for "In the Midnight Hour." A&M Records took notice of the record's popularity in Michigan and picked it up for national release. Despite topping the Detroit charts, it failed to catch on nationally. After several more unsuccessful releases, the Wanted called it quits.[14]

One of the more memorable songs to come out of the local scene in early 1967 was "Psychedelic Used Car Lot Blues," performed by the Southbound Freeway. Lead guitarist Marc Chover had been a friend and fan of a popular local folk music artist named Ted Lucas, who, aside from a solo career, spent some time in a band called the Spike Drivers. After listening to Lucas go on about how much fun it was to be in that band, guitarist Chover decided to start his own. He recruited some friends, and soon the South-bound Freeway was performing at the Chessmate, a popular folk music club at 17126 Livernois at McNichols. Later they became one of the first bands to appear at the Grande Ballroom, where they opened for the MC5.[15]

Southbound Freeway's one and only hit was recorded at Ralph Terrana's Tera Shirma Studios and released on the label of the same name. On the strength of the song, the group had been booked to appear on Robin Seymour's TV show, *Swingin' Time*. A few days before the show, Ralph received word that RCA, which was pressing the record, had fallen behind on schedule. They performed anyway and the audience really went for it. Unfortunately, the records had failed to ship. When the records finally did arrive in the stores, momentum was gone. Still the record did well enough to reach number 18 locally, and just missed the national "Hot 100" in *Billboard*.[16]

The Motor City's unofficial ambassadors of rock 'n' roll, Mitch Ryder and the Detroit Wheels, were at their peak of national popularity in February 1967, riding high on the huge success of their October 1966 smash, "Devil With The Blue Dress On/Good Golly Miss Molly." According to Mitch, the band had first come into contact with the song "Devil With the Blue Dress On" two years earlier, when it had been a minor Detroit R & B hit for Shorty Long on the Motown subsidiary Soul label. Long was also the song's composer. Ryder described the original as "much slower, much slinkier," and having a "much more serious rhythm to it."[17] One day, looking for something new to record, producer Bob Crewe had asked the band members if they "knew anything cool." The response, says Ryder, was, "Yeah, we know something *really* cool."[18] The band played their faster, up-tempo version of the song. Crewe connected it with Little Richard's "Good Golly Miss Molly." The resulting record spent fourteen weeks in the Top 40, cresting at number 4 and selling well over a million copies.

Their follow-up single, the extremely danceable "Sock It To Me Baby," had taken off and then stalled briefly after a number of radio stations voiced objections to a small portion of the lyrics, including the line "hits me like a puck."[19] The label forced Mitch to return to the studio, and rerecord the lyric, as, "hits me like a punt." Widespread airplay resumed, and in February 1967 the single climbed to number 6 on the national charts.

Mitch Ryder and the Detroit Wheels were selling a lot of records and getting booked on national tours with artists such as the Yardbirds, Simon and Garfunkel, and the Young Rascals. Still, Wheels drummer Johnny Bee says it seemed there was never any money left to set aside: "After we'd come in off the road, and they started deducting the hotels, food, transportation, you name it, there was nothing left. That's the way it was the whole time we were together."[20]

After "Sock It To Me Baby," Mitch Ryder and the Detroit Wheels returned to the medley formula, crossing "Too Many Fish in the Sea" with "Three Little Fishes." Although not a huge hit, it did chart at a respectable number 24 in May 1967. It would be the last in a string of hits for the group.

For sometime, Bob Crewe had been envisioning a different path for Ryder, one that would separate him from the band and place him squarely in the middle of more mainstream show biz. Mitch Ryder says that "Bob Crewe came from a time where the highest honor you could get was to be a Las Vegas star."[21]

At the same time, Mitch and Jim McCarty had been clashing over the direction the band should take. According to Ryder, "I wanted to add some horns, go a little more R&B, and compete with my idols, Wilson Pickett and James Brown. Jimmy, the guitar player, disagreed, and wanted to keep the group strictly rock 'n' roll. I thought we could do both, because R&B was what I did best, and they played rock with real passion."[22] Bob Crewe became aware of the dispute and viewed it as a "chink in the armor, a weakness." He did his best to exacerbate the disagreement. Ryder said, "I got my big band, but the Wheels left."[23]

Backed by a string-laden orchestra, Mitch Ryder next released a solo effort. He sang his way through a melodramatic version of "What Now My Love," a hit for Sonny and Cher a year earlier, and album filler for Herb Alpert and the Tijuana Brass, Robert Goulet, and a host of middle-of-the-road entertainers. Gone were Jim

McCarty's wicked guitar licks and Johnny Bee's thundering drums. Instead, Mitch entered the studio with sixty musicians. When Ryder asked Bob Crewe who was going to pay for the session, Crewe had responded, "You are." "I don't believe that," shot back Ryder. "Don't worry," advised Crewe, "it'll be a hit."[24]

Ryder's final high wail at the song's close was enough to push the record up to number 30, after which it quickly disappeared. Mitch Ryder stayed on the road, fronting a big show band featuring the horn section he had been dreaming of. For live performances, Crewe now dressed Mitch in flashy costumes and a cape. Instead of the raw, urban sound of his former band, Ryder was churning out a slick version of R & B with the members of his new band, simply paid employees, going through the motions.[25]

Fans shook their heads, wondering what had happened to that great rock band, Mitch Ryder and the Detroit Wheels. Why would they break up? "That was a fucking great band," recalled Ryder in a private conversation a few years later. "And they broke it up."[26] Asked how it happened, and if he was referring to the band members causing the breakup, Mitch commented: "No, not the guys in the band. I dunno how it happened. Nobody told them to do it. All I know is that the records, the singles came out, and there was 'Mitch Ryder' in huge bold-face type, and scrunched way down at the bottom they had 'and the Detroit Wheels.' And I stood for it, I stood for it right up till it was too late."[27]

Wheels drummer Johnny Bee says that Bob Crewe had never really wanted the band, right from the beginning, only Mitch, and had reluctantly accepted the whole group. "Now, here we are, just coming into our own, and they just pull the plug," he laments. "I think if we had gone on, we could of been like the Rolling Stones, but Crewe and his friends were just into a different scene, except for Charlie Colello, who was arranging the records. He advised that separating us was not a good idea, but Bob had his mind made up."[28]

In an interview with *Vintage Guitar* magazine, Jim McCarty concurred: "If we would have had management that really cared about the band as a whole, as opposed to just focusing on the singer, there's no telling what we could have done."[29] Johnny Bee feels that Mitch was just "caught up in the glitz and fame and just went along," adding that later on Mitch "felt bad and did regret what happened."[30]

While the Mitch Ryder Show toured the country, Jim McCarty headed to the West Coast to work with the Siegel-Schawll Band, while Johnny Bee kept a Ryder-less Detroit Wheels spinning for a while longer in the Midwest.

Following a rare Christmas rocker called "Sock It To Me Santa," Bob Seger returned to the charts in February 1967 with "Persecution Smith." As before, the record was first released on the Hideout label and then picked up for national distribution by Cameo-Parkway. Like "Eastside Story," this one zoomed into the top 10 locally, cresting at number 9, while failing to break beyond Michigan. The flip side of the release was "Chain Smokin'." During the previous five months, Bob Seger and the Last Heard had become the most popular attraction at the Hideout clubs and were drawing crowds wherever they appeared.

Disc jockey Tom Shannon, on the air at CKLW:

> You gotta make it to the Fifth Dimension, man, really. Michigan's most talked about teen club. In person tomorrow night and Friday, by popular demand, the all-girl group—how's this for a name: the Pleasure Seekers. I'm gonna go out there! Headlining is Bob Seger's Last Heard, all appearing in a fantastic show. The Fifth Dimension, featuring three exciting stages, carpeted sitting mound, fifty-foot bar and a boutique with mod fashions. The new world of the Fifth Dimension, so make it a date, tomorrow night and Friday, at eight o'clock! The Fifth Dimension, 218 West Huron, downtown Ann Arbor.[31]

Aside from recording, Seger was also involved in writing and producing for Hideout Records. Along with his cowriter credits on "Get Down On Your Knees" for the Underdogs, Seger, in the spring of 1967, had just penned "Miss You" for a new female group called the Mama Cats. He had also written "Burned" for a Hideout band called the Mushrooms. The leader of that group was Glenn Frey, formerly of the Subterraneans, a band he fronted while attending Dondero High School in Royal Oak. Seger and Frey shared producer-arranger credits on the record, which was the flip side of "Such a Lovely Child."[32]

In July 1967, Seger released "Heavy Music," his fifth single through Hideout productions. This time, it was pressed immediately on Cameo Records. Seger had first heard the term *heavy music* on a trip to New York, when a deejay referred to a Wilson Pickett record, saying, "That's some heavy music."[33] The rest of the song came about one night when the band was playing in a bar in Columbus, Ohio. "We got into this jam about 'deeper' and I really dug the jam," recalled Seger in a later interview. "We happened to be taping that night and then I went home and wrote the song around it."[34] Starting off with an irresistible bass line, running under the invitation, "Come on with me baby, we're gonna have a good time!" the record instantly became a Detroit call to "rock and roll!"

On past hits, Bob Seger's sound had been largely influenced by Van Morrison and Bob Dylan. But this time out, the sound was purely his own; a raw, hard-driving rhythm with his trademark raspy vocals: "Doncha ever listen to the radio when the big bad beat comes on?" wailed Seger. During late summer of 1967, "Heavy Music" *was* the big bad beat. Despite some controversy over whether the lyric "goin' deeper" was a sexual reference—or maybe partly because of it—the record was racing up the charts.[35] On August 16, CKLW made it a "Hitbound" pick. Earlier that year, CKLW had surged ahead of WKNR in popularity, and was now the number one Top 40 station in the area. Thanks to the station's huge fifty-thousand-watt signal, "Heavy Music" was being heard all over. Seventy thousand copies were sold in Detroit, where it reached number 3, and the record was expected to be listed as a "National Breakout" in *Billboard*.[36]

Excited and curious as to how national sales were going, Seger and manager Punch Andrews put a call in to Cameo-Parkway Records: "We couldn't get anybody to answer the phone," recalled Seger. "So we got a plane and went to New York, and knocked and knocked on the door of their office. Finally a janitor came out of the elevator and said, 'Nobody's there. They're gone.'"[37] The record label had gone out of business.

When the older members of the Fugitives had moved to Ann Arbor to enroll in college in 1965, lead guitarist Gary Quackenbush, who was still in high school, had stayed behind in Birmingham, joining a band called the Yorkshires. In November 1966, Gary rejoined the Fugitives, which now consisted of his brother Glenn, who played organ, drummer E. G. Clawson, and two new members, guitarist Steve Lyman and bass player Robin Dale. The band decided to "get serious" about a music career. "That's when we went after Jeep Holland," recalls Gary Quackenbush. "We got him to see our band, and he had the idea of putting Scott Richardson with the Fugitives."[38] At the time Richardson was lead singer for the Chosen Few. Just a month earlier, that band, which included Ron Asheton and James Williamson, had opened the Grande Ballroom.

The Fugitives, with Richardson on board, would now be known as the Scot Richard Case. "It rocked from the second we got together,' says Quackenbush. "The first gig we ever played was a hop for Bob Dell [of WTAC, Flint] out at the Fenton Community Center. Bob Seger, Mike Morgan from the Underdogs, and Scott Morgan from the Rationals were at that first gig just to check us out."[39]

In the late summer of 1967, the Scot Richard Case scored a hit on Holland's A-Square label, with Skip James's "I'm So Glad." But according to Gary Quackenbush, that song had not been his band's first choice for their initial release. "In the can was our version of a Pretty Things tune called 'Get the Picture.' Then, one of Jeep's friends went to England and bought the first Cream album. We heard 'I'm So Glad' and started doin' it, playin' it live and people just went nuts. Jeep saw that and decided that we're going to go in and record this and release it, and that's what happened."[40] The Scot Richard Case's recording of "I'm So Glad" became a statewide hit. "We went out and did in-house visits at all the stations we could find. Jeep was great about that," says Quackenbush. "We went to Grand Rapids, we went to Flint, we went everywhere in Michigan." Although it reached the top 10 on stations in Detroit and Flint, Jeep was unable to break it beyond the state line. "Jeep was more successful when it came to keeping people out of the draft," says Quackenbush. "He got me out, he got all of our band out, and quite a few others."[41]

E. G. Clawson told writer Debbie Burr that unlike many area

bands, the Scot Richard Case formed with the "stipulation" that the band would be "full-time work," so the members "dropped everything" else.[42] They played the Hideout circuit, and at Roostertail's Upper Deck on the Detroit River, as well as the Mt. Holly teen dances. According to Richardson, the band's repertoire consisted of all the "best rock and roll songs." Along with "every Stones song in existence," their set list included the unlikely "When the Lovelight Shines," the first hit for the Supremes.[43]

The group was also known for the "mod" Carnaby Street–style outfits they wore on stage. "The first Scot Richard Case gigs had the backing band in jackets, and Scott dressed pretty wild in front," says Gary Quackenbush. "That didn't last too long, 'cause things were changing in every way. Mod stuff was coming in, people were smoking pot and expanding their minds with LSD. I remember one time where we got in the van and drove to New York just to buy clothes. I think we were probably the wildest looking band at the time."[44] Scot Richardson, in particular, drew attention by swinging his microphone around and donning a suit covered with hundreds of miniature light bulbs that flashed to the beat of the music.[45]

# 14. Something in the Air

Jeep Holland's Ann Arbor–based operation continued to grow during 1967, as the Scot Richard Case, the Thyme, and the Apostles all signed contracts with his A-Square Management. The company was now also operating as a booking agency for Michigan rock bands and had begun to book for the Grande Ballroom.

Earlier in the year, after their unsuccessful release of "Hold On Baby," Jeep had convinced his primary outfit, the Rationals, to rerecord "Leaving Here," which had been the flip side of "Respect," their big hit in 1966. Scott Morgan recalled that Jeep was "really into that song for some reason, and really thought it could be a big hit."[1] The release of "Leaving Here" marked the end of a three-record deal with Cameo. Unfortunately, the record-buying public didn't share Holland's enthusiasm for the song, and the record failed to chart. On top of that, any hope for a first album for the Rationals vanished when Cameo-Parkway went bust.[2]

By the fall of 1967, Jeep had signed as an independent producer with Capitol Records, and arranged a one-off deal for the Rationals to do a single on the label. The band chose to record a Gerry Goffin–Carole King song called "I Need You," which had been a mild hit on the soul charts for Chuck Jackson. By January 1968, the Rationals found themselves back in Detroit's top 10. "I Need You," featuring the smooth "white soul" vocal of Scott Morgan, climbed to number 7. Although happy to have a local hit, the band was disappointed when the record failed to break out in other markets.[3]

After having been forced to relocate to Chicago with his family in 1965, Ted Nugent wasted no time in putting together a new band. He decided to call the group the Amboy Dukes, the name of a defunct Detroit R & B group. At the time, Nugent knew nothing about its true origin with a street gang in Perth Amboy, New Jersey, made famous in a 1950s novel.[4]

According to Ted, the band "practiced like Navy Seals on a mission," and within weeks had "killed the hottest bands in Chicago— The Ides of March and The Shadows of Night."[5] Ted Nugent claimed that the style of Chicago bands was to play covers of hit records as close to the originals as possible. Nugent's Detroit style was to "throw them into a dull blender and mutilate them into a high-energy, throbbing beef of sexuality and noise."[6] It wasn't long before Ted put in a call to John Drake, a former member of his old Detroit band, the Lourds. Drake moved to Chicago to handle lead vocals.

As soon as Nugent graduated from high school in 1967, he got in touch with an old Detroit contact named Bob Henkins. With Henkins signed on as manager, Nugent and Drake moved the band back to Detroit, where they put together a new lineup, including rhythm guitarist Steve Farmer, bass player Bill White, keyboardist Rick Lober, and drummer Dave Palmer. The Amboy Dukes quickly became regulars on the teen club circuit. On November 22, the Dukes and the Unrelated Segments opened for the Who at a big concert at Southfield High School, sponsored by the school's ten-watt FM station WSHJ. According to former Southfield student and Detroit deejay Pat St. John, the Who thought that WSHJ was a much larger station and agreed to appear, after hearing that the station "was really going 'push the show.'" Over three-thousand fans attended the concert.[7]

Henkins introduced the Amboy Dukes to Bob Shad, a veteran producer who had done jazz sessions with Charlie Parker back in the 1940s, before becoming artist and repertoire director for Mercury Records. After leaving Mercury, Shad launched a trio of small labels and found success recording rock 'n' roll hits such as "I've Had It" by the Bell Notes in 1959. He refocused on jazz in the early 1960s, founding Mainstream Records, where he signed jazz greats such as Maynard Ferguson, Shelly Manne, and Dizzy Gillespie. By 1967 Shad was again dabbling in rock, signing Big Brother and the Holding Company, the group that spawned Janis Joplin.[8]

On Henkins's recommendation, the Amboy Dukes signed a

recording contract with Mainstream. They recorded their first album, *The Amboy Dukes,* in one night on a four-track recorder.[9] Released in December 1967, it went to number 183 on the national charts. In January 1968, the band played at the Grande Ballroom where Ted's savage guitar attacks, aggressive stage attitude, and wild clothing made him the center of attention. By February, their first single from the album, "Baby Please Don't Go," another cover of a Them song, played at a dizzying speed, became a hit in Detroit, reaching number 15.

Before the release of their second LP, the band underwent a couple of personnel changes. Andy Solomon replaced Rick Lober on keyboards, and Bill White departed in favor of new bass player, Greg Arama. According to Nugent, they recorded the album *Journey to the Center of the Mind* on an eight-track in about five nights.[10] In May, the Amboy Dukes enjoyed an "era defining hit" with the album's title track. Nugent had written the music to go with Steve Farmer's lyrics. To most ears, the song sounded like an aural acid trip. Despite the album cover featuring what was obviously drug paraphernalia, Nugent claimed that at the time he didn't make the drug connection, saying: "I thought 'Journey to the Center of the Mind' meant look inside yourself, use your head, and move forward in life."[11] Nugent has always claimed "never to have smoked a joint . . . never done a drug" in his life. "Oh, drugs are cool," he sarcastically told writer Debbie Burr. "Numerous friends of mine have had good experiences . . . two died."[12] The record moved forward to the top of the Detroit charts and then rose to number 16 on *Billboard's* national list in July. Nugent felt that Detroit had an "edge" in music over other cities: it came "from having so much competition, and a strong work ethic."[13]

In February 1968, the MC5 were ready to record their second single. The song was an original, titled "Looking At You." John Sinclair, now officially serving as the group's manager, arranged to have it released on Jeep Holland's A-Square label. The recording session cost five hundred dollars. Russ Gibb paid the bill.[14]

On their previous recording, "I Can Only Give You Everything," producers and engineers had rushed through the sessions, dictating how they thought the song should sound. Although they were again recording at United Sound Systems, John Sinclair played the role of producer and kept the band from being intimidated by studio staff. Wayne Kramer recalls that studio engineer Danny Dallas was a rather "conservative type," but nonetheless "a good guy" who "got into the spirit" of what the group was trying to do. "We were really into a group consciousness and total sound," says Kramer.[15] John Sinclair recalled Dallas's "bewilderment" and "chagrin" when told to simply "open his pots and take down on tape what was coming out of the band."[16] According to Dennis Thompson, what was being recorded was also played through a PA system right in the studio: "It was probably just a couple of Vox columns and some horns, but that added clatter to the piece and gave it that metal edge which was ahead of its time."[17]

Despite having absolutely no experience producing records, John Sinclair was aware that AM radio tended to shave off the highs in a recording, so when he went into the booth with Wayne to mix the single, he "loaded" the recording with treble.[18] In spite of being under the influence of acid, or maybe because of it, they were able to get exactly the sound they wanted, capturing the band's maturing musical skills and its "fiery live" and jazz-influenced "free sound." Wayne Kramer felt that "Looking At You" was a "tour de force," thanks to Rob Tyner's "brilliant" melodies and harp playing.[19] Following Michael Davis's low-key opening on bass, Fred "Sonic" Smith's rhythm guitar slashed out in a duel with Wayne Kramer's lead guitar attack and then Tyner's vocal assault.

"Looking At You," with "Borderline," a Wayne Kramer original, on the flip side, was a unique release for A-Square. Rather than issuing it in the standard blank white 45 rpm sleeve, the label delivered it in a custom picture sleeve designed by Gary Grimshaw, featuring psychedelic images and John Coltrane looking toward the MC5. Even the label's design was custom tailored for the group. Unbelievably, they pressed only five hundred copies.

Although the MC5's recording of "Looking At You" impressed their fans as well as fellow musicians, it was highly unlikely it would ever reach the airwaves of the average Top 40 radio station, whose format and "sound" was designed to appeal to everyone from teeny-boppers to housewives. *Top 40* was actually a misnomer, as many of the big AM radio stations had scaled back their playlists. By 1968, following format techniques of national radio programmer Bill Drake, CKLW was playing the top thirty hits, two or three new "hit-bound" releases, and some selected oldies interspersed with fast a cappella jingles, commercial clusters, sensational "tabloid style" news, and high-energy disc jockeys in an incredibly tight, consistent presentation. Powered by its huge fifty-thousand- watt signal, the "Big 8" had become a broadcast giant, scoring number one ratings not only in Detroit, but in Cleveland and Toledo as well.

For years, the Top 40 stations had been the place to hear rock records. In fact most people referred to them as "rock stations," despite the fact that their playlists included virtually any style of music that was selling. On the one hand, Top 40 radio had a galvanizing effect, exposing a vast audience to a variety of musical styles, but the selection was always limited.

In the early days of pop and rock 'n' roll, the standard practice for record companies had been to focus on breaking hit singles. When an artist charted a hit, the record company would typically release a follow-up album featuring the hit single and eleven "filler" tracks, usually "cover versions" of other artists' hits. There were a few exceptions: the Kingston Trio, Roy Orbison, James Brown, and the Beach Boys, and the music coming out of small folk labels such as Vanguard and Elektra. But top-selling LPs tended to be such things as *West Side Story* and *Judy Garland Live at Carnegie Hall.*

Up until this point, the vast majority of young people listened to AM radio, associating FM with orchestral background music played in elevators and dentist offices. The fact that most radios were produced only with an AM dial didn't help. In 1966, WOR-FM in New York experimented with a "free-form underground" format featuring deejay Murray the K, but the station switched to a "Drake sound" Top 40 format after about ten months. In Detroit during 1966, Larry Miller was hosting a folk and blues music program called *Promenade* on WDTM-FM. But Miller's Saturday night show was buried among other classical and discussion programs on the station. While the AM Top 40 stations had audience shares as high as 20 and 30 percent, most FM stations did not draw an audience large enough even to show up in the ratings reports.[20]

Miller left to do an all-night free-form program on KMPX-FM, a struggling FM station in San Francisco.

By the fall of 1967, WABX-FM in Detroit had begun to air a new program of blues, folk, and rock music called *Troubadour* from seven to eight each evening. Station manager John Small hosted the program. The remainder of the day, WABX played a mix of mainly up-tempo middle-of-the-road music by artists such as Mel Torme, Frank Sinatra, Nancy Wilson, and Joe Williams. In the evening, there was an exceptional jazz program hosted by Jim Rockwell.

The response to *Troubadour* was strong enough to convince station owners Howard and Shelley Grafman to expand the rock programming on their station. On February 1, 1968, WABX threw out the rule book and started to program progressive rock in a free-form presentation for most of the day. For a time, contractual obligations kept a two-hour German-language program on the air from eight o'clock sign-on until ten each morning, when Dick Crockett would make a jarring transition into something like "Purple Haze."[21] Crockett, along with George Brown, was a holdover from the previous format; they were joined by Jim Hampton, who had been working for WXYZ, and two new announcers, Dan Carlisle and Jerry Lubin, who were going by the air-names Terry King and Jerry O'Neill respectively. Carlisle had started in radio at Michigan State University, then worked at Top 40 stations in Green Bay, Wisconsin, and Saginaw, Michigan. After losing interest and making plans to return to school, he took a job in a construction site trailer where they had an FM radio and he heard WABX shortly after they started playing rock. "So I went down there and John Small gave me an on the air audition and I passed," says Carlisle.[22] Lubin was working for WTAC in Flint when he was hired by WABX. By June, Dave Dixon joined the staff. A Birmingham, Michigan, native, Dixon had worked for a number of Michigan radio stations and had programmed WAUK AM and FM in Milwaukee, Wisconsin. Along with high school buddy Paul Stookey, he had cowritten "I Dig Rock and Roll Music," a Top 10 hit for Peter, Paul, and Mary in 1967. According to Dixon, it was he who convinced Lubin and Carlisle to drop their on-air personas of "Jerry O'Neil" and "Terry King" in favor of their real names.

Rather than limiting the play list to thirty preapproved selections, the deejays were encouraged to pick the music for their own shows. Suddenly, listeners were transported to a musical world without boundaries. Album cuts by the Beatles, the Rolling Stones, and other rock groups such as Jefferson Airplane, Cream, Vanilla Fudge, and Jimi Hendrix were programmed along with folk artists such as Bob Dylan, Tim Hardin, Judy Collins, Ritchie Havens, and Tim Buckley. Memphis R & B by Sam and Dave and Otis Redding appeared along with original rock oldies by Chuck Berry and Little Richard. WABX was also the only place for long cuts such as "Alice's Restaurant" by Arlo Guthrie, or the unedited versions of "Light My Fire," and "In-a-Gadda-Da-Vida." The station also gave exposure to recordings by local bands.

The deejays usually programmed "sets," several songs connected by a common thread, either in the style of the music or in the subject matter. In general, WABX deejays projected a hip, laid-back persona on the air. A listener might feel like he was in the living room of a friend playing some favorite tunes on his stereo. Nothing on the station was predictable. "Everybody liked to play their personal favorites," recalls Jerry Lubin, "but no one went too overboard in just one thing."[23]

"It was a fifteen-dollar converter that you could put in your car that really did it," says Dan Carlisle, regarding the rapid assent of WABX. "Detroit had more FM radios in the cars than anywhere else."[24] Carlisle was followed on the air each evening at eleven by Dave Dixon. The two made the transition with a nightly "Eleven o'clock rap" session where one evening they encouraged listeners to show support for WABX by "going naked for a day." On another night, the two turned their attention to some of the weird phone calls that came in to the station and promoted a "Sickest Listener Contest." The prize offered was a free hour of psychiatric help.

Although their listenership was growing, WABX posed no immediate threat to CKLW, which remained the big mass-appeal station in the Motor City. But when WABX started to broadcast more local community and political news from the left, and got more involved with the audience, it quickly became important to the late-sixties alternative scene in Detroit. Larry Miller returned from San Francisco in September and joined Carlisle, Lubin, and Dave Dixon, who all became well known in the community. "It didn't take long to realize that we were having an impact," recalls original "Air Ace" Jerry Lubin. "We were pioneering something new. We were the first in Detroit."[25]

# 15. Seger on the Rise

Following the demise of Cameo-Parkway Records in September 1967, Bob Seger watched helplessly as his "breakout" hit, "Heavy Music," lost momentum and fell off the national charts. His manager, Punch Andrews, at first thought of trying to place him with Motown, where the Underdogs had signed earlier in the year and were the label's lone "white rock band." But believing that the Detroit label's marketing machine would not be right for the job, Andrews approached some other labels. No one was interested. They told him Seger was "too guttural, too hard," and that he "wouldn't play well in other cities."[1]

Eventually, Andrews contacted Tom Gelardi, head of Capitol Records' Detroit office: "We were discussing Bob's career, and how he hadn't been able to break outside of Michigan," recalls Gelardi. "Punch told me that a disc jockey in Florida had been playing his records, and that Seger had just pulled in eleven thousand fans to a concert down there, so there was this great potential. Punch asked if I knew anybody at Capitol that might be interested in signing him. In fact, I had a good relationship with Carl Engelman, Capitol's A&R director, so I put in a call saying, 'Carl, I'd like to showcase a Detroit artist who is an amazing success in Michigan.' We set something up for the next Friday afternoon at a teen club out on Northwestern Highway. Bob performed for forty-five minutes, and did all those local hits, like 'East Side Story,' 'Heavy Music,' and some other originals."[2]

At the end of the set, Engelman told Gelardi and Andrews that he wanted to sign Bob Seger to the label. "The interesting thing was that Engelman was impressed more by Seger's writing ability than by his performance," says Gelardi. "He said, 'I want to sign him because he's an incredible songwriter.' And that's pretty much how Bob got with Capitol Records."[3]

Having been unhappy with the Last Heard moniker, Seger took the opportunity to change the name of the band to the Bob Seger System. The players remained the same, with bass player Dan Honaker and drummer Pep Perine at the core. Even with Seger's name at the front, the band was always democratic. "I was making as much money as the drummer and the background singer, we were all in it together," claimed Seger, who believed that "everybody went through the same amount of road torture."[4] Aside from money, the band also had a say in what they played, and how they should play it. Seger's insecurity often made him go along with band decisions even when he felt they were not right. "I just wanted to play and make records," he recalled. "I was afraid the band would break up."[5]

In April 1968, Seger's first Capitol single, the antiwar protest song "2 + 2 = ?" was released. Seger had undergone a transformation after a close friend was killed in Vietnam, and the record was an about-face from the hawkish "Ballad of the Yellow Beret" released two years earlier. The explosive "2 + 2" was a wild ride, with Seger questioning the demands of war. As usual, the record quickly raced up into the top 10 on Detroit charts, cresting at number 7, while failing to catch fire elsewhere. The song was included on Seger's first Capitol album, originally to be titled "Tales of Lucy," before producers settled on *Ramblin' Gamblin' Man,* the title of the second single taken from the album. This time out, a smashing drum rhythm opened the way for Pat McCaffery's hard-driving organ, as Seger sang with a swagger about being free. "Ramblin' Gamblin' Man" took off fast on both WKNR and CKLW, reaching number 3 in the Motor City. Along with Seger's regular band, friend Glenn Frey played rhythm guitar and sang backup on the hit.

On July 29, 1968, the Bob Seger System played at an outdoor concert at Oakland Mall in the Detroit suburb of Troy. It was one of the new, huge, enclosed malls designed to take business away from the older open-air shopping centers such as Northland and Eastland. The mall's marketing director, Bob Jones, thought that a great way to draw attention to the grand opening would be to stage a free rock concert in the parking lot, featuring top Detroit bands such as the Amboy Dukes, the Rationals, Savage Grace, and Third

Power. Bob Seger, having a string of local hits behind him, was slated to close the show.[6]

When the day of the grand opening arrived, there were indeed crowds swelling around Oakland Mall, but they were not the customers Bob Jones had been hoping to attract. Carloads of kids had showed up, not to shop but to see their local rock heroes. Because of the endless lines of cars exiting from I-75 onto Fourteen Mile Road in both directions, actual shoppers found it nearly impossible to get there. Every parking spot was taken. A stage with two banks of loudspeakers set high on scaffolding to each side filled the lot in front of Hudson's department store.

As the Bob Seger System came out to close the show, they faced a crowd of some twenty thousand fans, the largest audience Seger had ever performed for. "We did all our old hit songs," Seger recalled, "that's all we did."[7] Both Scott Morgan of the Rationals and Glenn Frey were more than impressed, with Frey telling Seger, "You just played hit after hit. I can't believe it."[8]

Jem Targal, bass player and vocalist for Third Power, recalls the concert being a "good turning point" for all the bands. "Nobody expected that kind of a crowd. It might have been one of the things that started kickin' off a lot of those kinds of outdoor concerts. Everybody enjoyed being together and seeing so many bands at one time."[9] While the concert was a great success, Bob Jones "caught hell" from the mall's management.[10]

Riding a high from his local popularity, things looked even brighter for Bob Seger in the fall when "Ramblin' Gamblin' Man," a number 1 single in Detroit, started to climb the national charts, eventually hitting number 17. Finally Bob Seger had a solid national hit on a major label.

# 16. A Night at the Grande

As 1968 began to unfold, the Grande Ballroom was drawing steady crowds every weekend. The talent on stage consisted mainly of Detroit-based bands, such as the MC5, Scott Richard Case, the Rationals, Thyme, Jagged Edge and the Apostles. But by late 1967, Russ Gibb was also financially able to begin booking a few national names. On Friday, December 15, Vanilla Fudge, best known for a slow, psychedelic version of "You Keep Me Hangin' On," played the first of a three-night stand, with the Thyme opening the show. On Saturday night the Rationals opened, and on Sunday the MC5, still the Grande's regular house band, earning $125 for a night's work.

Cream, the power trio featuring "guitar god" Eric Clapton, was on stage December 22 and 23, with the MC5 and Billy C. and the Sunshine opening both shows. Detroit blues legend John Lee Hooker came home to the Motor City the following week, December 29 and 30, and played to a young but appreciative audience. New Year's Eve was a family affair at the Grande as the "5" headlined, supported by Billy C. and the Sunshine, Prime Movers, and the Apostles. John Mayall's Bluesbreakers appeared in January 1968, Canned Heat and the Byrds in February. On March 1 and 2, Big Brother and the Holding Company, best known for bluesy lead vocalist Janis Joplin and their big hit "Piece of My Heart," took the stage. Al Kooper's Blood, Sweat, and Tears performed on the third.

The Who, popular in Detroit since their first release, "Can't Explain," became a local top 5 hit in 1965, performed an explosive set at the Grande on March 9, after which they loaded up their own equipment and headed for a Holiday Inn. According to tour manager Tom Wright, the Who had been on a grueling tour of one-nighters, and when they arrived in Detroit, "Everyone was shot."[1] Having played "the big deals, New York, San Francisco and LA," the band didn't have much energy or enthusiasm in reserve. Then the band arrived at the Grande, which Wright described as an experience similar to "dozing off in class and waking up in Times Square at five in the afternoon, and realizing you're on acid."[2] The Grande was packed for the performance, and although the Who had played before larger crowds, they had not seen an audience "so close together," looking like they were "stuck to the walls."[3] The band was more than pleased with their reception in Detroit and how familiar the crowd was with all their early material. Tom Wright "had never seen the Who try harder." Wright says that after that show, "the Who left Detroit convinced that they would be successful."[4]

"I went there the first time [the Grande] and my mind was just shattered," recalls Gary Quackenbush, formerly of the Fugitives, and at the time a member of the Scot Richard Case. "The Grande was the best place to go, and the best place to play that there ever was. It was a great stage, great acoustics, great vibe, great crowd, great time on the planet. The Grande made the Detroit audience. It made Detroit the place to play, and the place to be from."[5]

Where before music had been a part of the lifestyle of youth, now, in Detroit, it was becoming *the* lifestyle, and the Grande Ballroom was the epicenter of the scene. A night at the Grande was a unique experience. Entering the large building on Grand River Blvd., patrons climbed an expansive red-carpeted staircase to the second floor and the unique spring-suspended, floating hardwood dance floor built in 1930 to accommodate fifteen hundred people.[6]

At the rear of the massive stage hung a screen showing oil and water images, creating a psychedelic wash of color, splashing across the crowd, bouncing off a huge mirrored ball hanging from a very high ceiling in the center of the room. As the bands rocked on stage, standing on an old Victorian rug under semiadequate lighting, the smell of incense and marijuana hung heavy in the air. The dance floor was surrounded by a walkway where people would stroll or just hang out to talk, and at the same time, be able to view what was happening on the dance floor, looking through Moorish arches. "I realized that more than just music, we were selling an 'adventure,'" recalls Russ Gibb. "It was an opportunity for kids to get together, and we were always looking for ways to make it more fun. I remember spending one day covering an entire wall with Reynolds Wrap so we would get some great reflections."[7]

Across the dance floor from the stage was a raised platform where the light shows were produced by Trans-Love Energies' Magic Veil Light Company. The crew included Gary Grimshaw, Jerry Younkins, and Leni Sinclair. "There were five of us, and Russ paid us twenty-five dollars a night," recalls Grimshaw. "We spent twenty dollars on materials every night: food coloring, vegetable oil, rubbing alcohol, Twinkies, Visine, aspirin, etc. We shopped at a supermarket two blocks up from the Grande on Grand River Avenue—a gaggle of white freaks in an all-black 'hood."[8]

Gary Grimshaw, along with Carl Lundgren and Danny Dope, continued to produce the posters, handbills, and flyers that promoted upcoming shows. Russ Gibb would give free admission to kids willing to pass them out at school. All the Grande posters, with the exception of the first, were printed by Gary's Uncle Ivor, at his print shop, a half-mile or so from Russ Gibb's house. "Russ never interfered with the art," said Grimshaw. "He seemed happy to get any art, especially at the bargain basement prices he was willing to pay, and we were willing to accept."[9] As there were so many last-minute bookings at the Grande, much of the artwork had to be produced overnight. As a result, Grimshaw felt that although they "weren't executed as well as they could have been," the art's "strength was in its 'spontaneity.'"[10]

Grimshaw, who admits to having been a "hard-core communist" at the time, says that although Russ Gibb was a "hard-core capitalist," he was "into rock and roll and danger." Grimshaw says, "I know that Bill Graham caught flack for being a 'hip capitalist' in San Francisco, but in Detroit at that time, it was no big deal. Just to be hip was enough, it didn't matter if you were a capitalist or a communist. It ultimately was about putting on a killer show for the kids."[11] Gary says that Gibb was "always smiling and confident. He was fearless. He was 'Uncle Russ!' He *was* the Grande Ballroom. Sure, he had a team behind him, a very fine team, but he took all the media heat and dealt with it with style and grace."[12]

The Grande team now included Larry Feldman, who managed

the ballroom, Jeep Holland, who was booking the bands, and John and Leni Sinclair, who ran the Trans-Love store as well as a community information center, both inside the Grande. There was also George the "incense man." According to Russ Gibb, in the beginning, John Sinclair played a large role in the success of the Grande. "He had a better feel for the market than I when we started. I was familiar with the social structure of young people as 'frats' and 'greasers.' The kids coming to the Grande were different, and John understood them and the music they liked, so he wound up recommending a lot of the bands that were booked."[13] Gibb says that behind all the political rhetoric, he remembers Sinclair as the "sweetest guy, a really decent fellow."[14]

It was during this period that the MC5 started to enjoy popularity on a much larger scale, locally at least, as they took pride in overpowering national acts with their loud, high-energy Detroit style of hard-ass rock 'n' roll. They would sometimes heckle other bands they felt were underperforming, standing in the audience shouting: "*Kick out the jams* or get *off* the stage!"[15] Beacon Street Union, a band from Boston, was a so-called national act arriving at the Grande amid all sorts of hype from their record label. According to John Sinclair, the MC5 "destroyed them so badly that it was embarrassing."[16] News of the encounter spread across the country, so when Blood, Sweat, and Tears was booked to appear at the Grande, Columbia Records insisted that Russ Gibb take the MC5 off the bill.[17]

Soon Wayne Kramer and Rob Tyner picked up on the potential of their "kick out the jams" proclamation to be expanded into an explosive song. One day, while working on some new tunes at the kitchen table with a little amplifier and a lot of marijuana, the two decided to do something with the phrase. According to Kramer, after retreating to the bedroom for a minute or so, Tyner, who the other band members sometimes kidded for his curly hair and skinny legs, came back in yelling, "I've got it!" Although "Kick Out the Jams" became a rallying cry for Detroit's young rock 'n' rollers, Kramer realized that Tyner's lyric was also addressing the band: "He was saying, 'Let *me* be who I am.'"[18]

Although the MC5 made no attempt to yell anything when power trio Cream was performing, Wayne Kramer told writer Ken

Kelly about a moment when Fred "Sonic" Smith could not resist a backstage opportunity. After Ginger Baker had taken off on an extended drum solo, the band's bass player, Jack Bruce, accidentally walked into the MC5's dressing room on the opposite side of the stage. Without making eye contact, Smith posed a question to Bruce: "What about a second guitar? When you gonna add a second guitar?" An incredulous Bruce responded: "Well, we think Eric [Clapton] handles all the guitar duties quite well." Fred Smith, returned a low-key volley in a flat monotone while staring at the floor: "You-over-dubbed-a-guitar-player-on-the-album, when-ya-gonna-put-a second-guitar-in-your-show? Sounds-pretty-lame-now-Jack."[19] Kelly said that the exchange demonstrated that, while Fred was a "man of few words," they always "seemed well-barbed."[20]

# 17. Enter the Stooges

On March 3, 1968, a new group calling themselves the Psychedelic Stooges made their debut at the Grande Ballroom. Lead singer Jim Osterberg fronted the loud, raw, almost primitive-sounding rock band. The other members included Ron Asheton on guitar, his brother Scott on drums, and Dave Alexander on bass.

For their first show at the Grande, Osterberg, who was also known as "Iggy," arrived wearing an old floor-length white nightshirt. His face was painted white like a mime, and he was wearing an Afro wig made from twisted aluminum foil.[1] As the band droned on in a crude monotonous rhythm behind him, Iggy danced around the stage like a strangely tormented man. According to lead guitarist Ron Asheton, the band brought along some nontraditional instruments for that first show, including a water-filled blender into which they stuck a microphone. They played it through the PA system for fifteen minutes before coming onstage. They also brought along a vacuum cleaner and a washboard with contact mikes so Iggy could put on golf shoes and shuffle back and forth.[2]

John Sinclair was in the audience that night and thought this new band was "unbelievable," likening their songs to "demented grooves or trances."[3] Whatever it was, the Psychedelic Stooges made their mark. According to drummer Scott Asheton, they had accomplished what they set out to do, "knock down the walls and blow people's shit away." Although they didn't make believers of everyone, the ones they did win over, said Asheton, "started showing up at every gig."[4]

Jim Osterberg was born in Muskegon, Michigan, on April 21, 1947, the son of a schoolteacher and an executive secretary. The family lived in a trailer park called the Coachville Garden Mobile Home Court on Carpenter Road in Ypsilanti, a working-class community just a few miles southeast of Ann Arbor.[5] In school, despite being an honor student and member of the debating team, Jim described himself as being a "very unhappy person" before getting into bands, "very self-conscious and very schizoid."[6]

At the age of five, he began beating out rhythms with his Lincoln Logs and Tinker Toys. By 1962, Osterberg was playing drums in an Ann Arbor frat band called the Iguanas, who competed for gigs with the Rationals when that band was starting out. By 1965 the Iguanas had recorded a single, "Mona," with "I Don't Know Why" on the flip side. They also landed their first away-from-home gig, playing at a northern Michigan club called the Ponytail, located in Harbor Springs.[7]

At the start of 1966, Osterberg accepted an offer to replace the original drummer in the already established Ann Arbor–based blues band Prime Movers. Dan Erlewine, who sang and played lead guitar with the band (which also included his brother Michael and Robert Shefe), recalled that at the time, Jim was a "nice, well-mannered guy, even quite bashful around girls."[8] The members of the Prime Movers referred to Osterberg as "Iguana," after his old band, and eventually shortened the nickname to "Iggy."[9] At the time Wayne Kramer, who along with Fred Smith had seen the Prime Movers perform, believed that Iggy was "certainly the best drummer in Ann Arbor" and described his playing as "unbeatable."[10]

It was during his time with the Prime Movers that Iggy developed a real appreciation for blues artists such as John Lee Hooker, Muddy Waters, and Howlin' Wolf. One night at the Living End, a Detroit jazz and blues club, Iggy had the opportunity to meet Mike Bloomfield, the guitarist in the Paul Butterfield Blues Band. Bloomfield advised him: "If you really want to play [the blues], you've got to come to Chicago."[11] So with nineteen cents in his pocket and dreams of meeting his drumming idol Sam Lay, Iggy left for the Windy City.

As a child, Ron Asheton had lived for a time in Washington, D.C., and was inspired by his great-aunt and uncle, who had been vaudevillian performers. Ron took up the accordion and soon began performing recitals. After moving to Iowa with his family, he lost interest in the instrument.[12] But then the Beatles and Rolling

Stones hit, and his desire to play music returned. By eleventh grade, several years after moving back to Michigan, he dropped out of school and, with friend and fellow dropout Dave Alexander, made a trip to England in 1965. "We thought that if we went there, we'd learn something," Asheton recounted to writer Jason Gross. "It was amazing to be sixteen and to take a train to Liverpool to go to the Cavern. For one dollar in English money, we could go to afternoon sessions where five local bands would play."[13]

The two returned to London with just enough money to get back to the States. After arriving home they decided to get Ron's brother Scott and start a band. As their little group was going nowhere, Ron jumped at a chance to play bass with the established Prime Movers, after being recommended by Iggy Osterberg, an acquaintance of the Asheton brothers, from the days when they and Dave Alexander hung out at Discount Records, where Iggy worked for a time. Asheton's time in the Prime Movers was short-lived, and the seventeen-year-old was soon replaced by an older and more competent player.[14] But Iggy called Ron and told him about a band called the Chosen Few who were looking for a bass player. After meeting with Scot Richardson, Ron joined the band. Ron Asheton recalls, "I spent a year playing all the teen clubs, pretending I was Brian Jones."[15] As a member of the Chosen Few, Ron had the distinction of striking the first note on opening night at the Grande Ballroom.

In Chicago, Iggy spent a lot of time around authentic blues players, and he quickly came to the conclusion that what they did just came naturally and that it would be "ridiculous" for him to try and make a "studious copy," as many white bands did. Instead, after smoking his first marijuana joint, he thought about creating his own original sound.[16]

Soon he was on the phone to his old buddies Ron and Scott Asheton. After convincing them to come to Chicago and give him a ride back home, Iggy asked if they wanted to form a new band. At the time, the Chosen Few were breaking up, and Ron was faced with a choice of staying with Scot Richardson in a new band backed with money and good equipment, or going with his "true buds," brother Scott and Iggy. He chose the latter. After Ron switched to guitar, the band recruited Dave Alexander to play bass. The new, nameless band rented a house to live and practice in. Iggy waited tables at a restaurant, and Ron worked in a headshop to pay the rent.[17]

The original plan had been for Scott to sing lead and Iggy to play drums, but Ron recognized Iggy's "need to perform more freely," and recommended that he sing.[18] It was a performance by the Doors that really opened Iggy's eyes. Lead singer Jim Morrison had come on stage at the University of Michigan show and pro-ceeded to toy with the audience, singing in an irritating high-pitched voice, à la Betty Boop. He did the same thing with the second song, and the audience got even more pissed off. Iggy didn't think the band was very impressive, but he "loved" the way Morrison antagonized the crowd, at the same time "mesmerizing them."[19] The experience left him thinking, "Look how awful they are, and they've got the number one single in the country! If this guy can do it, I can do it."[20]

According to Ron Asheton, the band listened to a lot of Ravi Shankar as well as Frank Zappa and the Mothers of Invention. "OK, let's see, we take Harry Partch, Buddhist music, Gregorian chants and try to throw in a little Stones and a little Beatles and see what happens."[21] Then a friend who had attended the Monterey Pop Festival came back with a Jimi Hendrix album. Ron says that everybody got stoned and listened to the record, refusing to give it back for three days.

The Stooges' songwriting method consisted of Ron coming up with riffs; then he and Iggy would piece things together. Asheton's style of guitar playing was heavily influenced by the trip that he and Dave Alexander had made to England in 1965, where they had been impressed by the Who and the Move.[22] "So that was the start," said Asheton, "and basically, we just plugged away."[23]

Sometime later, while sitting around watching a Three Stooges Festival on TV, Iggy zeroed in on a name for the group.[24] The Psychedelic Stooges made their first public appearance at a concert at the University of Michigan student union on Halloween, 1967.[25] By March 1968, they were on to the Grande Ballroom and beyond, where a shirtless, sneering Iggy would roll around a stage covered with broken glass, or cut himself with a broken drum stick to draw blood, smear peanut butter on his bare chest, and make wild dives into the crowd. According to Russ Gibb, "Iggy was the show, but Ron was the sound."[26] Gibb's Grande Ballroom was like a "rock school" for Iggy: "It was a big sweatbox with one little window. You'd come out of there feeling like you'd really been through something," the singer recalled.[27]

One of the Stooges' more infamous early gigs came about after booking agent Jeep Holland convinced the owner of a Romeo, Michigan, club called Mother's to book the still unknown band in August 1968. Iggy arrived wearing a pair of skintight brown vinyl pants. During their performance, Iggy's crotch split open, momentarily exposing the singer's personal property. The brief incident would have probably been forgotten except for the fact that a girl in the audience happened to be the daughter of state police trooper stationed nearby. Later, as Iggy sat backstage with a towel wrapped around him, state troopers came busting through the front door, one yelling: "Where's that Iggy!"[28]

The lead Stooge beat it out the back door but was found a little later jumping from the trunk of a car in the parking lot, arrested, and taken to jail for the night. His parents came to get him in the morning. In court, Iggy pled guilty to disorderly conduct, a charge that had been reduced from indecent exposure. He paid a forty-one-dollar fine and nine dollars in court costs, and his folks took him home.[29]

"When I started out I was coming from an extremely anti-professional place; not a lot of professional spin behind it basically, not a lot of savior fare or know-how or anything," Iggy recalled years later. "So everything would go wrong. One night the bass player would set his shirt on fire, and another night I'd fall off the stage. You never knew what was up."[30] Ron Asheton felt that "because Iggy really wasn't a singer, he pulled everything that was humanly possible out of what he had."[31]

The Stooges formed a sort of unofficial alliance with the MC5 when they signed a booking deal with Trans-Love Energies. "I always admired them because I loved the big sound," said Ron Asheton, speaking of the "5." "I would learn things by watching them. 'How do they do that Chuck Berry, regular rock and roll thing?' I learned from them, being around the dressing room."[32]

In recalling the early days of the Stooges, MC5 drummer Dennis Thompson likened them to the "first true performance art band." At the time Thompson thought Iggy was forced to "overreact, over respond, over-dramatize" to compensate for the band's poor skills.[33] At the same time, Iggy viewed the MC5 as the "varsity," and the Stooges as the "dropouts."[34] Said Asheton, "We thought the MC5 were pretty accomplished musicians at a time when we really weren't."[35]

# 18.  On the Front Lines with the MC5

By late May 1968, the Trans-Love commune had been fire-bombed twice, and hassles with the Detroit police had escalated following a new curfew imposed following the assassination of Martin Luther King. As a result, John Sinclair moved the entire Trans-Love Energies operation to Ann Arbor, settling into two big Victorian-style houses next door to one another on a street not far from the University of Michigan campus. The commune included twenty-eight people, with Sinclair and his family and the MC5 and their ladies residing at 1510 Hill. Other assorted Trans-Love employees and hangers-on occupied the larger house at 1520 Hill. A carriage house out back accommodated additional guests.[1]

While Ann Arbor may have provided a more peaceful living environment, the MC5 seemed to find trouble whenever they left the area. On Friday, May 31, the "5" were booked at the original Hideout club in Grosse Pointe, which was trying to remain competitive. Although it was a small venue compared to the Grande Ballroom, Wayne Kramer says that the band "wanted to play everywhere they could and carry their message all over."[2] They were known for performing for free at many benefit shows around Michigan. The MC5's political posturing as a "revolutionary band" was becoming increasingly evident. Gary Grimshaw's handbill for the Hideout show featured a headline proclaiming, "Break Through American Stasis With The MC5." Below was a photo of the band standing naked from the waste up, in front of an American flag, hung backwards.

The Hideout was packed with four hundred fans that night, the largest crowd the small room had held in several months. Third Power opened the show, and as they played their set, Sinclair and Dennis Thompson headed to the parking lot for a smoke. There they ran into some kids offering to share some grass. While they passed around a joint, two rent-a-cops appeared, and thirty minutes later, the Harper Woods police. Informed of what was going down, Wayne Kramer, Fred Smith, Rob Tyner, Michael Davis, and Ron Levine, their equipment manager, came running out. A cop pushed Fred Smith in the chest and threatened further action if they didn't back off.3

Wayne Kramer says things got ugly inside when Levine grabbed the microphone and announced to the crowd: "Hey everybody, the pigs are out there busting the band. Are we going to take this?"4 Levine suggested that the kids surround the cops and demand to have Sinclair and Thompson freed. Before he could finish his plea, he was dragged offstage by a cop, and then the doors were closed with the kids inside. Not wanting anymore trouble, the manager requested that the police release all the suspects with the exception of the one who was actually caught with the marijuana. The police complied.

An excited crowd screamed when the MC5 returned to the stage, plugged in, and started a new set with, "Kick Out the Jams." Near the end of the set, as usual, John Sinclair joined the band on sax as they wailed on "Black To Comm." But tonight, the manager, in a hurry to get them offstage, turned off the electricity right in the middle of the song. Fred Smith chanted, "Power! Power! Power!" and the crowd joined him. The juice returned, and the band brought the whole night to a memorable climax. Wayne Kramer says, "It was a defining night for the MC5. Yeah, it was the people versus the pigs, and the people won."5

The following Sunday night, June 23, the MC5 was scheduled to open for Cream at the Grande Ballroom. Stoked by what had gone down at the Hideout, the band decided to make a statement by burning an American flag on stage. When Russ Gibb found out what the band was brewing, he threatened to send for the police. Gibb liked to align himself with the freaks, but even during the height of anti-Vietnam protesting, there were some things he would not allow.

It was a hot, humid night in Detroit; the temperature was over one hundred degrees in the Grande. The ballroom was packed with two thousand fans waiting to hear Cream and everybody's favorite local band, the MC5. In compliance with Gibb's request, the band decided that instead of burning a flag, they would rip one to shreds. That accomplished, they brought on to the stage a banner bearing a marijuana leaf and the word *Freek* across it. The place went crazy. Jerry Younkins stood on stage nude, cheering.[6]

It wasn't Russ Gibb, but the building's landlord, Gabe Glantz, who exploded after being told about the band's stunt with the flag. The next day, he fired Grande manager Larry Feldman and threatened to expel the MC5. However, they were back at the Grande two weeks later, on a triple bill with national act Blue Cheer, of "Summertime Blues" fame, and the Psychedelic Stooges. Gabe Glantz made a last-minute appearance, warning the band not to use "dirty words, nakedness on stage, and no incidents with the American flag, real or simulated."[7] John Sinclair intervened and an argument ensued, resulting in Glantz taking the group off the bill.

Informed of what was going down, Russ Gibb and his attorney arrived on the scene. When the Stooges finished their opening set, the crowd was ready for the MC5, what they got instead were records piped into the ballroom. The band was downstairs, listening as Gibb explained how volatile the situation could be. Three detectives were supposedly on site watching for anti-American activity. The Grande's license to operate was in danger of being yanked.

The argument between Sinclair and Gibb was showing no signs of compromise until a manager of the Blue Cheer came in and informed Gibb that his band would not go on if the MC5 were not allowed to play. It was after nine when Gabe Glantz came into the office and told Russ that the detectives had left the premises. Hearing the crowd chanting: "MC5! MC5!" in the background, Gibb relented, and the band ran out on stage to begin what was to be an hour and a half set. But after opening with a blistering rendition of "Ramblin' Rose" followed by the call to "Kick out the jams, motherfucker!" Gibb told Sinclair that because his attorney, who was monitoring the show, had to leave, the band would only be doing one more song. Sinclair passed the message to Rob Tyner, who berated Gibb as he stood in the audience. Uncle Russ retaliated by having the electricity to the stage shut off.[8] The MC5, who had opened the Grande and played several months for free, were being pushed out the door.

Although the MC5 were gone for the time being, the Grande Ballroom rocked on through the summer of 1968. Wayne Cochran and the C. C. Riders headlined all three nights of the last weekend in June. That month Gary Grimshaw disappeared from the light show company. Grimshaw and TLE member Pun Plamondon had been charged with possession and sale of marijuana by Traverse City police, stemming from an incident in March. While Plamondon went to jail, Grimshaw fled to California.9

During July, major acts such as the Jeff Beck Group, Pink Floyd, the Who, Spirit, and the Steve Miller Band pulled in big crowds at the Grande. In August, there were appearances by Country Joe and the Fish, performing their anti–Vietnam War anthem, "Fixin' to Die Rag," and Canned Heat, who had scored a top 10 hit with "On the Road Again." The band acknowledged that John Lee Hooker's "Boogie Chillen," recorded in Detroit twenty years earlier, had been the inspiration for their song.

All these acts shared the stage with Detroit bands such as Odds and Ends, the Rationals, Frost (from Saginaw), Thyme, Jagged Edge, and Flint's the Pack, sans Terry Knight. Terry had left the band to pursue a solo career.

Meanwhile, Mark Farner had returned from a stint with the Bossmen, switching from bass to guitar and taking over lead vocals in what was now being called the Fabulous Pack.10 The revamped band had charted two mild local hits during the preceding year, "Harlem Shuffle" reaching number 21 on WKNR's *Music Guide* in July, and "Wide Trackin'" charting at number 24 in September. Despite these records, the group was on an even playing field at the Grande Ballroom, where reputations were judged by performance, not by sales.

Another band of note at the Grande was the Stuart Avery Assemblage, which had been formed only three months prior to taking the stage as an opening act for the Yardbirds on May 3, 1968. Yardbirds lead guitarist Jimmy Page was so impressed with them that he invited the band to join his group in a postshow encore, which greatly helped the Detroit band build a name for themselves. The band wrote their own material demonstrating the influence of artists such as Jeff Beck, the Rascals, and the Stones. Stuart Avery was the soulful lead vocalist, and Paul Kingery played lead guitar. The lineup also included Tim Lambert on keyboards, Jim Borisen on bass, and John Orlich on drums.[11] Eventually the band shortened their name to just Assemblage.

By late July, the MC5 finally found trouble closer to home, when they attempted to perform a free concert in Ann Arbor's West Park. All through the previous summer, there had been free Sunday rock concerts in the park, featuring bands such as Seventh Seal, the Up, and the Prime Movers. But following complaints from neighbors about the noise, the city had passed an ordinance prohibiting "high output electronic musical instruments" in public parks. So when the MC5 applied for a ten-dollar permit to put on the concert, they were turned down.[12]

The band, believing the ordinance unfair, decided to go ahead and play there anyhow. On July 14, they set up their equipment in the picnic shelter, and played for about an hour before the police showed up. To both the cops and the mayor, who was also on hand, John Sinclair tried to argue that the band was just "donating their time and energy to the people so they could have some of the free music they need to survive."[13]

The music was over for the day, but the mayor indicated that he understood Sinclair's position and promised to get back in touch the next week regarding future concerts.

The dust was barely settling in Ann Arbor when the "5" packed their gear and headed out to play a paying gig at a teen club called the Loft, located in Leonard, Michigan, in northern Oakland County. The band had played there recently, but the club owner's checks had bounced. It seemed this was a common occurrence for bands who played at the Loft. When things got bad enough that the owner, Harold Baumer, was starting to have trouble booking a band, he got in touch with Sinclair and asked him to bring back the MC5. Not only would he "pay them all he owed but also 40% of the gate."[14]

When the band arrived the night of July 23, they were surprised to find a rent-a-cop warning them "not to play that song with *moth-*

*erfucker* in it." Baumer, however, told them not to worry and handed over one hundred dollars in cash; once again he promised big money at the end of the gig.[15]

The MC5 opened a killer set with Wayne Kramer's high-pitched lead vocal on "Ramblin' Rose" and then went right into "Kick Out The Jams." After "Come Together," the rent-a-cop, his warning ignored, ordered the show stopped. The band refused, and within a few minutes the Oakland County Sheriff's Department was on the scene.

Not wishing further problems, Sinclair had his equipment managers load up all the gear while everyone waited in the van. While John checked the stage area to make sure nothing of value was left behind, Baumer approached him, asking the band to return to the stage so he would not have to refund money to the audience.

As Sinclair informed Baumer that was not going to happen and then demanded to be paid, the rent-a-cops rushed up, ordering Sinclair to get out. Refusing to leave without the money, Sinclair was grabbed by the security cops but broke free, punching one of them in the face before being thrown to the floor, where he was beaten and maced. As 150 or so kids looked on, Fred "Sonic" Smith rushed to Sinclair's aid, joining in the bloody melee. They were both handcuffed, arrested, and hauled off to the Oakland County Jail, where they spent the night, charged with assault and battery. The following day they each were released on a twenty-five-hundred-dollar bond.[16] To the band it seemed Baumer had set them up. He'd managed to draw a crowd without having to pay the band.[17]

Back in Ann Arbor on July 26, two weeks went by with no word from city officials regarding free concerts, so Sinclair and the band decided to head back down to West Park. This time they rented a generator so they could play in the band shell. Word of the event spread quickly, and a big crowd was on hand. The Up opened the concert and played loud and hard until two uniformed cops showed up on the stage to shut down the music. As it happened, a police lieutenant named Staudmire was sitting in the audience, enjoying the concert. He was able to convince the other cops to back off, and the band to turn down the amps.[18] The Up finished their set, and the MC5 plugged in and rocked for an hour. All was well until Rob Tyner started to work the crowd, leading them into screaming, "Kick out the jams, motherfucker!" not once but three times. As the sound reverberated all over the neighborhood, residents dialed the police, and soon the cops arrived in force and arrested the band. Members of the MC5 were charged with disturbing the peace and with being "disorderly persons." Each member posted $125 bond before being released. The U of M paper, the *Michigan Daily*, covered the proceedings in detail, and soon the campus was rallying and protesting the ban on outdoor music concerts. After two weeks, the city council backed off, giving Trans-Love Energies permission to hold a series of free concerts at Gallup Park, located along the Huron River, on the outskirts of Ann Arbor.[19]

Like the May 31 confrontation at the Hideout, the West Park controversy was another major victory for Sinclair and the MC5. They had stood up to the police, defying what they thought were unfair laws, and with support from the "people," had won. Sinclair was now convinced that an "organized youth revolt" could be successful. MC5 concerts were expanding from musical events to political rallies where new followers could be recruited for the rock 'n' roll "revolution."

In keeping with the MC5's increasing political agenda, as well as his own professional aspirations, John Sinclair thought it sounded like a great idea to have the band play at a music festival to be held outside of the Democratic National Convention in Chicago, in late August 1968.[20] The concert was to be part of a much larger anti-war, anti-politics-as-usual protest, planned to counter the convention.

Almost a year earlier, a group known as the National Mobilization to End the War in Vietnam (MOBE), had decided to stage a major protest at the same time and place of the Democratic National Convention. At a meeting held in November 1967, Rennie Davis, the national coordinator for MOBE, stated that he "wanted the world to know that there are thousands of young people in this country who do not want to see a rigged convention rubber-stamp another four years of Lyndon Johnson's war."[21]

Three months later, Davis, along with Michigan activist Tom Hayden, announced a plan to attract as many antiwar people as they could to Chicago for demonstrations and teach-ins.[22]

Meanwhile, an antiwar group calling themselves the Youth International Party, better known as the Yippies, decided that they also would have a presence in Chicago. Founders Abbie Hoffman and Jerry Rubin, along with Ed Sanders and Keith Lampe, decided on a free music festival as an alternative to the more heavy-handed and militant groups such as MOBE and the Black Panthers. Their event would be called a "Festival of Life," and it would be held in the southern part of Lincoln Park, not far from the Amphitheatre, where the convention would be taking place. As part of the festival, Hoffman and Rubin announced plans to nominate a pig, "Pigasus the Immortal," for president.[23]

When Ed Sanders put in a call to John Sinclair, asking the MC5 to participate, Sinclair was more than enthusiastic. Arlo Guthrie, Country Joe and the Fish, Phil Ochs, and Sanders's group, the Fugs, were just some of the other artists committed to perform. Sinclair knew the MC5 would gain political credibility and reap a large amount of publicity by taking part in this national counterculture event.[24]

Plans for the festival, however, soon became complicated, as permits for the concerts were denied. On August 23, a federal district judge turned down a last-minute plea to overturn a previous decision to enforce an 11:00 P.M. curfew in parks, thus preventing demonstrators from sleeping there. Chicago's Mayor Richard Daley insisted that hippie demonstrators were not going to ruin the city's plan for an orderly political convention. Daly put the city's twelve thousand police officers on twelve-hour shifts, and his requests for seventy-five hundred army troops and six thousand National Guardsmen were granted.[25]

In order to pay for their trip, the MC5 had played a Saturday night gig at a northern Illinois teen club. Driving into Chicago at 4:00 A.M. the next morning, the band could "feel a really bad vibe."[26] After hooking up with some organization people, they were taken over to a church, where they attempted to sleep on wooden pews, surrounded by homeless people and derelicts. "The thought of a hotel never entered our mind," says Wayne Kramer.

"We lived in a world where if you needed a place to crash, it was usually a mattress on the floor of someone's apartment."[27]

Word spread quickly that things were not only bad, but downright dangerous in Chicago. As the MC5 rolled into the park at about three o'clock on Sunday, August 25, the band discovered that they were the only group to have actually shown up, all the others having been scared off by the bad publicity.[28] The band was also informed that there was no place to play. A flatbed truck, originally planned to be used as a stage, had not been allowed into the park. Never ones to back away from a challenge, the "5" unloaded their amps, guitars, and drums. According to Wayne Kramer, after past experiences in Detroit, the band "didn't find the possibility of police violence all that strange."[29]

In the midst of all the confusion, a couple of people came up and offered the band some hash brownies, cautioning that they were "very strong" and advising the musicians "to eat only one."[30] After devouring three brownies each, they decided it was show time. Searching for power, the band plugged into a electric socket in a hot dog stand nearby. Standing at ground level, surrounded by some two thousand kids sitting on the grass, and another two thousand milling about, the MC5 started to rock Chicago. Norman Mailer was covering the convention and witnessed the performance of the MC5. In an article for *Esquire* magazine, he described their music as "an interplanetary, then galactic, flight of song, halfway between the space music of Sun Ra and 'The Flight of the Bumblebee,' . . . the sound screaming up to a climax of vibrations like one rocket blasting out of itself."[31]

As soon as the band began playing, there were signs of trouble from what appeared to be agitators in the crowd. After just four of five songs, someone in the crowd threw a bottle and the Chicago police marched into the park from all sides, swinging billy clubs. The crowd responded by throwing more bottles. As police helicopters hovered above, Abbie Hoffman grabbed the microphone and started a tirade against the "pigs" and the "siege of Chicago."[32]

"It was just like 'Little Big Horn,'" recalls MC5 bass player Michael Davis. "The helicopters were flying overhead, the cavalry was charging over the hill, and the crowd was surging. At that point, we just wanted to save our guitars and amplifiers—that was the first priority."[33] High as a kite on the hash brownies, the band members and roadies pitched equipment into their van. They managed to retrieve their microphone from Hoffman, and within seconds the MC5 and crew were tearing off across the park, while all hell was breaking loose in the rearview mirror.[34]

For drummer Dennis Thompson, the whole experience had a sobering effect. If Chicago was supposed to be a show of solidarity, he wondered, where were the other bands? From that point on, Thompson had second thoughts about the "revolution."[35]

# 19. Total Assault: Kickin' Out the Jams

The MC5 were set to perform at the Oakland Pop Festival, at the Baldwin Pavilion at Oakland University in Rochester, Michigan, on September 1 when they received a tip: police were waiting there to arrest them on a year-old warrant issued after they had created a wild scene at a party held in an apartment complex. Rather than face the cops, the "5" turned around and headed home.[1]

After a week off at the Trans-Love commune in Ann Arbor, the MC5 returned to familiar territory near Wayne State University, where they were taking part in a much smaller festival called "Dialogue '68," held at the First Unitarian Church, located at the corner of Cass and Forest. In an effort to attract the hip young crowd, the church had enlisted John Sinclair and the "5" to help put it all together. The pastor of the church had officiated at the wedding of John and Leni three years earlier.[2]

Sharing the bill were the usual suspects: the Psychedelic Stooges and the Up. Also on hand were Billy C. & the Sunshine, the Wilson Mower Pursuit, and Saginaw's Popcorn Blizzard. Formed in the spring of 1967, the members of the Up were Franklin Bach on vocals, Bob Rasmussen on guitar, his brother Gary Rasmussen on bass, and Vic Peraino on drums. The band was managed by David Sinclair, John Sinclair's younger brother. While still in high school, the Rasmussen brothers had been in a band called the Citations that played at record hops with CKLW's Dave Shafer. Eventually, the band moved on to teen clubs, changing their name to Brand X. It was at this point, in the spring of 1967, that they met Franklin Bach, at the time the stage manager and announcer at the Grande Ballroom. Bach wound up joining the band as lead singer. After another name change, they became the Up and started to hang around the Wayne State campus, attracted by the evolving hippie scene. They played cover versions of Stones and Kinks hits, but their greatest influence was the MC5. The "5" began to feature the Up on its shows, including them as an opening act at the Grande Ballroom. In the fall of 1968, the Up moved to the Trans-Love Energies commune and became fully immersed in the revolutionary politics of John Sinclair. After the move to Ann Arbor, the band replaced drummer Vic Peraino with Scott Bailey.[3] John Sinclair thought that although the Up were not as "skilled in music and stagecraft" as the MC5, nor as "charismatic" as Iggy and the Stooges, the band did work hard at playing high-energy rock and roll that would inspire audiences to join the revolution against the status quo.[4]

When the MC5 took the stage on Saturday night, September 7, they were introduced to the audience by Jesse Crawford, a new spiritual associate of Trans-Love Energies. A native of Cleveland, J. C. had relocated to Ann Arbor in the mid-1960s, and had played drums for a time with the Prime Movers. He was a proponent of a spiritual movement called Zenta, whose beliefs were similar to those of Trans-Love, namely rock 'n' roll, drugs, and free sex. Crawford, known as the Oracle Ramus of Zenta, was now going along to all the band's gigs, delivering a "fire and brimstone" introduction sermon designed to get the crowd of "brothers and sisters" on their feet and rockin' in time with the MC5.[5]

Over the years, the "5" had tried to build a show similar to that of their heroes, especially James Brown. As Wayne Kramer recalls, "James Brown had an emcee that would come out and warm up the crowd. We took the spirit of the James Brown thing and then J. C. came up with his own text on it. 'Cause we wanted to entertain people and take them somewhere they hadn't been before."[6]

Shortly after the Unitarian Church concerts, John Sinclair left for New York to do some promotion for the band. He took along a copy of their recording "Looking at You" when he visited Bob Rudnick and Dennis Frawley in the studios of alternative radio station WFMU. The duo were hosting a program similar in content to their Kocaine Karma column, which appeared in the underground newspaper the *East Village Other*. Rudnick and Frawley both loved the record and began to talk up the exploits of the MC5 on the radio and in the paper. They described the band as "musical guerillas—an exploding theater formed by a fusion of avant garde jazz and primitive rock."[7] As Dennis Frawley later said, "We really liked John Sinclair and the way he did promotion. He was a sort of P.T. Barnum of the revolution. After sending us their first record, John would also send us raw tapes of the MC5, and we would put them right on the air at WFMU."[8]

Through Rudnick and Frawley, Sinclair also made contact with Danny Fields, the publicity director and "company freak" for Elektra Records, who had been responsible for urging the label to sign the Doors.[9] Fields thought that Sinclair was "bursting with charm, vigor, and intellect."[10] He was impressed by the look and size of the MC5's manager, and he too liked what he heard and agreed to come to Detroit to see the band perform live on September 21.

The MC5 met Fields at the airport and drove him out to their house on Hill Street in Ann Arbor. As he walked through the large Victorian home, Fields saw what seemed to be hundreds of rooms, each decorated in the psychedelic style of the times: mattresses on the floor, tapestries hanging from the ceilings, posters on the walls, and copies of Chairman Mao's Red Book lying everywhere. The basement held the various Trans-Love operations: printing press, design studios, workshops, and darkrooms. Danny Fields thought it was really "wild" that all the band members actually lived together in the house, as did their girlfriends, who gathered in the kitchen cooking meals that they served to the men, who ate alone.[11] Although the MC5 were the political "revolutionary band," their politics at the time did not extend to women.

On Saturday night, September 21, 1968, Danny Fields was present for the sold-out show at the Grande Ballroom. It was the first time the MC5 had played there since being barred after the flag controversy when they were supposed to perform with Blue Cheer on June 26. Fields saw the band come onstage dressed in colorful satin outfits and "spinning around really fast," as they began to play.[12] "These guys would show up dressed in wonderful colorful spangles and rhinestone costumes with American flags, and play loud and they did things in unison. . . . They were great," says WABX deejay Dan Carlisle, recalling the MC5. "They weren't some anarchist crazy people. I loved 'em. All of us in Detroit grew up on rhythm and blues. They were obviously inspired by that. They were a show band, that's for sure. The San Francisco bands is where we get all that hippie stuff from . . . you sort of shuffle on stage, and if you don't fall down into a drug coma, you play."[13]

"Wayne did a lot of dancing and gyrating," says Michel Davis, describing the MC5 on stage. "Rob would do the pony . . . Wayne and Fred got into choreography, back-bends . . . Fred did a lot of dramatic, bravado moves. He'd bend his knees and lean back."[14] Although they were not, according to Fields, "breaking the barriers of rock 'n' roll," the MC5 did put on a "great show"; he described their music as "fine blues-based rock & roll."[15]

After the show, Wayne Kramer felt that the band had scored high with Fields. He recommended that Fields also check out their "little brother band," Iggy and the Stooges, who were set to perform the following afternoon at the Union Ballroom in Ann Arbor. Danny Fields came away from the Stooges' performance impressed by Iggy's "high atomic energy." Fields felt that he had just experienced the music he "had been waiting to hear all his life."[16] After the show he approached Iggy, who was wearing a maternity dress and white powder makeup, and introduced himself as being from Elektra records. Iggy, unimpressed, responded with a flat, "Oh yeah, uh-huh" and referred Fields to his manager, Jim Silver.[17]

On Monday morning, Silver, Danny Fields, and John Sinclair were seated around the kitchen table of the MC5 house. Fields put a call in to Jac Holtzman, the president of Elektra Records in New York, telling him that the MC5 had sold out the Grande with fans lined up in the streets, adding, "They're really going to be big."[18] Fields continued to speak enthusiastically as he turned to the Stooges, telling Holtzman that the group played the "most incredibly advanced music" he had ever heard, describing their lead singer as a "star, really mesmerizing."[19] Holtzman, wishing to pump new blood into his primarily folk music label, which was enjoying success with the Doors, listened intently. Danny Fields strongly recommended that Elektra take both groups. Jac Holtzman agreed, as long as the MC5 would sign for twenty grand and the Stooges for five. According to Fields, John Sinclair "went white and fell backwards" when he heard the offer.[20] Jim Silver had a similar reaction to the idea of someone actually giving the Stooges five thousand dollars up front for a recording contract. For the MC5, all the long years of hard work were finally paying off. Wayne Kramer recalled, "I knew, finally, it was really going to happen. We were on the cusp of success."[21]

In his "Rock and Roll Dope" column appearing in the *Fifth Estate* the week of October 3, John Sinclair broke the news that on September 26 in New York, Elektra Records had signed the MC5 and the Stooges to "long-term recording contracts." He also announced that the MC5's first album would be recorded live at the Grande Ballroom later in the month. Recording the band live was a bold move, as live albums were not common and certainly not viewed as appropriate for a debut release. Wayne Kramer commented, "The live show was the central experience. That was who we were. We wanted to present that live."[22] Elektra's Jac Holtzman also felt at that recording live was the "only way to capture the MC5."[23]

In the meantime, the MC5 quickly put the twenty-thousand-dollar advance to use. "We paid off all outstanding bills and bought some new equipment," recalls John Sinclair. "Then we all headed right downtown and bought some expensive leather coats from Louis the Hatter."[24]

Jac Holtzman, John Sinclair, and Russ Gibb decided that the nights of Wednesday the thirtieth and Thursday the thirty-first of October would be the recording dates for the band's debut live album. Jac Holtzman put producer-engineer Bruce Botnick in charge of the project. Botnick had already demonstrated his skills as an engineer when he recorded the Doors' first album. After traveling to Detroit to do a sound check at the Grande, Botnick hired Wally Heider, the top remote recording engineer in the country. Heider flew equipment in from his home base in San Francisco and then rented a truck in Detroit, where they picked up the Universal Audio tube console, three L604 loudspeakers, and a 3M-79 model eight-track recorder.[25]

In addition to the two evening concerts, there were also plans to record on Thursday afternoon: "It was Jac Holtzman's idea to record the concert on the first night and then record the songs again on the following afternoon without an audience on hand," recalls Bruce Botnick. "Jac wanted some alternative tracks to work with, should something go wrong on the initial concert recording."[26]

On Wednesday evening, everyone was ready to make a great live recording. The Grande Ballroom was packed with fans for the free performance. There was electricity in the air as friends moved in and out of the MC5's dressing room. Danny Fields arrived wearing dark shades and a dark brown leather field jacket with epaulets. He reached into his pocket and pulled out two fat joints of African ganja, which he passed to the members of the band.[27] Wayne, Fred, and Michael were huddled around a small backstage amp, tuning their guitars. Stoked on the ganja, the band moved toward the stage on a mission to "play and destroy." As the crowd stomped out a beat, the whole band was onstage, and Brother J. C. Crawford was reaching for the microphone, speaking with the fervor of a southern Baptist minister standing before what was surely a crowd of sinners:

> Brother and sisters, I want to see a sea of hands out there! I want to see a sea of hands! I want to see a little *revolution* out there! Time has come, brothers. Time for you to choose. It takes five seconds to decide. Five seconds for you to decide your purpose here on the planet. Five seconds to decide if you are gonna be the problem, or if you are going to be the *solution.* You must choose. I want to know if you're ready to get down with it. I want to know if you're ready to testify. I give you a testimonial—*the MC5!*[28]

The crowd, whipped into a call-and-response frenzy, was going wild with screams and shouts as Wayne Kramer leapt into the air, spun around, and landed stage front, his hand sweeping down over the strings for the opening to "Ramblin' Rose."

Fred "Sonic" Smith was performing in his custom-made lime green suit. Bass player Michael Davis was decked out in a sequined "Uncle Sam" red, white, and blue matching vest, shirt, and trousers. Dennis "Machine Gun" Thompson was positioned solidly behind his massive double kit, savagely attacking the drums, while out in front Rob Tyner was wearing one of his original design yellow and pink outfits. According to Wayne Kramer, Tyner was "sweating, screaming and dancing like a man possessed by forces you don't even know about."[29] Extra cables and microphones on the stage gave minor interference as the band danced around, but nothing got in the way of the MC5's performance. At the time, Wayne felt that he was a "part of the best band in the world."[30]

Kramer recalled that he was "flying on pure adrenaline" and dancing his best "James Brown" through the first eight bars of their opening number. Then his E string slipped out of its saddle on the bridge, sending the guitar way out of tune. Kramer plunged into the solo, full throttle, without missing a beat, driving the song to its explosive conclusion, where upon striking a perfectly timed chord, the band made a dramatic final leap, hitting the floor in unison. Out in the audience, long-haired fans were jumping up and down and screaming loudly. Wayne Kramer took a second to retune his guitar, and instantly the band segued into the song everybody was waiting for, as Rob screamed: "Right now it's time to *kick out the jams, motherfuckers!*" The roof about lifted off the Grande Ballroom as the searing guitar notes of Fred and Wayne smashed into each other and the crowd cheered even louder.[31]

Out in the alley, behind the Grande, Wally Heider and Bruce Botnick were stationed in the mobile recording truck, capturing all they could of what many Detroiters believed was the best live band anywhere. A TV camera positioned on the stage enabled the two engineers to view the band's performance on a small monitor in the truck. "I knew at the time we were getting a good take," says Botnick. "The MC5 were always at their best when they were playing live."[32]

From "Kick Out the Jams," it was on to the sexually charged "Come Together" and then "Rocket Reducer No. 62" ("Ramma Lama Fa Fa Fa"), a song that provided Fred and Wayne the chance to "stretch out on their guitars." The band played "Borderline," John Lee Hooker's "Motor City Is Burning," and "I Want You Right Now." Then it was time for what Wayne Kramer called the band's pièce de résistance. It was called "Starship," which Kramer described as a "tone poem of space and the vistas of vistas": "The bass and drums are powering the starship, and the tools formerly known as electric guitars are signaling and probing other planets and star systems. We're all navigating through the nothingness. We've reached the purity of a new sonic dimension, and the whole crowd is right there with us."33

Fans were cheering as the feedback began to fade. As the concert ended, the exhausted band, soaked with sweat, left the stage and descended the three stairs to the dressing room, where they reunited with wives, girlfriends, and the whole extended family. Mission accomplished.

Following the two nights of recording, Bruce Botnick and Jac Holtzman packed up the tapes, and on Friday morning they grabbed a cab for the airport.34 Botnick, a self-described "twenty-three-year-old mod-dresser," seemed to have little in common with the looks and attitude of the MC5: "Actually, I thought they were nice guys," he recalls. "On stage they had the 'revolutionary persona,' but off stage, despite the political overtones, I thought they were like most rock bands who wanted to play music and have a good time."35

On November 1, 1968, immediately after the recording sessions for "Kick Out the Jams" had been completed, John Sinclair announced the formation of a new political division of Trans-Love Energies, to be known as the White Panther Party. Sinclair had been urged to create this new entity by Pun Plamondon, who, while serving a jail sentence over the summer, had spent time reading an interview with Huey Newton of the radical Black Panther Party. "I told Sinclair that changing the name to the White Panthers made perfect sense," says Plamondon. "We were being attacked politically, so we should respond in a political fashion and organize people."36 Sinclair, still charged by the events in Chicago the previous August and having had an affinity for black culture dating back to his formative years in Flint, agreed with Plamondon that the White Panther Party's name alone would give it instant credibility in radical circles.37 The WPP would take a stronger political stance than that of TLE. Sinclair would serve as "Minister of Information," and Plamondon "Minister of Defense." J. C. Crawford would be "Minister of Religion." On the East Coast, new recruits Bob Rudnick and Dennis Frawley were named "Ministers of Propaganda."[38]

As for the MC5, they would be the White Panther Party's "revolutionary band," authentic "rock and roll guerrillas," viewed as armed (with guitars) and dangerous.[39] The band and the WPP were ready to wage a "total assault on the culture by any means necessary, including rock and roll, dope and fucking in the streets." The declaration, with its vulgar reference to free sex, thrown in for shock value, was part of the White Panther's ten-point program, which, they took pride in pointing out, was similar to that of the Black Panthers.[40] William Leach, however, felt differently. His writings for the Black Panthers appeared in the *Inner City Voice* and the *South End,* the two issue-oriented newspapers read around Wayne State University. He wrote that White Panther principles espoused by Sinclair such as "Leaders suck" and "We are LSD-driven total maniacs in the universe" had nothing in common with the more serious tone set forth by the radical black organization.[41]

Leach also took exception to Sinclair's claim that "music is revolution," writing that "black folks have been singing, dancing and blowing instruments, and we still ain't free."[42] While labeling some white leftist organizations as militant but "inactive" or "undisciplined," Leach felt the White Panthers along with the Yippies were "making a joke out of the revolution."[43] Sinclair and the other WPP members, tripping on acid, seemed to be taking themselves quite seriously, as they railed against the "white honkie culture" declaring: "We demand total freedom for everybody! And we will not be stopped until we get it."[44]

# 20. Up against the Wall and Beyond

Wayne Kramer was asleep when the rough mixes of the Grande Ballroom concert arrived at the Hill Street house in Ann Arbor. John Sinclair had quickly threaded the tape onto their home deck and was playing it back at a high volume. "As I was waking up and listening to the music, I realized that it didn't sound very good," recalls Kramer. "There was too much distortion and a couple of screwups recorded, like when my string broke. I felt that we had material that had been recorded on much less sophisticated equipment that sounded better."[1] Kramer also says that the band hadn't played as well as they might have; they'd been "intimidated" by the live recording: "The MC5 was never a really consistent band. We took chances, tried different things. As a result we had some incredible nights of great music. But there was also the occasional train wreck."[2] At first Kramer wasn't worried. "When we first did the deal with Elektra, we were told that if we weren't happy with the results, we would be able to record live again. Well, when we told them we needed to cut it again, the answer was no. They thought the recording was fine."[3]

In December, the MC5 headed for Boston to begin a small East Coast tour, put together by Elektra Records to increase awareness of the band prior to the release of the *Kick Out the Jams* album, scheduled for early 1969. On December 12, the MC5 shared the bill with the Velvet Underground on the first of a three-day engagement at the Boston Tea Party, a rock venue similar to Detroit's Grande Ballroom. The first two nights went off without a hitch. Then, before the show on Sunday, John Sinclair came into contact with a group of community-minded radicals from New York's Lower East Side. Derived from a larger organization called Black Mask, twenty hard-core members of that group, led by Ben

Morea and Ron Hahne, had reformed as the Lower East Side SDS chapter in December 1967. They started identifying themselves as "Up Against the Wall Motherfucker!"[4]

Now they were asking the MC5 to help them raise defense funds on behalf of Morea, who had been arrested in Boston on charges of knifing a serviceman.[5] The MC5, being a "radical, revolutionary" band, saw no problem in letting one of the Motherfuckers address the audience for a couple of minutes between sets. Sinclair and the MC5, however, were not dealing with a harmless bunch of "protesting college kids," but a tough, ruthless gang of well-organized anarchists. At demonstrations they were known to break out of the main throng and smash windows, kick over trash cans, set fires, and disrupt traffic. Not satisfied with heckling, they would charge ahead, throwing karate chops, brandishing knives, and swinging bicycle chains while screaming: "Up against the wall, motherfucker!"[6] As the first group of radical young whites to connect with the black movement, they had won favor with Eldridge Cleaver's Black Panthers. They boldly took up community causes such as the Lower East Side garbage strike, during which they had hauled piles of stinking refuse by way of the subway, and dumped them in upscale Rockefeller Plaza.[7] They'd even rebuffed Abbie Hoffman's attempts to join their organization, viewing him as not radical enough.[8]

A month or so earlier, the Motherfuckers had pressured rock promoter Bill Graham to make the Fillmore available for free, once a week, to support the Lower East Side "community," where the theater was located. Graham had gone along with the idea, and on Wednesday evenings the Fillmore was inhabited by a strange array of belligerent street people, cooking food, taking care of babies, smoking dope, and being generally unpleasant.[9] The Motherfuckers and their people were loud, ugly, mean, and not to be taken lightly.

As the MC5 finished their opening set, the Motherfuckers took over the microphone. Following a plea for "defense fund" donations for Morea, they abruptly changed the subject and began ranting about how the "people" were being "ripped off" by the Tea Party. Declaring that the "music should be free," they encouraged the kids to tear the place apart.[10] Power to the mike was quickly killed, and the troublemakers were forcefully removed from the stage before the Velvets began their set.

Club manager Don Law blamed the MC5 for turning his stage over to the radicals, and after the show he banned the Detroit musicians from future appearances at the Boston club.[11] Unbeknownst to the band, Law also happened to be part of an influential group of rock concert promoters who controlled much of the national rock-and-roll touring circuit.

Undeterred, the band arrived in New York on Monday afternoon with plans to visit clubs as well as the offices of their new record label. They also found time to visit the headquarters of Up Against the Wall Motherfucker! where they were updated on the escalating conflict with promoter Bill Graham. Meanwhile, Elektra Records had rented the Fillmore East for an MC5 show on Thursday, December 26, and put together a big radio promotion involving an on-the-air ticket giveaway.[12] In spite of the Boston experience, the MC5 were still supportive of the Motherfuckers and agreed to do a free, unannounced performance the very next evening, December 16, a "free community night." The "5" arrived late for the free Fillmore show, which irritated many of the street people hanging out there. But despite some bad vibes, the "gig went down fine."[13]

The next day the group flew back to the Motor City to open for British rock act Crazy World of Arthur Brown at Olympia on December 23. The single "Kick Out the Jams" had just been released, and as the band drove across town, the record blasted over the car radio. Wayne Kramer recalled the moment as "overwhelming."[14] The MC5 went onstage that night to the thunderous hometown applause of seventeen thousand fans. They'd already put their recent experiences on the East Coast behind them.

Following a Christmas gig at the Crow's Nest in Saint Clair Shores, the band returned to New York for the highly publicized and possibly career-making appearance at the Fillmore East. Other forces, however, were at work and would cast a pall over their performance. Bill Graham had become unhappy with the behavior of the Motherfuckers and the street people who followed them. He didn't like the way they were treating his theater, smoking dope in the open and attracting the attention of the police, who were threatening to close him down. Graham had pleaded with the "community" for understanding when he canceled the free Wednesday policy. The Motherfuckers would hear none of it.[15] Worried about possible violence, Graham asked Jac Holtzman to cancel the upcoming MC5 appearance. Holtzman declined, not wanting to "back down on a commitment to the band."[16] On December 26, a defiant Bill Graham held back the five hundred free tickets that John Sinclair and Elektra had set aside for distribution to the Lower East Side community. Soon the Motherfuckers were pounding on the doors, demanding to be let in. It was at this point that the MC5 pulled up out front in a limousine, rented by Danny Fields. The site of this "radical" band stepping out of a limo enraged the Motherfuckers even more, and they started to berate the band members as "traitors" as they made their way into the theater.[17] As the band set up to play, the situation out front deteriorated into a shouting match between Graham and the Motherfuckers. John Sinclair tried to make peace by telling Graham that the band wouldn't play unless he let everybody in. Graham acquiesced.[18]

Inside, the band tore through a few numbers while some of the Motherfuckers were standing by in the wings. According to Wayne Kramer, they were waiting for the MC5 to give the word to "burn the place down."[19] Instead, Rob Tyner spoke to the audience about how the MC5 hadn't come to New York for "politics," but to "rock and roll."[20] This displeased the Motherfuckers, and the mood got uglier as the evening wore on. At the conclusion of their set, some street people rushed the stage, and a brawl ensued. According to Dennis Thompson, the Motherfuckers, now as angry at the MC5 as they were at Bill Graham, started smashing the band's equipment as well as slashing the curtain and setting seats on fire.[21] In all the pushing and shoving, someone swung a chain at Bill Graham, breaking his nose.

The band members were pushed toward the middle of the theater, where they found themselves surrounded and fighting off a knife attack on Wayne Kramer. Making a run for the doors, they were greeted by the sight of two waiting limousines. As some of the band and roadies jumped inside, the Motherfuckers and their women banged on the limo, shouting and screaming. Wayne

Kramer recalls, "They were smashing our promo records against the Cadillac limo's tail fins and crying at the top of their lungs: 'Bastards! Pigs! Phonies! Sellouts!' "[22]

As the limos pulled away, Kramer was left standing in the middle of the street, surrounded by an angry mob. He says, "I felt I needed to deal with this situation. I needed to speak up for the band and convince these people that we were not a bunch of phonies."[23] It quickly became obvious that things were out of control, and two higher-ups in the Motherfuckers literally picked Kramer up, at first going back inside and then rushing him down the street and safely depositing him a couple of blocks away.

Back inside the Fillmore, Bill Graham was mistakenly telling people that Rob Tyner had been the person who had hit him with the chain. Understandably upset, Graham declared then and there that the MC5 would never again play the Fillmore or, if it was up to him, anywhere else.[24] As the band flew back to the Motor City, they reflected on the evening's events. Dennis Thompson remembers, "We're all going, 'What are we doing? Fuck this revolution shit. We should have just stayed in Detroit.' "[25]

Thompson was probably right. Like Don Law in Boston, a vengeful and influential Bill Graham put the word out to other promoters around the country: "Watch out for this band. Don't have anything to do with them or any of their ilk."[26]

The MC5's fabulous East Coast tour had now resulted in the band being blackballed by two of the biggest concert promoters in the country.

Back in Michigan after their New York adventure, the MC5 were enjoying the notoriety of a cover story in the January 4 edition of *Rolling Stone*, written by the magazine's influential rock critic, Jon Landau. Danny Fields had initiated the contact the previous October, telling Landau that Elektra had just signed "the best goddamn band in the world" and convincing him to fly to Detroit to see them perform live.[27] Like Fields before him, Landau was duly impressed, though somewhat intimidated by John Sinclair and the White Panther Party, commenting that they were "just too far out."[28]

That same evening, Jon Landau heard the band perform, and while he did express "reservations about the group's musical abilities," he was "bowled over by their energy."[29] After the show, Landau offered his opinions for making the MC5 a better band. Suddenly, in addition to his position as a music journalist, he found himself a paid consultant to Elektra Records.[30]

The *Rolling Stone* article was a long, glowing piece that heralded the MC5 as the next big thing, despite the fact that they hadn't put out an album. Rock critic Robert Christgau described Landau's piece as "adulatory to the point of sheer credulousness."[31] Apparently Landau saw no conflict of interest in writing about a band that he was also being paid to advise. Landau urged pop critic Richard Goldstein to write positive articles about the MC5 for both the *Village Voice* and the *New York Times*.[32]

Meanwhile, the single "Kick Out The Jams" entered the Detroit record charts at CKLW and WKNR on January 30, reaching number 2 by the middle of February. Although Elektra had encouraged the band to record the "Motherfuckers" version of "Kick Out the Jams" for the album, John Sinclair claims to have insisted that the band also record a version of the song as "Kick Out the Jams, Brothers and Sisters," so as to get play on Top 40 radio stations.[33] That version was recorded during the afternoon session at the Grande when there was no audience present. Wayne Kramer remembers, "We weren't complete idiots about it. We knew *that* would never be played on the radio, so we recorded an alternative intro for the 45 rpm version. We told the record company to 'let the single get as firmly established in the charts as it can. Wait until it starts coming back down before you put the album out. Then they won't be able to stop us—we'll be a bona fide hit band. Then the controversy will work in our favor.' "[34] But, when Elektra saw how fast the single was selling, they rushed out the album, and, according to Kramer, "the shit hit the fan." When the kids played the album version at home, parents took offense not only to the objectionable lyrics in the song, but also to the word "fuck" in the liner notes by John Sinclair.

Out of nowhere, clerks in record stores were being arrested for selling the "obscene" album and stores were complaining to distributors, who in turn were giving Elektra a hard time.[35] In Detroit, Hudson's, the major department store chain, refused to stock the album. In retaliation, the band placed a full-page ad in the February 13–27 edition of the *Argus,* Ann Arbor's underground newspaper. The ad read, "KICK OUT THE JAMS, MOTHERFUCKER! . . . and kick in the door if the store won't sell you the album . . . FUCK HUDSON'S!" They sent the bill for the ad to Elektra Records.[36]

Jac Holtzman hit the roof when he found out that the "Fuck Hudson's" ad had included the Elektra logo. Hudson's reacted by removing all Elektra products from their shelves, including albums by Judy Collins, Phil Ochs, Theodore Bickel, and the Doors.[37] Holtzman put a call through to John Sinclair, telling him that he did not have the right to use their logo in a political statement. When Sinclair told Holtzman that the record executive "needed to support the revolution," Holtzman fired back that he "supported their music," but not "their revolution."[38]

According to Sinclair, Elektra had been completely behind the album in its original form, and Holtzman had gone so far as to say, "If there are any problems, our legal department will back you up."[39] Holtzman had undertaken the whole project with what Sinclair felt was "considerable naivete."[40]

Bill Gavin, who published an influential music tip sheet for radio stations, was calling the record "obscene" and asking that stations ban both versions of the controversial song.[41] Large record distribution chains were backing off from carrying the album in its current form. In a panic, Holtzman flew to Ann Arbor for an emergency meeting with the band, proposing that Elektra put out a new LP featuring the "brothers and sisters" version of "Kick Out the Jams."[42] According to John Sinclair, he and the band were opposed to this strategy, and felt that they should "push the original and kids would demand it."[43] By the end of their meeting, Holtzman appeared to be coming down on the side of the band.

On March 7, the MC5 headed out to Seattle for the start of a self-financed tour of the West Coast. Manager John Sinclair and Dennis Frawley, minister of propaganda of the White Panther Party, had flown out to San Francisco the day before to do advance work. They were met at the airport by Gary Grimshaw, self-exiled to the Golden State, who had offered to drive them around.[44] The first stop was the offices of *Rolling Stone* for an uncomfortable visit with publisher Jann Wenner. Sinclair wanted to know why Wenner had sent back five hundred free copies of "Kick Out the Jams" provided by Elektra for the magazine to give away to subscribers. Wenner denied being influenced by stories that the MC5 was more hype than good music, saying that he had decided to go with a similar record promotion from Phil Spector for his new Ike and Tina Turner release, "River Deep Mountain High."[45]

Next stop was the local record distributor. "When we got there, we found that there were no MC5 records in stock. Sinclair was really perturbed," recalls Dennis Frawley.[46] Sinclair then contacted the Avalon Ballroom, which he had been calling from Ann Arbor with little success. After getting one of the owners on the phone, Sinclair made a deal to have the MC5 play there for five days the following week. Thirty minutes later the same guy called back to cancel. Sinclair was told that Gary Scanlon, the other partner, "didn't like their record and the word was out that the MC5 is a hype."[47]

Things went better at the Straight Theater in the Haight-Ashbury district, where the band set up a three-day engagement for the following weekend. Sinclair was more than pleased with the arrangements because the Straight Theater had a strong reputation for being a "people's theater" with "great community rock 'n' roll scenes and the best vibes in town."[48] The Straight Theater was the site for the premiere screening of a "Kick Out the Jams" promotional film produced by Trans-Love Energies. In January, Leni had shot the MC5 performing their signature song during concerts at the Grande Ballroom, the Village Pub in Birmingham, and at the Delta Pop Festival in Midland, Michigan. Pun and Genie Plamondon, Dave Sinclair, Robin Summers, and Audrey Simon had provided the lighting. John and Leni Sinclair did their best to edit the rough footage to run in time with the MC5's single version of "Kick Out the Jams."[49]

Despite Bill Graham's not wanting to hire the MC5, things were looking good with the Straight booking. Gary Grimshaw quickly produced a promotional poster as Sinclair and Frawley grabbed a flight north to hook up with the band, who were set to play at Seattle's Eagles Auditorium on the seventh and eighth of March, opening for Jethro Tull.

According to John Sinclair, the "people of Seattle weren't ready for the MC5." Although there were some freaks who dug the Detroit high-energy sound, most were "stunned and even offended" at the conclusion of the band's two sets, and some had complained that the band played too loud.[50]

While in town the MC5 and company connected with the local underground newspaper, the *Helix*, whose staff had started a West Coast White Panther chapter. The "5" agreed to play at a benefit for the paper on Sunday. There were far more people in attendance than the previous two nights because other acts were added to the bill. The group was bummed to have to wait seven hours to perform. It was two in the morning when the MC5 finally plugged in, and by then the crowd had thinned considerably. John Sinclair felt that most of the music on the show was "pretty tired," and that the locals seemed to prefer "low-energy folk-rock."[51] As the band played, Sinclair heard a guy in the audience shouting "Plastic!" at Wayne Kramer. According to Sinclair, "Wayne called him down from the stage and told him to 'suck out his ass.' The same dude started throwing eggs at us and other shit. It was a drag."[52] The wild band from the Motor City had no regrets as they departed Seattle the following morning for the Bay Area.

After arriving in San Francisco, the "5," for unknown reasons, once again hooked up with New York's infamous Motherfuckers, who were in town. Together they shared some joints and decided that the MC5 would put on a free concert for the street people at the Straight on Thursday night, one day before their regular three-day engagement running on April 14, 15, and 16. The free show, featuring the MC5 and Nimbus, attracted a large noisy crowd of scruffy, tough street types like those the Motherfuckers were associated with in New York.[53]

On April 14, the roadies for the MC5 had arrived early to set up the band's huge wall of Marshall amps at the rear of the stage. Mike Walters, a roadie for Clover, the opening band, felt that his band's amps "looked like toys in comparison."[54] Unlike other bands, Clover hung around to check out the performance of the MC5. After spending the evening sitting around in Levi's and T-shirts, the band hit the stage in their trademark colorful satin costumes, playing music that was "beyond loud."[55] For the finale,

Wayne Kramer coaxed a girl on stage. The two gyrated together, the girl ripped Wayne's clothes off, and they dropped to the stage on top of one another. "Wow!" was Walters's response, after finding out that the girl had been a plant.[56]

At the end of the show, Clover drummer Mitch Howie invited the MC5 to come out to the band's house in Mill Valley. The band got lost on the way and arrived late. After a few refreshments, Wayne Kramer decided he wanted to jam a little and plugged into someone's amp. Because it was so late, Clover asked Kramer to play quietly. Of course the MC5 never played quietly, and Wayne started blasting away. Annoyed, Mitch Howie ordered Kramer out of his house. The MC5 members tumbled out the door and into their car, crashing into a neighbor's house before escaping from peaceful Mill Valley.[57]

Before their final night at the Straight Theater, the MC5 performed in front of twenty thousand people in Golden Gate Park on Sunday afternoon. The audience, which included members of the Hell's Angels, saw the band open with a scorching version of Little Richard's "Tutti-Frutti." A witness to the performance was Art Johnson, who wrote in an article for the *Fifth Estate* that the MC5 were "almost like an acid test," and that their music appealed to "the lowest on the social strata" and "speaks of more anarchy and more destruction."[58] Wayne Kramer says that "West Coast hippies just didn't connect with the MC5. We had too much macho energy, our clothes were too shiny, our amps were too big. We did too much leaping, spinning, screaming and hollering. We were out of sync with the West Coast."[59]

In the early morning hours of March 18, the band members and eleven others crammed into a station wagon and were rolling down the Bayshore Freeway when suddenly they were pulled over by authorities, and accused of "speeding, drunk driving, the possession of marijuana and other dangerous drugs."[60] According to an account by John Sinclair, the cops found an unidentified pill on the floor of the car, and a pipe with alleged residue on the ground away from the vehicle. An altercation ensued, and Jerry Younkins was almost pushed over a guard rail on the skyway. The police punched and kicked Fred Smith. Sinclair, who had been driving another vehicle, escaped across the bridge to Berkeley.[61]

After spending the night in jail, the group was arraigned on Wednesday with charges reduced to driving while drinking, and Fred Smith was charged with resisting arrest. Having posted bail, the band made its way over to the East Bay for a benefit show in Berkeley for the Liberation News Service and Newsreel.[62]

The whole San Francisco trip seemed to be spinning out of control. The Detroit band was getting bad-mouthed all over, including in Ralph Gleason's influential column in the *San Francisco Chronicle*. Lester Bang's negative album review in *Rolling Stone* was adding to the talk that the band was all hype. Bangs wrote that the MC5 "comes on more like Blue Cheer than Trane and Sanders," and that "musically the group is intentionally crude and aggressively raw."[63]

Local deejays were playing the commercials for the new MC5 album, but then calling them "Detroit's answer to Blue Cheer." Sinclair was desperate to get the MC5 in front of a West Coast crowd, but he was having a hard time lining up any other gigs. The Avalon had turned them away. After offering to play on a benefit for the San Francisco State Strike Fund at the Fillmore, they were refused entry by Bill Graham, who was still seething over the incident in New York: "The MC5 aren't qualified to play on my stage," Graham screamed at Danny Fields. "They're a *shuck* and they'll *never* play in my halls!"[64] Graham also had the band removed from a planned gig the following weekend at a new club of which he was a partner, located in Pasadena. Sinclair, who had spent the previous Monday in the company of Charles Bursey, a Black Panther and candidate for Berkeley City Council, committed the MC5 to performing at a benefit dance-rally for him the night of the canceled Pasadena gig.[65]

Prior to leaving the Bay area for Los Angeles, where the MC5 would begin sessions for their second Elektra album, Sinclair and Frawley revisited the Elektra Records distribution center. To their surprise, they found a stack of newly redesigned *Kick Out the Jams* albums. The gatefold was gone, along with the offensive liner notes. The title song had been switched to the "brothers and sisters" 45 version, all without the knowledge or consent of the band.[66] John Sinclair immediately flew to New York to have it out with Jac Holtzman, but the head of Elektra Records was in no mood for compromise. He released the MC5 from their contract.[67] When Danny Fields criticized Holtzman for not supporting the MC5 as he had Jim Morrison when the Doors' lead singer had been arrested for supposedly exposing himself in concert, the label chief fired him.[68]

Following the Elektra meeting, Sinclair flew to Florida to hook up with the MC5, who were booked to play at the Miami Pop Festival, with Chuck Berry and Creedence Clearwater Revival. Upon arriving he was tipped off that the State of Florida had issued a warrant for the MC5's arrest. Sinclair advised the band to cancel their trip and return directly to Michigan.[69]

# 21. The Detroit Pop Festival

Two popular Michigan bands were going through significant changes at the start of 1969. Both were managed by Jeep Holland, and were part of his A-Square management, record, and booking business. Although the Rationals had enjoyed a local hit in the early part of 1968, it had been a one-off on Capitol, arranged by Holland through an independent deal with the label. The band was in debt, owing several years of back taxes.[1]

Meanwhile, the members of the band were experiencing growing pains and felt that Jeep was the reason they "hadn't become bigger." Now all out of high school and living on their own, they had come to resent Holland's "babysitter kind of management."[2] Rationals drummer Bill Figg felt that "Jeep was just handling too many bands and wasn't doing a good job promoting his major act."[3] Influenced by gigs they shared with the MC5 and the Stooges, the Rationals wanted to move away from the "white soul" sound that they had become identified with and start to write and perform some original material with a harder edge. Jeep also had not been able to interest Capitol in anymore of his productions.[4]

In April 1968, the group had approached Larry Feldman, manager of the Grande Ballroom, about taking over as their manager. "We knew Larry through the Grande, and I knew that he had a real good business sense," recalls Bill Figg. "He knew how to handle money, and that was the one area that Jeep wasn't good at."[5] Although Figg, Steve Correll, and Terry Trabandt wished to move on, Scott Morgan had reservations. He believed that Jeep "had done a lot" for the band. But at the same time he felt that Holland had become "out of touch" with the group, perhaps the result of being too busy with other acts and responsibilities.[6]

"The first thing Larry did after taking over management was to hire a CPA to figure out our financial situation," says Figg. "We each owed ten thousand dollars to the government, and they were threatening to seize everything we owned. Larry worked out a payment schedule with the feds, and that took off some of the heat."[7]

On their own, with Feldman on board, the Rationals recorded a single they had written together called "Guitar Army." Capitol hadn't thought much of it, so the song stayed on the shelf until January 1969, when the band put it out on the new local Genesis label. A "screaming rock and roll song with lyrics branded at the time as subversive," it "was too much for some people," according to Terry Trabandt.[8] The last Rationals record the public had heard had been the soulful "I Need You" a year earlier. Now the band not only sounded different, but looked different as well, losing their trademark matching outfits and "boyish" image.

The Rationals' split with Jeep Holland came in the footsteps of the Scot Richard Case, who had severed ties to A-Square several months earlier, in the summer of 1968. The group had complained that Jeep Holland had wanted to "exercise artistic control more and more strongly" at a time when they were becoming more serious about their music.[9] After receiving standing ovations at the Toronto Pop Festival in June, the Scot Richard Case replaced Holland with Pete Andrews, who owned a paint company in Ann Arbor and a rock club in Tawas. "Pete had been involved in some band stuff by booking Mother's, and all the Hideout bands played there," recalls Gary Quackenbush. "We chose him although he had no real experience being a band manager. He really kind of left us alone in some regards, which was good because we were pretty headstrong. But he could book a show—boy, could he book a show, and that's really what he did."[10]

Absorbing Andrews, and wishing not to focus on any individual member, the band changed their name to SRC. Producer John Rhys introduced them to Herb Hendler, vice president of Capitol Records' publishing company, and soon the band signed with the label.[11] They released their first album, produced by Rhys, in the fall. The self-titled LP featured Motor City–style rock with a psychedelic edge. One of the standout tracks was "Black Sheep," which received substantial airplay on WABX. In the best Detroit tradition, the LP sold well in Michigan but nationally stalled at number 147 after four weeks in *Billboard*. Now, in the spring of 1969, following two personnel changes (Al Wilmot replacing bass player Robin Dale, and the departure of Steve Lyman), SRC was releasing its second Capitol LP, *Milestones.*

The first Capitol album had been cut at the Tera Shirma studios on Livernois, but this time out SRC was recording all the basic tracks in its own studio in the band house near the intersection of Plymouth and Broadway in Ann Arbor. "We took our advance money and bought our own equipment, including a Skully half-inch, four-track machine that we purchased from United Sound. Skully stuff was built like a tank. It was the standard of the industry. We rigged a studio right in our house where we could work more freely," says Gary Quackenbush.[12] The band's second LP bested the first by staying on the national charts for nine weeks, climbing to number 134.

After losing two bands, Jeep Holland had the "wind knocked out of his sails," especially by the Rationals, which had been his first band. "I think he just had enough at that point. He didn't really do too much after that," Scott Morgan recounted.[13]

By Monday, April 7, the MC5 had sold twenty thousand copies of *Kick Out the Jams* locally, and the album had reached number 30 in *Billboard*. The MC5 were back in the Motor City and headlining the Detroit Pop Festival. Staged at Olympia Stadium, it was a ten-hour event running from two in the afternoon until midnight. All but one of the twenty acts on the bill were from Detroit and the surrounding area.[14]

Promoters Mike Quatro and Pete Andrews had put together an opening lineup including SRC, Amboy Dukes, Bob Seger, Frost, Rationals, Red, White and Blues Band, Frijid Pink, Wilson Mower Pursuit, Savage Grace, Sweetwater, Train, Früt of the Loom, the Up, Third Power, Unrelated Segments, and the Pleasure Seekers (performing in see-through shirts, pants, and vests). Two stages had been constructed to accommodate all the bands and to keep the breaks to a minimum. The atmosphere was loose, and kids were able to move about freely. Some sixteen thousand people showed up for the event, enticed by Detroit's growing reputation as a unique rock culture and high-energy alternative to the San Francisco scene.[15] Tickets were sold for $3 advance, $3.50 at the door.

Usually home to sporting events, in particular Detroit Red Wings hockey, Olympia Stadium was not regarded as an ideal setting for music performance. The MC5's feedback bounced all over while Rob Tyner rolled on the stage, simulating copulation. The MC introduced Bob Seger as "the finest musician in the field of rock ever to come out of Michigan." Unfortunately, Olympia's poor acoustics made it impossible for the audience to hear anything but the bass and the drummer's cymbals.[16] Seger's latest Capitol single, "Ivory," was among Detroit's current top sellers.

The Frost was one of the most popular bands playing at the Detroit festival. Led by guitarist Dick Wagner, the group had come out of Saginaw. In 1964, Wagner had put together his first band, the Bossmen, which specialized in Beatles and Yardbirds covers. As the twenty-one-year-old leader of the band, Wagner had displayed an unusual entrepreneurial spirit: "We put our records out on our own label called Dicto, and we would carry the records with us and sell them at our gigs, and we'd go visit all the radio stations too," he recalls. "We were able to get played on big stations like WTAC and WKNX in the Flint-Saginaw area and stations wherever we would be playing."[17] The Bossmen scored a huge hit in the Saginaw Valley in 1965 with "Baby Boy." They continued to play the most popular clubs and dances in the area, and by 1966 had their sights on Detroit, where their reputation eventually landed them a one-time appearance at the Grande Ballroom shortly after it opened.

After the breakup of the Bossmen in 1967, Wagner got together with another area group, the Chevelles, which included Bobby Rigg and guitarist Donny Hartman. The band, going by the name Dick Wagner and the Frosts, continued the tradition of a thousand other cover bands, playing their versions of hits made popular by others. Things changed however, after Wagner returned from a trip to New York, where he had the opportunity to audition for Blood, Sweat, and Tears: "I came back determined to make the new band happen and to write original music," says Wagner.[18]

To go along with the new music, they cut the name of the band down to plain Frost. In addition to Wagner, Rigg, and Hartman, the new group included Gordy Garis on bass. By February 1968, they were onstage at the Grande Ballroom, earning one of the heaviest reputations in Motor City rock.

Aside from leading the band, Wagner also served as manager, making all the business decisions. One of those decisions was signing the band to a contract with Vanguard Records. "What happened was that several record companies were showing interest in signing the Frost," says Dick Wagner. "Columbia was calling to talk, but Vanguard sent their A&R guy to see us. His name was Sam Charters. He had been a blues historian or something, but he really liked us and flew in to see us several times. Looking back, we probably should have gone with Columbia, but Vanguard was really convincing in regards to how they were going to promote us, so we signed with them."[19]

At first, things looked promising, with the label seemingly committed to breaking the band nationally. When the group's first album *Frost Music,* was released in March 1969, Detroit area record shops had plenty of product on hand, and the LP, fueled by the top 20 single "Mystery Man," came flying off the shelves. Unfortunately, Vanguard didn't follow through in other markets. Wagner recalls, "When we played the Fillmore West, there were no records in the San Francisco stores."[20]

The group played all over, from L.A. to Canada, to support the new album, and according to Wagner, "There were never any records."[21] Local deejays didn't know who the band was, so to compensate Wagner did what he had done in the old days with the Bossmen, "go to radio stations and just go in and meet people."[22] In 1969, there were many free-form FM stations, and deejays would take the time to listen to something new. The band was able to get some songs on the air. Regional sales pushed the LP to number 148 in *Billboard,* but Vanguard's inadequate distribution held back further sales. In Michigan they were stars, drawing big crowds and selling lots of records. Everywhere else, Frost was just another unknown band from out of town.

Third Power was a Detroit band that seemed to be included on every important bill in town. The power trio featured Drew Abbot on lead guitar, Jim Craig on drums, and Jem "Turk" Targal on bass and lead vocals. As a young child, Targal studied violin. He met

Abbott while attending Oakland Community College at Auburn Hills. The two decided to start a band, and Targal made the transition to bass. After a couple of failed drummers, Jim Craig came on board. After a name change from the BVD's to Third Power, they made their way into the teen clubs, such as the Fifth Dimension and Crow's Nest. The band also played frequently at the Psychedelic Midway, at Royal Oak's Kimball High School, where the stage was set up on the tennis courts.[23] They made their first appearance at the Grande Ballroom on July 14, 1968. Following their performance at the Oakland Mall concert in the fall, a newspaper reporter dubbed Craig "Big Beat."[24] The band itself played loud and hard, in the style of Cream and Mountain. Their recording "We, You, I," with "Snow" on the flip side, for the local Baron Records label received some airplay on WABX.

When they weren't performing, Third Power retreated to their band house in Farmington Hills. "We had an eighty-acre farm, forty acres of it was woods, and we made an Indian village back there," recalls Targal. "We used to have the best parties on Saturday nights about once a month. Everyone would come out to our place 'cause it was such a cool place to hang out."[25] Along with the Frost, Sam Charters signed Third Power to Vanguard Records, where they too experienced problems with promotion and distribution of their first album, *Believe,* released six months later. "We went with Vanguard because they were a smaller company, and we thought they really wanted to promote their rock and roll side of things," says Targal. "It seemed like the good way to go but probably turned out not to be."[26]

The Wilson Mower Pursuit's current mixed-gender lineup was a radical change from the band one might have seen a year earlier. Formed in 1967 as a blues-based rock group, they were supposedly named for a fictional blues singer (Wilson Mower) of whom the band was in "pursuit." Paul Koschtial, the lead guitarist, had aspired to play blues licks in the style of B. B. King and Albert King, but his desire for a recording contract led the group down a more commercial path. By the fall of 1968, their manager, Dick Sloss, jumped at the opportunity to sign Stoney Murphy, the lead singer of the popular all-female bar band Feminine Touch. The "new" Wilson Mower Pursuit, built around the sex appeal and vocal talent of Stoney and the blistering guitar of Koschtial, became more popular than before.[27]

The Detroit Pop Festival also presented Früt of the Loom, which projected a campy "hippie band" image. Their lead singer, Norm Lieberman, went by the name Panama Red. Their musical style was all over the place, ranging from country to hard rock to 1950s-style rock and doo-wop ballads that shared little with the slicker sounds of Sha Na Na or Flash Cadillac.[28]

Along with the performances of the bands, some of the highlights of the Detroit Pop Festival included a naked man walking through the crowd and a repo man from a finance company showing up to repossess an organ. WABX deejays emceed and did their "usual tried and true unprofessional job," wrote station "Air Ace" Dan Carlisle, in a follow-up piece in *Creem,* a new monthly rock music magazine published out of Detroit.[29]

# 22. Voices of the Counterculture

*Creem* was the brainchild of Tony Reay, a former musician from England, who was working as a clerk at a head shop called Mixed Media in the spring of 1969. The store was owned by a music enthusiast named Barry Kramer.

Like Kramer, Reay was caught up in the artsy community happenings around the Wayne State University campus in the late sixties. He was associate music editor at the *Fifth Estate*, wrote a music column for the *Detroit Free Press*, and could be heard on the Mixed Media–sponsored *Tea Party* radio show on WABX.[1]

Reay noticed that the Detroit music scene was incredibly scattered, spread throughout the city and suburbs. He came up with the idea for a locally focused, music-oriented newspaper that would unite all the musically hip kids. He took his idea to Kramer, who showed little interest. Reay took it upon himself to get things going. His friend and a former bandmate Chuck Pike helped with the layout of the first issue, which they produced in Tony's apartment on Gladstone Street. Dated March 1, 1969, the cover displayed the word *Creem* growing up like a vine from the open mouth of a hippie character. The paper featured profiles of local bands, record and concert reviews, music-oriented news items, and gossip.[2]

When that first issue quickly sold out, Barry Kramer stepped back in to the picture and funded the second issue, which was produced in the basement of his Full Circle Record Store at 4860 Cass Avenue. Tony continued to produce the publication but now under the direction of Barry Kramer.[3]

According to Reay, the paper had started off serving "the entire community: the music, the artists, and the consumers (mass and otherwise)," and it "paid for its initial print run on newsstand sales alone."[4] Reay says that *Creem* had such an immediate impact because "even the existing radical broadsheets were still precariously balanced on the cusp of good journalism . . . or plunging headlong into the morass of political rhetoric."[5]

The paper's somewhat irreverent approach and support of local bands made it stand out. Reay commented, "When *Creem* began, many words saw the light of ink that perhaps were not in the best fashioned grammar, or even good enough English to deserve print in any other vehicle . . . but what they said needed to be written and read and that was enough reason."[6]

Soon though, Reay began to butt heads with Kramer over the direction the magazine should be taking. Although they continued to cover the local counterculture scene, "*Creem* magazine's importance to Michigan was short lived," according to Reay, because "Barry [Kramer] never had any interest in publishing a local magazine."[7] Feeling that his original vision was being hijacked after only a few issues, Tony Reay left the publication to which he had given life, and Barry Kramer cemented his position as publisher and guiding force of *Creem*.

Dave Marsh was a self-described "skinny nineteen year-old suffering from overexposure to LSD and the MC5, with absolutely no prospects" when Kramer gave him a job at the publication. "In those days, this magazine was not so much a job or even a publication as it was a non-stop raving, brawling family," Marsh later recalled.[8] In addition to Marsh, the early staff included Charles Auringer, who handled graphics and photos, and writers Richard C. Walls, Richard Siegal, Robin Summers, Debbie Burr, Deday Larene, and Sandra Stretke. The Boy Howdy image became an identifying signature of the publication.

Most of the *Creem* staff lived and worked in a dilapidated three-story cast-iron loft building at 3729 Cass Avenue, where, according to Dave Marsh, "Barry Kramer was the architect and center of everything that went on."[9] Marsh described Kramer as the "eternal psych student" who "enjoyed creating chaos and attempting to control it."[10]

Kramer produced an increasingly professional publication, reflecting the raw energy of Detroit rock and roll, while giving it a more national appeal. "When we saw something that scared us, we moved toward it," said Marsh, describing *Creem*'s pioneering style of rock journalism.[11]

As for WABX, after a year with a "free-form" music policy, and despite new competition, the station remained the favorite among Detroit's alternative community. In June 1968 WKNR-FM hired John Small as program manager and started moving in on WABX's turf. And now WXYZ-FM was taking a more cautious approach, carrying prerecorded progressive rock programming featuring deep-voiced announcer "Brother John." WXYZ-FM was one of seven ABC-owned and -operated FM stations around the country, and Brother John aired on all of them. He never mentioned Woodward Avenue or the Grande Ballroom, or any local bands. Most Detroit kids smelled the corporate odor and dialed out.

WABX, on the other hand, had made a point from the beginning of identifying itself with the rock 'n' roll community, shunning the glitter and gloss of AM Top 40 radio. They were openly against the war in Vietnam and favored legalization of marijuana. Their national news content reflected those views. Locally they gave complete coverage to the Detroit music scene, as well as devoting air time to community causes such as Open City.

In August 1968, WABX had organized a free concert in Rouge Park featuring the MC5, SRC, and the Red, White and Blues Band, plus the first local appearance of Teegarden and Van Winkle, a folksy two-man, organ and drum band that had adopted Detroit as home base after splitting from Tulsa, Oklahoma. Ripple wine flowed freely as over two thousand WABX listeners—or as they referred to themselves, "freaks"—danced and partied in celebration of having what they felt was their very own radio station.[12]

WABX scored its greatest success on the morning of October 21, 1968, when it received a set of secret tapes from an "anonymous donor." Dick Crockett, who was on the air during the midday hours at WABX, recalls where the tape really came from: "Dave Dixon's friend Paul Stookey, of Peter, Paul and Mary, had the tape with him when he dropped by the station to visit after a concert at Masonic Temple. Of course we couldn't reveal that at the time."[13]

Dan Carlisle says that Stookey, who had recently been to England, had told Dixon, "I'm gonna leave something downstairs with the guard. I don't want to give it to you personally, because I don't want you to be able to say I gave it to you."[14] Dick Crockett recalls, "We sat around discussing what we should do with it because obviously, we didn't have any legal right to air it. But it was too good a thing to pass up, so we decided that Dan would play the tapes that evening and started announcing that 'something big' was going to happen on Dan's show at nine o'clock."[15] That evening, people all over town were tuned to 99.5 on the FM dial. "We emptied the Grande," recalls Carlisle. "The Grande had Procol Harum that night, and the kids left to get to their car radios. Everybody knew that it was probably either the Beatles or the Stones."[16]

The tapes contained ten songs from the unreleased new double album by the Beatles. The tapes were so secret they hadn't even been played yet in England. The album was not set for release in the United States until November 15. About forty-five minutes into the broadcast, Carlisle received a Trans-Atlantic phone call from Northern Songs Limited in London. A Detroit record distributor had contacted Capitol Records in Hollywood with news that the new Beatles release was being aired without authorization. Carlisle was warned that if he "did not immediately stop playing the tapes an injunction would be issued against the station."[17] Carlisle agreed but asked for permission to play the remaining songs. "It was the world premiere of the White Album," says Carlisle, adding, "I loved it."[18]

"It was so exciting," says Dick Crockett. "The phones were lighting up like crazy and the word of mouth was tremendous. This was the event that really put the station on the map. Before that night, it had always been the big AM's like CKLW and WKNR that managed to get exclusives of a new song by the Beatles or Stones. Now here's little WABX-FM playing a new Beatles album for the first time. The excitement just permeated the station for days."[19]

In the spring of 1969, with the aid and approval of the city of Detroit, WABX said thanks to its listeners with two free concerts at Tartar Field on the Wayne State campus. Four thousand showed up to party.[20] In July, Dan Carlisle was surprised when he started receiving mail from prisoners at Jackson State Prison who had been allowed to listen to an hour of his nightly show. For them, WABX and *Creem* partnered to put together a rock concert inside the walls of Jackson Prison. The Wilson Mower Pursuit, Third Power, and Savage Grace performed two shows.[21]

As a result of *Creem*'s new rock journalism, the *Fifth Estate*'s politics, and "underground" progressive rock stations WABX and WKNR-FM, Detroit's rock 'n' roll community was connected as never before. Across the metropolitan area there were stores catering specifically to the new youth culture, selling records, black light posters, strobe candles, incense, pipes, denim, and paisley bell bottoms. Groove Shop on Mack Avenue, Other Place on Lahser Road, Head Shop on Grand River, Poster Pit in Lincoln Park, Plum Pit in East Detroit, Paper Lion in Mt. Clemens, Paraphernalia in Birmingham and Bell, Book and Candle in Westland were some of the most popular stores.[22]

As for the music—it was everywhere. A seemingly inexhaustible supply of local bands were booked into the teen clubs all over town. *Creem* magazine stated that "Detroit is such a hotbed of rock and roll because the kids are so deeply involved in it," describing the relationship between the bands and their audiences as "nearly symbiotic."[23] At the same time, the trend of major pop concerts continued. Just seven weeks after the Detroit Pop Festival at Olympia, Russ Gibb staged a huge "First Annual Rock 'n' Roll Revival" at the Michigan State Fairgrounds. John Sinclair and Trans-Love Energies produced the show. This time local bands such as the MC5, Stooges, Amboy Dukes, SRC, Frost, Third Power, Rationals, and the Lyman Woodward jazz-soul group shared the stage with national acts including Chuck Berry, Sun Ra, Dr. John, Johnny Winter, and an English band known as the Bonzo Dogs. Other up-and-coming Detroit acts on the bill included Savage Grace and Brownsville Station.

The daytime weather was fine, but it rained both nights, the crowds staying dry under the covered grandstands as the bands performed on a stage built especially for the concert. The MC5 were in top form, with Rob Tyner out front, spinning like a "demented bee." As the set drew to a close, Fred "Sonic" Smith, outfitted in silver lamé, and Wayne Kramer jumped up and grabbed the overhang of the canopy covering the stage. They hooked their legs to it, and continued to play while hanging upside down, smashing their guitars together at the climax: rock and roll, Detroit style.[24]

In his book *Fortunate Son,* Dave Marsh wrote: "So powerfully did the MC5's music unite its listeners, that leaving those 1968 and 1969 shows, one literally felt that anything, even that implausible set of White Panther slogans, could come to pass."[25]

Since returning from the West Coast, John Sinclair had continued to run into legal problems. In April, a Pontiac judge acquitted Fred Smith of charges stemming from the incident at the Loft club a year earlier, but found Sinclair guilty. On his way to an MC5 gig in Sarnia, Ontario, Sinclair was stopped at Port Huron, where U.S. Customs agents arrested him for "leaving the U.S. without registering as a convicted narcotics violator."[26] The leader of the White Panther Party was held in the St. Clair County jail for three days. Forced to focus on his own legal problems, Sinclair decided to share more of the responsibilities in the Trans-Love/White Panther organization.

Sinclair, who was hosting a Sunday broadcast with Jerry Lubin on WABX, recommended Ministers of Propaganda Bob Rudnick and Dennis Frawley, who had been fired from New Jersey's WFMU, for a job at the station. WABX manager John Detz, who had heard their show in New York, agreed to put their "Kocaine Karma" show on every night, from 2:00 to 7:00 A.M. Sinclair hired Danny Fields, who'd been fired by Jac Holtzman, to take charge of publicity, and also hired David Newman to handle the group's finances.[27]

Shortly after Danny Fields learned that Elektra had dropped the MC5, he got in touch with Jon Landau and asked that the critic put in a call to Jerry Wexler at Atlantic Records.[28] Landau had kept up steady contact with Wexler, offering insight and advice on the burgeoning underground music scene. Now Landau was urging Wexler to sign the controversial Detroit band, claiming that "Atlantic could succeed where Holtzman and Elektra had failed."[29]

In early May, John Sinclair flew back to New York to meet with Wexler and Fields. Atlantic agreed to give the MC5 total control of their recording and production as well as a fifty-thousand-dollar advance, a staggering amount at the time.[30] Jerry Wexler named Jon Landau producer for the band's debut Atlantic album, *Back in the USA*. In mid-May, Landau dropped everything and moved in with the MC5 at their new digs on a ten-acre farm in Hamburg, Michigan, to begin preparations for the new sessions. Landau quickly came to see that the band had serious problems with discipline and motivation, owing in part to frequent drug use. As part of a new regime, Landau had the band members running ten laps around their circle drive and eating a high-protein diet. Dennis Thompson said, "Well, he was trying to cure us. Before we'd get up in the morning, he'd already blasted through *The New York Times* and did the crossword puzzle."[31]

Fields and Landau also recommended that the MC5 end their relationship with John Sinclair, Landau going so far as to calling Sinclair "an amateurish manager."[32] After spending a little time around the band, Landau began to sense that "John Sinclair's personality was more of an influence on the band than his political teachings."[33] The MC5, tired of being treated as "good little communists supporting everybody," began to agree.[34] According to Wayne Kramer, none of the MC5 "ever got anything out of being in the band," saying that all earnings "always went into one central account that paid the bills." They had always had a roof over their heads and food on the table, but they "never had any money and never had any personal possessions."[35]

The politics of John Sinclair "confused" Dennis Thompson: "John was getting too biased toward the politics. At the time, there was a lot of camaraderie happening, with SDS, the riots, the war in Vietnam and so forth. So there was some polarization on the left and because John's in that mix, we become part of that mix. It was hard for us to separate the politics from the music at that point."[36] What about photos of Thompson wearing a bullet belt strapped across his chest? "It was done tongue in cheek," says the MC5 drummer. "It wasn't like we were guerillas in the mountains. We weren't guys with guns. People should know that there was an awareness inside the band [and] that we weren't that fuckin' stupid. It was veering from the music, and the music is what it was about. It was about rock 'n' roll music. Sure, politics got us a lot of press, but we really wanted to be a big, big rock 'n' roll band, not just Sinclair's personal political platform. We believed in politics and philosophy, but we didn't want to teach."[37]

Landau and Fields argued that if the MC5 really wanted to be the "greatest rock 'n' roll band in the world," they needed to have more professional management and a more focused approach to their music. Regarding Sinclair and the entire White Panther/Trans-Love operation, Landau urged the band to "get rid of all these freeloaders."[38]

Still hesitant to make a final break with the man who had been their guiding force, the band called a meeting on their turf in Hamburg. They put a new deal on the table, one that would remove Sinclair as manager but would still pay him 15 percent of all bookings, 20 percent of Elektra royalties (already paid up), but nothing on future Atlantic recordings. The band, feeling that Sinclair had not been instrumental in putting the Atlantic deal together, gave credit and a five-thousand-dollar finders fee to Danny Fields. Sinclair rejected the deal. As a compromise, the band agreed to give him 5 percent of all income.[39]

The way Sinclair saw it, Landau had convinced the MC5 that his "musical and performance ideas were all wrong." He also felt that David Newman, for his part, had convinced them that their money had been "mismanaged for two years."[40] Sinclair felt "betrayed."[41] He had been the one who "carried the band when they were making twenty-five dollars a night," and had "driven them around and set up their equipment and wrote their press releases."[42] He was also the one who had helped to get them the first record contract. Now he was being accused of "using *them?*" He left the meeting that night feeling that "things would never be the same again."[43]

Not only was John Sinclair given the boot, but Brother J. C. Crawford was too. Although the members of the MC5 said that J. C. was "one of us," they also felt that his whole warm-up routine had run its course, and wouldn't work with the band's new image.[44] Meanwhile, the various members of that radical "people's band," the MC5, figured out what to do with the advance money from Atlantic. After paying off their outstanding debts, each member received a thousand bucks. Parental cosign agreements signed, Wayne Kramer bought an XKE Jaguar, Michael Davis a Buick Riviera, Fred "Sonic" Smith a 1966 fastback Corvette with a 327 engine, and Dennis Thompson a 1967 Vette with 390 horsepower. Family man Rob Tyner bought a sensible station wagon.[45]

On June 7, the MC5 and their brother band, the Stooges, headlined a concert at the Eastown Theatre. Ron Asheton had to fill in for Michael Davis because the MC5 bassist had been arrested on a shoplifting charge. He'd walked out of an Ann Arbor store wearing a pair of sunglasses he thought Wayne Kramer had paid for.[46]

A former movie palace built in 1930, the Eastown had reopened under new owner Bob Bageris. The opening night show on May 29 had featured SRC, Teegarden and Van Winkle, and Savage Grace. Up until this point, the Grande Ballroom had been the big rock gig in the Motor City, attracting national headliners (the Who debuted their rock opera *Tommy* at the Grande on May 9) and top Detroit groups. The small teen clubs developed local band talent that aspired to play there. The Eastown Theatre had a seating capacity of fifteen hundred, and now Bageris was going to give Russ Gibb a run for his money.[47]

On July 22, 1969, following two postponements, the long-awaited trial of John Sinclair, charged with possession of 11.50 grams of marijuana, finally got underway. Prosecutor Gerald Celesky had built his case on shaky witnesses, including Vahan "Louie" Kapagian, the undercover narcotics cop who had infiltrated Sinclair's organization on two occasions. Kapagian testified that his memory was "better now than two years ago" and that he could see no problem with having failed to record an incriminating conversation with John Sinclair on December 22, 1966. Nor did he think it was a problem that he had destroyed his logbook sheets that may have been helpful to the defense.[48]

When Celesky called chemist Martin Goreman to testify, the witness admitted that his testing methods were outmoded and not sufficient to prove beyond a reasonable doubt that the substance in question was marijuana. Defense Attorney Justin C. Ravitz, believing that the substance couldn't be proven to be marijuana, called no witnesses. But he did a credible job of cross-examining each witness in an attempt to show that there was a plot to "get" John Sinclair. When all was said and done, the jury needed only an hour and five minutes to decide that Sinclair was guilty as charged. He was immediately taken to jail for the weekend to await sentencing.[49]

On Monday, July 28, the head of the White Panther Party stood before Judge Robert J. Columbo in Detroit Recorder's Court. Offered the microphone, Sinclair took the opportunity to state that the charges against him had been "fabricated" by the Detroit Narcotics Squad. Specifically, said Sinclair, it had been a conspiracy to frame him, put forth by Warner Stringfellow, Vahan Kapagian, and Joseph Brown among others. Sinclair denied possessing the two marijuana cigarettes. "Everyone who is taking part in this, is guilty of violating the United States Constitution and violating my rights and everyone else's that's concerned."[50]

Sinclair's defense attorney took the microphone. At first he seemed to plea for mercy, mentioning that Sinclair was married, that his two-year-old daughter—"a beautiful child"—was in the audience, and that his wife was pregnant. Ravitz went through the litany of unfair convictions and accusations carried out against his client. He referred to "illegal entrapment" in an earlier marijuana case, as well as a conviction of assaulting a police officer "who wasn't even a police officer" in another. Addressing the stringent Michigan marijuana laws, Ravitz told the court that such "sumptuary legislation . . . is on the books to go after and to impress politically unpopular people and groups and minorities." He cited studies showing that "twenty-five percent of future doctors, lawyers and indeed judges have possessed and smoked marijuana."[51]

Unimpressed, Judge Columbo responded that Sinclair was "not on trial and never was on trial in this courtroom because of his beliefs," but rather that he represented "a person who has deliberately flaunted and scoffed at the law."[52] Columbo went on to say that the system had "tried to understand John Sinclair" and had even "tried to reform and rehabilitate" him. Then the judge turned directly to the defendant: "Well, the time has come," he said. "The day has come. And you may laugh, Mr. Sinclair, but you will have a long time to laugh about it. Because it is the judgement of this Court that you, John Sinclair, stand committed to the State Prison at Southern Michigan at Jackson or such other such institution as the Michigan Corrections Commission may designate for a minimum term of not less than nine and a half nor more than ten years."[53]

After giving Sinclair credit for the two days spent over the weekend in county jail, Columbo stated his belief that if released on bond, Sinclair was likely to "violate the law and flaunt the law," so bond was denied pending appeal. Sinclair expressed his outrage at the sentence and bond denial and then was taken directly to prison to begin serving his nine-and-a-half-year sentence for two marijuana joints.[54]

The big rock shows continued to roll out during the summer of 1969. On July 4 and 5, twenty thousand people showed up near Lake Michigan for the Second Annual Saugatuck Pop Festival. Set to perform were SRC, Bob Seger, Frost, the Stooges, Muddy Waters, Procol Harum, and Rotary Connection.

On Sunday, August 3, it was the Mt. Clemens Pop Festival at Sportsman Park, located at Twenty-eight Mile Road and Gratiot in New Haven, Michigan, produced by Dave Dubray and Michael Quatro. The national-name lineup included Country Joe and the Fish, John Mayall, Eric Burdon, Muddy Waters, T-Bone Walker, Cat Mother and the All-Night Newsboys, the McCoys, and Alice Cooper. They shared the bill with Detroit's MC5, the Stooges, the Up, Früt of the Loom, Red, White and Blue Blues Band, Savage Grace, Ted Lucas, the Pleasure Seekers, and Frijid Pink. Admission to the twelve-hour event cost five dollars.

As successful as the Michigan concerts were, a much more ambitious festival was about to take place in New York state. It was billed as the "Woodstock Music and Arts Fair," though the town of Woodstock ultimately passed on the opportunity to be its host. Instead, the event moved to Wallkill, N.Y. Scheduled for August 15–17, the festival was being promoted as "three days of peace and music." In addition to the music, advertisements claimed there would be "hundreds of acres to roam on, art shows, a crafts bazaar, work shops and food." Attendees would be able to "fly a kite, sun yourself, cook your own food and breathe unspoiled air."[55]

The roster of national and international talent was more than impressive: Joan Baez, Arlo Guthrie, Canned Heat, Grateful Dead, Janis Joplin, Jefferson Airplane, Santana, the Who, The Band, Joe Cocker, Crosby, Stills, and Nash, and Jimi Hendrix. Tickets were on sale in advance and priced at seven dollars per day or eighteen

John Lee Hooker *(second from right)* on the stage of the Apex Bar in Detroit, after switching to electric guitar, circa 1950. (Courtesy: Howard DeWitt.)

Hank Ballard came off the Detroit assembly line to join the Royals, who soon became R & B stars as the Midnighters. It was Ballard who wrote "The Twist," made famous by Chubby Checker. *Top, left to right:* Charles Sutton, Sonny Woods, Lawson Smith. *Bottom left,* Arthur Porter and *right,* Hank Ballard. (Courtesy: Marv Goldberg.)

One of Detroit's pioneer R & B groups, the Imperials, in 1954. *Left to right:* Robert Adams, Ben Knight, Lee Goodwin, and Milton Harris. (Courtesy: Marv Goldberg.)

The Serenaders evolved into the Royal Jokers. Their most popular comedy dance routine involved throwing an imaginary bug on each other and doing a wild dance to shake it off. *Left to right:* Willie Jones, Norman Thrasher, Ted Green, Theron "T-Man" Hill, and Noah Howell. (Courtesy: Marv Goldberg.)

The Diablos featuring Nolan Strong in 1954. The group recorded for Detroit's Fortune Records. *Left to right:* Juan Guiterriez, Willie Hunter, Quentin Eubanks, Nolan Strong, and Bob "Chico" Edwards. (Author's collection.)

The "Frantic One," Ernie Durham, arrived at WJLB in 1955 and became Detroit's best-known and best-loved R & B disc jockey. (Author's collection.)

"FRANTIC" ERNIE DURHAM SHOW W J L B
Mon.-Fri.: 9:30-11:30
Saturday 2:30-3:30

Bud Davies at the CKLW mike in 1954. The popular radio deejay soon brought early rock 'n' roll to television on his *Top Ten Dance Party*, aired each afternoon on channel 9. (Author's collection.)

opular Detroit vocalist Bunny Paul at a 955 recording session. In 1963, she became he first white female artist to record for 1otown. (Courtesy: Bunny Paul.)

d McKenzie ushers in the rock 'n' roll era in etroit with Bill Haley and the Comets. The hoto was taken on the set of Ed's popular *aturday Party* TV show, broadcast on WXYZ-V, channel 7, in 1955. Haley was born in the etroit enclave of Highland Park. Courtesy: Carol McKenzie.)

Pop deejays and friendly rivals Robin Seymour of WKMH and Ed McKenzie of WXYZ in 1953, deciding what selections to make on the new Wurlitzer 1500 automatic play jukebox. (Courtesy: Carol McKenzie.)

ill Haley and the Comets in action on nother broadcast of *Ed McKenzie's Saturday Party* in 1956. (Courtesy: Carol McKenzie.)

Kingpin deejay Mickey Shorr of WXYZ, signing autographs outside of the Michigan Theater in downtown Detroit at his "Record Stars of '57" stage show. (Courtesy: May Shorr.)

Promotional photo for Jack Scott's appearance at Mickey Shorr's "Rock 'n' Rollorama Easter Edition," 1957. Scott became the first white rock star to be identified with Detroit. (Courtesy: May Shorr.)

A rare early photo of Jackie Wilson *(second from right)* making a hometown TV appearance during his time as a member of Billy Ward's Dominos in 1955. (Courtesy: Carol McKenzie.)

Legendary rock deejay Tom Clay of WJBK just before climbing to the top of a three-story-high sign to broadcast his show in the summer of 1958. (Author's collection.)

Besides their own recordings, the Royaltones played on many Detroit sessions for other artists. Despite a number of personnel changes, sax player George Katsakis was a constant. This 1959 lineup includes *(left to right)* Karl Kay (Kamenski), twins Greg and Mike Popoff, and George Katsakis. (Courtesy: George Katsakis.)

The Larados, a popular vocal group with an R & B doo-wop sound, performing at a high school record hop in 1957. *Left to right:* Ron Morris, Tommy Hurst, Bob Broadrick, Bernie Turnbull, and Don Davenport. (Courtesy: Gary Banovetz.)

The Thunder Rocks were one of the most popular Detroit bands of the late fifties and early sixties. Pictured in 1960 are *(back row, left to right)* Bruce Penner, Jerry Kowalski, and Jerry Polleky; *(front, left to right)* Pat LaRose, Tom Pozniak, and Larry Skover. (Courtesy: Bill Hennes.)

Michigan rock star Del Shannon of "Runaway" fame.
(Courtesy: Brian C. Young.)

the SUNLINERS

The Sunliners were one of Detroit's top club bands. In New York they appeared at the Peppermint Lounge. By the late sixties the band evolved into Rare Earth. *Left to right:* Fred Saxon, John Parrish, Gil Bridges, Russ Terrana, and Ralph Terrana. Drummer Pete Rivera was the group's lead singer. (Courtesy: Russ Terrana.)

Detroit club and record act Jamie Coe and the Gigolos posing in the Rose Bar in 1960. *Top, left to right:* the club's singing bartender George ("Heigh Ho Silver") Elikis; Dave Kovarik, saxophone; Dennis Kovarik, bass. *Bottom, left to right:* Lynn Bruce, drums; Jack Rainwater, guitar; Jamie Coe, vocals. (Courtesy: Lynn Bruce.)

Terry Knight was a charismatic radio deejay before fronting the rock band Terry Knight and the Pack. Later he engineered the successful launch of Grand Funk Railroad. (Author's collection.)

Promotional photo for the Reflections, taken a few months before they scored their first and biggest hit with "(Just Like) Romeo and Juliet" in May 1964. *Top to bottom:* Phil Castrodale, Dan Bennie, Ray Steinberg, John Dean, Tony Micale. (Courtesy: Tony Micale.)

Although it was a number 1 record in Detroit, "Mind Over Matter" by Nolan Strong missed the national charts in 1962.

The Fortune Records building on Third Avenue. (Courtesy: Charles Auringer.)

Even after "Fingertips Pt. 2" topped the national charts, "Little Stevie Wonder" continued to make local appearances. Here he performs at a high school record hop hosted by CKLW's Dave Shafer in 1964. (Courtesy: Dave Shafer.)

*Left,* Johnny "Bee" Badanjek and *right,* Earl Elliott of Billy Lee and the Rivieras with Motown star Smokey Robinson at Walled Lake Casino in 1964. (Courtesy: Johnny "Bee" Badanjek.)

Original publicity photo for Mitch Ryder and the Detroit Wheels following a name change from Billy Lee and the Rivieras, February 1965. *Standing, left to right:* Jim McCarty, Earl Elliott, Johnny "Bee" Badanjek, and Joe Kubert. *Seated:* Mitch Ryder. (Courtesy: Johnny "Bee" Badanjek.)

A changed music scene: the Underdogs in front of the stage at the Hideout teen club in Harper Woods, Michigan, 1965. *Left to right:* Jack Louisell, Chris Lena, Dave Whitehouse, Steve Perrin, Mike Morgan, and Tony Roumell. (Courtesy: Chris Lena.)

The Pleasure Seekers, the first all-girl rock band to gain popularity in Detroit. They got their start at Dave Leone's Hideout club in 1965. *Top:* Nancy Ball; *bottom, left to right:* Arlene Quatro, Suzi Quatro, Mary Lou Ball, Patti Quatro. Later, Suzi became a star in Europe. (Courtesy: Suzi Quatro.)

The Rationals performing on Robin Seymour's *Swingin' Time* show on CKLW-TV, channel 9, in 1966. *Left to right:* Steve Correll, Terry Trabandt, Bill Figg, and Scott Morgan. (Courtesy: Bill Figg.)

The Woolies played rock with a true blues influence. Pictured in 1966 are *(top, left to right)* Bob Baldori, Jeff Baldori, Bee Metros, and *(in front)* Stormy Rice. (Courtesy: Bob Baldori.)

The Tidal Waves in a publicity shot at Metropolitan Beach in 1966. *Top row, left to right:* John Wearing, Tom Wearing, Dennis Mills. *Bottom row, left to right:* Bill Long, Rick Jackson. (Courtesy: Bill Long.)

The main studio at United Sound Systems on Second Avenue in Detroit. John Lee Hooker, Jack Scott, the Rationals, and Bob Seger were just a few of the many artists who recorded at United Sound over the years. (Courtesy: Dr. Ed Wolfrum, Audio Graphic Services.)

What was at the time the futuristic recording console at United Sound Systems Studios, built by engineers Bill Beltz and Les Cooley in 1965. The four-track Class A console was modified for eight-track recording by Beltz and Ed Wolfrum in 1968. (Courtesy: Dr. Ed Wolfrum, Audio Graphic Services.)

Producer, manager, and booking agent Jeep Holland at a late sixties recording session. (Courtesy: Dr. Ed Wolfrum, Audio Graphic Services.)

The first promotional poster designed by Gary Grimshaw for opening night at the Grande Ballroom, October 7, 1966. (Courtesy: Gary Grimshaw.)

A "paisley vibe" with the MC5 and fellow members of Trans-Love Energies Unlimited, 1967. *Top row, left,* Dennis Thompson holding cup and *right,* Rob Tyner. *Middle row, left to right:* Fred "Sonic" Smith, road manager Steve Hardenek, unidentified female, Michael Davis, Wayne Kramer, and band manager and Trans-Love wizard John Sinclair. *Bottom row, left to right:* Becky Tyner (sewing MC5 costumes), Pun and Genie Plamondon. (© 1967 Leni Sinclair.)

Onstage at the Grande Ballroom, 1968. Iggy balances on a mike stand while Ron Asheton unleashes power chords from his guitar. (© 1968 Leni Sinclair.)

Russ Gibb, before and after opening
the Grande Ballroom.
(Courtesy: Russ Gibb.)

Ron Asheton of the Stooges, backstage
at the Grande Ballroom in 1969.
(© 1969 Leni Sinclair.)

Ted Nugent performing
with the Amboy Dukes at
Sherwood Forest Dance Hall
near Davison, Michigan, in
1969. (© 2004 Pat Appleson
Studios, Inc., Ft. Lauderdale,
Fla.)

The MC5 "on the attack" at West Park in Ann Arbor.    (© 1968 Leni Sinclair.)

Dave Dixon, "Captain of the Air Aces" at "underground" radio station WABX-FM, 1969. (Author's collection.)

Members of the WABX air staff in late 1969. *Left to right:* Dennis Frawley, Bob Rudnick, and Dan Carlisle. (© 1969 Leni Sinclair.)

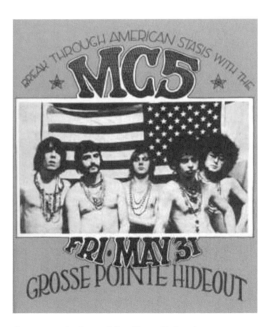

A poster designed by Gary Grimshaw promotes a 1968 appearance by the MC5. (Courtesy: Gary Grimshaw. Photo © 1968 Leni Sinclair.)

Mitch Ryder sans the Detroit Wheels in 1969. (Courtesy: Charles Auringer.)

Commander Cody and His Lost Planet Airmen. Cody was George Frayne *(holding mike)*. The quasi country-rock band also included (*left to right*) Steve Davis on steel guitar, George Tichy, Andy Stein, and Lance Dickerson on drums; (*at second mike, left to right*) Bill Kirchen on guitar, Billy C. Farlow on guitar, and "Buffalo" Bruce Barlow on bass. (© 1970 Leni Sinclair.)

The Frost, 1969. *Standing,* lead vocalist and guitarist Dick Wagner; *below, left to right:* bassist Gordy Garris, guitarist Donny Hartman, and drummer Bobby Rigg. (Courtesy: Dick Wagner.)

John Sinclair, manager of the MC5 and leader of the White Panther Party. (© 1968 Leni Sinclair.)

The Third Power on the steps of the Detroit Public Library, 1969. *Left to right:* Jem Targal, Jim Craig, Drew Abbott. (Courtesy: Jem Targal.)

The Up striking a revolutionary pose in 1969. *Left to right:* Gary Rasmussen, Frank Bach, Scot Bailey, and Bob Rasmussen. (© 1969 Leni Sinclair.)

Michigan rock legend Bob Seger headlines another show at the popular Mt. Holly Ski Lodge in Mt. Holly, Michigan. (© 2004 Pat Appleson Studios, Inc., Ft. Lauderdale, Fla.)

The Bob Seger System in action, 1970. *Left to right:* Dan Honaker on bass, Pep Perine on drums, and Bob Seger. (© 2004 Pat Appleson Studios, Inc., Ft. Lauderdale, Fla.)

The MC5 displaying some "Detroit attitude" in an advertisement for their *Back in the USA* album, February 1970. *Top from left:* Dennis Thompson, Wayne Kramer. *Below from left:* Rob Tyner, Fred "Sonic" Smith, and Michael Davis. (Author's collection.)

Alice Cooper performing at Mt. Holly Ski Lodge, 1970. (© 2004 Pat Appleson Studios, Inc., Ft. Lauderdale, Fla.)

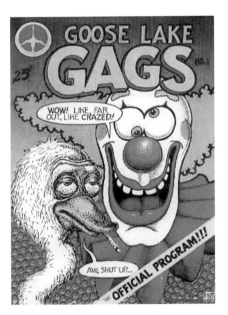

Program cover from the Goose Lake International Music Festival held near Jackson, Michigan, August 1970.

ggy of the Stooges grabs a smoke while SRC plays on stage: E. G. Clawson on drums, Scott Richardson, vocals, and Al Wilmot on bass. (© 1971 Leni Sinclair.)

The Früt. Eventually the band had its own club in Mt. Clemens, Michigan, known as the Früt Cellar. (© 1971 Leni Sinclair.)

An exhausted Grand Funk Railroad following a 1971 show in Atlanta. *From left:* Mark Farner, Mel Schacher, and Don Brewer. (Courtesy: Carter Tomasi.)

The band known as Detroit in 1971. *Left to right:* Equipment manager J.B. Fields, drummer Johnny "Bee" Badanjek, road crew person *(inside car)*, keyboard player Harry Phillips, conga player "Dirty" Ed, lead guitarist Steve Hunter *(sitting on hood)*, bass player Ron Cooke, Mitch Ryder in black T-shirt *(far right)*. (Courtesy: Charles Auringer.)

Veteran "blue-eyed" Detroit R & B vocalist Rusty Day performing as a member of the Amboy Dukes in 1970. (© 2004 Pat Appleson Studios, Inc., Ft. Lauderdale, Fla.)

The Flaming Ember, a veteran Detroit band with a heavy R & B sound, in 1970. *Back row, left to right:* Bill Ellis, Joe Sladish, Jim Bugnel. *Front left,* Jerry Plunk and *right,* Larry Greg. (Courtesy: Jim Bugnel.)

Bob Baldori of the Woolies with Chuck Berry at rehearsal for a 1971 concert at Oakland University in Rochester, Michigan. (© 2004 Pat Appleson Studios, Inc., Ft. Lauderdale, Fla.)

Chuck Berry inspired countless Detroit rockers including Ted Nugent and Wayne Kramer. Backed by the Woolies, Chuck rocks a Motor City audience in 1971. (© 2004 Pat Appleson Studios, Inc., Ft. Lauderdale, Fla.)

Guitarists (left) Mike Lutz and (right) Cub Koda of Brownsville Station in the dressing room before a concert, 1971. (© 2004 Pat Appleson Studios, Inc., Ft. Lauderdale, Fla.)

John Sinclair, reunited with wife Leni and daughter Sunny following his release from prison. (Courtesy: *Flint Journal*, all rights reserved, December 15, 1971.)

After escaping the collapse of the Detroit rock scene, Alice Cooper returned for a 1973 concert at Ann Arbor's Crisler Arena. (Courtesy: © Leni Sinclair.)

dollars for the entire three-day event. As the festival unfolded, some three hundred thousand people swarmed into the area, and the biggest celebration of youth and rock and roll got under way.[56]

Back in Michigan, a "Free John Sinclair" movement had begun to form soon after the White Panther leader entered Jackson State Prison. To the Panthers, the Woodstock festival looked like a great opportunity to drum up some support for the cause. Leni Sinclair, Pun and Genie Plamondon, and two other members piled into a broken-down van and headed for Wallkill. They arrived on Saturday afternoon and connected with radical activist Abbie Hoffman, who had sent them two hundred dollars gas money for the trip. Leni Sinclair remembers, "We went there to make an announcement about John Sinclair, and to hand out some literature and collect some money. We waited and waited backstage. Everybody refused to let us speak."[57]

At a little past midnight, as the Who were performing "See Me, Feel Me," a stoned and frustrated Pun Plamondon urged Abbie Hoffman to climb onto the stage and speak to the audience. After grabbing the microphone from Pete Townsend, Hoffman began to ramble on about the plight of John Sinclair. Townsend reacted quickly, hitting him over the head with his guitar.[58] Hoffman, Leni, and the others were taken to "Movement Village," in an adjoining valley. According to Sinclair, "All the movement people were over there with their tents and their literature, far away from the people. Movement people mingled with movement people and didn't do much educating."[59] Detroit's White Panthers had believed they could "use rock 'n' roll to reach and radicalize young Americans" at Woodstock, says Sinclair, but "we left with our tails between our legs."[60]

On the return trip, Leni, Pun, and the rest were pulled over and arrested by New Jersey State Troopers. Sinclair says, "When we had first arrived, we drove the van over a tree stump and it broke something underneath. So to drive it we had to tie a long string around the gas pedal and pull on it to raise the pedal. Well, we were driving very slow on the freeway, trying to get it to a garage. All of the sudden there was a police car behind us, and I guess we looked suspicious. The police stopped us, and they found some weed. Off we went to jail!"[61] Pun Plamondon recalls that roadblocks had been set up specifically to catch "hippie types" leaving Woodstock. "I had a hunting knife on the dashboard when we were stopped, so they used a dangerous-weapons charge as a reason to search the vehicle, and they found some hash."[62]

During the same week that John Sinclair was on trial, the MC5 had been rehearsing for their new record in Guido Marasco's GM recording studios, at 14611 Nine Mile Road near Mound Road in East Detroit. The new facility featured eight- and sixteen-track recorders, a Newman master cutter, and a high-speed duplicator, as well as beds and a sauna. As John Sinclair settled in to the daily routines of prison life, the MC5 had moved on. According to Wayne Kramer, the band felt that their main responsibility was to themselves: "If Trans-Love isn't together enough to be doing all the things that a production-management company does, that doesn't stop us," Kramer stated at the time.[63]

Moving on meant replacing John Sinclair. The MC5 announced that Danny Fields, who had been "working in close conjunction with John," would be taking over as manager on a trial basis.[64] The Trans-Love organization accused the band of turning their back on not only Sinclair but the whole TLE community and the "revolution." Leni Sinclair disputed the way the band wanted to handle the earnings due her husband. Wayne Kramer denied all the accusations, saying that TLE was upset because they wanted the money to go to them. Instead, the MC5 announced that "all John's percentages would go to the John Sinclair Defense Fund."[65]

It was obvious that the MC5 was trying to distance itself from the entire Trans-Love/White Panther operation. Rob Tyner now spoke of the band not wanting to indulge in "romantic adventurism." "We're trying to elevate ourselves to a position where our program will come first," said the band's lead singer.[66] Citing the growing influence of rock 'n' roll, Tyner said that the MC5 wanted to "try and bring things together in a congenial and musical atmosphere so that change can go down."[67]

Regarding the MC5's new stance, John Sinclair later commented, "They kind of left me in prison, didn't even help take care of my pregnant wife. Even gangsters do that."[68]

# 23. I Wanna Be Your Dog

At the time Elektra Records cut the MC5 loose in April 1969, the label had yet to get the Stooges into the recording studio. Jac Holtzman, feeling that the band "could barely play their instruments," wondered how he was going to "get them on record."[1] Finally, in mid-May, John Cale of the Velvet Underground was called in to produce the band's sessions, scheduled to take place at the Hit Factory in New York. Things got off to a bad start, when the band arrived with only five songs ready to record. "You guys got enough material to do an album, right?" Jac Holtzman queried Ron Asheton. "Oh sure," the Stooge's guitarist replied.[2] Retreating to their room at the Chelsea Hotel, Asheton worked up some riffs, and Iggy "bashed out some lyrics," and within two hours, the two came up with three new songs.[3]

Once in the studio, the band turned up their amps and bumped heads with John Cale. "We were used to playing on 10, and he's saying, 'No, that's not the way it's done!'" recounted Ron Asheton. The Stooges practically had to stage a sit-down strike over the issue, telling Cale: "We're not playin', we gotta do it our way."[4] According to Asheton, they reached a compromise, and the band recorded with the amps on 9.

When the sessions were done, Iggy was unhappy with Cale's finished product, so Jac Holtzman did a remix. The completed album, titled simply *The Stooges,* was released on July 19 and entered the *Billboard* charts on August 23.[5]

The attitude of the Stooges on their debut effort was pretty much captured in the lyrics of one of the standout tracks, "1969." Iggy laments: "Another year for me and you, another year with nothing to do." They continued the theme on "No Fun." On another track, Iggy offers a darker declaration of love and obedience. Instead of promising the girl of his desire "trips to the moon," he proclaims, "I wanna be your dog." In addition to three block chords, the song features the sound of sleigh bells and a one-note piano. According to Iggy, he "loved the way that worked against a heavy guitar."[6] The bells were inspired by free jazz artist Pharoah Sanders's 1966 recording of "Upper Egypt and Lower Egypt." Although the Stooges were not as openly into the free jazz sound as were the MC5, they did feel that it "loosened up the music in bands."[7]

"Little Doll," "Not Right," and "Real Cool Time" were the songs Iggy and Asheton had written in a hurry at the Chelsea Hotel. The lyrics for the songs, said Ron Asheton, evolved from "just things we said in life at the band house. Like 'Oh, she's not right. Man, she's so cool, I wanna be your dog.'"[8] Dave Alexander contributed a plodding ten-minute track entitled "We Will Fall."

To make the Stooges' instrumental trio sound bigger, Ron Asheton performed open-neck drones, such as on "I Wanna Be Your Dog." Asheton said, "You make a three-fingered chord, and keep that first E chord droning; that gives you that mysterious, 'what's going on there?' sound."[9] He cites Ravi Shankar, who used a prolonged drone "while picking all those notes," as an influence.[10] Asheton played a Gibson Flying V guitar on five of the album's eight songs, switching to a Fender Stratocaster on the three tunes composed at the Chelsea.[11]

"The dangerous Psychedelic Stooges manage to quickly get down to the nitty gritty of sensual frustration for all of neo-American adolescent malehood," read a review in *Creem*. The magazine described Ron Asheton's work on "Not Right" as "physically abusive" and his overall playing as "probably the guitar style of the future."[12]

Elektra put Steve Harris in charge of the Stooges marketing project. He chose "I Wanna Be Your Dog" to be the single promoted to Top 40 stations, for which there turned out to be few takers. On September 5, the Stooges made their New York debut, opening for the MC5 at the Pavilion in Flushing Meadows. Reviewer Fred Kirby, writing in *Billboard* magazine, described the scene: "Iggy, attired in cut-away blue jeans, swayed and gyrated, caressed and licked the Mic stand, flung it into the audience, scraped his chest until bleeding and rolled on the floor."[13] Kirby also stated that while "the MC5 showed they rated their headliner billing, the erotic performance of the Stooges was coolly received by most of the 2,000 in attendance."[14]

The Stooges were also cooling on the charts, as the album peaked out at number 106. Many record buyers were having a hard time getting into their brutally simplistic approach. Writer Lenny Kaye put the group into the context of the times, saying that while the "musical mainstream had become more sophisticated," the Stooges had "shifted the transmission into reverse, grinding the gears."[15] As for the Stooges' popularity or lack of it, Iggy told writer Dave Marsh, "Mass recognition is not what's important to me, what's important is individual recognition. In other words, it's not how many people recognize you, it's what the people who *do* recognize you, recognize you for."[16]

Aside from the music, the Stooges were being recognized for their sheer audacity. And it wasn't just Iggy who drew the stares. Heads turned when Ron Asheton walked around attired in an SS jacket. He didn't wear it to make any kind of "pro-Nazi statement." He just thought it "looked cool."[17] On one occasion, the Stooges' guitarist wore an SS tunic while boarding a plane. As he walked down the ramp, the shocked pilot wanted him thrown off the flight. Asheton recalled that the stewardess intervened on his behalf, telling the pilot, "He seems like a nice guy," and adding, "I think the uniform is cute."[18]

As for the band's image at the time, Asheton says that there were some bands and critics in the early days who viewed the Stooges as "a joke, a clown band, and a novelty act."[19] Asheton found some of Iggy's antics on stage dangerous, more than one time thinking, "Oh my God—a mike stand's just missing my head." He also recalls how difficult it was to concentrate on his guitar playing: "I'd just be watching [Iggy] and just cracking up."[20]

# 24. "Uncle Russ"

In the fall of 1969, WABX was still the most popular of the three FM stations programming "progressive rock" in the Motor City.[1] But WKNR-FM received a big boost in August when Dan Carlisle joined the station, going on the air in the afternoon after jumping ship from WABX. Carlisle cited "the unwillingness of the station to offer a competitive salary" as the main reason for leaving.[2] Aside from money, Dan was also upset that Rudnick and Frawley had been dumped from the all-night show for allegedly making nasty remarks about the bathrooms at the Grande Ballroom. Carlisle typed a letter of resignation and left it on the desk of station manager John Detz. Unfortunately, he forgot to add his signature, so Detz wound up having to quiz each deejay to find out who had actually quit.[3]

At WKNR-FM, Carlisle joined an air staff that included former Keener-AM Top 40 deejay Jerry Goodwin, who had gone through some sort of transformation after embracing "underground radio." The station also benefited from having Russ Gibb, the proprietor of the Grande Ballroom, on the air each weekend. Along with playing the records, "Uncle Russ" would "rap" with listeners on the air. Gibb says, "We sort of made things up as we went along. It was all sex, drugs, and rock 'n' roll. The McDonald Drop-outs, Kilo the Dog, and Roger Goodtime were some of the characters I dreamed up for skits on my show."[4] "Russ's show was giant," says Dan Carlisle. "It was great. It worked for him, worked for WKNR, and worked for his club."[5]

In addition to the Grande Ballroom and his weekend radio shows on WKNR-FM, Russ Gibb's business interests kept expanding. For a time he was operating the Grande-Cleveland, as well as promoting concerts in Toronto and St. Louis. During the last weekend of May he had produced the big "Rock and Roll Revival" at the Michigan State Fairgrounds. A week later, on June 6 and 7, it was "Under the Stars, Russ Gibb Presents," a concert headlining the Who. In September Gibb would organize the Meadowbrook Pop Festival. He had also signed a deal with the J. L. Hudson Company, owners of the big department store chain, to stage a series of free concerts at the company's various store locations. If that wasn't enough, "Uncle Russ" was set to appear in a new TV show airing on channel 62.[6]

The only thorn in Gibb's side had been the emergence of the Eastown Theatre. Aside from some of the Grande crew who rebelled to operate the See Theater at the site of the old Village on Woodward for a short time in 1969, the Eastown posed the first serious challenge to the Grande. Russ had even shown interest in buying the Eastown from owner Bob Bageris, who, despite drawing good crowds, quickly found himself struggling on the business side. The deal fell through, and the Eastown closed for a while. Then Bageris contacted Aaron Russo, a promoter from Chicago who owned the Kinetic Playground, that city's major rock ballroom. Russo visited the Eastown and felt that it had "potential," commenting on the "good acoustics."[7] He entered into an agreement with Bageris to manage the venue. After checking out the competition at the shabby Grande, Russo announced that he was in a "state of shock." He "couldn't believe *that* was the Grande Ballroom."[8]

The Grande had in fact become run-down. Earlier in the year *Creem* magazine had chided Russ Gibb because the ballroom was "rapidly deteriorating."[9] The bands that played at the Grande, as well as the fans who paid to see them, complained about the horrible condition of the bathrooms. Uncle Russ claimed that it was difficult to replace the bathroom fixtures because they were "old fashioned and out of date."[10]

As the Eastown was threatening his livelihood, Gibb decided to shut down the original Grande Ballroom. After striking a deal with the Nederland brothers, who owned the Riviera Theater just around the corner, he opened the hybrid Grande-Riviera, in its place. The Eastown held around seventeen hundred people. Gibb's Grande-Riviera, with a legal capacity of around twenty-seven hundred, would now jump way ahead. After securing a dance license, a concert license, and a theater license, and Russ opened the new location on Friday, September 26, 1969.[11] SRC, the Amboy Dukes, and the Alice Cooper band were set to play the opening night show. Saturday it would be the Who and Alice Cooper, on Sunday, the Who and the Frost.

Aaron Russo countered, booking the Steve Miller Band and Pacific Gas and Electric into the Eastown, followed by Sly and the Family Stone and Lee Michaels. The two rock impresarios took shots at one another, Gibb claiming that Russo *had* to come to Detroit because the competition had gotten too hot in Chicago, Russo firing back that he "never would've been able to come to Detroit if Russ had done things right here and taken care of the people and the talent in a proper way."[12]

The big question was whether Detroit would be able to support two ballrooms. While Aaron Russo leaned toward booking national acts exclusively—admitting he didn't know which local ones to book—Russ Gibb remained committed to booking top Detroit bands along with national talent.

On Sunday, October 12, away from the club scene and on the air at WKNR-FM, Russ Gibb answered the studio phone. It was a listener from Ypsilanti, identifying himself only as Tom: "Did you know that Paul McCartney is dead?" he queried the radio host. After Gibb expressed doubts, the caller suggested that he try playing the Beatles' recording of "Revolution No. 9" backwards. Still dubious, Gibb spun the track counterclockwise on the turntable. Sure enough, the phrase "number nine," repeated throughout the song, sounded eerily like "turn me on dead man."[13]

The two stayed on the air for two hours, discussing more evidence of McCartney's death, such as the musical fadeout at the end of "Strawberry Fields," where John Lennon seemed to be saying, "I buried Paul" and the cover shot from the *Sergeant Pepper* album showing a left-handed bass guitar made from grave flowers. There were a lot more clues. "The phones lit up within thirty seconds and stayed lit for four days," Gibb recalled. "Before long, people were in front of the station, banging on the windows."[14] On Monday, the station had to put extra help on the switchboard. "I vacillated back and forth from thinking he was really dead to the fact that he was playing a game of being symbolically dead," Gibb told *Creem* magazine.[15]

The McCartney death rumor had actually aired first on WOIA, a small FM station in the Ann Arbor area, on October 8, after all-night deejay Larry Monroe had received some calls on it from listeners. According to Monroe, "Published accounts of the rumor trace it back to an article in the September 23 edition of *Northern Star,* the student newspaper at the University of Illinois."[16]

Meanwhile, the story just kept getting bigger. On Monday, Fred LaBour, a University of Michigan student, was starting to write a review of the new *Abbey Road* album for the school paper, the *Michigan Daily.* After hearing Gibb's show on Sunday, he decided that instead of a straight review, he would embellish the McCartney rumors and write a lengthy story detailing how it had all come about.[17] Many of the clues he mentioned came from Gibb's broadcast, while he discovered others for himself. The whole article was pure fiction but fed the public's appetite for information.

Russ Gibb, John Small, and Dan Carlisle decided to put together a special program. John Small edited down material on thirty-six reels of tape into a two-hour presentation. *Life* magazine was in the studio the night of the first broadcast, and a story soon appeared in the popular magazine.[18]

Tom Gelardi of Capitol Records' Detroit office recalls his label also benefiting: "Sales of Beatles albums started taking off almost instantaneously after Russ got the initial calls on Sunday. The E.J. Korvette store chain were quickly wiped out of Beatles product by Monday."[19]

In the middle of all the excitement, Russ Gibb received a phone call from someone claiming to be Paul McCartney.[20] As for Gibb's, Small's, and Carlisle's take on the situation, they pointed out that they had "never actually said that Paul McCartney was dead," only that they had "suggested that *that* message is contained in Beatle artifacts, and that the conclusions that can be drawn there are variable."[21] In the end, the Paul McCartney death hoax provided a windfall of publicity for Uncle Russ and WKNR-FM.

Around the same time that he was squabbling with Aaron Russo, Gibb began a new relationship with local booking agent and promoter Mike Quatro whereby the two would produce a series of concerts. As a child, Quatro—who was the older brother of Suzi Quatro of the Pleasure Seekers—had been an accomplished keyboard player and had even performed on the Lawrence Welk TV program. By the late sixties, when a substantial performing career failed to materialize, he turned to concert promotion.[22]

Gibb and Quatro billed their first venture as "A Black Arts Festival" taking place at Olympia on Halloween night, October 31, 1969. The lineup was impressive: MC5, Stooges, Frost, Bob Seger System, Teegarden and Van Winkle, the Coven, Amboy Dukes, All the Lonely People, Savage Grace, Pleasure Seekers, and Früt of the Loom. English bands Pink Floyd, Arthur Brown, and Bonzo Dog Band were also listed on advertisements for the concert, along with appearances by LSD advocate Timothy Leary and several magic acts.[23]

Although Quatro, Gibb, and Mike Keener produced the event, it was Quatro who was responsible for the advertising. When fourteen thousand fans arrived, they found out that the MC5, Bonzo Dog Band, Pink Floyd, Arthur Brown, and Bob Seger would not appear. It seemed the promoter had done his ads before actually signing contracts with many of the acts. Michigan's fundamentalist Baptists had convinced Olympia management to block the appearances of Tim Leary and the Coven.[24]

Even with a shorter list of acts, the concert was overbooked for the time allotted, and with so much dope and cheap wine on hand, the Detroit police shut the whole thing down at 1:00 A.M., right in the middle of a set by Savage Grace. After announcing that the plug had been pulled, WABX deejay and show emcee Jerry Lubin introduced Dick Wagner of the Frost and Ted Nugent of the Amboy Dukes. Both bands had been unable to perform. As the crowd screamed: "We want more!" Ted Nugent, his face painted green and black, grabbed a hanging stage rope and swung out over the cheering audience.[25] It was the last entertainment of the night. Later, Lubin devoted most of WABX's "Rock and Roll News" to discussing the ill-conceived concert. Despite the debacle, Russ Gibb went ahead with an agreement for Quatro to start booking bands into the Grande-Riviera,[26] which put him into competition with Jeep Holland, who had handled all bookings up to that point.

# 25. First Train out of Town

The Eastown Theatre was closing out 1969 with a New Year's Eve appearance by the new power trio known as Grand Funk Railroad. The group had risen from the ashes of the Fabulous Pack, the Flint-based band that had carried on following the breakup of Terry Knight and the Pack. Grand Funk Railroad was comprised of guitarist–lead vocalist Mark Farner, drummer Don Brewer, and bass player Mel Schacher. The trio had made an unimpressive Michigan debut the previous May as a last-minute add-on at the "Rock 'n' Roll Revival," held at the State Fairgrounds. Some attendees had called their performance "a bomb."[1]

In the months that followed, Grand Funk Railroad's popularity with fans had grown steadily in other parts of the country, but despite plenty of national bookings and fairly strong national record sales of their first album, locally they were perceived as lightweight hype.[2] There was resentment among Detroit's rock community that this Michigan group had been able to explode on the national rock scene without coming up through the ranks of local bands playing the teen clubs, the Grande, and the big Michigan rock festivals. The slow, grinding careers of Detroit favorites such as Bob Seger, the MC5, and the Rationals made quick success of Grand Funk Railroad all the more amazing.

"Detroit has been built up," Don Brewer commented in *Creem.* "It's been socked into Detroit kids' heads that Detroit is the musical capitol of the world or something."[3] "What happens in Detroit is that they devote too much time thinking, 'make it in Detroit and you can make it anywhere,' when in fact, 'make it in Detroit and you *can't* make it anywhere,'" sarcastically preached the group's manager, Terry Knight, who had been determined that Grand Funk Railroad make it nationally first.[4]

After splitting from the Pack in April 1967, Knight had gone down several roads, all of which seemed to place him in advantageous positions. While performing in Cleveland with his horn-driven Terry Knight Revue, Ed McMahon, of Johnny Carson's *Tonight Show,* happened to be in the audience, and signed Knight to a management contract. He wanted Terry to write the musical score for a motion picture Ed was involved with called *The Incident.* McMahon gave Terry Knight twenty-five thousand dollars up front.[5]

At the conclusion of filming, Terry began wearing love beads, and returned to performing as a singer-songwriter in coffeehouses, such as the Chessmate in Detroit, where folksingers Chuck and Joni Mitchell also performed. Appearing in Florida, he met Twiggy, the 1960s supermodel, and joined her on a national tour, warming up the audience with a few songs. It was Twiggy who brought Terry to the attention of Paul McCartney, who was looking for talent to sign to the Apple record label.[6] Twiggy's manager suggested that Knight join them on their return trip to London. But when he arrived, the four Beatles were embroiled in business arguments, and a meeting with McCartney never took place. Still, Knight benefited from the whole experience. Paul McCartney made some calls that resulted in Terry being signed by Capitol Records.[7] The label then released a song Terry had written about McCartney on his return plane ride called "Saint Paul." The record spent a couple of weeks on the charts at Detroit's WKNR in May 1968.

Although he wasn't setting the world on fire, things were going well for Terry Knight at the beginning of 1969. Meanwhile, his old bandmates in the Fabulous Pack had not been able to keep up momentum from their two 1967 regional hits "Harlem Shuffle" and "Wide Trackin'." Their producer, John Rhys, who also had an arrangement with Capitol Records, had not been able to coax the label into releasing an album they had recorded. The Pack had also bombed at a high-profile East Coast gig at the Boston Tea Party. In late 1968, bass player Rod Lester and keyboardist Craig Frost bailed out in the middle of a freezing New England tour, leaving Mark Farner and Don Brewer to ponder their future.[8]

Upon returning to Michigan, the two decided to reform as a trio because, as Don Brewer recalled, "the power trio thing—with Cream, and Hendrix, and Blue Cheer and all that kind of stuff—

seemed to be the thing that was happening. We figured, 'We can do that!'"[9] In search of a strong bass player, Farner and Brewer approached Mel Schacher, who had joined Question Mark and the Mysterians after their success with "96 Tears." Schacher accepted, and the still nameless trio started practicing. Brewer felt that the new band needed help, and thought back to how quickly Terry Knight had pulled things together after joining their old Jazz Masters band. After having changed the name of the group to the Pack, Terry had done what he had promised he would—get the group a record contract, and concert and TV appearances. So without Mark Farner's knowledge, Brewer sent a letter to Terry in New York.[10] Although there had been some bad blood in the old band, especially between Farner and Knight, Terry was interested in what Brewer was telling him about the band's new sound. Mark, Don, and Mel came to see Knight at one of his Detroit gigs at the Chessmate, and then he traveled to Flint to hear them perform. "The power was just totally, absolutely, entirely unusual," thought Knight after hearing the trio. Admitting that he didn't "admire their music" and "could never figure out what the hell it was," Terry Knight instantly sensed that he could "package it, market it, and sell it."[11]

Searching for a name for the band, Terry suggested they use the title of a song he had recently written called "The Grand Funk Railroad," which had been inspired by Michigan's Grand Trunk Railroad line. Terry believed the name had "power, forward motion, strength and longevity."[12] It also had a copyright licensed to Terry Knight.

The three hungry musicians, believing that he held the formula for success, agreed to having Terry as their manager. "I told them the only thing I demand is that you do what I say," said Knight.[13] A three-year deal was arranged. Because the members were under twenty-one, the contracts were cosigned by their parents.[14]

After unsuccessfully shopping the band around to several record labels in both New York and Los Angeles, including Capitol, Terry turned his attention to getting the band in front of a live audience. As he still performed occasionally at the Limelight Gallery in Buffalo, Knight was able, through a friend, to get Grand Funk Railroad a last-minute booking at a big rock show in that city.

According to Knight, the band went on "stiffer than a board," trying to emulate Cream, and played to a "gigantic vacuum of applause." "Well," said Knight, "we broke that mold right then and there. Grand Funk was told, not asked, 'to move like their assholes were on fire.'"[15]

In April, Knight turned to a friend named Ken Hamann, who owned a recording studio in Cleveland. Hamann agreed to let Knight and the band record there with no money up front.[16] There the group recorded some songs, including "Heartbreaker." Mark Farner was the band's principal writer, although Don Brewer was quoted as saying, "Basically we all write the songs. It's just that he [Farner] writes the original song and we arrange it."[17] Terry took the tape containing two of the tracks back to Capitol in Los Angeles. Knight said, "I guess it was [Paul] McCartney that called Mauri Lathower, the head of A&R at Capitol and said, 'This guy [Knight] knows what he's talkin' about.'"[18] Knight convinced Lathower to give the group a small deal for a one-shot single, and then pressed on, eventually securing an appointment with Sal Ianucci, the president of Capitol. Don Brewer recalled that Knight "had a way of walkin' through any door, and coming across very impressive, and very knowledgeable about what he was doin' in the music business."[19] Ianucci was impressed with Knight's enthusiasm and salesmanship in trying to win an album deal: "If you like this—you'll love 'em. You've gotta trust me on this," Knight had pleaded.[20] The Capitol execs gave their approval, and Grand Funk Railroad had their record deal with Capitol . . . well, not quite. It was actually Terry's company, Good Knight Productions, that had the deal, and the band was signed to that production company, where Terry would produce their recordings for Capitol. Knight also created a corporation called GFR Enterprises to handle the money, and he saw to it that his company, Storybrook Music, published the band's songs.[21]

Despite their cool reception at the "Rock 'n' Roll Revival," Grand Funk Railroad fared well at a series of rock festivals in the South during the summer of 1969, where Knight had booking agent Jeep Holland arrange for them to perform for free in order to gain exposure.[22] After going on as the first act on the first day, the band made such an impression in Atlanta that they were quickly moved up on the bill and invited back for the next year. At the Texas Pop Festival, the trio received no less than four standing ovations and two encores from a crowd of 180,000. *Billboard* called them "a Detroit-based trio with individually perfected talents fused into a tight unit of exciting projection."[23] At the same time, Knight worked the phones, calling deejays around the country to remind them that Grand Funk Railroad was surely going to be bigger than the Beatles!

The high-profile shows; a hit single, "Time Machine"; and heavy press coverage, including a three-page ad in *Billboard,* pushed the band's first album, *On Time,* to number 27 and gold record status. A second album was about to be released at the end of December. "It's just hard, hard rock," said Don Brewer, describing the music of Grand Funk Railroad.[24] Hard rock hyped to the max by the man serving as their "mentor, manager, publisher and producer"— Terry Knight. On New Year's Eve, 1969, Grand Funk Railroad, red hot in most parts of the country, would again try to win over the Motor City.

# 26. 1970

In the GM Studios on Nine Mile Road in East Detroit, Jon Landau was feeling his way through the sessions for the MC5's second album, his first shot as a rock producer. The band seemed more than pleased to have him at the helm. Wayne Kramer referred to Landau as "the killer catalyst of all time."[1] According to Kramer, Jon Landau was "the first person they had met who had a working knowledge of rock and roll music that could relate it to the band."[2] The "5" were now buying completely into the Landau hype, calling their days with John Sinclair "amateur."[3] Landau himself rubbed salt into the wounds of the White Panthers, saying he "related to rock and roll a lot more than political things."[4]

Landau told the press that the new MC5 record would be a "rock 'n' roll album" but not one "pretending" that it was recorded twenty years ago. While the band would record "Tutti-Frutti," they would make it more contemporary, while at the same time "retain the energy" of the Little Richard classic.[5] Aside from Chuck Berry's "Back in the USA," the rest of the album would consist of originals such as "Call Me Animal," "Tonight," "Teenage Lust," "High School," "American Ruse," "Shakin' Street," and the band's take on society as "The Human Being Lawnmower."

Although the MC5's split with John Sinclair was discussed by many people in the rock community and criticized by some, most fans remained loyal to the band and were looking forward to the release of their second album. Meanwhile, on October 7, 1969, the already imprisoned Sinclair had been indicted by a federal grand jury in Detroit, along with fellow White Panthers Pun Plamondon and Jack Forest, with conspiring to bomb the head office of the CIA in Ann Arbor on September 29, 1968. Plamondon, who was also charged with carrying out the bombing, was printing flyers in the basement of the White Panther headquarters when he heard the news about the indictment broadcast on WABX. He immediately went underground, making his way to Europe.[6]

The MC5 had stayed busy both in the recording studio and onstage, joining the Stooges on September 1, 1969, for a benefit concert at the Grande Ballroom for the *Fifth Estate.* Peter Werbe had assumed the editorship of the radical paper following the departure of Harvey Ovshinsky. On September 14, the MC5 traveled down the road to perform at the Toledo Pop Festival along with the Amboy Dukes, Frost, SRC, the Rationals, the Früt, and L.A.'s Alice Cooper band, which was starting to play more frequently in the Detroit area. Folk-rockers the Turtles, of "Happy Together" fame, headlined the concert. On October 25, the MC5 were back on the East Coast, opening for Led Zeppelin and Johnny Winter at Boston Gardens. A single, "Tonight," from their forthcoming Atlantic album, had been released on the fifteenth and spent four weeks on the WKNR *Music Guide,* reaching number 21.

Having been forgiven by Bill Graham, the "5" headed back out to San Francisco for a four-day stand at the Fillmore West, sharing the bill with Jethro Tull and Sanpaku. Back in Detroit, they played the Eastown on January 9, 1970. Connie White, who covered the concert for *Creem,* reported that while the MC5 had "tightened up and gained a degree of polish," their tunes were not as "progressive" and "sophisticated" as in the past. She also felt that the band had lost some of their "rapport" with the audience.[7]

The MC5's Atlantic LP *Back in the USA* hit the store shelves on January 15. Despite the single released earlier, fans were still taken off guard when they put the needle in the grooves of the band's second album. The big, powerful, high-energy sound everyone had been expecting had been replaced on every cut by a tight, thin veneer that lacked "bottom." Dennis Thompson placed most of the blame squarely on Jon Landau, calling him a "typical brilliant liberal intellectual" who loved R & B but had a "tin ear."[8] Because of Landau's lack of experience as a rock producer, and the MC5's lack of experience in the studio, Thompson says, the *Back in the USA* album came out "balls-less, thin sounding, sterile and too fast."[9]

Wayne Kramer said that in the studio the band had listened to the playback "full blast and didn't realize how thin it sounded."[10] Regarding the extreme tightness of the album, Kramer confided that the band was still "stinging" from Lester Bangs's brutal review of their first album. As a result, he wanted *Back in the USA* to be a "note-perfect" recording, where guitars were "gonna be in tune, tempos are gonna be right on."[11] For a while it seemed like Kramer and Landau were on the same page. Dennis Thompson says, "We overcompensated, and that was Landau and our combined naïveté."[12]

Greil Marcus, writing in *Rolling Stone*, said that although the album had "some first rate songs" and some "good musical ideas," he considered "the idea of a 'solid, clean, tight and together' sound . . . self-conscious."[13] Marcus was positive about three of the original songs on the album: "Teen Age Lust," "American Ruse," and "Human Being Lawnmower." He called the title song "stiff" and "Tutti-Frutti" the "worst cut."

The album turned out to be a commercial failure. Whereas *Kick Out the Jams* had climbed to number 30 on the *Billboard* album charts, *Back in the USA*, heralded as the triumphant follow-up, stalled at number 137. According to Dennis Thompson, the album "confused" their audience. Gone was the "relentless fire-and-brimstone" of the *Kick Out the Jams* live set. "We were this rebellious pirate crew, and now all of a sudden we're tight."[14] Despite mixed reaction to *Back in the USA*, the MC5 kept the songs in front of audiences as they played at the popular Daniel's Den in Saginaw on February 20. Then they traveled back to where their infamous 1968 East Coast tour had begun eighteen months earlier, appearing at the Boston Tea Party on March 6.

On January 24 and 25, 1970, Detroit's alternative rock and political community came together at a special two-day event to raise money for the John Sinclair Defense Fund and one of Sinclair's favorite causes, decriminalization of marijuana. The two-day event was produced by the STP Coalition (Serve the People), made up of various cultural and radical organizations in the Detroit and Ann Arbor areas. Both the reopened and renovated Grande Ballroom—sans Russ Gibb—as well as the Eastown Theatre, hosted.[15]

Things got underway Saturday afternoon at the Grande, with a set from the White Panthers' own band, the Up. Although scheduled to speak, Abbie Hoffman and Jerry Rubin, currently on trial in the Chicago Seven case, were no-shows, as was Ed Sanders of the Fugs. The radical flame was kept burning, however. Brother J. C. Crawford, late of the MC5, read an hour-long message from John Sinclair that spoke of the "historical and political rationale for the benefit."[16] White Panther Party minister of education Skip Taube also spoke, and Genie Plamondon made an unannounced appearance. She read a special message from her exiled husband, Pun, who was spending time in Algeria in the company of Eldridge Cleaver: "The newest prison in the world cannot hold Brother John if the people won't let it. And we are the people, we are a people. We are the people of the Woodstock Nation," declared Pun Plamondon.[17] (Three months later, Plamondon was arrested while attempting to reach a safe house in Michigan's Upper Peninsula.)

On Saturday evening, sixteen hundred "brothers and sisters" filled the ballroom, and on Sunday another nine hundred showed up to hear SRC, the Amboy Dukes, and Brownsville Station perform. The latter group, fronted by Cub Koda, had recently scored a local hit with "Rock 'n' Roll Holiday," released on Hideout Records.

Over at the Eastown on Sunday, a crowd numbering one thousand saw a "killer" show featuring the MC5 and Mitch Ryder with a new group of Detroit Wheels. Both bands received standing ovations. There were however, some bad vibes between the audience and the "5" over the band's split from Sinclair and the Trans-Love organization. Other popular area bands performing at the Eastown show included the Rationals, the Früt, and Commander Cody and His Lost Planet Airmen. When it was all over, they had raised eight thousand dollars on behalf of the John Sinclair Defense Fund.[18] Unfortunately, Sinclair had been transferred the previous September to the state prison in Marquette, five hundred miles to the north, making it more difficult for him to communicate with his attorneys or anyone else who could help him fight his case.[19]

Of all the high-energy performers appearing at the Sinclair benefit, the Commander Cody outfit was a different breed. Playing a laid-back, country and western style of primitive rockabilly and boogie, the band had first come together in Ann Arbor in 1967.

Cody, the band's piano player, was actually George Frayne. Back in 1963, while attending the University of Michigan, he had become friends with John Tichy, who was studying engineering and playing guitar in the Amblers, the only student band on campus. In the fall of 1964, Frayne, playing a Farfisa Combo Compact keyboard, joined Tichy in launching a new band called the Fantastic Surfing Beevers. They drove to their first gig in an old hearse with a surfboard mounted on the roof. When Frayne graduated in the spring of 1966, the band found itself at a crossroads. Tichy was going on to grad school at U of M. Frayne had not yet made up his mind, but after receiving a scholarship, he stayed. In the fall of 1967, Frayne and Tichy decided to start yet another band. It was Frayne who chose the name, inspired by the 1952 movie called *Lost Planet Airmen*. The film's hero had been rocket man Commando Cody, sky marshal of the Universe.[20]

According to Frayne, the band was made up of "various assortments of honking, blowing and strumming neo radicals who specialized in a form of quasi-social mayhem."[21] Along with Frayne and Tichy, musicians in the band included Steve Davis on steel guitar, John Copley on snare drum, John Farlow playing standup bass, and Steve Schwartz strumming rhythm guitar. Bill Kirchen from Seventh Seal joined as lead guitarist. Lead vocals were handled by Kirchen and singer–harp player Billy C. Farlow, who joined after leaving the band he fronted, Billy C. and the Sunshine.

Commander Cody and His Lost Planet Airmen began drawing steady crowds to appearances around Ann Arbor, such as those at the Canterbury House at 721 East Huron. Still unsure about a full-time music career, Frayne accepted a position as assistant professor of art at Wisconsin State University. He wound up driving fourteen hours a week back and forth to hook up with the band for sold-out weekend gigs in Ann Arbor.[22] Searching for new challenges, Bill Kirchen split for San Francisco. By the end of the summer of 1968, at Kirchen's urging, Frayne resigned from his teaching position and jumped in a van with Billy Farlow and Steve "The West Virginia Creeper" Davis, and the three of them headed West. Upon arriving in the Bay Area, they recruited bassist Buffalo Bruce Barlow and drummer Lance Dickerson and started playing local gigs, including the 1968 Berkeley Folk Festival.[23] In January 1970,

Commander Cody and His Lost Planet Airmen returned to Michigan to perform at the Sinclair benefit.

Mitch Ryder's appearance at the Sinclair benefit marked a major change in direction for the already legendary performer. After splitting from the original Detroit Wheels midway through 1967 to front a horn-driven nine-piece show band, Ryder had found something less than success. The idea of packaging rock 'n' roll and R & B in a Las Vegas–style presentation just never rang true. "We had costumes and lighting and swirling discs; fantastic incredible makeup and garb, but it never came off," Ryder recalled.[24] Although he tried to "make that show band become a group," the musicians never related to themselves as anything but paid employees.[25]

Ryder had built his reputation on a raw R & B style that was not well served by the show band's slick professionalism. It was while headlining a big package show in New York staged by disc jockey Murray the K that Mitch had begun to realize how important the Detroit Wheels had been. Billed fourth and fifth behind Ryder were British rockers Cream and the Who respectively. When Cream guitarist Eric Clapton asked Ryder how Jim McCarty was doing, Ryder began to feel his status at the show owed entirely to his past work with the Wheels, who "weren't there to reap any of the benefits."[26] In fact, with the exception of "What Now My Love," which made a mild dent in the charts, Mitch Ryder had scored no hits since leaving his original band. People were coming to see the Mitch Ryder show, but they were coming to hear the hits he had cut with the Detroit Wheels.

Financially, Ryder was taking a beating. He was paying the band's salaries, $250 per week (show or no show, low or high gross), plus transportation. Mitch accused his managers of taking "every penny" he had, roughly $110,000, and putting it toward the production of his show. Ryder's costumes alone cost $1,000 each, and he had four or five of them.[27]

Although Ryder and the Wheels had sold six million records for Bob Crewe, a $15,000 advance and one royalty check for $1,000 is all the singer had ever been paid, aside from personal appearance fees. Deep in debt, Ryder felt that Bob Crewe was treating him like "slave labor."[28] After becoming aware of Ryder's unhappiness, Crewe threatened that if he ever left him, he would see to it that Mitch "died musically."[29] Things had definitely reached a breaking point, and Ryder filed a suit against Crewe. "We went to court in New York and he won," recalled Mitch.[30] Losing an appeal, Ryder continued to perform, but the show band was coming to an end. "It was really attrition that finished it off," said Ryder. "They had all my money locked up and things were so tight that we had to let a horn player go. Then a few weeks later, we'd lose another horn."[31] Crewe finally sold Ryder's contract to Paramount, and Mitch wound up with a choice of going to L.A. to record with pop music producer Jeff Barry or going to Memphis to do a project with Booker T. and the MG's. For Mitch Ryder, the choice was obvious.

In June 1969, Mitch arrived at the Stax recording studios in Memphis, recently acquired by Dot Records, to begin work on what would eventually be called the Detroit-Memphis Experiment. The idea of combining Ryder's tough Detroit vocals with the gritty Memphis sound of Booker T. and the MG's was ripe with potential. Unfortunately, according to Ryder, it was a "rush job" and didn't work because there was "no direction to it" and "no concept."[32] Originally, Mitch had wanted it to be "more like an Otis Redding kind of thing."[33] Ryder and producer Steve Cropper of the MG's had worked separately on musical ideas and then gotten together with other writers in the upstairs cubicles at Stax to try to come up with complete songs that they would go into the studio to record. "We called it the 'Detroit-Memphis Experiment,' because it was thrown together," said Ryder.[34] The other problem, according to Mitch, was that the young audience at the time was "going into psychedelia," while he was turning out a heavy R & B album. Although it was a disappointment, Ryder believed that there were "a couple of brilliant moments" on the record. He cited "Liberty" as his favorite: "That's where everyone cooked, everything came together."[35]

In the album's liner notes, Ryder spoke of "being raped by the music machine that represents that heaven-on-earth, New York b/w Los Angeles." He also informed the world that "Mitch Ryder is the sole creation of William Levise Jr." Looking back, he admitted that venting anger in print had been a mistake, adding, "It's something you just don't do if you want to keep a career."[36]

In the late summer of 1969, Mitch returned to the Detroit area and struck up a relationship with Barry Kramer, the publisher of *Creem*. Anxious to get something going, Mitch contacted Johnny "Bee" Badanjek about getting the Wheels back together. Since they last parted, Bee had fronted his own Detroit Wheels band and even cut several sides for Harry Balk's Inferno label, most notably, a record called "Linda Sue Dixon." Having folded the Wheels, Bee was playing with a new group in Birmingham called Blueberry Jam. "Mitch called and wanted to start a new band right away because he owed a lot of money to the unions, after the big horn band fell apart," recalls the former Wheels drummer. "So we got some players together."[37]

In addition to Ryder and Badanjek, the new Wheels included Steve Hunter on lead guitar, Ray Goodman on rhythm guitar, Tony Suhy on bass, Mike McClellan and Chuck Florence on horns, and Boot Hill, formerly of Billy C. and the Sunshine, on piano. Barry Kramer took over as the band's manager, and *Creem* magazine's offices provided a rehearsal space. "We were practicing on the third floor of this old building, and some of the *Creem* writers were living on the second floor," recalls Johnny Bee. "Man, I'd come in there and start beating on those drums and those people down below would get real upset."[38]

Following their appearance at the John Sinclair benefit, the band made plans for a spring tour. This time there would be no jet planes or huge arena shows in major cities. The musicians hit the road in a used 1967 Fleetwood Limousine trailed by a U-Haul truck carrying their equipment. First stop: Dwogiac, Michigan, followed by an appearance in Terre Haute, Indiana, where the rockin' Wheels played for a sit-down, junior class dinner dance and party. From there they made their way south on the redneck circuit, deep into Mississippi. No longer big-time headliners, they faced an endless stream of small-town shows in high school gymnasiums, Baptist colleges, local teen clubs, county armories, and somewhat suspect clubs with names such as the Copa and the Shangri-La.[39] Ryder may have been off the charts for three years, but he was still a celebrity. At fried chicken and hamburger stands along the way, Mitch would accommodate fans, including local police officers, with a photo or an autograph. To women he gave a hug. By the time it was over, the band had played in twenty-three towns, crossing the Deep South and up through the Carolinas before eventually returning to home turf in the Motor City.[40]

From a distance, the rock scene in Detroit in the spring of 1970 still appeared to be the same mix of music and politics, of and for the people. Up close it was less about the people and more about the business of rock, and the small group of men who controlled it in the Motor City. *Creem* magazine described the state of the rock music industry in Michigan as resembling a "classical model of oligopoly," where "competition and the economies of scale dictate merger, consolidation and clandestine cooperation."[41]

Following much public feuding, Russ Gibb had entered into a joint business arrangement with his former adversaries, Bob Bageris and Aaron Russo at the Eastown Theatre. Dan Carlisle, who was booking bands for the Grande at the time, remembers what went down: "I got a call from Russ saying for me to come over to his house. After arriving, Russ said that we were going to go meet Bob Bageris, and we did. We went and met him in a parking lot. Gabe Glantz, who was really the money behind everything, was also there. They all signed some sort of contract. Gabe said to me, 'If you'll just shut up, I'll give you a hundred bucks a week,' or something. I didn't know what he was talking about. I didn't really understand until Russ explained to me that they were signing a deal. They were not going to be competing anymore, because it was going to destroy them both. Together they were deciding that they wouldn't let the booking agents work them anymore."[42] Gibb ceased operations at the Grande-Riviera and reopened the original Grande Ballroom in January. He then staged his final show at the legendary venue on January 23, supposedly to cut back on competition for the Eastown. Not long after, Aaron Russo left town and returned to Chicago.

*Creem,* claiming that "Glantz owns fifty percent of everything Gibb does," also reported a confrontation that may have led to the closing of the Grande.[43] On January 2, Glantz had shown up at the

Eastown, of which he, along with Gibb, was now part owner, to collect money. Bageris refused to turn over any cash, believing that if the Grande was still open, the contract for the merger of the Grande and the Eastown was broken. Bageris had Glantz hauled away by the police. Glantz then returned to the Eastown the following evening brandishing a gun. He was quickly asked to leave, which he did. In the end, Glantz won out. Later that week the courts ruled that the merger was in effect.[44] After a couple of concerts put on by the "Grande Family," the ballroom's doors remained closed for the next six months.

On the booking front, Mike Quatro sold his agency to Dave Leone, who renamed it Diversified Management Associates. Punch Andrews was helming his own agency, Punch Enterprises, and booking the Frost, the Bob Seger System, SRC, and Third Power, among others.[45]

Jeep Holland's A-Square Productions was going downhill following the loss of the Rationals and SRC. Gale and Rice and Kramer-Day Associates were the other major agencies booking Michigan bands, which numbered around four hundred. There was also a new agency, Seventy Plus, formed by Robin Seymour and former Grande Ballroom manager, Larry Feldman, who was now managing the Rationals.[46] Robin was planning a show at the Michigan Theater downtown, featuring the MC5, and Frijid Pink, along with some revival films on screen. Tickets were priced at $3.50 and $4.50.

Frijid Pink, a band originally known as the Detroit Vibrations, was a hot ticket after scoring a number 1 hit in Detroit in February, with a heavy, distortion-drenched, guitar-driven version of "House of the Rising Sun." The single had also become a national hit, reaching number 7 in *Billboard* and attaining gold record status. The six-man lineup from Detroit's downriver suburbs featured vocalist Kelly Green, lead guitarist Gary Thompson, rhythm guitarist Tom Yehley, bassist Tom Harris, drummer Richard Stevers, and keyboard player Larry Zelanka. In the beginning they played parties and record hops at teen clubs such as the Chatterbox in Allen Park, where they connected with Robin Seymour. The

Detroit Vibrations wound up appearing on Seymour's afternoon TV show *Swingin' Time* some seventeen times.[47]

One day in the late spring of 1967, Richard Stevers was painting the bathroom of his parent's house with the help of his bandmate Tom Yehley. "We ended up with pink paint in our hair," Stevers recalls. "This was when we were thinking about changing our name and back when women were doing all the frosting of their hair. My mom sees us and suggests Frosted Pink as a good name for our band. I said, 'No, Mom, that ain't gonna happen.' Now, we had a Frigidaire refrigerator at the time. We were all sittin' around the kitchen, and she says, 'How about Frigid Pink?' I said, 'Nah, nothing with the pink thing.' Two weeks later we were Frijid Pink."[48]

Midway through 1967, the band introduced its new identity during a performance at the Harbor Lights Theater in Ecorse, Michigan. Richard Stevers recalls, "We came out on stage as the Detroit Vibrations for the first set and we had all our old outfits on, playin' the old Motown kind of sound. Second set, we came back up on stage and everybody was all done up in pink velvets and satin. We had the smoke machine going, we had the pink lights, and we had a guy with us who created a kind of psychedelic oil and water show on the screen."[49]

In the fall, Frijid Pink was playing at the annual Alsac show at Cobo Hall. Also on the bill was a rockabilly singer named Jerry Jaye, who had recently had a hit with "My Girl Josephine." The record had been released on Hi Records, which was owned by the much larger London Records, home to the Rolling Stones. When Jaye's band failed to materialize, his label representative, Alan Mitnick, asked Frijid Pink if they could help out and play backup. After running through a couple of songs backstage, they performed with Jaye, and at the end of the show he asked the band to go on the road with him. As the musicians were all still in high school, it was out of the question. But Alan Mitnick asked the band to send him a tape. Impressed by what he heard, Mitnick managed to get them signed to another London subsidiary label, Parrot Records.

The label chose "Tell Me Why" as the first single release, and it became a hit in Detroit, reaching number 14 in March 1969, although failing to take off elsewhere. Their next release, "God Gave Me You," was not doing as well until fate stepped in. At the time, Frijid Pink drummer Richard Stevers was dating the daughter of Paul Cannon, the music director at WKNR. "When we recorded the first batch of songs at the Tera Shirma studio, we had some time left over on the session," Stevers recalls. "The guitar player and myself had been practicing 'House [of the Rising Sun],' so we recorded it, and when we left the studio, it was the last song on the tape. Later I took my reel-to-reel tape machine with me when I went to visit my girlfriend, and I asked Paul to listen to the songs. I played a couple of bars from each one, and after we went through the whole thing, he didn't say much. Then 'House' started up, and I immediately turned it off because it wasn't anything I really wanted him to hear. Then Paul says, 'No, start that over, turn it back on.' He says, 'Tell Parrot to drop "God Gave Me You" and go with this one.'"[50] A few weeks later, Stevers and his girlfriend were parked in the Cannon's driveway after a date, sharing a few kisses, when her father tapped on the window. "I went, 'Oh wow, am I in trouble,'" says Stevers. "Anyhow, Paul says, 'Come in the house, I got something I want you to hear.' I walked inside and 'House of the Rising Sun' was blaring out of the radio."[51] Besides reaching the U.S. top 10, the Frijid Pink single became a huge hit in Europe, where it held the number 1 position in Germany for eleven weeks, and hit number 4 in the United Kingdom, spending some four months in Britain's top 75.[52] A self-titled Frijid Pink album was released and quickly entered the top 10 in *Billboard*.

Management was a family affair, handled by Richard Stevers's father, Clyde, an ex-cop, and Marv Wilson, who was the brother-in-law of bass player Tom Harris. Although Frijid Pink had played at the Grande Ballroom and at a slew of Michigan festivals, after the success of "House of the Rising Sun," they spent less time in Detroit. The band toured Australia and Canada, as well as the United States, including an impressive date at Unganos in New York. An article in *Creem* said Frijid Pink had experienced an "overnight rise," and that everyone in Detroit seemed surprised.[53]

While the "5," the Stooges, Frost, and other Detroit bands were having problems selling records away from home turf, Frijid Pink had seemed to come out of nowhere and go international.

The Stooges kept rockin' into 1970, and on April 12 they were booked into Sherwood Forest, the rock club owned by Don Sherwood in Richfield Township near Davison, Michigan, just to the east of Flint. The Sherwood Forest dances were staged by Peter C. Cavanaugh and Johnny Irons, two enterprising disc jockeys from WTAC in Flint who had pooled their resources to promote rock concerts. Sherwood Forest had moved ahead of Mt. Holly ski lodge, becoming the most important rock venue in the Saginaw Valley.

Prior to introducing the Stooges, who were standing behind him waiting to play, Irons took a few moments at the microphone to plug some upcoming shows. The disc jockey droned on and on, and Iggy suddenly yelled, "Shut up!" Irons, not known for having a great sense of humor, shot back, "That's a good way not to get paid."[54] Despite the bad vibes, Iggy and the Stooges rocked—a shirtless Iggy moving out into the crowd.

At a past concert with the MC5, Cavanaugh had run into problems with the police and the band's famous "Kick Out the Jams" proclamation. From then on, Sherwood Forest contracts included a no-profanity clause. That night, when the lead Stooge began singing some lyrics Cavanaugh found objectionable, he had electricity to the band cut. Iggy, whose microphone was plugged into a separate PA system, continued with his performance, swinging a chair in the air and aggravating a biker in the audience by staring at his girlfriend. After a minute or so Iggy became aware that the music behind him had stopped. "What the fuck's wrong? Where's the music?" His words reverberated throughout the hall and into the ears of a still-pissed off Johnny Irons, who immediately ran to the edge of the stage and grabbed the long mike cord, which was wrapped several times around Iggy's neck. Irons reeled in the lead Stooge.[55] The scene was getting ugly, as Cavanaugh stood onstage giving the audience a blow-by-blow account. It took several police officers to pry Iron's hands from Iggy's neck.

Upon returning to the stage, Johnny Irons took the mike and looked for support from the audience: "We don't want any acts like that here, do we?" According to Iggy and his manager Jim Silver, the crowd responded with "Fuck you, Irons" and "Eat shit." In retaliation, an angry Irons accused the band of breaking the no-obscenities clause in their contract and refused to pay them. Not wanting to aggravate the marginally influential disc jockey any further and cause problems with potential bookings elsewhere, the Stooges packed up and headed back to Ann Arbor.[56]

In May, the Stooges were ready to record their second album for Elektra, titled *Fun House*. The album's name was inspired by the rambling twelve-room farmhouse in which the Stooges resided at the corner of Eisenhower and Packard roads in Ann Arbor. Iggy maintained quarters in an attic bedroom. *Fun House* would have the distinction of being the first Elektra record to feature the label's new butterfly logo. The sessions were held over eight days at the label's new West Coast studios under the direction of staff producer Don Gallucci, who seemed a perfect choice. As a teenager, he had been the keyboard player in the Kingsmen when they recorded the grunge classic "Louie, Louie."[57]

Gallucci recorded the Stooges live in the studio through a PA on twelve reels of 3M Scotch tape. "We were a little more professional by then," recalled Ron Asheton. "It was more relaxed, and we were really able to work with Don."[58] Asheton also remembers being introduced to Ross Meyer, the engineer, who exclaimed: "I just got done doing Barbra Streisand and now I'm doing you guys!"[59] In addition to the regular lineup, Steve McKay was brought in to play tenor saxophone.

If the general listening audience had been offended by the Stooge's first album, they were savaged by the sounds of *Fun House*. It was Don Gallucci's idea to record the songs in almost the same order as the band performed them in their shows.[60]

Ron Asheton described *Fun House* as "good old rock 'n' roll" with elements of "funk and jazz."[61] The title cut and the psychedelic "Dirt" were built on riffs started by Dave Alexander. The other songs were combinations of ideas from Ron and Iggy. On "Loose," "TV Eye," and "Down on the Street," Iggy can be heard sneering out in front of Ron's blues-rock guitar strokes and Scott's relentless drumming. "LA Blues" was five minutes of wild, jarring, searching sound. A single, "Down On the Street" paired with "I Feel Alright," was released on July 8, and the album followed on August 18. Bassist Dave Alexander left the band before the album's release and was replaced by Zeke Zettner. On June 13, the Stooges played at the Cincinnati Pop Festival, a performance memorable for Iggy's walking across the audience, stepping from hand to hand.

The Stooges were conspicuously absent from a major event at Sherwood Forest in Davison, Michigan, on June 24. This time out, Peter C. Cavanaugh and Johnny Irons were promoting "Wild Wednesday," advertised as "12 Groups in 12 Hours." Twin stages had been constructed to accommodate all the bands at the huge outdoors festival. Twenty thousand kids came out to see Bob Seger, Ted Nugent, the MC5, Rationals, Brownsville Station, Alice Cooper, and Frijid Pink.[62]

Just three days later, the "5," the Rationals, and Frijid Pink were onstage at Windsor Arena, just across the river from the Motor City, for the Detroit-Windsor Pop Festival. Also on the bill were Third Power; Blues Train; the horn-driven rock band All the Lonely People; the Up; and the Sunday Funnies. J. C. Crawford, late of the MC5 and currently a deejay at WKNR-FM, emceed the show. On July 19 it was time for another WABX free concert at Tartar Field on the Wayne State campus featuring the MC5, Commander Cody, Catfish, Früt of the Loom, and Savage Grace, who were on the local charts with their recording of "Come On Down."

The members of Savage Grace, formed in early 1969, had far more experience than the average rock band starting out. Lead guitarist and vocalist Ron Koss began playing at age thirteen while growing up in Detroit's inner city. Two years later he was playing the bar scene as well as doing session work for a number of R & B acts. Keyboard player John Seaner also had experience in bar bands, but that was tempered by the seven years he studied classical piano. It was Seaner's background in classical and jazz along with his ability to play harpsichord that won him his spot in Savage Grace. Drummer Larry Zack had a jazz influence and, along with Koss, had done session work.

After the three musicians played together on the small stages of various Motor City bars for a while, they recruited Al Jacquez, a seventeen-year-old singer and bass player from Ann Arbor, and Savage Grace was born. Debbie Burr, writing in *Creem,* likened

Jacquez's vocals to "bestial, lust-thirsting scream[s] stimulating the sexuality of men and women alike." Savage Grace quickly managed to attract the attention of Warner/Reprise Records, which signed them to a recording contract.[63]

The Goose Lake International Music Festival was to be Michigan's rock mega-event of 1970. The promoter was thirty-five-year-old Richard Songer, a successful businessman who had made big money in construction. He was now fulfilling "a dream of building a park where young people could get together and have a good time."[64] Taking place on a 390-acre site just outside of Jackson, Michigan, on August 7, 8, and 9, the festival would feature Jethro Tull, Ten Years After, Mountain, Chicago, Rod Stewart and Faces, the Flying Burrito Brothers, the Mighty Quick, the New York Rock Ensemble, the James Gang, and John Sebastian. The Motor City was well represented by the MC5, Bob Seger, SRC, the Stooges, Savage Grace, Third Power, and John Drake's Shakedown. Also on the bill was Mitch Ryder, fronting his new band, Detroit. Three-day tickets were available by advance purchase for fifteen dollars.

In a newspaper ad, Songer had written a personal message to all the "brothers and sisters" expounding all the amenities of "Goose Lake Park—The World's First Permanent Festival Site." Free parking, huge restrooms, a clean lake for swimming, dune buggy and motorcycle trails, custom-designed music bowl and sound system, and open kitchens. The message concluded with a salutation of "peace."[65]

Although sixty thousand people were expected, a staggering two hundred thousand arrived, hoping to recapture some of that 1969 Woodstock magic. Instead they encountered a scene more reminiscent of Attica, as they were herded inside a metal link fence topped with barbed wire that surrounded the festival site. Once inside, no one was allowed to leave. Overhead, Songer directed park security from a helicopter continually dipping and zig-zagging over the huge captured crowds.[66]

Right in front of the stage was a special walled-off area for press and celebrity visitors, secured by mounted guards sporting cowboy hats. The main audience area was behind the wall.[67] The bands performed on a revolving stage built and operated by former

Grande Ballroom manager Tom Wright and his company, Hard Corps Productions. Jem Targal, of Third Power, recalls that his band following the Stooges: "On Saturday night, Iggy and the Stooges were playing on one side and then they spun the stage around and someone announced, 'The Third Power!' Drew [Abbott] starts playin' a real wild, long intro—*dah, dah, dah!* The place went crazy."[68] A surprising highlight of Third Power's set was their rendition of "Little Drummer Boy." Jem Targal recalls, "I sang all the crazy rock songs, but I could also sing clean, like Andy Williams. So we would deliver a message that 'Christmas is an all-year thing,' and do 'Little Drummer Boy,' real straight. When we played it at Goose Lake, everybody did the lighters thing [holding up lit lighters]. Afterward, people said, 'What a cool thing.' That was on Saturday night. Yeah, we were all pretty high, for sure. The next morning I woke up in a tent at Biker's Meadows. A band canceled, so we got to play again during the day on Sunday."[69]

Despite the impressive array of talent, drugs took center stage at Goose Lake. As dopey eyed fans moved through the dusty garbage-strewn paths at the concert site, they were greeted at every turn by dealers hustling deep inventories of grass, acid, speed, mescaline, and specialty items such as balloons filled with nitrous oxide: "Step right up! Two tokes full for only twenty-five cents!" One enterprising youth from Chicago reportedly sold fifteen thousand dollars' worth of narcotics. Operating out of a panel truck, he "shouted like a barker at a circus midway" as he peddled some fourteen varieties of drugs to the passers-by.[70] Drug overdoses? No problem. Just drag your bummed-out friend to the Open City LSD Rescue tent at the rear of the audience area—just don't try to exit the festival. On just the first day, on-site doctors reported that five hundred attendees were treated for "bad trips." Some had become ill after ingesting a horse tranquilizer being sold on the park's open drug market.[71] Former WABX "Air Ace" Dennis Frawley recalls that there were "little booths set up like lemonade stands" with kids standing in line to shoot up meth. "What was really bad was that they were using the same works over and over," says Frawley. "It was really quite decadent."[72]

Jackson County sheriff Charles Southworth estimated that "75 percent of the youths were on drugs," but the activities inside the park went completely unsupervised. "We can't go in after them. We'd get mobbed," said Southworth.[73] Although police didn't interfere with the drug scene inside the park, they made over 160 arrests outside of the festival site, mainly for narcotics violations. Some six hundred illegally parked cars were towed away from narrow dirt roads leading to the site.[74]

A squabble broke out between Richard Songer and the people from Open City, the Detroit-based underground services organization, who were operating one of two free-food kitchens. Open City had been given eighteen thousand dollars to operate the kitchen for a crowd much smaller than the two hundred thousand who had been let in. Songer accused Open City of "trying to cheat him," while officials for that organization charged that they had been underfunded. Eventually more food arrived from private donations, but in the meantime there were many standing hungry in the food lines.[75]

Liza Williams, writing in the *Los Angeles Free Press,* gave her take on the festival: "Instant slum, overcrowding, all the disadvantages of a ghetto—recreated folks, for your listening pleasure."[76]

Many members of Detroit's rock community felt that the "people's culture" was quickly being overtaken and exploited by business types bent on making a fast buck. Still, the STP (Serve the People) Coalition had been involved with the planning of the Goose Lake Festival. They reported at the time that although he was an outsider, Songer seemed "to be a man we can work with."[77] The presence of the White Panthers, who were trying to raise funds on behalf of the imprisoned John Sinclair, added some "people's credibility" to the event. But there was criticism of both the Panthers' poorly delivered message and the apathetic mood of the crowd.[78] Although Goose Lake was not as dark as the Rolling Stones' debacle at Altamont, California, it did leave a bad taste. "Goose Lake, I felt, signaled the end for all that era," says Dan Carlisle, at the time a deejay for WKNR-FM. "That was really horrible. . . . There was a lot of heroin at Goose Lake, not just from the performers either. I saw people with needle stalls, and selling needles on a blanket. I thought . . . geez, what the heck is goin' on here?"[79]

An outraged Governor Milliken condemned the "deplorable

and open sale and use of drugs" at Goose Lake. "The promoters may condone it. Some parents may condone it. But I do not," stated Milliken, speaking from the National Governors Conference in Missouri.[80] He requested that State Police director Fredrick Davids "insure that evidence is carefully collected and documented so that drug pushers can be arrested and prosecuted."[81] State attorney general Frank J. Kelley announced that he would seek an injunction against another festival at the site unless the crowd would be limited to fifteen thousand. "I think we have seen the first and last rock concert of that size in Michigan," said Kelley.[82] Jackson County prosecutor Bruce A. Barton indicated that he would try to "permanently close" the park. The sheer size of the festival crowd had made policing "virtually impossible," commented Barton, who went on to say that he had "enough evidence so there will never be another rock festival."[83]

At the same time, a seemingly sanctimonious Richard Songer stated that he was "shocked" at the "flagrant use of drugs" at his rock festival. "If I am guilty or the park is guilty of allowing dope to be sold or used on this site, then every school principal, every state park official, every state, federal and city official is much guiltier than I."[84] When it was all over, Richard Songer was indicted by the state of Michigan for promoting the sale of illegal drugs. Dennis Frawley comments, "It was too bad about Songer. He was a nice guy and meant well, but I think the whole thing just got too big to maintain that 'peace and love' thing. It got ugly. Goose Lake was really the beginning of the end for the whole pop festival scene that had been going on in Michigan."[85]

Several months after the release of the "Guitar Army" single, the Rationals had recorded an album "on spec" at the Artie Fields studios and then shopped it around with little success. By this time, their manager, Larry Feldman, had gone into business with Robin Seymour, creating a production company. Seymour, by way of an old relationship with Bob Crewe, was able to get the *Guitar Army* LP released on the Crewe label in early 1970. Fred Saxon produced the session along with the Rationals for Robin Seymour Enterprises.[86]

Unfortunately, the album they had waited so long to release

sold poorly. "Robin wanted Fred Saxon to produce it, and he wasn't very flexible," recalls Bill Figg. "If we had had more say, I think it would have turned out different."[87] Saxon, on the other hand, felt "frustrated" that there were "so many people putting their input into every tune on the album."[88] Bill Figg says that the only place the *Guitar Army* album sold well was in Spain, although he could "never figure out why."[89]

Soon Larry Feldman moved on, leaving the band with Seymour as temporary manager. In the late summer of 1970, with their finances still in disarray and members arguing over direction, the Rationals, a band that after nine years together appeared to have what it took to move on to national fame, decided to call it quits. "We had no management, and the band was just kinda floating at that point. We seemed disconnected from everything, we weren't getting along, and nobody seemed to have a clue," said Scott Morgan,[90] who in late 1968 had turned down an opportunity to audition to replace Al Kooper in Blood, Sweat and Tears because he didn't want to leave the Rationals. Bill Figg recalls, "We played our last job at a little bar in Windsor, then we just quit. Everybody wanted to do something different."[91]

Two Detroit bands having success in 1970 were both in a separate orbit from the Grande Ballroom and counterculture scene. In fact, both bands had come together before all of that had begun to take place.

The first was the Flaming Ember, originally billed as the Flaming Embers (after the downtown Detroit restaurant) when they recorded for Fortune Records in 1964. Jerry Plunk played drums as well handling lead vocals. Bill Ellis played keyboards, and Joe Sladich, guitar. Jim Bugnel joined on bass in 1966, when the original bass player left. That was the year that the versatile blue-eyed soul band came to the attention of Ed Wingate of Golden World Records. Signed to Wingate's Ric-Tic label, they had an R & B hit with "Hey Mama Whatcha Got Good For Daddy." The single was written and produced by Golden World staffer George Clinton. Rather than the white teen clubs, the Flaming Embers were booked into black nightclubs such as the 20 Grand. As early as 1968, Wingate had even managed to get them into the Sands

Hotel in Las Vegas, where they appeared on a bill with Louie Prima, Solomon Burke, and Tamico Jones. Upon returning to Detroit, the group was informed that Ed Wingate had sold Golden World to Berry Gordy along with most of the label's artists (the GW studio became Motown's new Studio B). But Wingate gave the Flaming Embers an outright release from their contract so they would be able to negotiate a new deal on their own.[92]

At about the same time, the famous production and songwriting team of Holland-Dozier-Holland had walked out on Motown in a dispute over money. H-D-H decided to form their own company and established the labels Invictus and Hot Wax. On Ed Wingate's recommendation, the Flaming Embers signed with H-D-H and modified their name, dropping the *s*.[93]

In September 1969, the Flaming Ember scored their first national hit on Hot Wax with "Mind Body and Soul." It was a number 1 smash in Detroit and in much of the South. Nationally, it reached number 26 in *Billboard*. Their release in the summer of 1970, the rousing "Westbound No. 9," gave the band a second gold record and spent ten weeks in the national Top 40.

Jim Bugnel says that Eddie Holland had held the band back from *American Bandstand* because there were two big soul stations in L.A. that would not play a record if they knew the musicians were white. "He waited until we hit number 1 on those stations before he booked us on *Bandstand*. Then they couldn't do anything about it because it was such a hit. When we finally did *American Bandstand*, Dick Clark says, 'Sorry, but when I booked the Flaming Ember, I thought I booked a black group.' They were shocked when they saw us."[94]

According to Bugnel, the band was very popular in the South: "We went down there and did twenty-six one-nighters in thirty days in nine states. Now we were on a tour situation where Rod Stewart was a day ahead of us and Chicago was a day behind us, you know, on the same circuit. We out sold all of 'em. We were thinking, 'This is really something,' because those acts were huge at the time. We come down there with the long hair and they look at us . . . and they were always expecting a black group. The South was like three years behind, back then."[95]

Recording for Holland-Dozier-Holland meant that the band would be augmented by other players. "We'd do stuff and then they'd take it and layer it, and so on and so forth," Bugnel recalls. "I'd do my bass thing and then they'd have Bob Babbitt come in and add another bass part and when I'd hear the song back later, I'd say, 'Gee . . . I don't remember doing that.'"[96]

The other big "soul"-oriented white band making noise was Rare Earth. They were originally known as the Sunliners when they formed in 1961, their name inspired by the 1956 Ford Sunliner owned by their sax player, Gil Bridges. The early lineup also included Pete Rivera (drums), Ralph Terrana (keyboards), Russ Terrana (guitar), Fred Saxon (saxophone), and John Parrish (bass). The Sunliners developed a reputation as one of the best all-around club and show bands in Detroit, and were also popular on the East Coast circuit. Despite their popularity as a performing act in nightspots such as Detroit's Club Cliche, the band had been unable to come up with a hit record. Meanwhile there had been ongoing personnel changes. By 1966, Ralph Terrana had left to open the Tera Shirma recording studio. Russ Terrana became an engineer at Golden World, and Fred Saxon went into record promotion. Guitarist Rod Richards, percussionist Eddie Guzman, and keyboard player Kenny James had come on board to join Bridges, Rivera, and Parrish.[97]

By 1968, the musical landscape was changing. "Those were the days when rock and roll was emerging from music into a culture," recounted Pete Rivera.[98] Feeling that the Sunliners moniker had a dated sound, the band opted to make a change. "We chose 'Rare Earth.' It was cool, back to nature, and reflective of the time," said Rivera.[99]

Searching for a record contract, Rare Earth made an unexpected connection to Motown Records. At the time, the band's manager was also co-owner of a Detroit hair salon frequented by Margaret Gordy, former wife of Berry Gordy. Whenever Margaret would stop into the beauty parlor she would hear the latest about Rare Earth. When she finally accepted an invitation to hear them play, she brought along Barney Ales, Motown's director of marketing. "Barney heard our sound and coincidentally already had been urging other Motown executives to expand from their R&B roots to take advantage of the exploding popularity of rock and roll," recalled Pete Rivera.[100] Thanks to Barney Ales's influence, Rare Earth was signed to Motown. Although there had been other white rock bands on the label, such as the Ones and the Underdogs, they had pretty much been "one-hit affairs," with the label showing little long-term interest. Now Motown wanted to create a dedicated "rock 'n' roll" label, and they decided to call it Rare Earth Records.

The band was allowed five late-night sessions in the Motown studio to record their first album. They cut six or seven of their best club songs but came up around ten to twelve minutes short. To fill the space they decided to record "Get Ready," which had been a big hit for the Temptations on the R & B charts, though it hadn't done nearly as well with pop audiences. According to Pete Rivera, they lengthened the track by adding "expanded solos for everyone and a bit of a rock and roll edge."[101] When completed, Rare Earth's heavy bass and drum-led track clocked in at twenty-one minutes.

Upon its release in August 1969, sales of the album were sluggish. As a remedy, Barney Ales suggested that the "Get Ready" track be edited down to three minutes and released as a single. Six months down the road, the record was finally making it onto radio playlists at major R & B stations, and then it went pop. By April 1970, "Get Ready" was a smash, reaching number 4 in *Billboard* and spending seventeen weeks in the Top 40, far longer than the average hit record. In the end, Rare Earth's debut single sold four million copies. Album sales shot up when the long version received play on FM progressive rock stations.[102] A second "rock" version of a Temptations hit, "(I Know) I'm Losing You," went to number 7 in the summer of 1970. The string of hits continued with "Born to Wander," "I Just Want to Celebrate," and "Hey Big Brother."

Motown itself was moving in new directions since losing its most prolific songwriting and production team, Holland-Dozier-Holland. Although the label didn't abandon their commercial pop and R & B roots, they were releasing more socially conscious music. In the wake of David Ruffin's departure, the Temptations had found success with topical material such as "Cloud Nine" (featuring Dennis Coffey's wah-wah pedal), "Runaway Child Running Wild," and "Ball of Confusion," all of which were produced by the innovative Norman Whitfield. Whitfield also produced Edwin Starr's "War," a number 1 smash in the summer of 1970. Bob Babbitt played bass on that recording. "They [Motown] were expanding. There was more work—too much work for [James] Jamerson," Babbitt recalls. "James had become very self-destructive for the talent he had, the great player he was. When he started missing sessions, I was able to step in for him, although I know that wouldn't have happened without his acceptance of me."[103]

That same year, Marvin Gaye began working on a song called "What's Goin' On," which had a smooth, mellow, sax-led progression and jazzy feel, with Marvin's vocal floating above and Jamerson's bass groove below. Although Berry Gordy didn't like it and wanted to release more typical Gaye material, Marvin wouldn't budge. Meanwhile an acetate demo of the song mistakenly came across the desk of Harry Balk, at the time Motown's A&R director. Harry loved it and played it for anyone who would listen. Only Stevie Wonder seemed to share Balk's enthusiasm.[104] When the single was finally released in January 1971, it shot up the charts and spent three weeks at number 2 pop. A groundbreaking album was in the works.

In October 1970, the MC5 started work on their third album, the second for Atlantic. In July, the band had embarked on their first European tour, where, after arriving on the continent, they discovered that their original dates had not been secured. A series of hasty phone calls garnered some last-minute bookings. On the twenty-fifth, the Detroit band performed alongside British rock groups such as the Pink Fairies and Demon Fuzz at the Phun City Festival, a major concert event in Worthing. On the twenty-sixth they appeared on a bill with Matthews Southern Comfort at the Roundhouse in London. On July 31, they played at the Marquee, another London date. "The responses of the crowds were better than they get over here," reported road manager Steve Harnadek upon the MC5's return to the states.[105] According to Wayne Kramer, although the *Back in the USA* album had been poorly received in the States, it was a different story in Europe: "In England people didn't like Kick Out The Jams. It was too loose, too untight, too much hollering and ranting. But they really liked Back in the USA."[106]

As production for the new album got underway, Jon Landau was out of the picture. Atlantic staff engineer Geoffrey Haslam was serving as a sort of coproducer on the sessions being done at the Head Sound Studio in Ypsilanti, Michigan. The band had already done some recording with Haslam at the Landsdown Studio in England on their recent European tour. Out of those sessions came a tough rocking track titled "Sister Anne," penned by Fred Smith. Sensing that this might be their last chance, the band was making the decisions on the selection of the music and the way it would be recorded. Wayne Kramer commented, "You have to look at the larger context of our band learning the process of making records, learning as we went, with no guidelines."[107] "Sister Anne" would be included on the new LP, to be titled *High Time.*

While the MC5 were attempting to put the fire back in their music, Grand Funk Railroad was enjoying amazing success on the national front. The group's second album, *Grand Funk,* released at the end of 1969, had gone gold, and Terry Knight's nonstop promotions kept increasing the band's visibility. GFR's success came despite bad coverage from much of the national press. Don Brewer said, "Terry's way of promoting us was to piss everybody off, bad press, good press, it didn't make any difference."[108] Knight tried to promote the band "too good to speak to the press." If the press needed to know anything, they would have to speak with Terry. "The press really hated that whole thing, that whole approach," said Grand Funk's drummer. "So every chance they had to blast us, they did."[109]

In the summer of 1970, GFR released their third LP, *Closer To Home.* Terry Knight arranged for a huge billboard of Mark, Don, and Mel to go up in Times Square. According to Knight, "the billboard was 120 feet high and two city blocks long." It cost him one hundred thousand dollars, which was eventually reimbursed by Capitol.[110] The standout track on the album was "I'm Your Captain," also known as "Closer To Home," to which Terry Knight had added the Cleveland Symphony Orchestra to the mix. Panned by critics, the album was loved by fans, who seemed to like everything about Grand Funk Railroad. "Something about the overwhelming simplicity of the music hit the audience," wrote critic Robert Christgau. "Something about Farner's presence—striding the stage gracefully, his compact torso gleaming with sweat, his gorgeous auburn hair swinging and shimmering beneath the lights—inspired countless mid-adolescent males to spread the word."[111]

Although they were becoming a famous national act, an article in the May 17, 1970, edition of the *Detroit Free Press* stated, "Ironically, their hometown has yet to discover them," and that the "$1 million they'll earn in 1970 will be for music made everywhere in the world but Michigan."[112] Mark Farner felt that their lack of popularity in Michigan was the result of all those years playing as the Pack: "We had to go prove to the rest of the world who we were and then we would be accepted in our hometown."[113]

While Terry Knight carefully orchestrated every move for Grand Funk, there was no one looking out for the MC5. Since John Sinclair's departure, John Landau and Danny Fields had served as pseudomanagers. Then Fields had set the group up with Dee Anthony, who worked closely with Frank Barsalona of Premier Talent, the biggest booking agent in the country. "That didn't work for a variety of reasons," recalls Dennis Thompson. "The collective personality of the band was too difficult for Dee Anthony to handle. He liked handling all those English bands like King Crimson and whatever. At the same time, because we didn't have strong management, Atlantic Records wasn't giving us much in the way of finances for promotion. So after a while, here we are back on our own again."[114]

The business side of the Detroit music scene continued to tighten up. Russ Gibb had gone into a partnership with Punch Andrews at the newly opened Birmingham Palladium at 136 Brownell. The fifteen-hundred-person club was originally known as the Birmingham-Bloomfield Teen Center, and later as the Village Pub. Punch's own acts, Bob Seger and SRC, played on opening night, November 7, 1970.[115] Gibb's former venue, the Grande Ballroom, reopened under new management on December 31 and closed again soon after.[116]

Dave Leone's Diversified Management Associates had recently become the exclusive booking agents for the MC5, Amboy Dukes, Brownsville Station, Stooges, Savage Grace, and Früt. They were also representing two transplants to the Detroit music scene: Alice Cooper and Parliament/Funkadelic.

Although Alice Cooper was the name of a band, not an individual, it was lead singer Vincent Furnier who was becoming identified as "Alice." A native Detroiter, Furnier was born on February 4, 1948, the son of a minister. From an early age, Furnier suffered from bronchial asthma. In the interest of his health, his family relocated to Phoenix when he was ten. He grew up in the typical suburbs and became a high school track star.[117] By the end of high school, Furnier had developed a serious interest in music. He played in local Phoenix bands such as the Earwigs, the Spiders, and the Nazz, the latter of which turned out to have the same name as a band led by Todd Rungren. In a search for a new moniker, the band settled on Alice Cooper, after a seventeenth-century witch.[118] The band included Michael Bruce on guitar and keyboards, Glen Buxton on guitar, Dennis Dunaway on bass, and Neil Smith on drums.

After departing Phoenix for Los Angeles, the band hooked up with Frank Zappa, who had seen them open for the Doors. Vincent Furnier recalled that although the band "identified" with Zappa, they were more "affected" than "influenced" by him. "We understood that there was someone thinking the same way and so when we got together with him it worked perfectly."[119]

Alice Cooper recorded two albums for Zappa's Straight label. But the mix of hard rock and psychedelia on the band's early releases did not sell well. After being well received at several Michigan rock concerts, they decided to make a move to Furnier's hometown, attracted by Detroit's reputation as a hard rock haven.[120]

In September 1969, several months before making a permanent move to the Motor City, Alice Cooper performed at the Toronto Rock 'n' Roll Revival with John Lennon's Plastic Ono Band and the Doors. While the Cooper band was playing, someone threw a live chicken on stage. Thinking that it would fly, Alice tossed it in the air. Instead it fell into the audience, where it was promptly torn to pieces and tossed back on stage. By the time the story made the papers, rumors were spreading that Alice had ripped the head off the chicken and drunk its blood. News of this bizarre happening spread across the country, adding to the group's already strange reputation.[121]

According to Furnier, "the sex and violence of TV and the movies" was the "heart" of the Alice Cooper band. "We weren't brought up under a blues influence. We were brought up under an electronics influence. You just let your lower self go, and then it takes on all these aspects of the society—the city with horns blowing, the people yelling things at each other, and the all-in-all violence and chaos of the city. Put that on stage with music, and that's what this is."[122]

After relocating to the Motor City in 1970, Alice Cooper quickly found a home along side other bands performing in the countless clubs frequented by the city's music-hungry youth culture. "Detroit understood us, totally," recalled Furnier. "The first gig we played was with the Stooges and the MC5 and we fit like the missing piece of a puzzle."[123]

Alice Cooper was totally accepted as a "Detroit band." "It was the best audience in the world," recalled the singer years later. "In any other city, people went home from their work to put on their Levi's and black leather jackets for a concert. In Detroit, they came from work like that."[124] Detroit audiences got into Alice Cooper's theatrical shock rock. The band appeared on stage wearing eyelashes and thick makeup, skintight leotards, leather microskirts, and marquis de Sade riding boots. Furnier would shock the crowd by appearing with a boa constrictor wrapped around him. Their stage act also featured a gallows where the singer would suffer a mock execution. Alice Cooper: "We like reactions. A reaction is walking out on us, a reaction is throwing tomatoes at the stage. Reactions are applauding, passing out or throwing up. I don't care how they react, as long as they react."[125]

It was, however, a Top 40 single that moved Alice Cooper from Detroit cult act to national recording status. Rosalie Trombley, music director at influential market leader CKLW, scheduled regular—if brief—meetings with promotional representatives from the various record companies. They were given a few minutes each to pitch their latest releases, and to tell Rosalie just why she should be playing their new record rather than someone else's. There were only thirty records plus a "hitbound" release on the station's playlist each week. "Rosalie had a feel for the street retailers and would always be loaded with information on how product was doing," recalls Tom Gelardi, who was the Capitol Records rep in Detroit. "It was no use bullshitting her. If you didn't have an accurate and honest story to tell, you were better off not even talking about records."[126]

One day, Warner Brothers rep Dave Ursel showed up in Rosalie's office saying that Warner Brothers "had a 45 out on Alice Cooper." Trombley was more than familiar with the name. "That's all you heard around at that time: 'Alice Cooper, Alice Cooper, Alice Cooper,'" recalls the former CKLW music director. "I told Dave, 'I want to hear this damn record. I've heard so much about him,' because I had my son at home who was bugging me, and there were transcription operators at the station who were into a 'Whoa man . . . you gotta listen to WABX' type of thing. I also wanted to be able to use a piece of product that they [WABX] were playing and making noise with."[127]

The record was "Eighteen," and Rosalie was surprised when she heard it. "I said 'Wow!' Then I took the record off the turntable, and Dave Ursel asked if I liked it. Well, at the time we were just getting into this Canadian content thing, and when I took it off the turntable I saw Jack Richardson's name listed as producer. He was a Canadian. I told Dave that in fact I loved the record, and I was loving it more after seeing that it would qualify for Canadian content. We ended up putting the record on the air that day. The next morning when I came in, when I checked the hitline and the records that were requested, "Eighteen" was already number 3 on the phones! I'm not saying I wouldn't have played the record, probably would have, but that's how it got the immediate attention it did."[128]

By Friday of that week, Rosalie received a phone call from Jack Richardson in Toronto thanking her for playing his record. Rosalie Trombley: "I told Jack, 'Yeah, it's huge! Good grief, it's really going to be a big record.' He said, 'I understand you're using it as a Canadian content record.' I said, 'Yeah, well, you produced it!' He said, 'Yes, I produced it but not in Canada.' I told him, 'Well, there's not anything I can do about that now. I'm playing a hit record and I'm staying with it, I'll just unqualify it.'"[129]

Powered by CKLW's fifty thousand watts, "Eighteen" became a top 10 hit in Detroit, reaching number 7 at Rosalie's station and charting even higher at competitor WKNR, where it went to number 5. The record spent eight weeks in the national Top 40, cresting at number 21 in March 1971, setting the stage for Alice Cooper's emergence as a major national act.

After Alice Cooper, the newest, hippest thing happening on the Detroit music scene in 1970 was Parliament/Funkadelic, a wildly dressed, flamboyant twin-group led by George Clinton. The band found its inspiration in the soul and psychedelic musical trail blazed by Jimi Hendrix as well as Sly and the Family Stone.

George Clinton was born in an outhouse in Kannapolis, North Carolina, July 22, 1941, and moved to Newark, New Jersey, with his mother and eight siblings. By 1956 he was dividing his time between membership in a street gang called the Outlaws and his job as a hairdresser at the Uptown Tonsorial Parlor in Plainfield, New Jersey. It was in the back room of that barbershop that Clinton and friends Calvin Simon, Grady Thomas, and Clarence "Fuzzy" Haskins started singing together and formed a typical 1950s doo-wop group called the Parliaments.[130]

In 1963, after struggling for several years with limited success, Clinton convinced the other members to relocate to Detroit, home of the fledgling Motown record company. After hanging around the label's offices on West Grand Boulevard, singing for anyone who would listen, they attracted the attention of Martha Reeves. She arranged an audition, and Motown signed them to a contract. But unlike groups such as the Temptations and the Four Tops before them, this was not for the Parliaments a happy ending. After three hitless years, the group departed the label.[131]

In 1967 the group signed a new recording contract with Revilot records, a small local label owned and operated by LeBaron Taylor, the afternoon disc jockey on R & B station WJLB-AM. Taylor also happened to be the Parliaments' manager. In June 1967, the group exploded on the charts of the local R & B and Top 40 stations with their first Revilot release, "(I Wanna) Testify." The hard-edged soulful track with a gospel bent seemed tailored to Detroit tastes. The record topped the local soul music surveys and also reached number 1 on pop music station WKNR the week of June 6. Then it began to break nationally, cresting at number 5 on the R & B charts and number 20 pop in early August.

After making local TV appearances, including one on Robin Seymour's *Swingin' Time* on channel 9, the Parliaments were booked into New York's famed Apollo Theater. Like most other contemporary R & B groups, they were dressed in matching suits and sported processed hair. They attempted to perform slick routines such as those perfected by the Temptations. "We only had half a routine," recalled Clinton. "We would always get carried away somewhere in the song and forget about the routine."[132]

The success of "Testify" should have provided a springboard for the Parliaments. Instead, things came grinding to a halt. They followed with a few less successful releases, and then they began arguing with LeBaron Taylor over missed royalty payments. The Parliaments, however, remained tied to a contract with Revilot.[133]

By 1969, with the royalty issues still not resolved, George Clinton took the Parliaments' backup band, the Funkadelics, and signed them to Detroit's Westbound Records, recently founded by Armen Boladian, one of Detroit's most successful record promotion reps. Clinton signed on as their producer.[134] Funkadelic was led by guitarist Billy Nelson, who had been playing behind the Parliaments since their old New Jersey days. In the new formation, Nelson moved to bass, and Eddie Hazel became lead guitar. Other members included drummer Tiki Fulwood, guitarist Tawl Ross, and organist Mickey Atkins. The band's first album, *Funkadelic,* was released in early 1970, and the single "I'll Bet You" became a local top 10 hit after Rosalie Trombley added it to the playlist at CKLW. Other cuts included "Mommy, What's a Funkadelic?" "Music for My Mother," and the eight minute blues-rock track "Good Ole Funky Music." The songs provided a gritty, urban soundtrack for the 1970s. Funkadelic also broke new ground as a soul act by appearing at gigs with Detroit hard rockers, such as the MC5 and the Stooges.[135]

As Funkadelic was breaking on the charts, Clinton won back the rights to the Parliaments name. After dropping the *s*, Parliament signed their own record deal with Holland-Dozier-Holland's Invictus label, home to Chairman of the Board ("Give Me Just a Little More Time") and Freda Payne ("Band of Gold"). Parliament and Funkadelic began appearing together, and musicians and singers crossed back and forth between the two entities. Gone were the slick suits—in were crazy costumes. George might come on stage wearing an Indian headdress, while Grady appeared as a genie, and Calvin wore a pointed wizard's hat. Jim Bugnel of the Flaming Ember recalls a conversation he had with George Clinton one night at the 20 Grand: "We knew George pretty well at the time, and he says to us, 'I'm gonna form a new group and we're gonna rehearse for six months and you're not going to hear from me until then.' He says, 'And when we come back, we're gonna *blow* the music scene away.' He sure did. You couldn't follow that act."[136]

The first Parliament album, *Osmium,* released in late 1970 was a musical quilt of gospel-rock, some county-western hooks, and some "sleazy, greasy funk." George Clinton said of his two bands, "Funkadelic was the guitar and rock side and Parliament was for the singers and the horns, but stuff was always crawling over to the other side—and it was really about makin' sure we had two paychecks coming in."[137]

# 27. The Big Bust

Toward the end of 1970, having been transferred back from Marquette, John Sinclair surveyed the post-Woodstock scene from his cell at Jackson State Prison. He and other members of the White Panthers decided on a change in identity to something less threatening and more inclusive. "We wanted to 'demilitarize,'" says Pun Plamondon.[1] Sinclair thought they should become the "Woodstock People's Party." But recent events such as the shootings at Kent State, the murder and beatings at Altamont, and the continued oppression from the Nixon administration had already cast a pall over the memories of "three days of peace and love" at Yasgur's Farm. In a letter sent to his brother in early 1971, David Sinclair wrote: "We're not feeling very Woodstocky out here."[2] On May 1, the White Panthers dissolved and were replaced by the "Rainbow People's Party," Plamondon's name of choice. John Sinclair remained imprisoned, with seven and a half years to go.

In July 1971, Atlantic released the MC5's new album, *High Time*. Fred "Sonic" Smith made his growth as a songwriter evident through his contribution of four of the album's eight lengthy cuts. Dennis Thompson wrote "Gotta Keep Movin'" with Fred to "show off Fred's ability to play thirty-second notes." Thompson says that *High Time* was the "best record" the band ever made. "We got a good sound, we were happy with our sound on the third album and we were happy with the material, and it is by far the best work we have ever done."[3] Despite the strong material and outstanding production, Thompson says, the band was still not getting support from the record company, which was "threatening to drop" them.

In a September 1971 *Rolling Stone* review, Lenny Kaye wrote: "It seems almost too perfectly ironic that now, at a time in their career when most people have written them off as either dead or dying, the MC5 should power back into action with the first record that comes close to telling the tale of their legendary reputation and attendant charisma."4 Although commenting that *High Time* was not "a perfect album," Kaye cited "Sister Anne" as a "top flight piece of work in the old tradition." He also singled out "Baby Won't Ya" for its "rollicking choruses and guitar breaks," and commented on how "strong" Rob Tyner's voice sounded. Despite the positive review, *High Time* failed to chart, leaving the MC5 without a commercial record or record label, as Atlantic released the band from its contract. "We'd alienated two different factions of our audience," commented Dennis Thompson. "The industry didn't like us, the kids didn't know what to think about [us]."5 Concerning the MC5, writer and fan Dave Marsh said: "They were the best band any of us had seen. When they didn't conquer the world, it was very confusing."6

Meanwhile, Grand Funk Railroad were the conquering rock heroes in the summer of 1971. A live album released in November 1970 had climbed to number 5, and in April 1971, the *Survival* album went to number 6. All five of their albums had been certified gold. Later that month, the hometown Detroit audience had finally come around, buying twelve thousand tickets for Grand Funk Railroad's concert at Cobo Hall.7 Terry Knight then booked the band to play a concert at Shea Stadium in New York on July 9, and all fifty-five thousand seats went so quickly that the band set a new sales record—breaking the one established by the Beatles in 1966.[8] "They were a good rockin' band," says Dennis Thompson. "There was a little bit of bitterness and resentment on our part because they were sucking up our audience. I mean, we're having all these hassles with the police and we're shooting ourselves in the fuckin' feet, and Grand Funk's getting what we wanted all along, which was to be a big-time huge touring band. See, they didn't have a political profile—they just picked up the Detroit high-energy act that we started. It was a smart move."9

Michael Davis shares some of Thompson's bitterness, but at the same time says that the guys in Grand Funk were "pretty good players, pretty good musicians": "They did this boogie thing, they had that boogie sound, and they could go and just kind of jam and pull it off. The people of Detroit who had seen the MC5 knew that what they were doing was just a shadow, that it was nothing compared to what the MC5 was doing. But we had pretty much crossed the line, too much an enemy of our own ambitions. I guess because what we had talked about doing and then what we wound up having to do, it didn't hold water. It was empty."[10]

Midway through 1971, the Stooges finally had material ready for their third Elektra LP, tentatively titled *Raw Power*. Danny Fields had replaced Jim Silver as the band's manager, although he was operating long distance from New York. Dave Alexander was gone too. To ward off his fears of playing in front of such a large crowd at the Goose Lake festival, he had downed a pint of Kessler, smoked a bunch of pot, and taken some downers. When the band came onstage, he couldn't remember any of the songs. The band played on, but at the conclusion a "furious" Iggy fired him.[11]

For their part, Iggy and Scott Asheton had come to embrace heroin to the point that it was practically supplanting their music. Scott Asheton's apartment in the Fun House had become the official "shooting gallery." Ron Asheton, who remained clean, recalled that there used to be "blood dripping from the TV room ceiling after the guys would clear their syringes."[12] Iggy was so consumed by heroin that he moved from the Fun House into the University Towers in Ann Arbor, where it would be easier for him to buy and sell drugs. The band was spending virtually every dollar it made on heroin.

In the middle of the drug chaos, Danny Fields put a call through to Bill Harvey at Elektra, reminding him that it was time to "pick up the option" on the Stooges' third album. The two flew to Ann Arbor so Harvey could hear the band play their new songs. Ron Asheton gave Harvey earplugs to wear during the audition. Danny Fields was more than pleased with what he heard, but after returning to their motel Bill Harvey told him: "Frankly, I heard nothing at all."[13] Fields was taken aback, believing that *Raw Power* was "genius" and that the track "Search and Destroy" was "one of the greatest rock & roll songs of all time."[14] It may well have been, but Harvey felt the material was not commercial enough. The Stooges' first two albums had sold poorly and to Bill Harvey *Raw*

*Power* sounded like more of the same. In the end, his opinion was what mattered, and Elektra dropped the Stooges. Iggy and Scott could now devote 100 percent of their time to drugs. A few months later Danny Fields quit, saying he "couldn't handle it."[15]

Michigan legend Bob Seger was also feeling a great deal of frustration midway through 1971. After finally scoring a top 20 national hit with "Ramblin' Gamblin' Man," by the spring of 1969 Seger's career had quickly returned to the old familiar pattern. The follow-up, "Ivory," had reached number 13 on the Detroit charts, but had stalled at number 97 in *Billboard*. His next single, "Noah," came out in July and rose quickly to number 14 in the Motor City. It failed to chart nationally. For a short time, Bob Seger contemplated leaving the music behind and enrolling in college to study criminology.[16] Instead he returned to the road. In April 1970, he released "Lucifer" and made a predictable sprint up the Detroit charts, cresting at number 10. Nationally it could do no better than number 84.

The Bob Seger System continued to play wherever they could book a gig. "We would play Kentucky, Tennessee, and Ohio, we'd go down to Florida and play. I always saw that we had something," Seger recalled. "Whenever we'd play Florida, which was my only decent market besides Detroit, we'd drive down there in twenty-four hours and play without rest."[17] On one return trip, Seger himself drove twenty-five straight hours from Miami to Grosse Pointe, Michigan.

His third Capitol LP, *Mongrel*, received some good reviews and went to number 171 on *Billboard's* album chart. According to Bob, that album was "very big" for about six months in Michigan. It also sold well in Florida: "We got something like $15,000 a night there, which was ridiculous for us in those days, because we'd go into Georgia or some place the next night and make $500 tops. And the club owner probably lost money on us at that price."[18]

Released in the spring of 1971, "Lookin' Back" was a great rock single, chiding conservatives for not being open to new ideas. Detroit made it a number 3 smash hit. The rest of the country hardly took notice, as it barely made the top 100, clocking in at number 96.

By the summer of 1971 Bob Seger felt he needed to make a change. As he owed Capitol one last album in order to fulfill his contract, he decided to switch gears and record an all-acoustic collection of introspective songs. "Brand New Morning" would be the title. "Everyone has down periods," commented the veteran rocker. "The acoustic album was the depths for me."[19] Alone after a failed marriage, and seemingly unable to advance his career, Seger "felt kind of defeated" and without direction: "I knew I wanted to play music, I just needed time to figure on how to go about it again."[20]

As for the Frost, it was all over in 1971. The distribution and promotion problems that the group had experienced with their first album, *Frost Music,* in early 1969 had continued. Their second album, *Rock and Roll Music*—half of which they recorded live at the Grande Ballroom—stalled at number 148 in *Billboard,* and a third album, *Through the Eyes of Love,* failed to break outside of Michigan. Despite live concert successes on the West Coast, in Canada, New England, and throughout the Midwest, Wagner says that there was never an ample supply of records in the stores outside of Michigan. Vanguard Records would not take the financial risks involved in breaking the band nationally.[21]

Dick Wagner tried to bring in someone from New York to manage the band, but the other members didn't care for him. Instead, Wagner decided to call it quits. For over three years Frost had been one of the biggest draws in Michigan. Now they were no more.

The band fronted by Mitch Ryder also continued to struggle. After the revamped Detroit Wheels tour of the South in the spring of 1970, the group's lineup and name—now simply Detroit—were revised. In addition to Mitch on vocals and Johnny Bee on drums and vocals, Steve Hunter remained as lead guitar. The rest of the band included W. R. Cooke on bass and vocals, Dirty Ed on congas and tambourines, Bret Tuggle on guitar, and Harry Phillips on keyboards. "It was a rough street band," recalls Ryder. "Two of the members were bikers, and there were a lot of drugs, a lot of hard living—the band lived their image."[22]

One of Detroit's earliest gigs was in Kelawna, British Columbia, near Vancouver, in July 1970. They did not take the town by storm. Possibly due to a lack of advertising, the local newspaper reported that only three hundred people had seen the band over three days. Detroit's manager, Barry Kramer, expected to lose ten thousand dollars, which, according to Mitch at the time, "would have been the best [payday] in a long time."[23]

One thing that Mitch had to deal with was having to answer fans who wanted to know why he didn't do more of the old songs: "I tried to explain to them that this isn't the Detroit Wheels—it's Detroit. It's not Mitch Ryder and Detroit—it's a great rock and roll band, and I happen to be their singer."[24]

Meanwhile, the band had secured a recording contract with Paramount and headed to the RCA studios in Chicago to begin sessions for a new album, most of which Mitch and Johnny had written. After recording the first half in Chicago, the band moved to the Manta Sound Studios in Toronto to complete the project under producer Bob Ezrin. The LP, titled *Detroit,* came out in mid-1971.[25] Paramount released "Long Neck Goose" as the first single, but the album's standout track was the Lou Reed composition "Rock 'n' Roll," done first by the Velvet Underground. Steve Hunter opened Detroit's version with a ferocious guitar riff, while Johnny Bee kept hard time on a cowbell and Mitch Ryder sang about the days when you could still "dance to a rock and roll station, and it was *all right.*" After hearing the version by Detroit, Lou Reed commented: "That's the way it was *supposed* to sound."[26]

Despite positive reviews, hopes of returning to the days when Mitch and the Wheels had been the hottest rockers in America were dashed. The *Detroit* album was only a moderate commercial hit, staying for six weeks on the national charts, where it peaked at number 176. The single "Rock 'n' Roll" reached number 12 on the Detroit charts but failed to make the national Top 40. It did however, receive heavy play on FM progressive radio.

The band continued a grueling schedule of less than prestigious gigs. Following a week playing in a Boston bar, the musicians asked for their pay and received their answer from the barrel of a shotgun instead. Then they arrived at what they thought was going to be a festival in Indianapolis, only to find a grubby little racetrack with a flatbed truck for a stage. There had been a mini-riot the day before during a free concert by the Guess Who, and now there were more police and sheriff's deputies on hand than audience members, who numbered roughly twenty-five.[27]

Looking out over the small, static crowd, Mitch reached for the microphone: "Hello Indianapolis, I'm Mitch Ryder and this is Detroit. We'd like to see you dance." Johnny Bee kicked in on the drums as the band fired up "It Ain't Easy." Within a few minutes cops were tapping their feet and people were starting to move. A girl jumped on stage and yelled: "C'mon everybody, *dance!*"[28] By the time Mitch ripped into "Devil With the Blue Dress On," no one in the band was focusing on the size of the audience. The small crowd was there to rock 'n' roll, and everything *was* just all right.

In the late summer of 1971, the Grande Ballroom opened its doors for a series of "People's Ballroom" benefit concerts on behalf of the still imprisoned John Sinclair. The MC5, Frijid Pink, the Up, Detroit featuring Mitch Ryder, and Third Power were some of the performing acts. A year earlier, the Up had released a blistering single called "Just Like an Aborigine." Their current release was a rallying cry for John Sinclair, titled "Free John."

On December 10, 1971, Leni Sinclair and David Sinclair, John's brother, joined with promoter Pete Andrews to stage a major media event, a "Free John Sinclair" benefit concert at the Crisler Arena on the University of Michigan campus. Some fifteen thousand people paid three dollars each to attend the ten-hour show featuring Stevie Wonder, Bob Seger, and other top Detroit talent, plus a special appearance by John Lennon and Yoko Ono. As a huge cloud of marijuana smoke floated overhead, poet Allen Ginsberg opened the event with a reading of his own lines: "Dear John Sinclair, we pray you'll leave your jail box."[29] Abbie Hoffman, Black Panther Bobby Seale, and yippie Jerry Rubin were also on hand for rousing antiestablishment speeches. Rubin told the crowd: "This rally's publicity will make it ridiculous to keep Sinclair in jail for smoking a flower."[30]

Unbeknownst to prison officials, John Sinclair was even heard over the loudspeakers by way of a telephone hookup direct from Jackson Prison. An emotional Sinclair could be heard choking up as he spoke with his wife Leni and their four-year-old daughter,

Sunny. "I'm totally wiped out. I don't know what to say," he told the rally.[31]

Stevie Wonder sang "Heaven Help Us All" and then dedicated "Somebody's Watching You" to all the undercover agents in the audience.

It was a little past 3:00 A.M. when John and Yoko finally appeared on stage for a twenty-minute acoustic set that included four recently composed songs. Lennon closed the show with one titled "John Sinclair," which lamented the harsh sentence handed down. "They gave him ten for two, what else can the bastards do?" he sang. "Let him be, set him free. Let him be like you and me." At three-thirty in the morning, the inspired audience marched out of the arena chanting: "Free John Sinclair."[32]

Leni Sinclair had been so busy she didn't have a chance to meet the Lennons until after the show: "I had two children and I was sitting at the literature table trying to sell posters. You know, we didn't get any money out of the thing. After it was over we were as broke as ever."[33] Transportation and arena rental costs had eaten up a large portion of the estimated forty-five thousand dollars in ticket sales, leaving twenty-eight thousand to help pay Sinclair's legal fees.

But all the publicity from the event paid off. Only three days later, following two and a half years behind bars, John Sinclair was released from Jackson Prison, his bond finally granted.[34] During an earlier incarceration, local police had cut off most of Sinclair's long hair. This time, as a result of legal action, John had prevented authorities from doing it again. As he stepped into a room just outside his cellblock, he "swept his family up in his arms," including two-year-old Celia, born during his time away. Leni Sinclair says, "We were just as dumbfounded as when he went in—'Wow! . . . we can't believe it.' But there he was, as quickly out as he was in."[35]

After hugging his mother and his brother David, John Sinclair turned to the attending press, telling them that what he had gone through had been a "burden but worth it if it works." He had been a "political prisoner," he said, but would "do it again" if it led to the legalization of marijuana laws. He thanked his wife, John Lennon, and the fifteen thousand people at Crisler Arena, saying that "the people made 'em let me out." When a reporter asked whether the prison experience had changed his attitude toward marijuana, Sinclair shot back: "I'm gonna smoke some joints."[36] His attorney, Dennis Hayes, could be heard sighing: "Oh for chrissake, here we go again." As Sinclair and his family drove off in the same 1960 Bentley limousine that had been used by the Lennons, Sinclair's mother was heard cautioning her son, calling out, "Take it easy now!"[37]

In March 1972, the Michigan Supreme Court overturned John Sinclair's conviction and ruled unconstitutional the state's strict marijuana law that had put him behind bars. The new laws would go into effect on April 1. In the meantime, there was a three-week grace period in which pot smokers could enjoy their favorite pastime without threat of arrest.[38] According to Sinclair, they had "exerted pressure to change the laws and in Ann Arbor marijuana possession was penalized with a five dollar ticket."[39] In addition, a lawsuit filed by the White Panthers against the federal government resulted in the Supreme Court's ruling, on June 19, 1972, that the practice of wiretapping a person without first obtaining a warrant from a judge would no longer be allowed.[40] The illegal wiretapping of Pun Plamondon's telephone had prompted the government to indict Plamondon, Sinclair, and Jack Forest two and a half years earlier.

After his release from prison, John Sinclair took over as chairman of the Rainbow People's Party. Although Sinclair resumed a "frantic pace" as a "concert promoter, politico-cultural activist and tireless propagandist," he missed managing a band. The Up was still around and carrying the revolutionary banner, but John's brother David was managing them. Sinclair joined David and SRC manager-promoter Pete Andrews to form a new production and management company as an offshoot of the Rainbow People's Party. It was going to be called Rainbow Multi-Media. At the same time in the spring of 1972, Detroit, featuring Mitch Ryder, parted company with Barry Kramer, citing business differences. Ryder asked John to take over management of Detroit.[41] Although Ryder had not been part of the political-cultural scene in Michigan during the late sixties, he had since embraced it, hanging out in Ann Arbor and becoming involved with the Committee to Free John

Sinclair. John decided to make Mitch and the band the company's "first working project."[42]

At the time, John Sinclair and the counterculture community were still looking forward to ending the war in Vietnam, ensuring the success of the black liberation movement, bringing about the legalization of marijuana, and removing Richard Nixon from the presidency. Aside from involving Mitch and the band in these political causes and getting them a gig at the April 1972 "Get Out the Vote Rally" for the Ann Arbor city council elections, nothing much happened. Detroit never got a shot at a second album. "You could see the end coming," says Johnny Bee. "Things had gotten real ugly where the band was concerned."[43]

With frequent in-fighting and Mitch worried about a possible throat operation, the dream of a major comeback fell apart. Toward the end of the year, Mitch dropped out. The band carried on with little success, a little while longer with Rusty Day, recently ousted from the Amboy Dukes, taking over vocals. After Detroit, Ryder picked up a few bucks singing at local gigs with friends in what they called the Knock Down, Drag Out Party Band. A few months later a disillusioned Mitch Ryder packed up his belongings and moved to Denver, Colorado, where he went to work in a warehouse.

The Amboy Dukes were also running out of steam. "There never was a break-up of the Amboy Dukes," recalled Ted Nugent. "It just got to be such a revolving door mentality with the musicians."[44] According to Ted, the big problem was drugs: "They were *all* stoned."[45] Nugent also cited attitude problems: "A lot of our band members became frustrated because we weren't making much progress and we played a lot of gigs. We would play up to two-hundred gigs a year."[46]

Nugent had fired John Drake "because he wouldn't conform to rehearsal schedules or to the vocal styles within the musical progress of the band." Steve Farmer was let go because Ted felt he was "so high and so irresponsible."[47] Greg Arama, who played the signature bass line on "Journey to the Center of the Mind," went on a heroin journey of his own and Ted wouldn't let him come back.

Rusty Day, the 350-pound singer who replaced John Drake, had been somewhat of a Detroit legend while fronting his R & B band, Rusty Day and the Midnighters. Day recorded a modest local hit called "I Gotta Move" on the Maltese label in 1967. Nugent had "admired Day's status and vocal capabilities."[48] But the singer never really tapped his potential in the Amboy Dukes. He sang on the Duke's third LP, *Migrations,* and its follow-up, *Marriage on the Rocks.* Neither album was successful. Nugent said that Day "ended up doing so many drugs, I had to throw him out of the band as well."[49] Andy Solomon took over vocals.

By the release of 1971's *Survival of the Fittest,* recorded live at the Eastown Theatre, the band was being billed as Ted Nugent and the Amboy Dukes, but only Nugent had survived from the original lineup. Besides acting as road manager, Ted was also booking the band, maintaining the equipment, handling the hotels, and keeping the ledgers. It all began to take its toll. After complaining of constant "muscle spasms in the ass," he decided to take some time off, and the last incarnation of the Amboy Dukes came to an end.[50] The final album reached number 129 in *Billboard.*

After a meteoric rise, Frijid Pink was spiraling down. Although their second album, *Defrosted,* hadn't sold as well as the first, bookings had remained strong and the LP had done better in Europe. But the band was experiencing problems from within. "It had to do with management and personnel clashes," says original drummer Richard Stevers. "I thought things were going really smooth. Apparently we had a couple of others that did not. They thought they were the 'superstars' and Zach [bass player Tom Harris] and I were . . . just there. If these guys could have just kept their heads, we could have gone on for a few more years and made the big money, but that's not the way it worked out."[51]

As they were having little success in the states, the MC5 decided to turn their focus on Europe. Wayne Kramer says, "We had met Roan O'Rahilly at Phun City. He was an Irish [Republican] Army revolutionary working with the Irish struggle. He founded Radio Caroline. He was into film and arts, a producer. He wanted to save the MC5 and almost did. He tried to place us with a couple of new record companies and helped us get a house to live in England."[52]

Before the band started their first tour of the UK in 1972, Michael Davis fell by the wayside after failing to show up for a concert at the London School of Economics. "At that point in time I was so disenchanted with the whole MC5 thing. I didn't like anybody in the band anymore," admits Davis. "Everybody was on their own trips. We had no spirit as a group. It was such a burden to carry on this pseudopolitical torch, always having to defend ourselves. I got into the drug world on a more intense level, to where I had all the money I needed for drugs—all the drugs and all the money."53

When it came time to leave for Europe, Davis told the other band members to "go ahead," that he would buy his own ticket and meet them there. "When I arrived in London, I got busted at the gate," the bassist recalls. "I had some paraphernalia. They let me go, but I had to go back home and fly in again, so I missed the first concert."54 Dennis Thompson met Davis at the airport and let him know that "everybody's pissed." Davis says, "My response was to ask, 'Where's the dope?' Then we went to Chinatown and scored."55

Shortly thereafter, the band called a meeting and Davis learned that he was no longer in the MC5. "It was just the biggest relief in the world," says Davis. "I felt like a new person. I went back to the States and resumed my career as a drug addict."56 Meanwhile the band picked up Steve Moorhouse as a replacement bass player for the tour.

On Sunday February, 13, 1972, the MC5 played at the Fox in Croydon. Reports said that the stage was "too small," and the poor lighting wasn't worthy of the name. The gig was underadvertised, and there was every reason to doubt that any significant proportion of the audience knew who the MC5 were.57 Rob Tyner commented at the time: "If they don't know who we are now, they sure as hell will when we're through."58 Wayne Kramer came onstage dressed in a striped Lurex draped jacket, and in a review he was described as looking like "a nasty little rock and roll punk hoodlum." Fred Smith was wearing a skintight superhero costume in black and silver Lurex with SS emblazoned on the front and a silver cap and cowl. Tyner was described as looking like "a huge mouth rimmed with an immense puffball of Afro hair."59

A reviewer called them "masters of kinetic energy." But the

energy was rapidly draining out of the MC5, and as the weeks went by, the group began to disintegrate. In addition to the drug abuse, they were experiencing the financial strain of going through bankruptcy. Dennis Thompson says, "After we lost John [Sinclair], the rot started to set in, and the whole band, which had always experimented with drugs, was doing heroin a lot, especially Michael. We did it to numb ourselves. The government was after us, we didn't have a manager, the audience had turned against us. There was never a chance to repair ourselves. It was like being in a boxing match with Joe Frazier—you're up against the ropes taking shots."[60]

The MC5 played on through gigs in Cambridge and Liverpool. In March, they managed to lay down some tracks at the Herouville Castle studios, including the "pedal to the metal" car song "Thunder Express," which was not released. After a brief tour in France, they returned to the UK and played solo gigs in Lanchester, Scarborough, and Canterbury. In April the band came home for a short stay and then returned to England for a high-profile appearance at the "First Annual London Rock 'n' Roll Revival" at Wembley Stadium. The "5" were billed fourth, following Little Richard, Jerry Lee Lewis, and Chuck Berry.[61]

After returning to the States, the four remaining members of the MC5 held a meeting at Rob Tyner's house. Dennis Thompson announced that he did not wish to immediately go back on tour in Europe: "I had made a decision to go into a clinic and go into rehab. I wanted to get on the methadone program so in a few months I would be free and clear. I had tried cold turkey and it just didn't work. I said, 'Guys, just, let's wait on this tour, just let me clean up.' Instead of having the brains to say, 'Yeah, that's a good idea,' nobody said that. I said, 'I'm not goin' on this trip.' Then Rob, who only used grass, says, 'Dennis isn't going, then I'm not going.' Rob used to room with me. He knew I needed to clean up—it was a matter of life and death. It was a show of solidarity on Rob's part. He thought the others would say 'Okay, we'll wait a couple of months.' We wouldn't have broken up. I didn't want to quit the band, but they decided to go over—just the two of 'em! Wayne and Fred are gonna be the MC5! Well, that just didn't work, and they came home with their tails between their legs."[62]

According to Wayne Kramer, he and Fred, had "felt it was important to honor prior commitments."[63]

The MC5's last European tour was a disaster. Kramer says, "We had Derek Hughes on bass. We met our drummer in the dressing room the night of the gig. He didn't know who the MC5 were. We sucked. Fred and I were trying to sing, and we didn't even know the words to our own songs. It was terrible. We tried to play some songs that everybody would know, like old Chuck Berry stuff. Anything to get through the gig."[64] Despite bad reactions from the crowd, the MC2 and their pickup players trudged on. A Scandinavian promoter threatened to sue when he found out that Rob Tyner wasn't in the current lineup. There were angry confrontations and cancellations. Wayne and Fred returned home in November.[65]

On December 31, 1972, a promoter decided to get all five members of the MC5 back together for a New Year's Eve show, and reopened the Grande Ballroom, which had been closed for over a year. "It was nasty," recalls Michael Davis. "After all the shit that had gone down and the band had failed and broken up . . . and then had gone on to become ridiculous caricatures in attempts to survive. It was really pitiful. Still I was glad, because in my mind it brought some kind of closure to the whole deal. You know . . . 'One more time.'"[66]

Dennis Thompson recalls, "My best memory of that night is that 'I'm clean, I'm not high and I'm not likin' what I'm hearin.' There's no life to the music. The spiritual connection that we had is totally dissipated. There's maybe two hundred to four hundred people there. It's a failure as a draw. It was a futile fucking attempt to try and resurrect something that was unresurrectable at the time."[67]

"By that performance we were damaged and hurt people," testifies Wayne Kramer. "We were completely estranged from each other. Fred and I were the only two that had some communication, but even that was strained through drugs. It was a terrible show . . . we sucked. Memories of it are in grainy black and white. I felt we were a fraud, fakes. The only thing that mattered was heroin. Halfway through the show, I told Fred, 'I just can't play anymore.' I'd been paid up front, so I just left and went to a dope house."[68]

The Grande, which had been the scene of their "greatest triumph," had now become the scene of what Wayne Kramer calls a "pathetic last attempt," for which the band was paid five hundred dollars. "I guess you could look at the MC5 at that point as an allegory for what was happening in Detroit," says Kramer. "It went from being a boomtown to guns, heroin, and murder. An urban nightmare."[69]

There were many factors that brought an end to Detroit's explosive rock music scene. Dan Carlisle had begun to "sense a change" after Alice Cooper moved to the Motor City. "Alice became the hottest act in Detroit. He eclipsed the MC5, the Stooges, and everybody else. That was also the beginning of the glitter rock thing, when David Bowie and groups like Roxy Music became really big in Detroit. Here is a very bizarre band, Roxy, [that] sold out Cobo Hall in a working-class city and were still playing clubs in L.A. and New York, so you knew there had been a change in the audience. You could sense a shift."[70]

Again citing Goose Lake, Carlisle says that heavy heroin use took its toll on the local scene. "It was really getting bad. I remember seeing musicians making junk buys before playing. There were bands stealing equipment from each other. That kind of thing just wouldn't have happened a few years before. The whole scene had developed an air of danger."[71] According to Ron Asheton, "Once heroin was introduced into the picture, it was the beginning of the end." He recalled waking up everyday to find that "another piece of equipment had been taken and traded for spoon. A thousand dollar piano for a $40 spoon."[72]

"I felt like we had turned the corner on, you know . . . magic time," says Michael Davis of the MC5. "The coach had turned into a pumpkin. It was over man. We had all stayed out past twelve and anything good was over. The pattern in drugs had changed from smoking pot to smoking angel dust. Instead of LSD or mushrooms, people were taking Quaaludes or sleepers. It was like an epidemic. Instead of doing things for stimulus, the stimulants became crystal meth. To get laid back, instead of smoking weed, people were doing heroin."[73] Davis also says that at the time many of those still involved in the revolutionary movement believed that the "drugs of the capitalist pigs were being infiltrated into the counterculture to destroy it from within." Davis also felt that "the tone of the music was changing into something more dreary and plodding and not fun."74

"It was painfully obvious that the Detroit scene was dead," says Dennis Thompson. "It went from an atmosphere of hope and expectations, to one of fear and dread. The whole momentum was gone, it died. It literally just passed away."75

Third Power's Jem Targal says that along with hard drugs, alcohol played a part in finishing off the era: "Eighteen became the legal drinking age about that time and it changed the complexion of things in town, because all of the sudden, the young kids could go and drink. I remember Drew [Abbott] saying, 'I guess we're going to have to start playin' the bars.' . . . It was especially hard after being so spoiled, because we were right in the middle of that whole concert scene. Right at the end, when things were really slowing down, I started writing some of my best stuff and I kept thinking: boy, if we only had had another year, I think we could have made that jump to the next level. Just realizing that wasn't going to happen . . . it was sad."76

SRC suffered a similar fate, says Gary Quackenbush: "SRC was about as far from a bar band as you could ever imagine, but we found ourselves playing in them, so we knew it was sliding at that point."77

If drugs, alcohol, and changing musical tastes were not enough, bad management was also a major contributor to the destruction of Detroit's vibrant music scene. In addition to the Rationals, Frost, and several other bands, it finished off SRC, which played its last gig in January 1973. "The whole last year of that, we were without a manager. We did it all ourselves, and we were deep in debt," confides Gary Quackenbush. "We had to fire Pete [Andrews]. He was a lousy bookkeeper, and if it wasn't for the people he hired to help, we would have been in worse shape."78 In light of dwindling record sales, which the band partially blamed on Capitol Records, as well as on Pete Andrew's inability to deal effectively with the label, SRC "moved to get out" of their contract with Capitol. Then Gary Quackenbush, who'd been fighting with the rest of the group, got into a motorcycle accident. Ray Goodman replaced him on lead guitar. SRC's third and final LP for Capitol was *Traveler's Tale,* which they recorded entirely on an eight-track deck in the band's own studio. Gary Quackenbush returned to SRC's lineup after six months. Toward the end, the band performed under the name Blue Scepter.

At the same time, work opportunities were disappearing. "There was no club action," says Dan Carlisle, recalling the Detroit scene by late 1972.[79] Rising costs involved in promoting rock 'n' roll were rapidly leaving the smaller local promoters and local talent behind. The major booking agencies on the east and west coasts had been signing all the most popular bands. The prices they charged were far beyond what a small or medium-sized club could afford, as they required much higher guarantees and percentages of the gate. Agencies such as Premier out of New York or IFA had no interest in placing local talent on the same bill as their major acts. Being a thousand miles away, they knew nothing about local Michigan bands. And besides, they preferred to send along one of their own midlevel acts to open. Russ Gibb says, "It was called 'piggy-backing.' If a venue wanted to book a certain act, they would have to take another lesser band the promoter was handling as the opening act."[80]

Slowly but surely, most of the Detroit bands were disappearing from national headliner concerts staged at Cobo Hall, Olympia, and other large venues. Following Russ Gibb's departure, the Grande Ballroom had struggled on and off under various promoters and then ceased operations, unable to compete for the big-name groups. The Eastown Theatre shut down in the fall of 1971 for violating city health and safety codes. An investigation by the *Detroit Free Press* had described the theater's mezzanine as being "a veritable drug supermarket."[81]

Skyrocketing ticket prices forced kids to save their money for the major concerts, leaving them unable to patronize what small clubs were left. By the end of 1972, most were shuttered. The multiact rock festivals vanished, as fees for individual acts escalated and memories of Goose Lake lingered.

Soon many of Michigan's better midlevel bands called it quits. Things had come a long way from the days when Jeep Holland ran a thriving booking business out of his one-bedroom apartment in Ann Arbor, and Dave Leone was able to build a mini recording and performance empire from a VFW hall he dubbed the "Hideout." Rock 'n' roll had suddenly gone corporate. "Everyone was aware that the alternative culture we had been building was as sick as the culture it was supposedly an alternative to," wrote Dave Marsh in the pages of *Creem*.[82]

When Richard Nixon soundly defeated George McGovern in the November 1972 elections, the rock community's hunger for "revolution" began to wane. Rather than worrying about how to save the world, maturing longhairs were suddenly more concerned with the oil crisis and the inflation of the early 1970s, including rising gas prices. "Yeah, so what happened to the revolution? We got beat," offered John Sinclair. "And then we went home and took up our ploughshares, or typewriters or what-have-you. Licked our wounds and hoped that there weren't reprisals. Hoped they wouldn't come after us and pummel us some more, even though we weren't causing them any more problems."[83] "Things had definitely changed," says Pun Plamondon, who was released from prison in July 1972. "There was less brotherhood and more capitalism."[84]

Detroit took another blow when Motown Records, which had provided the rhythm of the city, packed up and left in June 1972. "One day we went to the studio and we were supposed to record," recalled Eddie Willis, one of the legendary Funk Brothers. "There was a big sign on the door, saying there won't be any work here today—Motown's movin' to Los Angeles."[85]

It would be simplistic and false to say that the Detroit rock music and counterculture scene came to an end at the stroke of midnight on one particular day. But the spirit, the pride, the community involvement, and the infrastructure that had nurtured it at its peak in the very late sixties was in a rapid decline. Within just a few years people would be able to look back on the years spanning from 1965 to 1972 and recognize an era gone by.

New bands would continue to form, although at a much slower pace. Some with veteran players, and some with those who were inspired by them. These groups, good as many were, however, would not be identified with the city's "classic" bands of the late sixties. The door to that club was closed and locked.

# Epilogue

**Ed "Punch" Andrews:** As the band-booking business consolidated in the early seventies, Andrews focused exclusively on managing the career of Bob Seger, which he continues to do today. In the nineties, on Seger's recommendation, Kid Rock signed with Andrews, who still calls his Birmingham-based business Hideout Productions, a link to the sixties.[1]

**Bob Bageris:** After the Eastown Theatre closed, Bageris went on to become the leading promoter of major rock concerts in Detroit. Helming his company, Bamboo Productions, he booked concerts by such artists as the Rolling Stones and Jefferson Airplane at Olympia Stadium, Cobo Hall, and other large venues throughout the Midwest. In 1975 he brought the Who to the Pontiac Silverdome for the stadium's first major concert. On April 1, 1985, Bob Bageris died at the age of thirty-seven, following a yearlong battle with a bone marrow disorder.[2]

**Harry Balk:** The former independent producer stayed on as A&R director at Motown until around 1977. He is retired and living in California, where he occasionally returns to the studio with a promising new talent.[3] Balk's former partner, Irv Micahnik, moved to New York in 1964 to manage Chubby Checker. Micahnik died in 1978.

**Hank Ballard:** In 1960, long after their ties to Detroit had been forgotten, Hank Ballard and the Midnighters came charging back on the pop charts with two Top 10 hits: "Finger Poppin' Time" and "Let's Go, Lets Go, Lets Go." Hank wrote "The Twist," which became a number one 1 hit twice for Chubby Checker. By the seventies Ballard was working as a single, sometimes touring with

James Brown. In 1999, Hank Ballard was inducted into the Rock and Roll Hall of Fame. He died on March 2, 2003, the victim of throat cancer.4

**Brownsville Station:** The party band led by Cub Koda scored a national hit when "Smokin' in the Boy's Room" hit number 3 in *Billboard* in December 1973. Koda remained active in the Detroit music scene as a solo performer and as a music journalist until his death on July 1, 2000.5

**Dan Carlisle:** One of the original announcers on "underground" radio station WABX and at WKNR-FM, Dan left Detroit in the mid-seventies. Stops along the way have included KLOS in Los Angeles, KSAN in San Francisco, and WNEW-FM in New York. He recently returned to KLOS in Los Angeles, a classic rock station.6

**George Clinton, Parliament/Funkadelic:** When the Detroit rock scene collapsed, Clinton's dual aggregations rolled on. Funkadelic albums were released on Detroit's Westbound Records through 1976. After Holland-Dozier-Holland's Invictus label folded, Clinton took his Parliament group to Casablanca Records, and in 1974 released *Up for the Down Stroke.* The title cut became a number 10 R & B single. It was followed by *Chocolate City.* Their next album, *The Clones of Dr. Funkenstein,* was a rather dark look into the future. Then, *Mothership Connection* launched the P-Funk era. Parliament earned gold records with 1976's "Tear the Roof Off the Sucker ('Give Up the Funk')" and 1978's "Flashlight." In the early eighties, the Clinton scene came crashing down amid infighting over rights and royalties. George released a few solo projects and did some producing. Around 1987, the emerging hip-hop scene tuned in on the P-Funk legacy. In the nineties Clinton reassembled his crew as the P-Funk All Stars and hit the road, performing three- and four-hour shows. In 1996 the whole Parliament-Funkadelic family was inducted into the Rock and Roll Hall of Fame. As of 2004, George Clinton and his band continue to tour.7

**Jamie Coe:** Although he was never able to fulfill his dream of becoming a national recording star, Jamie remained a popular entertainer in his hometown. During the seventies he appeared nightly in his own club, Jamie's, on Seven Mile Road. As of 2005 he continues to perform at his Jammer's club on Plymouth Road in Livonia.[8]

**Alice Cooper:** In 1972, the boys from Phoenix, who had successfully transformed themselves into a "Detroit band," made a hasty exit from the Motor City. They made Connecticut their new home base. In 1974, the Alice Cooper band released its final album, *Muscle of Love*. At that point, Vincent Furnier legally changed his name to Alice Cooper and embarked on a solo career, leaving behind the other band members.[9] Three of those players, Michael Bruce, Dennis Dunaway, and Neal Smith, started a new band in 1976 called Billion Dollar Babies. They released one unsuccessful album and then disbanded. Meanwhile, Alice Cooper (the singer) carried on without missing a beat. His 1975 solo release, *Welcome to My Nightmare*, featured Michigan guitar legends Dick Wagner and Steve Hunter, drummer Johnny Bee, and the rest of Lou Reed's former backing band. The LP included the hit single "Only Women Bleed." Although his stage show continued to evolve and singles such as "I Never Cry," "You and Me," and "How You Gonna See Me Now " scored high on the Top 40 charts, heavy drinking, weaker albums, and stage performance competition from a group called Kiss took their toll. Television appearances with the likes of Bob Hope also helped to chip away at Cooper's rock image in the late seventies. He rebounded in 1986 with noticeably improved material on the LP *Boa Constrictor*. In 1989, *Trash* was a big album, producing the hit single "Poison." Although record sales again fell off in the nineties, Cooper continues to tour, delivering the kind of live show that caught Detroit's attention back in the Eastown Theatre days. In 2003, he released the LP *Through the Eyes of Alice Cooper*.[10]

**Barry Kramer/*Creem* Magazine:** Although *Creem* had successfully transformed itself into a national magazine, it remained based in the Detroit area. Lester Bangs, Jaan Uhelzki, and Ben Edmonds pumped new blood into the writing staff in the seventies. Barry Kramer oversaw all aspects of the operation until his untimely death in 1981.[20] The magazine continued to publish until 1991, when dwindling circulation forced it out of business. New owners reactivated *Creem* in 2003. Dave Marsh, who coined the term "punk rock" in a 1971 *Creem* column, went on to write for publications as diverse as *Rolling Stone, Newsday,* and *Playboy.* He also authored two biographies on Bruce Springsteen as well as a book dedicated to the grunge classic "Louie, Louie."[21] In October 2004, *Kick Out the Jams! With Dave Marsh,* began airing on the Sirius Satellite Radio Network.

**The Funk Brothers:** In 1983, Allan Slutsky, a lifelong Motown fan from Philadelphia, read James Jamerson's obituary in *Rolling Stone,* which had been written by Detroit musician Marshall Crenshaw. It inspired Slutsky, who also happened to be a guitarist, writer, and producer to write a book about the musician's life. After *Standing in the Shadows of Motown* was published, Slutsky had the idea of searching out the remaining Funk Brothers and attempting to get a film about them produced. In November 2002, the motion picture *Standing in the Shadows of Motown* was released, two months after the death of drummer Richard "Pistol" Allen. While touring to promote the film, keyboard player Johnny Griffith died of a heart attack. A combination of storytelling by the Funks, mixed with archival footage, reenactments, and new performances, the film is a testament to the Detroit musicians who made some of the most exciting and memorable music ever recorded.[11]

**Russ Gibb:** After ending his association with the Grande Ballroom in January 1970, Gibb traveled to London, where he stayed for a time with Mick Jagger. While there he was impressed by Jagger's state-of-the-art home video system. Along with a friend, he bought franchise rights for the yet undeveloped cable television system in Dearborn and Wayne, Michigan. When both areas were wired for cable in the eighties, Gibb became a millionaire. He and his partner Michael Berry set up a fund called the Dearborn Cable Communication Fund, to promote local programming and education. Russ also worked at the White House as National Director of Youth and Education for the Bicentennial. In July 2004 Gibb retired from his position at Dearborn High School, where he had taught video media education classes.[12]

**Berry Gordy:** Following his move to Southern California, Gordy focused on the film career of Diana Ross. Aside from Stevie Wonder and the Commodores, there wasn't a lot of Motown music hitting the airwaves by the midseventies. Although Michael Jackson had emerged as a major solo artist with the release of the *Off the Wall* album in 1979 and the record-breaking *Thriller* in 1982, by the early eighties Motown was in financial trouble. On Tuesday, June 29, 1988, after months of tough negotiation, Berry Gordy sold Motown Records to MCA. In the end, Gordy had parlayed his eight-hundred-dollar investment into sixty-one million dollars.[13]

**Grand Funk Railroad:** In 1972, Mark Farner, Don Brewer, and Mel Schacher took legal action, hiring attorney John Eastman to extricate themselves from the control of manager Terry Knight, on grounds of "accounting irregularities." Knight countersued, and the nasty litigation went on for two years. When the case was settled in 1974, the band won their freedom. Terry Knight won ownership of all the group's early publishing.[14] In the meantime the band continued to record for Capitol, where for legal purposes they were billed as Grand Funk. In 1973 with keyboard player Craig Frost joining as a fourth member, they released the Todd Rungren–produced platinum-selling album *We're An American Band*. The LP's title song became a number 1 smash. The band hit number 1 again in 1974, with their re-make of "The Locomotion." Toward the end of the year, the soulful "Some Kind of Wonderful" reached number 3, and in April 1975, "Bad Time" charted at number 4. In 1975 after all the wrangling with Knight, bad blood developed between the band members, and Grand Funk Railroad broke up. Mark Farner went on to a solo career and became a born-again Christian. The others played for a while in a band called Flint. Later Don Brewer went out on the road with Bob Seger. In 1996, Farner, Brewer, and Schacher reunited and played for sell-out crowds across the country on a tour that lasted close to three years. Today Mark Farner continues to play with his own band, while Don Brewer and Mel Schacher, augmented by other musicians, perform as Grand Funk Railroad. Terry Knight eventually settled in Arizona, writing children's books and cashing his royalty checks from the GFR days.[15] On November 1, 2004,

Terry was living with his sixteen year-old daughter in Temple, Texas, when he was stabbed to death defending her from her twenty-six-year-old boyfriend, who was charged with murder.

**Gary Grimshaw:** Grimshaw rejoined John Sinclair and became art director for the Ann Arbor Blues and Jazz festivals in 1972 and 1973. He was the associate art director of *Creem* magazine from 1976 to 1984. During this time he also produced posters, record album art, logos, and graphics for major promoters and dozens of Detroit bands and clubs. A turning point in Gary's career occurred in 1986 when his work was chronicled in the book *The Art of Rock: Posters from Presley to Punk,* by Paul Grushkin. The book became known as the bible of rock and roll poster collectors. In it, Gary was credited as "one of the originators of the form."[16] In 1988, Gary and his wife Laura moved back to San Francisco, where he served as art director of ArtRock, a major supplier of concert posters. When that association ended in 1991, he returned to freelance work. In the spring of 2004, Grimshaw moved back to Detroit.[17]

**Jeep Holland:** Holland left the Detroit/Ann Arbor music scene as it imploded in 1972. He moved to Boston and managed Discount Records' Harvard Square store in Cambridge. In 1984, Jeep donated his 125,000-piece-record collection to the Archive of Contemporary Music. He was working for the Diamond Comic Distributors in Baltimore at the time of his death in 1998 at the age of fifty-six.[18]

**John Lee Hooker:** In 1970 Hooker moved to the San Francisco Bay area, where he teamed up with the rock group Canned Heat for the successful *Hooker and Heat* album. John Lee continued to record and tour through the rest of the seventies and eighties. In 1989, his career received a boost after signing with independent Chameleon Records. His initial album for the label, *The Healer,* featured collaborations with fellow musicians and fans such as Carlos Santana, Robert Cray, Charlie Musselwhite, Los Lobos, and Bonnie Raitt, among other notables. *The Healer* became the first million-selling blues album. His follow-up LP was titled *Mr. Lucky.* Hooker continued to perform and record until he died in his sleep on June 21, 2001. His definitive Detroit recordings, including "Boogie Chillen," were reissued in 2003 as part of a Blues King Pins series by Virgin Records America.[19]

**Dave Leone:** He continued to operate the influential Diversified Management Agency until 1987, booking acts nationwide, such as Aerosmith, Ike and Tina Turner, the Romantics, Nazareth, Chuck Berry, and Iggy Pop. He was described by one musician as a "mentor" who "got you excited about what you were doing."[22] Dave Leone died of a heart attack at age fifty-seven, in October 1999.

**Barbara Lewis:** Her string of midsixties hits continued with "Puppy Love," "Baby I'm Yours," "Make Me Your Baby," and "Make Me Belong to You." By the late seventies Lewis had embarked on a career in the security industry. Today she resides in Florida and has resumed her singing career.[23]

**MC5:** Unable to find enough work to support his drug habit, Wayne Kramer turned to hustling, stolen goods, and drugs. In 1975, after being busted for selling cocaine to undercover cops, he began serving a sentence at the Federal Correctional Facility in Lexington, Kentucky.[24] During his two years behind bars, he developed a relationship with fellow prisoner Red Rodney, who had played bebop trumpet with Charlie Parker in the early fifties. The two inmates played together in the prison band for Sunday concerts in the big yard. Rodney became a mentor to Wayne, helping him pass a correspondence course from the Berklee College of Music.[25] Following his release, Wayne relocated to New York City, where he produced underground and anarchist rock bands. With Johnny Thunders, he cofounded Gang War. In the early eighties, he joined with Don and David Was in the "acid funk" band Was (Not Was). In 1994, Wayne moved to Los Angeles and signed with Epitaph Records, releasing the solo albums *The Hard Stuff* in 1995, *Dangerous Madness* in 1996, *Citizen Wayne* (produced by Don Was), in 1997, and a live effort called *LLMF: Live Like a Motherfucker* in 1998. He reunited with John Sinclair to coproduce and cowrite the album *Full Circle,* for Sinclair and his Blues Scholars. In 2001, after going to business school, Kramer received a small-business loan from the federal government and started his own label, Muscle Tone Records. In 2002, the label's initial release was Wayne's *Adult World.*[26]

As for Michael Davis, aside from playing briefly in 1973 with Fred Smith and Dennis Thompson in a band called Ascension, the former MC5 bassist lived the life of an addict. After two or three drug-related arrests, like Wayne Kramer, he also found himself doing time in the federal prison in Lexington, Kentucky. While incarcerated, Davis returned to his artist roots, decorating the visitor's room with Navaho sand paintings done in acrylics. After one year behind bars, his work earned him an early release, and in 1976, he returned to Ann Arbor, Michigan. Not long after, Ron Asheton came over with Cary Loren and convinced Michael to play bass in their new Detroit band, Destroy All Monsters. After a seven-year run, Davis moved to Arizona, where he has led a drug-free life concentrating on painting. In 2003, he and his family relocated to Los Angeles.[27]

Dennis "Machine Gun" Thompson, the MC5's stick-breaking power drummer, played in bands such as the New Race, the New Order, Sirius Trixon and the Motor City Bad Boys, and Dodge Main, and then taught drums and found employment outside of music, always with the hope of again playing professionally. He still resides in the Detroit area and is writing a book and working on an album.[28]

Rob Tyner upset his bandmates by fronting a new group of players using his former band's name for a short time in the midseventies. Later he led the Rob Tyner Band and released several records. He also was successful with a photography career. Toward the end of the seventies, Rob was invited to come to England and write an article for the *New Musical Express.* While spending time with the Sex Pistols and the Clash, Tyner learned of the MC5's influence on these and other bands of the new "punk" movement.[29] Back in Detroit during the eighties, he continued to perform around town. His last recording was on *Bloodbrothers,* done with the group Weapons. The LP contained a track titled "Grande Days," which saluted the famous ballroom where the MC5 had forged their hard-rocking reputation. While sitting behind the wheel of his car in the driveway of his home on the morning of

September 17, 1991, Rob suffered a fatal heart attack. On February 22, 1992, Smith, Kramer, Davis, and Thompson got together for the first time in twenty years to perform a tribute concert for their former lead singer.[30]

Fred "Sonic" Smith, the band's creative rhythm guitarist, formed the influential Sonic's Rendezvous Band, which also included Scott Morgan, Scott Asheton, and former Up bassist Gary Rasmussen. Primarily a "live" band, their 1977 single release, "City Slang," has become an underground classic. After leaving the band, Fred wed singer Patti Smith. On November 4, 1994, "Sonic" died of heart failure.[31]

In 2003, the three surviving members of the MC5 were reunited for a one-shot "tribute" performance at the 100 Club in London, sponsored by Levi's, who were using the band's image in advertising. After all those years apart, the MC5 once again became a lightening rod for controversy. While many fans were thrilled, others were quite distressed because the MC5 were "going corporate."[32] Wayne Kramer countered by reminding critics that the band's stance had been "by any means necessary."[33] Aside from the London reunion, the year 2003 also saw the release of a documentary motion picture about the band called *MC5: A True Testimonial.*[34]

In March 2004, Michael Davis, Wayne Kramer, and Dennis Thompson announced a worldwide tour. Billed as DKT/MC5, they would be joined by a rotating cast of guest musicians at concerts in Japan, Australia, and Europe as well as major cities across North America. The tour kicked off with a concert before a hometown audience of one thousand fans at Detroit's Majestic Theatre on June 10, 2004. Opening for DKT/MC5 was John Sinclair, backed by a band that included Jim McCarty from the Detroit Wheels.[35]

**Ollie McLaughlin:** The Ann Arbor–based producer was preparing for the release of an album by the Gospel group the McAllisters, when he died of a heart attack at age fifty-eight, on February 19, 1984. Also in the works at that time was a four-album retrospective of his career. "He was one of the last of those giants who really knew the roots of producing a good product," commented a former disc jockey at the time of McLaughlin's death.[36]

**Scott Morgan/The Rationals:** Following the breakup of Guardian Angel, Morgan was a member of the now legendary Sonic's Rendezvous Band. After Fred Smith's departure, that group continued on as the Scott Morgan Band, which was followed into the eighties by Scott's Pirates. Morgan's original group, the Rationals, got together for a while in the early nineties, but old differences made it a short-lived reunion.[37] Bill Figg, Terry Trabandt, and Steve Correll all found work outside of music.[38] In 1999, Scott recorded with the Swedish band the Hellacopters, which was inspired by the Motor City rock of the late sixties. As of 2005, Scott Morgan continues to perform.

**Ted Nugent/The Amboy Dukes:** After the unraveling of the Amboy Dukes, Ted took some time off to go deer hunting in Colorado. In 1976, he signed a new recording contract with Epic Records and his solo career took off with the release of the album *Free For All*. In 1977, *Cat Scratch Fever* was huge and spawned the Top 30 hit single of the same name. Album successes continued with *Double Live Gonzo, Weekend Warriors,* and *State of Shock.* Ted was the top-grossing tour act in 1977, 1978, and 1979.[39] Although Nugent's popularity waned in the eighties, he carried on with a seemingly endless schedule of touring, in support of albums such as *Scream Dream, Nugent,* and *Penetrator.* In the nineties he formed a new "supergroup" called Damn Yankees, which also included former Styx guitarist Tommy Shaw. They had a number 3 hit with "High Enough." Aside from rock 'n' roll, Ted has become almost as famous for his skills at bow and arrow hunting and for his right-of-center political views. He has also written for over forty magazines, has placed books on the *New York Times* best-seller list, and published his own magazine, *Ted Nugent's Adventure Outdoors.* All in all, Ted Nugent has recorded twenty-nine albums including 2001's *Full Bluntal Nugity.*

Steve Farmer, former rhythm guitarist, and the man who wrote the spacy lyrics to the Amboy Dukes' most famous song, "Journey to the Center of the Mind," has continued to play over the years. In 2000 he released a new CD titled *Journey to the Dark Side of the Mind.* Along with updating the original theme, the CD includes a track called "Detroit after Dark," which harkens back to the sixties. Original Dukes keyboard player Ric Lober is also featured on the

CD. Greg Arama, who played bass beginning with the Amboy Dukes' second album, was killed in a motorcycle accident on September 28, 1979, at the age of twenty-nine. Andy Soloman became a top recording engineer. John Drake was last sighted selling cars in Detroit.[40] Rusty Day, who replaced Drake, was murdered in a 1982 drug deal gone bad in Orlando, Florida.

**Harvey Ovshinsky/*The Fifth Estate:*** An award-winning filmmaker, Ovshinsky continues to reside in the Detroit area and serves as president of HO Productions.[41] Now published quarterly, the *Fifth Estate* remains the longest-running English-language antiauthoritarian newspaper in American history. In September 2002, the *Fifth Estate* relocated to a commune in Pumpkin Hollow, Tennessee, with editorial contributions from the former Detroit staff. Former editor Peter Werbe, who transformed the already left-leaning publication into an outlet for anarchist ideas, continues to broadcast his Sunday night talk show *Nightcall* on WRIF.[42]

**Bunny Paul:** In 1960, after several releases on labels such as Dynamic, Brunswick, and Roulette, Bunny's career came to a halt after she was diagnosed with a brain tumor. Following surgery she was left with partial paralysis. By 1963, looking to add some white artists to its roster, Motown asked Bunny to record for its Gordy label.[43] Backed by singers including Martha Reeves, and with Joe Hunter and the Motown house band laying down a solid and funky groove, the thirty-eight-year-old singer delivered a soulful, poignant performance on "We're Only Young Once." The medium tempo rocker was written by Bunny, along with Mike Valvano and the song's producer Clarence Paul (no relation). On the flip side was a bouncy Berry Gordy composition called "I'm Hooked." These two lost Motown gems failed to make the national charts. They were Bunny Paul's last recordings.

Bunny still resides in the Detroit area, where for the last sixteen years she has been a volunteer with the "Meals for Wheels" program for the elderly.[44]

**Pun Plamondon:** After thirty-two months in prison, Plamondon was released in July 1972. He returned to Ann Arbor and worked for a while with John Sinclair at the Rainbow People's Party. Over the years he struggled with alcohol addiction and drifted. After learning that his birth parents had been American Indians, Plamondon began studying their culture and telling Indian history by way of legends and stories. Pun currently resides in western Michigan and is writing his autobiography.45

**Iggy Pop/The Stooges:** When Elektra passed on Raw Power and dumped the Stooges, Iggy descended deep into the drug world. On a trip to New York, he met David Bowie, who helped him find decent management and invited him to come to England, where he reformed the band as Iggy and the Stooges with James Williamson playing lead guitar and Ron Asheton moving to bass.46 Signed to Columbia, the band was finally able to release their third album, *Raw Power,* in 1973. "Search and Destroy" and "Penetration" were highlights, although the record reflected the somewhat glittery production values of Bowie. Despite much anticipation, *Raw Power* flopped, and the reunited Stooges were short-lived. Iggy returned to drugs, specifically downers. After a series of bad shows in Detroit during the winter of 1973–74, Iggy quit the band.47 In the late seventies, David Bowie again pulled Iggy out of the drug world and into the recording studio in Berlin to record the albums *Lust for Life* and *The Idiot,* both released in 1977. Later Iggy Pop albums included *American Caesar, Beat 'Em Up,* and *Instinct.* While Iggy's solo career rolled on, Scott Asheton played drums in Sonic's Rendezvous Band in the seventies, while his brother Ron founded Destroy All Monsters. Original Stooges bassist Dave Alexander died on February 10, 1975. In 2003, after some thirty years apart, Iggy along with Ron and Scott Asheton reunited as the Stooges for a series of well-received concerts.48 In 2003, Iggy released the album *Skull Ring.*

**Suzi Quatro/The Pleasure Seekers:** By 1969, the Pleasure Seekers had been transformed into Cradle and were playing music with a harder edge. After seeing the group perform in Detroit in 1971, British producer Mickie Most signed Suzi to a solo contract. She became a star in the UK starting with her number 1 single "Can the Can" in 1973. She went on to have ten more international hits, although she reached the U.S. charts only once with 1979's "Stumblin' In," a duet with Chris Norman. She is best remembered by American audiences for her role as Leather Tuscadero on TV's *Happy Days* in the late seventies. She still resides in London, where she hosts a radio program on the BBC. She recently made her twenty-first tour of Australia.[49]

**Mitch Ryder and the Detroit Wheels:** In Denver, Mitch made friends with local musicians, and at night he worked on his songwriting skills.[50] In 1978, Ryder returned home to Detroit. He formed a band and released an autobiographical album on his own Seeds and Stems label titled *How I Spent My Summer Vacation.* He followed it in 1980 with *Naked but Not Dead.* Neither album sold well, partially as a result of business-related problems. Ryder returned to a major label with his 1983 release, *Never Kick a Sleeping Dog,* produced by John Mellencamp. A standout cut was Mitch's version of Prince's, "When You Were Mine." Meanwhile, interest in Mitch Ryder music had really taken off in Europe, especially Germany, where he remains popular today. In the United States, he performs mainly his oldies.[51]

After the Detroit band fell apart toward the end of 1972, Johnny Bee reunited with original Detroit Wheels guitarist Jim McCarty. Together they founded the Rockets, one of the first notable groups to emerge in the post classic era of Detroit rock. Aside from his duties as drummer, Bee also handled lead vocals for the band until 1976 and made major contributions as a songwriter. The Rockets, with Bee, McCarty, bass player John Fraga, guitarist Dennis Robbins, keyboard player Donnie Backus, and lead vocalist David Gilbert, continued on into the early eighties, releasing albums such as *Love Transfusion, Turn Up the Radio,* and *No Ballads.* The single "Oh Well" became a top 30 hit in 1979.[52] Over the years Johnny Bee has toured and recorded with artists such as Edgar Winter, Alice Cooper, Dr. John, Bob Seger, Ronnie Montrose, Nils Lofgren, and Detroit's Romantics. Johnny has recently become known in art circles for his talents as a serious painter of modern art.[53] At the same time he continues to play great rock 'n' roll as a member of the recently formed Detroit band Jack Lord.

After leaving the Wheels, and prior to forming the Rockets, Jim McCarty recorded with Jimi Hendrix and Buddy Miles. Along with fellow Detroiter Rusty Day and the former Vanilla Fudge rhythm section of Tim Bogart and Carmine Appice, he formed a new band called Cactus in 1970. After three not very successful albums, they called it quits. After the Rockets, McCarty formed the Detroit Blues Band, which in 1995 evolved into his current band, Mystery Train. The band continues to perform a mix of original blues as well as cover versions.[54] When Ted Nugent was asked if he had a hero, the outspoken guitarist named McCarty, speaking of his "amazing tonal projection beyond the times," saying McCarty's "Chuck berry-on-steroids approach had been unprecedented and insanely energized for the times."[55]

The Detroit Wheels' rhythm guitarist Joe Kubert passed away in 1991. Original bass player Earl Elliott, who left the band for an army stint (to be replaced by Jim McCallister) later went into business, owning a successful import company in Detroit. As of 2004, Elliott works as a real estate investment broker. He resides in a house on Walled Lake where he can look across the water to the site of the old Walled Lake Casino, where he performed with Billy Lee and the Rivieras some forty years earlier.[56]

**Jack Scott:** In 1977, Scott headlined a sold-out fifties rockabilly revival tour in England. Retro rocker Robert Gordon recorded Scott's "The Way I Walk" in 1978 and that recording was later featured in the film *Natural Born Killers.* In 1980, Jack's original version of "Good-bye Baby" was included in the soundtrack for the motion picture *Diner.* Later, Dave Marsh named "Good-bye Baby" as one of the 1001 greatest singles ever made in his book *The Heart of Rock and Soul.* In 2001, Jack returned to England for a successful tour. A British deejay attending one performance said that Scott "sang with clarity and strength" throughout an amazing seventy-five minute show. Jack continues to live and perform in the Detroit area.[57] In Hazel Park, a portion of Nine Mile Road near John R has been renamed Jack Scott Boulevard in honor of the city's favorite son. *Jack Scott's Greatest Hits,* featuring all his best songs from the Carlton and Top Rank days, is still in release.

**Bob Seger:** In 1972, "Punch" Andrews put a deal together whereby Warner Brothers would release Bob Seger material on Punch and Bob's own subsidiary label, Palladium. Seger teamed with Teegarden and Van Winkle on Smokin' OPs. The LP *Back in '72*, a hard-rocking collection released in 1973, included a track titled "Rosalie," written about CKLW music director Rosalie Trombley, who later did much to further the singer's career.[58] Despite the inclusion of the highly regarded cut "Get Out of Denver," the album stiffed and became his last for that label. Seger resigned to Capitol in 1975 and put together a new group of players including Alto Reed (sax), Drew Abbott from Third Power (guitar), Robyn Robbins (keyboards), Chris Campbell (bass), and Charlie Allen Martin (drums). When the next Capitol LP came out in 1975, the credits read "Bob Seger and the Silver Bullet Band." The LP was *Beautiful Loser* and it reached number 131 in *Billboard*. In 1976, Seger released a two-disc live album the band had recorded at Detroit's Cobo Hall a year earlier. *Live Bullet* was the title, and this time the album reached number 34, winning Seger his first gold record. Live Bullet stayed on the *Billboard* charts for three years. In 1977, he finally attained rock superstar status with the release of *Night Moves*. The album went platinum and the title song single hit number 4 in *Billboard*. In 1978, the album *Stranger in Town* produced hit singles such as "Still the Same," "Hollywood Nights," and "We've Got Tonight," as well as the all-time jukebox smash "Old Time Rock & Roll." Bob Seger scored his first number 1 album with the release of the multiplatinum-selling *Against the Wind* in 1980. The LP spawned memorable hit singles including "Fire Lake," "Against the Wind," and "You'll Accompany Me." His next album was another "live" release titled *Nine Tonight*. It sold three million copies during its first year in release.[59] Although his popularity decreased somewhat in the later half of the eighties, his voice can still be heard nightly on television commercials for Chevy trucks, built "like a rock." Bob Seger was finally inducted into the Rock and Roll Hall of Fame in the spring of 2004.

**Robin Seymour:** One would be hard pressed to name a midsixties Detroit band that did not appear on Seymour's *Swingin' Time* TV Show on channel 9. Robin survived some tough times and today lives in Southern California, where he operates a successful infomercial production company.[60]

**Del Shannon:** A few years after his last hit, Del turned his attention to producing. He had a hit with a group he discovered called Smith. They recorded Del's arrangement of the old Shirelles hit "Baby It's You" and had a number 5 hit in 1969. The following year Del produced and played guitar on "Gypsy Woman," a number 3 hit for Brian Hyland. In the early seventies, he toured extensively in England and other parts of the world. The rest of the decade saw Shannon slip into what he described as a "dormant" period, where he took to drinking heavily.[61] After Del gave up alcohol, it was Tom Petty who brought him back to the charts, producing the critically acclaimed album, *Drop Down and Get Me* in 1981. The album included Shannon's first Top 40 hit since 1965, with his cover of Phil Philips's "Sea of Love." Although longing for contemporary success, Del stayed busy on the lucrative oldies circuit. On February 3, 1990, he played his final performance as part of a memorial show for Buddy Holly, Ritchie Valens, and J. P. Richardson, at the Civic Auditorium in Fargo, North Dakota. Five days later, sitting in a rocking chair in his Canyon Country, California, home, Del took his own life.[62] In 1999, Del Shannon was inducted into the Rock and Roll Hall of Fame. A memorial marker was erected along with a museum in his hometown of Coopersville, Michigan.

**John Sinclair:** During his time in prison, John Sinclair published *Guitar Army* which chronicled his life. He coproduced the Ann Arbor Blues and Jazz Festival starting in 1972. After suffering major financial losses in 1974, the Rainbow Multi-Media Corporation that he had formed with Pete Andrews went out of business. John and Leni and other former members of RMM then formed Rainbow Productions in Detroit, specializing in advertising and public relations as well as club management. Sinclair also served as arts editor and later as editor-in-chief of the *Detroit Sun*. When the publication folded in October 1976, he went on to be named state coordinator of Michigan NORML (National Organization for the Reform of Marijuana Laws). He remained active in the Detroit community for many years, serving on numerous committees. After being fired from his position as editor of the Detroit Council of Arts' *City Quarterly*, Sinclair filed an unsuccessful lawsuit against the city.[63] He moved to New Orleans in 1991 and for over a decade hosted a weekly blues show on public radio station WWOZ-FM. He also began performing spoken word gigs backed by a group of musicians he called the Jazz Scholars. In 1995, Sinclair launched a small record label called Total Energy and released his own CD titled *Full Moon Night* and vintage material from the MC5, the Rationals, and Mitch Ryder. When John lost his position as editor of a New Orleans jazz publication, he reached another major crossroads in his life. In November 2003, he announced that he was relocating to Amsterdam, Holland,[64] but he continues to spend much of his time in Detroit when not on the road performing.

In 2004, production was completed on *Twenty to Life: The Life and Times of John Sinclair*, a film by Steve Gebhardt. Looking back on the years from 1967 to 1971, Sinclair recalled: "So much was going on back then, every day seemed like six months."[65]

**Leni Sinclair:** Her life continued to run parallel with that of her husband John until their marriage dissolved in 1977. Together they donated their papers and memorabilia to the Michigan Historical Collections of the University of Michigan in 1979. Leni continued with her photography career and lived for a time in New Orleans before returning to Detroit in the late nineties. Her work has been well documented over the years through magazine articles, record albums, posters, CDs, John Sinclair's book *Guitar Army*, and her own book, *The Detroit Jazz Who's Who*. In 1998, a retrospective show of her work took place at the Boijman's museum in Rotterdam, Holland. She continues to produce exhibitions of her work in various galleries.[66]

**SRC:** The band briefly performed under the name Blue Scepter before the final breakup. Scott Richardson moved to California and was last known to be working on a project with Ray Manzarek of the Doors. Gary Quackenbush, SRC's slashing lead guitarist, put his instrument down and worked in a sales career for a number of years. He has recently been playing again and was a major draw at a "Nights of the Grande" concert staged at the Magic Bag club in Detroit in 2003. He has new recordings available at his web site, www.srcrecords.com. Drummer E. G. Clawson died in early 2003.[67]

**Nolan Strong/Fortune Records:** The Detroit legend continued to record for Fortune until five years before his death on February 21, 1977, at the age of forty-three. Although his recordings have been out of print for many years, bootleg compilations can be found. Fans look forward to the eventual re-release of original masters after a rumored purchase of the Fortune catalog. Meanwhile the career of label mate Nathaniel Mayer has taken off again, and he is an in-demand performer in the United States and Europe. His new album on Fat Possum Records is titled *I Just Want to be Held*. Devora Brown, long retired, still lives in the Detroit area with her son Sheldon Brown. The Fortune Records building on Third Avenue was demolished in 2001.[68]

**Third Power:** In 1974 Third Power lead guitarist Drew Abbott began a long run with Bob Seger and the Silver Bullet Band. Bassist Jem Targal has had a successful career in photography and animation.[69] His current work and vintage photos of Third Power can be viewed at www.diamondjems.com.

**The Underdogs:** After the Underdogs broke up in 1968, Tony Roumell worked as a session guitarist at Motown, while some of the other members played in a short-lived band called Nickel Plate Express. Eventually Tony became a financial adviser and is currently based in Hawaii. Chris Lena runs a recording studio in Los Angeles.[70]

**United Sound Systems Studios:** In the early 1970s, Jimmy Siracuse sold United Sound to former session guitarist and producer Don Davis, who ran the business until the mid 1990s. When Davis left the recording industry, the legendary studio closed its doors for what seemed like the last time. In 2003, local attorney Roger Hood and Detroit music enthusiast Kevin Powell purchased the business for the cost of back taxes and existing debt. Now equipped with the latest recording gear including Pro Tools, the studio is again producing music with a Detroit edge.[71]

**The Up:** When the "revolutionary band" broke up in 1972, the Rasmussen brothers, Bob and Gary, joined with three members of a Mt. Clemens–based band called Brat to form Uprising. In the midseventies, Gary Rasmussen then became bass player in Sonic's Rendezvous Band. He continues to play professionally today.[72]

**WABX:** Detroit's original "underground" radio station hung on with its free form programming until the midseventies when new ownership instituted a more restrictive format. The station changed call letters in 1984.[73]

**Dick Wagner/The Frost:** Following the breakup of Frost, Dick Wagner moved quickly and formed a new power trio called Ursa Major that included former Amboy Dukes bass player Greg Arama. Wagner's guitar work was also displayed on recordings with Lou Reed *(Berlin, Rock 'n' Roll Animal)* and Alice Cooper *(Welcome to My Nightmare, Alice Cooper Goes to Hell, Lace and Whiskey)*. Later he did session work with artists such as Peter Gabriel, Etta James, and Hall and Oates. He returned to his hometown of Saginaw, Michigan, in 1995, and founded Wagner Music Group, which houses a forty-eight-track recording studio and production facilities. He also performed again with the original members of Frost at occasional reunion gigs. In 2000, Wagner was given a lifetime achievement award from the Detroit Music Awards, and the Michigan House of Representatives passed a resolution thanking the Frost for its contributions to Michigan rock and roll.[74]

# Notes

## Chapter 1

1. Barbara Hoover, "Paradise Is Found in Neighborhood Reunion," *Detroit News*, February 28, 1998, C1.

2. Marianne Yared McGuire, "Memories of Black Bottom Stir as Reunion Nears," *Detroit Journal*, August 4, 1996.

3. Author's interview with historian Beatrice Buck.

4. Lars Bjorn and Jim Gallert, *Before Motown: A History of Jazz in Detroit, 1920–1960* (Ann Arbor: University of Michigan Press, 2000), 65.

5. John Lee Hooker, quoted in Jim O'Neal and Amy Van Singel, *The Voice of the Blues: Classic Interviews from Living Blues Magazine* (New York: Routledge, 2002), 216.

6. Howard DeWitt, "John Lee Hooker: From Clarksdale to Detroit," *Rhythm and Blues News*, December 1999–January 2000, 9.

7. Greg Johnson, "John Lee Hooker: RIP." *Blues Notes*, August 2001, http://www.cascadeblues.org/History/JohnLeeHooker.htm.

8. Jay Obrecht, *Rockin' and Tumblin': The Postwar Blues Guitarists* (San Francisco: Miller Freeman, 2000), 307.

9. John Fredrick Cohassey, "Down on Hastings Street," *Detroit Blues,* spring 1997, 14.

10. Charles Shaar Murray, *Boogie Man: The Adventures of John Lee Hooker in the American Twentieth Century* (New York: St. Martin's Press, 2002), 141.

11. Ibid.

12. Author's interview with Bill Randle.

13. Ibid.

14. Ted Carroll, "John Lee Hooker: A Tribute," 2001, http:////acerec001.uuhost.uk.uu.net/whoweare/hooker.html.

15. Author's interview with Ed Wolfrum.

16. Author's interview with Jack Surrell.

17. Ibid.

18. Murray, *Boogie Man,* 118.

19. Paul Oliver, *Story of the Blues* (Boston: Northeastern University Press, 1977), 180.

20. O'Neal and Van Singel, *Voice of the Blues,* 204.

21. Ibid., 205.

22. Murray, *Boogie Man,* 132.

23. O'Neal and Van Singel, *Voice of the Blues,* 204.

24. Ibid., 211.

25. Johnson, "John Lee Hooker."

26. DeWitt, "John Lee Hooker," 11.

27. John Lee Hooker, quoted in Obrecht, *Rockin' and Tumblin','* 288.

28. John Lee Hooker, quoted in Murray, *Boogie Man*, 142.

29. Ibid.

30. John Lee Hooker, quoted in O'Neal and Van Singel, *Voice of the Blues*, 217.

31. Dave Sax, quoted in Ron Weinstock, "Boogie on John Lee," http://www.dcblues.org/articles/hooker.html.

32. O'Neal and Van Singel, *Voice of the Blues*, 214.

33. Mark Bego, *Aretha Franklin: The Queen of Soul* (New York: St. Martins Press, 1989), 17.

34. Murray, *Boogie Man*, 142.

35. Author's interview with Jack Surrell.

36. Marv Goldberg, "The Royals," *Discoveries,* June 1996.

37. Johnny Otis, quoted in Steve Propes, "Johnny Otis, the Rock 'n' Roll Years: Doin' the Crazy Hand Jive," *Goldmine*, March 25, 1988, 8.

38. Ibid.

39. Hank Ballard, quoted in Howard DeWitt, "Hank Ballard: From Alabama Gospel to the Early Hits," *Rhythm and Blues News,* August–September 1999, 5.

40. Ibid., 5.

41. Ibid., 6.

42. Ibid., 6.

43. Ibid.

44. Ibid.

45. Ibid.

46. Marv Goldberg, "The Imperials," *Discoveries* 149, October 2000.

47. Ibid.

48. Goldberg, "The Serenaders," *Discoveries* 98, July 1996.

49. Theron Hill, quoted in ibid.

50. Goldberg, "The Serenaders."

### Chapter 2

1. James Austin, liner notes, *The Fortune Records Story,* http://www.lex.jansen.demon.nl/fortune/.

2. Devora Brown, quoted in Dan Nooger, "Devora Brown: The Fortune Teller Speaks," *Goldmine,* June 20, 1986, 18.

3. Author's interview with Artie Fields.

4. Ibid.

5. Bob Merlis and Devin Seay, *Heart and Soul: A Celebration of Black Music Styles in America, 1930–1975* (New York: Stewart, Tabori and Chang, 1997).

6. Devora Brown, quoted in Nooger, "Devora Brown," 18.

7. Richard Roberts, "Fortune Records," *Goldmine,* April 1997.

8. Devora Brown, quoted in Nooger, "Devora Brown."

9. "Nolan Strong and the Diablos," 1998, http://members.aol.com/Dowopdowah/diabls.htm.

10. James Austin, liner notes, *Daddy Rock,* http://www.lexjansen.com/fortune/diablos.htm.

11. Devora Brown, quoted in Nooger, "Devora Brown," 20.

12. Ibid.

13. Author's interview with Gary Banovetz.

14. Ibid.

15. Ibid.

16. J. C. Marion, "Detroit's Nolan Strong and the Diablos," in *Doo-Wop Nation* no. 19, 2000, http://home.earthlink.net/~jaymar41/diabolos.html.

17. Author's interview with Gary Banovetz.

18. Ibid.

19. Marion, "Detroit's Nolan Strong."

20. Rick Roberts.

21. Author's interview with Sheldon Brown.

22. Devora Brown, quoted in Nooger, "Devora Brown," 18.

23. Nooger, "Devora Brown."

24. Cohassey, "Down on Hastings Street."

25. Joe Louis Walker, "1998 Blues Estafette Lineup," 1998, http://www.bluesworld.com/Estafette98.html.

26. Carlo Wolff, "Fortune Records," *Goldmine*, May 3, 2002, 32.

27. Marv Goldberg, "The Five Dollars," *Discoveries*, September 2001.

28. Andre Williams, quoted in Epstein, "A Conversation with Andre 'Mr. Rhythm' Williams," *Ugly Things* 17, http://www.ugly-things.com/andre.html.

29. Author's interview with Gary Banovetz.

30. Andre Williams, quoted in Devora Brown.

31. Ibid.

32. Devora Brown, quoted by Andre Williams in Epstein, "Conversation with Andre Williams."

33. Ernie Durham, quoted by Andre Williams in Epstein, "Conversation with Andre Williams."

34. Goldberg, "The Five Dollars."

35. Andre Williams, quoted in Wolf, "Fortune Records," 33.

36. Ibid.

37. Johnny Powers, quoted in Nooger, "Devora Brown," 18.

38. Devora Brown, quoted in ibid.

## Chapter 3

1. David Carson, *Rockin' Down the Dial: The Detroit Sound of Radio from Jack the Bellboy to the Big 8* (Troy, Mich.: Momentum Books, 2000), 2–3.

2. Ibid., 4.

3. Ibid., 18.

4. Loraine Alterman, "Ernie Durham, First Record Hop Man," in *Detroit Free Press,* April 9, 1967.

5. Nat Tarnapol, quoted in Frances DeHondt, "DJ Mickey Shorr Proves Showbiz Real Friendly," *Detroit Times,* June 1957.

6. Ibid.

7. "Rock 'n' Rollorama Breaks All House Records at Fox Theater, Detroit," *Billboard,* January 1956.

8. "Teeners Rally to Mickey," *Detroit News,* April 30, 1956.

9. Author's interview with Bud Davies.

10. Ibid.

11. Jay Warner, *The Billboard Book of American Singing Groups* (New York: Billboard Books, 1992).

12. Author's interview with Bunny Paul.

13. Klaus Kettner and Tony Wilkenson, liner notes, *Such a Rock and Roll Night,* August 2002.

14. Author's interview with Bunny Paul.

15. Ibid.

16. Ibid.

17. Ibid.

18. Marilyn Bond, "Rockin' in the Motor City," *Rock and Blues News,* August–September 2000, 27.

19. Ibid.

20. Official Jack Scott homepage. http://www.history-of-rock.com /jack_scott.htm.

21. Alan Adler, "Rock 'n' Roll Survivor Still Enjoys Singing His Own Way," *Oakland Press,* March 7, 2002.

22. David McLaughlin, "A Detroit Legend Reborn," *Jam Rag,* May 2002.

23. Jack Scott, quoted in Vivian DeGain, "Hazel Park's Jack Scott Brings Back His 'Good Music,'" *Daily Tribune* (Royal Oak, Mich.), November 11, 2002.

24. Program notes, "Rock 'n' Roll O'Rama Easter Edition," Broadway Capitol Theater, April 1957.

25. Author's interview with Jack Grenier.

26. Author's interview with George Katsakis.

27. Billy Poore, "Great Scott," *Rock and Blues News,* December 1998–January 1999, 28.

28. Lee Cotton, "The Hawk Rocks Again," *Rock and Blues News,* May–June 1999, 7.

29. Bill Dahl, "Jack Scott," *All-Music Guide,* http://www.allmusic .com/cg/amg.dll?p=amg&token=&sql=11:ygae4j87owaw.

30. Author's interview with William Levise Jr. (Mitch Ryder).

31. Jack Scott, quoted in McLaughlin, "A Detroit Legend Reborn."

32. Poore, "Great Scott."

33. Author's interview with George Katsakis.

34. Ibid.

35. Ibid.

36. Ibid.

37. Ibid.

38. Ibid.

39. Author's interview with Clark Reid.

40. Author's interview with Lee Alan.

41. "Disc Jockey Tom Clay Fired by WJBK," *Detroit News,* November 23, 1959.

42. Tom Clay, quoted in James Hart, "One Fired, Two Quit in Payola Furor," *Detroit Times,* November 23, 1959, 2.

43. "Tom Clay Fired."

44. Ed McKenzie, quoted in "A Deejay's Expose," *Life,* November 23, 1959.

45. "Jac LeGoff Fired for Payola Talk," *Detroit Free Press,* November 20, 1959.

46. Ibid.

47. Tom Clay, quoted in Hart, "One Fired, Two Quit," 1.

48. Ibid.

49. Ibid.

50. Mickey Shorr, quoted in "I'm a Goat," *Detroit News,* 2a.

51. Ibid., 1a.

52. Author's interview with George Katsakis.

53. Ibid.

54. John Collis, *The History of Rock,* part 24, 2002, http://www.rocka-billyhall.com/JackScott.html.

55. Poore, "Great Scott," 31.

56. "The Larados." http://www.reflections-music.com/larref.html.

57. Don Davenport, quoted in ibid.

58. Steve Propes, "Lamont Dozier: An Insider's Look at Motown," *Goldmine,* June 20, 1986, 16.

59. Author's interview with George Katsakis.

60. Author's interview with Bill Hennes.

61. Author's interview with Johnny Powers.

62. Author's interview with Clark Reid.

## Chapter 4

1. Lars Bjorn with Jim Gallert, *Before Motown: A History of Jazz in Detroit, 1920–1960,* 193–94.

2. Cohassey, "Down on Hastings Street," 16.

3. "Jackie Wilson," http://www.history-of-rock.com/jackie_wilson .htm.

4. "Jackie Wilson," http://ourworld.compuserve.com/homepages/ DYaros/jwilson.htm.

5. J. C. Marion, "The Dominos Theory," *Doo-Wop Nation* no. 14, http://home_earthlink.net/-jaymar41/doowoptp.html.

6. Jackie Wilson, http://ourworld.compuserve.com/homepages/ DYaros/jwilson.htm.

7. Marv Goldberg, "The Thrillers/5 Jets," *Discoveries* 98, July 1996.

8. Berry Gordy, *To Be Loved* (New York: Warner Books, 1994), 13–15.

9. Ibid.

10. Ibid.

11. Ibid., 97.

12. Ibid.

13. "Smokey Robinson Biography."

14. Smokey Robinson with David Ritz, *Smokey: Inside My Life* (New York: McGraw-Hill, 1989).

15. Don Waller, *The Motown Story* (New York: Charles Scribner's Sons, 1985), 28.

16. Gordy, *To Be Loved,* 107.

17. Ibid.

18. Ibid., 110.

19. Ibid., 109.

20. Author's interview with Larry Dixon.

21. Gordy, *To Be Loved,* 118–19.

22. Barrett Strong, quoted in Don Waller, "Earth to Cloud Nine: Barrett Strong on 'Money,' Motown, and the Muse," *LA Weekly,* January 15–21, 1999.

23. Gordy, *To Be Loved,* 122–23.

24. Waller, "Earth to Cloud Nine."

25. Author's interview with Harry Balk.

26. Harry Balk, quoted in interview by John Rhys, 1999, www.blue power.com.

27. Ibid.

28. Ibid.

29. Author's interview with Lynn Bruce.

30. Author's interview with Harry Balk.

31. Harry Balk, interview by Rhys.

32. Ibid.

33. Author's interview with Lynn Bruce.

34. Harry Balk, interview by Rhys.

35. "Del Shannon," in *History of Rock.com,* http://www.history-of-rock.com/del_shannon.htm.

36. Max Crook, http://www.maxcrook.com.

37. Brian Young, "The Making of 'Runaway,'" http://go.zibycom .com/members/002222119/Site4/maxrunaway.html.

38. Del Shannon, quoted by Max Crook in "Del Shannon Rock On," http://d21c.com/spacebeagle/delshannon.html.

39. Harry Balk, quoted in Rhys interview.

40. Young, "The Making of 'Runaway.'"

41. Author's interview with Harry Balk.

42. Ibid.

43. Ibid.

44. Ibid.

45. Susan Whitall, "R&B Great Reclaims His Fortune," *Detroit News,* December 5, 2002.

46. Devora Brown, quoted in Nooger, "Devora Brown," 19.

47. Whitall, "R&B Great Reclaims His Fortune."

48. Devora Brown, quoted in Nooger, "Devora Brown," 19.

49. Author's interview with Sheldon Brown.

50. Devora Brown, quoted in Nooger, "Devora Brown," 19.

51. Jay Johnson, quoted in "Nolan Strong and the Diablos," http://members.aol.com/Dowopdowah/diablos.htm.

52. Author's interview with Sheldon Brown.

53. Devora Brown, quoted in Nooger, "Devora Brown," 19.

54. "The Falcons," in *Soulful Kinda Music,* http://members.tripod .com/SoulfulKindaMusic/falcons.htm.

55. Wilson Pickett biography, *Rock + Hall of Fame and Museum,* 1993, http://www.rockhall.com/hof/inductee.asp?id=167.

56. Soulful Kinda Music, http://www.soulfulkindamusic.net/vol umes.html.

57. Author's interview with George Katsakis.

58. Author's interview with Barbara Lewis.

59. Ibid.

60. Ibid.

61. Ibid.

62. Ibid.

63. Ibid.

64. Ibid.

65. Ibid.

66. Author's interview with Jamie Coe.

67. Ibid.

68. Bond, "Rockin' in the Motor City."

69. Ibid.

70. Author's interview with Lynn Bruce.

71. Author's interview with Dave Kovarik.

72. Ibid.

73. Ibid.

74. Author's interview with Lynn Bruce.

75. Author's interview with Jamie Coe.

76. Author's interview with Marc Avery.

77. Author's interview with Jamie Coe.

78. David Meikle, "The Golden World Story," in *Soulful Detroit.com,* 2002, http://www.soulfuldetroit.com.

79. Ibid.

80. Author's interview with Tony Micale.

81. Fred Gorman, quoted in Bill Dahl, liner notes, *Rock, Rhythm and Doo Wop: The Greatest Songs from Early Rock 'n' Roll,* Rhino Records.

82. Author's interview with Tony Micale.

83. Ibid.

84. Ibid.

85. Ibid.

86. Ibid.

87. Ibid.

88. Author's interview with Gino Washington.

89. Ibid.

90. Earl Dowdy, "The Amazing Empire on West Grand Boulevard: Million Dollar Music in Four Flats," *Detroit News,* July 25, 1965, 1g.

## Chapter 5

1. Entertainment listings from *Detroit News.*

2. Author's interview with Mitch Ryder.

3. Author's interview with Ronnie Abner.

4. Author's interview with Mitch Ryder.

5. Ken Settle, "Mitch Ryder, No More Vacations," *Goldmine,* May 20, 1988, 20.

6. Dave Marsh, "Put the Bacon on the Paper So's the Grease'll Run Off," *Creem* (October 1969), 13.

7. Author's interview with Mitch Ryder.

8. Ibid.

9. Ibid.

10. Author's interview with Ronnie Abner.

11. Author's interview with Thomas Hester.

12. Author's interview with Ronnie Abner.

13. Marsh, "Bacon on the Paper," 14.

14. Author's interview with Mitch Ryder.

15. Author's interview with Thomas Hester.

16. Ibid.

17. Marsh, "Bacon on the Paper," 17.

18. Nathaniel Mayer, quoted in Settle, "No More Vacations."

19. Author's interview with Mitch Ryder.

20. Author's interview with Johnny Bee.

21. Jim McCarty, interview, *Vintage Guitar,* May 1999.

22. Author's interview with Johnny Bee.

23. Ibid.

24. Ibid.

25. Author's interview with Lee Alan.

26. WXYZ audiotape recording, 1963.

27. Dick Osgood, *Wyxie Wonderland* (Bowling Green, Ohio: Bowling Green University Press, 1981), 398.

28. Mitch Ryder, quoted in Trowbridge, "Mitch Ryder: Doctor Detroit," *Eye Weekly* (Toronto), November 28, 2002, http://www.eye.net/eye/issue/Issue_11.28.02/music/ryder.html.

29. Marsh, "Bacon on the Paper," 14.

30. Settle, "No More Vacations," 20.

31. Mitch Ryder, quoted in Trowbridge, "Doctor Detroit."

32. Dave Prince, quoted by Earl Elliott in Settle, "No More Vacations," 20.

33. Mitch Ryder, quoted in "Mitch Ryder: Naked But Not Dead," 2003, http://www.cucamonga.be/interviews/mitchryder0303.htm.

34. Mitch Ryder, quoted in Trowbridge, "Doctor Detroit."

35. Author's interview with Johnny Bee.

36. Author's interview with Mitch Ryder.

37. Mitch Ryder, quoted in "Mitch Ryder: Naked But Not Dead."

38. Mitch Ryder, quoted in "Mitch Ryder Interview," interview by Al Sorenson and Rick McGrath, June, 17, 1970, *The Georgia Straight,* http://www.rickmcgrath.com/mitchryder.html.

39. McCarty, interview, *Vintage Guitar.*

40. Author's interview with Johnny Bee.

41. Marsh, "Bacon on the Paper."

42. Author's interview with Mitch Ryder.

43. Ibid.

44. Mitch Ryder, quoted in "Mitch Ryder: Naked But Not Dead."

45. Michael B. Smith, "The Super-energized Ted Nugent: It's the Nature of the Beast," *Goldmine,* February 25, 2000, 15.

46. David Segal, "Musicians Play Deejay: Ted Nugent's Most Influential List," *Washington Post,* 2002.

47. Ibid.

48. Steve Olsen, "I Am the Original Caveman in Year 2002," *Juice,* http://www.juicemagazine.com/tednugentintw.html.

49. Ibid.

50. Ted Nugent, quoted in Segal, "Musicians Play Deejay."

51. Bob Gulla, "The Motor City Madman," *Guitar,* August 1999.

52. Segal, "Musicians Play Deejays."

53. Alan Vorda, "Interview with Ted Nugent," February 24, 1988, http://web.wt.net/~duane/nugent.html.

54. Segal, "Musicians Play Deejays."

55. Smith, "Super-energized Ted Nugent."

56. Ted Nugent, quoted in article reprinted at http://www.mitchryder.de/guitarworld.php.

57. Ted Nugent, quoted in Peter Kautto, "The Ted Nugent Show," Rock United.com, http://www.AOR-Europe.com. Must click on Ted Nugent name.

58. Ibid.

59. Vorda, "Interview with Ted Nugent."

60. Ibid.

## Chapter 6

1. Michael Flores, "It Came from the Garage," 1998, http://www.psychotronic.info/10am/hideout_records.htm.

2. Jeff Gerritt, "David Leone: Managed, Inspired Detroit Rockers," *Detroit Free Press,* October 9, 1999, 11a.

3. Flores, "It Came from the Garage."

4. Author's interview with Gary Quackenbush.

5. Ibid.

6. Flores, "It Came from the Garage."

7. Author's interview with Gary Quackenbush.

8. "No Obscene Dancing: The Hideout Story," liner notes to *Friday at the Hideout,* Norton Records, 2001.

9. Author's interview with Gary Quackenbush.

10. "No Obscene Dancing."

11. Author's interview with Gary Quackenbush.

12. "No Obscene Dancing."

13. Flores, "It Came from the Garage."

14. Dave Leone, quoted in "It Came from the Garage."

15. Ibid.

16. Author's interview with Gary Quackenbush.

17. "No Obscene Dancing."

18. Punch Andrews, quoted in *Detroit Free Press,* 1999.

19. Author's interview with Gary Quackenbush.

20. "No Obscene Dancing."

21. Author's interview with Chris Lena.

22. Ibid.

23. Ibid.

24. Ibid.

25. Author's interview with Tony Roumell.

26. Aaron Rosenbaum, "Teen Music: Smokey Soul Sound Sizzles a Go-Go," *Acorn* (Dondero High School), December 16, 1966.

27. "No Obscene Dancing."

28. Author's interview with Chris Lena.

29. Author's interview with Tony Roumell.

30. Flores, "It Came from the Garage."

31. Loraine Alterman, "Underdogs Reach for a Star," *Detroit Free Press,* October 22, 1965, 4c.

32. WKNR audio tape recording, December 1965.

33. Author's interview with Chris Lena.

34. Author's interview with Tony Roumell.

35. Ibid.

36. "No Obscene Dancing."

37. Ibid.

38. Ibid.

39. Ibid.

40. Flores, "It Came from the Garage."

41. Suzi Quatro biography, in *Suzi Quatro Web Page,* http://www.comnet.ca/-rina/suziquatro.html.

42. "No Obscene Dancing."

43. Suzi Quatro, quoted in radio interview, February 14 2003, www.abc.net.au/hobart/stories/5784161.htm.

44. Ibid.

45. "No Obscene Dancing."

46. www.artistdirect.com/music/artist/bio/0,,481985,00.html ?artist= suzi+quatro.

## Chapter 7

1. Sue Ellenbush, "Bands and Night Spots Become Big Business," *Acorn* (Dondero High School), December 16, 1966.

2. Steve Marcus, obituary of Jeep Holland, *Boston Globe,* 1998.

3. Author's interview with Bill Figg.

4. Ken Shimamoto, "Let's Get Rational: Scott Morgan's Garage Days Revisited," http://www.scottmorganmusic.com/scott_rationals.html.

5. Shimamoto, "Pirate Music: The Scott Morgan Story," in *Addicted to Noise,* http://www.i94bar.com, www.i94bar.com/ints/scottmorgan1.html.

6. Author's interview with Bill Figg.

7. Shimamoto, "Let's Get Rational."

8. Author's interview with Bill Figg.

9. Scott Morgan, quoted in "The Rationals: Michigan Sounds of the Sixties," in *The Rationals,* http://www.therationals.com/12oclock.html.

10. Steve Morse, "Boston's 'Ultimate Music Fan,'" *Boston Globe,* 1984.

11. Remembrance of Jeep Holland by Dave Kamminga, www.ewwvi.net/jeep/remembrances/dkamminga.html.

12. Scott Morgan, quoted in Richie Unterberger, *Urban Spacemen and Other Wayfaring Strangers: Overlooked Innovators and Eccentric Visionaries of '60s Rock* (San Francisco: Backbeat Books, 2000), 214–21.

13. Ibid.

14. Author's interview with Bill Figg.

15. Dave Marsh and Debbie Burr, "The Rationals: Your Average High School Band Seven Years Later," *Creem,* April 1970.

16. Author's interview with Bill Figg.

17. Ibid.

18. Ibid.

19. Terry Trabandt, quoted in Marsh and Burr, "The Rationals."

20. Shimamoto, "A Brief History of the Rationals," www.scottmorganmusic.com/scott_rationals.html.

21. Unterberger, *Urban Spacemen,* 214–21.

22. Ibid.

23. Ibid.

24. Shimamoto, "Brief History of the Rationals."

25. Marsh and Burr, "The Rationals."

26. Scott Morgan, quoted in Marsh and Burr, "The Rationals."

27. Author's interview with Bill Figg.

28. Terry Trabandt, quoted in Marsh and Burr, "The Rationals."

29. Author's interview with Bill Figg.

30. Steve Terrell, quoted in Marsh and Burr, "The Rationals."

31. Author's interview with Tom Wearing.

32. Ibid.

33. Ibid.

34. Ibid.

35. Vernon Joynson, *Fuzz, Acid, and Flowers: A Comprehensive Guide to American Garage, Psychedelic and Hippie Rock (1964–1975)*, Borderline Productions, 1993.

36. Ibid.

37. Ibid.

38. Steve Roeser, "The Tumultuous Times of Terry Knight," *Discoveries* 141, February 2000, 139–41.

39. Ibid.

40. Author's interview with Marc Avery.

41. Terry Knight, quoted in Roeser, "Tumultuous Times," 40–41.

42. Ibid.

43. Ibid.

44. Author's interview with Marc Avery.

45. Audio tape recording from CKLW, December 18, 1964.

46. Roeser, "Tumultuous Times," 43.

47. Ibid.

48. Ibid.

49. "96 Tears," http://www.pharaohweb.com/Qmark/bio.html.

50. James Thompson, "Detroit's Play-It-Extra-Loud Rock 'n' Roll Scene," *Goldmine*, February 25, 2000, 28.

51. Tom Simon, "? Question Mark and the Mysterians," http://www.tsimon.com/mysteria.htm.

52. Thompson, "Play-It-Extra-Loud," 28.

53. Ibid.

54. Ibid.

55. Author's interview with Tom Shannon.

56. "No Obscene Dancing."

57. "Bob Seger."

58. Doug Brown, quoted by Dave Leone in "No Obscene Dancing."

59. Ibid.

60. Various on-line bios.

61. Greg Kot, "Devotion Keeps Detroit a Rock City," *Chicago Tribune*, December 18, 2003.

62. "Bob Seger, in His Own Words," in *Super Seventies.com*, http://www.superseventies.com/ssbobseger.html.

63. Timothy White, "The Loneliness of the Long Distance Rocker," *Crawdaddy*, November 1977.

64. Segerfile.com/bands.html.

65. Chris Cioe, "Hymns from the Heartland," *Musician*, http://www.segerfile.com/earlydays.html.

66. Ibid.

67. "Bob Seger, in His Own Words."

68. Bob Seger, quoted in Cioe, "Hymns from the Heartland."

69. Ibid.

70. Author's interview with Bill Figg.

71. Roy Trakin, "Bob Seger: The Creem Interview," *Creem*, September 1986.

72. "No Obscene Dancing."

73. Bob Seger, quoted in Dave Marsh, "Bob Seger, Not a Stranger Anymore," *Rolling Stone*, June 15, 1978, 68.

74. Trakin, "Bob Seger."

## Chapter 8

1. Nelson George, *Where Did Our Love Go? The Rise and Fall of the Motown Sound* (New York: St. Martins Press, 1985), 103.
2. Author's interview with Gary Quackenbush.
3. Seger, quoted in Kot, "Devotion Keeps Detroit a Rock City."
4. Steve Propes, "Lamont Dozier," 14.
5. Propes, "Lamont Dozier," 15–16.
6. Ibid.
7. Ibid.
8. Ibid.
9. Ibid.

10. Dowdy, "Amazing Empire," 7G.
11. Lamont Dozier, quoted in Waller, *The Motown Story*.
12. Ibid.
13. Earl Van Dyke, quoted in Waller, *The Motown Story*, 158.
14. James Jamerson, quoted in George, *Where Did Our Love Go?*
15. Uriel Jones, quoted in Kim Heron, "The Unsung Heroes of the Motown Sound," *Detroit Free Press*, July 31, 1983.
16. Earl Van Dyke, quoted in Waller, *The Motown Story*, 60.
17. Dan Forte, "Motown's Funk Brothers: The Greatest Hit-Making Guitarists in the History of Pop Music," *Vintage Guitar*, April 2003, 86.
18. Don Was, quoted in ibid., 90.
19. Author's interview with Gary Quackenbush.
20. James Jamerson, quoted by Suzi Quatro in "Lighting Flash," *Sun-Herald*, January 6, 2003.
21. Joe Messina, quoted in Forte, "Funk Brothers," 27.
22. Ibid.
23. Eddie Willis, quoted in ibid., 82.
24. Author's interview with Richard Stevers.
25. Waller, *The Motown Story*, 164.
26. Ibid.
27. Author's interview with Ed Wolfrum.
28. Author's interview with Bob Babbitt.
29. Ibid.
30. Ibid.
31. Ibid.
32. Ibid.

## Chapter 9

1. Author's interview with Russ Gibb.
2. Ibid.
3. Ibid.
4. Ibid.
5. Russ Gibb, quoted in Bill Dow, "Psychedelic Posters Rock: The Art of Collecting," *Hour Detroit*, February 2000, 68.
6. Ibid.
7. Author's interview with Russ Gibb.
8. Peter Gavrilovich and Bill McGraw, "A Detroit Rock Shrine," *Detroit Free Press*, October 13, 2000.
9. Author's interview with Russ Gibb.
10. Dennis Thompson, quoted in James Thompson, "MC5 Kickin' Out the Jams," *Goldmine*, March 10, 2000, 28.

11. Author's interview with Gary Grimshaw.

12. Gary Grimshaw, "Lincoln Park Tribe," in *Tribes of the Cass Corridor,* 2001, http://www.corridortribe.com/tribes/Lincoln_Park_Tribe/.

13. Ibid.

14. Ibid.

15. Author's interview with Wayne Kramer.

16. Wayne Kramer, quoted in Jimmy Guterman, liner notes, *The Big Bang! A Best of the MC5,* 1999.

17. Author's interview with Wayne Kramer.

18. Wayne Kramer, interview by Jason Gross, *Perfect Sound Forever,* http://www.furious.com/perfect/mc5/waynekramer.html.

19. Author's interview with Wayne Kramer.

20. Ibid.

21. Wayne Kramer, quoted in Ken Kelly, "Interview with the MC5's Other Guitarist," in *Addicted to Noise,* 1995.

22. Wayne Kramer, quoted in liner notes from *'66 Breakout,* March 12, 1999.

23. Wayne Kramer, quoted in ibid.

24. Wayne Kramer, quoted in Peter Werbe, "You Don't Turn Your Card In," *Vintage Guitar,* December 1998.

25. Author's interview with Wayne Kramer.

26. Ibid.

27. Ibid.

28. Ibid.

29. Jerry Goodwin, quoted in on-line remembrance, *Make My Day.com,* http://www.makemyday.free.fr/jgrecalls.htm.

30. Wayne Kramer, quoted in liner notes, *'66 Breakout.*

31. Author's interview with Wayne Kramer.

32. Author's interview with Michael Davis.

33. Ibid.

34. Ibid.

35. Ibid.

36. Ibid.

37. Ibid.

38. Author's interview with Dennis Thompson.

39. Author's interview with Michael Davis.

40. Wayne Kramer, quoted in Kelly, "MC5's Other Guitarist."

41. Dennis Thompson, quoted in Ken Shimamoto, "Dennis Thompson: Phantom Patriot," in *I94 Bar,* http://www.i94bar.com/infa/thompson.html.

42. Ibid.

## Chapter 10

1. John and Leni Sinclair Papers, Bentley Historical Library, University of Michigan.

2. Author's interview with John Sinclair.

3. John and Leni Sinclair Papers, Bentley Historical Library.

4. Leni Sinclair, quoted in Christopher M. Singer, "Radical Captured 1960s in Photos," *Detroit News,* December 5, 2001.

5. Author's interview with Leni Sinclair.

6. Author's interview with John Sinclair, who was given his Red Squad file during Mayor Coleman Young's administration.

7. John Sinclair, *Guitar Army* (New York: Douglas Book Corporation, 1972), 191.

8. Ibid., 190.

9. Ibid.

10. John and Leni Sinclair Papers, Bentley collection.

11. Sinclair, *Guitar Army,* 189.

12. Ibid.

13. Sinclair, letter to the *Michigan Daily* (University of Michigan), September 28, 1969.

14. Ibid.

15. Sinclair, letter to *Michigan Daily.*

16. Sinclair, *Guitar Army,* 192.

17. Leni Sinclair, quoted in "Leni Sinclair: Through the Camera's Lens," interview by Ken Shimamoto, http://www.i94bar.com/ints/leni.html.

18. Wayne Kramer, quoted in Kelly, "MC5's Other Guitarist."

19. Ibid.

20. Leni Sinclair, interview by Ken Shimamoto.

21. Wayne Kramer, quoted in Kelly, "MC5's Other Guitarist."

22. Author's interview with Wayne Kramer.

23. Author's interview with John Sinclair.

24. Author's interview with Wayne Kramer.

25. Author's interview with Michael Davis.

26. Author's interview with Wayne Kramer.

27. Ibid.

28. Author's interview with Dennis Thompson.

29. Sinclair, quoted by Wayne Kramer in Kelly, "MC5's Other Guitarist."

30. Sinclair, *Guitar Army,* 197.

31. Bob Manardo, "56 Arrested in Drug Raids in WSU Area," *Detroit News,* January 25, 1967, 10a.

32. Ibid., 1a.

33. Author's interview with John Sinclair.

34. Sinclair, *Guitar Army,* 197.

35. Sinclair, letter to *Michigan Daily.*

36. "Trans-Love Special," a descriptive essay, 1967. John and Leni Sinclair Papers, Bentley collection, University of Michigan.

37. Ibid.

38. Ibid.

39. Sinclair, *Guitar Army,* 32.

40. Ibid., 33.

41. Author's interview with Pun Plamondon.

42. Sinclair, quoted in John Strausbaugh, *Rock 'Til You Drop* (London: Verso, 2001), 97.

43. Allan Blanchard, "Riot at Love-In: Ten Jailed," *Detroit News,* May 1, 1967, 1.

44. Gary Bronston and Susan Holmes, "Belle Isle Love-In Turns to Hate," *Detroit Free Press,* May 1, 1967, 1a.

45. Author's interview with Michael Davis.

46. Julie Morris and Jenny Nolan, "Sex, Drugs, Rock 'n' Roll, and Plum Street," *Detroit News Rearview Mirror,* http://www.detroitnews.com/history/hippie/hippie.htm.

47. Blanchard, "Riot at Love-In," 10a.

48. Wayne Kramer, "Riots I Have Known and Loved," *Pop Smear,* http://www.popsmear.com/popculture/features/24/riotsknown.html.

49. Ibid.

50. Author's interview with Leni Sinclair.

51. Sinclair, quoted in Morris and Nolan, "Sex, Drugs, Rock 'n' Roll."

52. Sinclair, quoted in Rob Tyner Interview, *Warren-Forest Sun,* May 1967.

53. Dennis Thompson, quoted in Shimamoto, "Dennis Thompson: Phantom Patriot."

54. Author's interview with Wayne Kramer.

55. Wayne Kramer, quoted in Guterman, liner notes, *The Big Bang!*

56. Ibid.

57. Marshall Crenshaw, quoted in discussion forum in *Soulful Detroit.com,* http://www.soulfuldetroit.com.

58. Wayne Kramer, quoted in Kelly, "MC5's Other Guitarist."

59. Ibid.

60. Wayne Kramer, "Rocket Reducer," *LA Weekly,* 1998, http://www.laweekly.com/ink/98/50/reverb-kramer.shtml.

61. Ibid.

62. Billy C. Farlow biography, http://www.billycfarlow.com/bio.html.

## Chapter 11

1. Author's personal experience.

2. Herbert Boldt, "Johnson Sends Five Thousand Troops Ready for Riot Duty," *Detroit News,* July 24, 1967, 1.

3. Sidney Fine, *Violence in the Model City: The Cavanagh Administration, Race Relations, and the Detroit Riots of 1967* (Ann Arbor: University of Michigan Press, 1989), 160.

4. Ibid., 160.

5. Boldt, "Johnson Sends Troops."

6. Author's interview with Robin Seymour.

7. Ibid.

8. Author's interview with Russ Gibb.

9. Ibid.

10. Ibid.

11. Ibid.

12. Wayne Kramer, quoted in Kelly, "MC5's Other Guitarist."

13. Ibid.

14. Ibid.

15. "The Fire This Time," *Time,* August 4, 1967, 13.

16. Ibid.

17. Kevin Boyle, "After the Rainbow Sign: Jerome Cavanagh and 1960s Detroit," speech delivered November, 30, 1999, Walter P. Reuther Library, Wayne State University, http://www.reuther.wayne.edu/exhibits/cavanagh.html.

18. Ray Girardin, quoted in Fine, *Violence in the Model City,* 96.

19. "The Fire This Time," 13.

20. Ibid., 13.

21. *Fifth Estate,* August 1967.

22. Author's interview with Leni Sinclair.

23. Sinclair, interview by P. T. Quinn, *Perfect Sound Forever,* http://www.furious.com/perfect/mc5/johnsinclair.html.

24. Ibid.

25. Kramer, quoted in Kelly, "MC5's Other Guitarist."

26. Author's interview with Wayne Kramer.

27. Ibid.

28. Wayne Kramer, quoted in Kelly, "MC5's Other Guitarist."

29. Wayne Kramer, interview by Terry Gross, *Fresh Air,* NPR, August 19, 2002.

30. Author's interview with Dennis Thompson.

31. Author's interview with Michael Davis.

32. John Sinclair, "The MC5: How the Jams Were Kicked Out," *Zig Zag,* 1977.

33. Sinclair, *Guitar Army,* 195.

## Chapter 12

1. Morris and Nolan, "Sex, Drugs, Rock 'n' Roll."

2. Pat Halley, "Plum Street Redux," http://www.prweb.com/releases/2004/2/prweb102916.htm.

3. Author's interview with Harvey Ovshinsky.

4. Ibid.

5. Ibid.

6. Harvey Ovshinsky, quoted in Bill McGraw, "*Fifth Estate* Turns Twenty, as Radical as Ever," *Detroit Free Press,* November 22, 1985, 1b.

7. Author's interview with Harvey Ovshinsky.

8. Jacob Brackman, "The Underground Press," *Playboy,* August 1967, 83.

9. Ibid.

10. Ibid.

11. *Fifth Estate,* February 1–15, 1968, 1.

12. Author's interview with Harvey Ovshinsky.

13. Ibid.

14. Sinclair, *Guitar Army,* 195.

15. Radio commercial aired on Jim Rockwell's program at WABX, December 1967.

## Chapter 13

1. Author's interview with Tony Roumell.

2. Ibid.

3. Ibid.

4. Waller, *The Motown Story,* 57.

5. Author's interview with Tony Roumell.

6. Ibid.

7. Ron Stults, liner notes, "The Unrelated Segments: The Story of Their Lives," http://www.cicadelic.com/segments.htm.

8. Ibid.

9. Ibid.

10. Ibid.

11. Author's interview with Bob Baldori.

12. Ibid.

13. Ibid.

14. "Fuzz and Acid," on-line.

15. Ralph Terrana, "The Tera Shirma Story," in *Soulful Detroit.com,* 2002, http://www.soulfuldetroit.com.

16. Ibid.

17. Ryder, quoted in interview with Jay Burstein in *Official Mitch Ryder Web Site,* August 28, 2001, http://www.mitchryder.de/tradecenter_inter view.php.

18. Ibid.

19. Author's recollection.

20. Author's interview with Johnny Bee.

21. Ryder, quoted in "Mitch Ryder, Naked but Not Dead."

22. Ibid.

23. Ibid.

24. Bob Crewe, quoted in Marsh, "Bacon on the Paper," 16.

25. Ibid.

26. Ryder, quoted in Ed Ward, "In Detroit: Mitch Ryder, No Wheels," *Rolling Stone,* March 2, 1972, 31.

27. Ibid.

28. Author's interview with Johnny Bee.

29. Ibid.

30. McCarty, interview, *Vintage Guitar.*

31. Audio tape recording, CKLW, 1966.

32. "No Obscene Dancing."

33. Bob Seger, quoted from radio interview, http://www.segerfile .com/singles.html#music.

34. Seger, quoted in Dave Marsh, "Doncha Ever Listen to the Radio . . . How to Remain Obscure through Better Rock 'n' Roll; Bob Seger, Best in the Midwest," *Creem,* May 1972.

35. Ibid.

36. Marsh, "Not a Stranger Anymore," 69.

37. Bob Seger, quoted in ibid.

38. Author's interview with Gary Quackenbush.

39. Ibid.

40. Ibid.

41. Ibid.

42. E. G. Clawson, quoted in Debbie Burr, "SRC Music Is Like between Easy Rock 'n' Roll and Scary," *Creem,* April 1970.

43. Richardson, quoted in ibid.

44. Author's interview with Gary Quackenbush.

45. Clawson, in Burr, "SRC Music."

## Chapter 14

1. Morgan, quoted in Unterberger, *Urban Spacemen,* 217.

2. Vorda, "Interview with Ted Nugent."

3. Author's Interview with Bill Figg.

4. Nugent, quoted in Smith, "Super-energized Ted Nugent," 15.

5. Ibid.

6. "Amboy Dukes," http://www.classicbands.com/amboy.html.

7. http://www.patstjohn.com/wshj.asp.

8. Ron Wynn, "Bob Shad Profile," http://www.music.com/per son/bob_shad/1/.

9. Vorda, "Interview with Ted Nugent."

10. Ibid.

11. Nugent, quoted in Debbie Burr, "A Stone for Danny Fisher," *Creem*, February 1970.

12. Ibid.

13. Nugent, quoted in Wayne Bledsoe, "Rocker Nugent Revels in Goofy Theatrics," *Albuquerque Tribune Online,* http://www.abqtrib.com/archives/diversions/082799_nugent.shtml.

14. Author's interview with Wayne Kramer.

15. Ibid.

16. Sinclair, liner notes, *Get Out the Vote,* Total Energy Records, April 10, 1997.

17. Thompson, quoted in Mike Johnston, "Pen Up the Limits: An Interview with Dennis Thompson," in *Divine Rites Records,* 1995, http://www.divinerites.com/in_thom1.htm.

18. Sinclair, "The MC5: How the Jams Were Kicked Out."

19. Kramer, quoted in Guterman, liner notes, *The Big Bang!*

20. ARB ratings for Metro Detroit, 1968.

21. Author's interview with Dick Crockett.

22. Author's interview with Dan Carlisle.

23. Author's interview with Jerry Lubin.

24. Author's interview with Dan Carlisle.

25. Author's interview with Jerry Lubin.

### Chapter 15

1. Author's interview with Tom Gelardi.

2. Ibid.

3. Ibid.

4. Marsh, "Not a Stranger Anymore," 70.

5. Ibid.

6. Recollection of Rob Maisch, http://www.segerfile.com/concerts.html#oakland.

7. Seger, quoted in Marsh, "Not a Stranger Anymore," 68.

8. Frey, quoted by Bob Seger in ibid.

9. Author's interview with Jem Targal.

10. Bob Jones, http://www.segerfile.com/concerts.html#oakland.

### Chapter 16

1. Tom Wright, quoted in *Creem,* May 1969, 22.

2. Ibid.

3. Ibid.

4. Author's interview with Tom Wright.

5. Author's interview with Gary Quackenbush.

6. Recollections of author; author's interview with Russ Gibb; author's interview with Wayne Kramer.

7. Author's interview with Russ Gibb.

8. Author's interview with Gary Grimshaw.

9. Ibid.

10. Grimshaw, quoted in Dow, "Psychedelic Posters Rock," 68.

11. Author's interview with Gary Grimshaw.

12. Ibid.

13. Author's interview with Russ Gibb.

14. Ibid.

15. Gary Graff, "Wayne Kramer of the MC5 Still Kickin," *Guitar.com*/cda/columncorner/article_display.aspx?ssection=tl8spath=8 10000007492.

16. Sinclair, "The MC5: How the Jams Were Kicked Out."

17. Ibid.

18. Kramer, quoted in Gary Graff, "MC5er Still Kicks Out the Jams," *Detroit Free Press*, February 11, 1990.

19. Kramer, quoted in "MC5's Other Guitarist."

20. Kelly, quoted in ibid.

## Chapter 17

1. Legs McNeil and Gillian McCain, *Please Kill Me: The Uncensored Oral History of Punk* (New York: Grove Press, 1996), 41.

2. Ibid.

3. John Sinclair, quoted in McNeil and McCain, *Please Kill Me*, 41.

4. McNeil and McCain, *Please Kill Me*, 41.

5. Jim Osterberg (Iggy), liner notes for *American Caesar*, 1993.

6. Jim Osterberg (Iggy), quoted in interview with David Walley, in *Jazz and Pop*, July 1969.

7. Jim Osterberg (Iggy), liner notes for *American Caesar*.

8. Erlewine, "Prime Movers Bio," Rusted Chrome.com, http://home.att .net/~s.m.geer/bands.htm.

9. Radio interview, WHFS, Bethesda, Md., December 1980, http://www.geocities.com/mnennoburke/iggyinterviews.html.

10. Wayne Kramer, quoted in McNeil and McCain, *Please Kill Me*, 35.

11. McNeil and McCain, *Please Kill Me*, 11.

12. Ron Asheton, interview by Jason Gross, *Perfect Sound Forever*, February 2000, www.furious.com/perfect/ronasheton.html.

13. Ibid.

14. Ibid.

15. Ibid.

16. McNeil and McCain, *Please Kill Me*, 37.

17. Ron Asheton, interview by Gross.

18. Dave Marsh, "Is It Bizarre Music or Merely Better Music: The Incredible Story of Iggy and the Stooges," *Creem*, June 1970, 30.

19. McNeil and McCain, *Please Kill Me*, 40.

20. Ibid.

21. Ron Asheton, interview by Gross.

22. Marsh, "Bizarre Music," 31.

23. Ron Asheton, interview by Gross.

24. Author's recollection.

25. Marsh, "Bizarre Music," 30.

26. Russ Gibb, quoted by Jim Dunbar in "Wylde in the Streets," *Ray-Gun Magazine* 62, December 1998.

27. Jim Osterberg (Iggy), quoted in Brian McCollum, "Detroit's Pop Music Landmarks," *Detroit Free Press*, August 3, 1997, 1H.

28. David McLaughlin, *Mother's and Others: The Rock and Roll History of Romeo, Michigan* (Lakeville, Mich., 1997).

29. Ibid.

30. Jim Osterberg (Iggy), quoted in Jaan Uhelszki, "The Importance of Being Iggy," *Rollingstone.com*, July 13, 2001, http://www.rollingstone.com/news/newsarticle.asp?nid=14229&ct=85.

31. Ron Asheton, quoted in Dunbar, "Wylde in the Streets."

32. Ron Asheton, interview by Gross.

33. Dennis Thompson, quoted in Shimamoto, "Dennis Thompson: Phantom Patriot."

34. Jim Osterberg (Iggy), interview by Walley.

35. Ron Asheton, interview by Gross.

## Chapter 18

1. Sinclair, *Guitar Army*, 44.

2. Author's interview with Wayne Kramer.

3. John Sinclair, "Rock 'n' Roll Dope," *Fifth Estate*, June 19–July 1, 1968.

4. Ron Levine, quoted by Wayne Kramer in interview with the author.

5. Author's interview with Wayne Kramer.

6. John Sinclair, "Rock 'n' Roll Dope," June 19–July 1, 1968.

7. Glantz, quoted in "Rock 'n' Roll Dope," *Fifth Estate*, July 4–18, 1968.

8. Sinclair, "Rock 'n' Roll Dope," June 19–July 1, 1968.

9. Sinclair, *Guitar Army*, 3.

10. Billy James, *An American Band: The Story of Grand Funk Railroad* (London: SAF, 1999), 3.

11. Steven Geer, on-line bio at *Rusted Chrome* web site, http://home.att.net/ ~s.m.geer/bands.htm.

12. Doug Fulton, "Gallup Park—Where the Action Is," *Ann Arbor News*, August 16, 1968.

13. Sinclair, "Flash! MC5 Arrested in Ann Arbor for Playing Free Music in the Parks—Charged with Disturbing the Peace!" *Ann Arbor Sun*, July 28, 1968, reprinted in Sinclair, *Guitar Army*, 94.

14. Sinclair, "Rock 'n' Roll Dope #5," reprinted in Sinclair, *Guitar Army*, 91.

15. Author's interview with Wayne Kramer.

16. Sinclair, *Guitar Army*, 91.

17. Ibid.

18. Ibid., 94.

19. *Michigan Daily* (University of Michigan). Referenced in *Ann Arbor Sun*, Aug. 7, 1968.

20. Ibid.

21. Douglas O. Linder, "The Chicago Seven Conspiracy Trial," http://www.law.umkc.edu/faculty/projects/ftrials/Chicago7/Account.html.

22. Ibid.

23. Ibid.

24. Author's interview with Dennis Thompson.

25. Linder, "Chicago Seven Conspiracy Trial."

26. Author's interview with Wayne Kramer.

27. Ibid.

28. Ibid.

29. Kramer, "Riots I Have Known."

30. Kramer, quoted in McNeil and McCain, *Please Kill Me*, 43.

31. Norman Mailer, *Miami and the Siege of Chicago* (Cleveland: World Publishing, 1968), 142.

32. Sinclair, quoted in McNeil and McCain, *Please Kill Me*, 44.

33. Author's interview with Michael Davis.

34. Ibid.

35. Author's interview with Dennis Thompson.

## Chapter 19

1. Author's interview with Wayne Kramer.

2. John Sinclair, liner notes, *MC5—Power Trip*, July 1994.

3. Ken Shimamoto, "In the Trenches with the Guitar Army: Gary Rasmussen Reflects," in *Addicted to Noise*.

4. Sinclair, liner notes, *MC5—Power Trip*.

5. Ibid.

6. Kramer, interview by Terry Gross.

7. Dennis Frawley, quoted in Abe Peck, *Uncovering the Sixties: The Life and Times of the Underground Press* (New York: Pantheon, 1985), 173.

8. Author's interview with Dennis Frawley.

9. Ibid.

10. Fields, quoted in McNeil and McCain, *Please Kill Me*, 45.

11. Ibid.

12. Fields, quoted in McNeil and McCain, *Please Kill Me*.

13. Author's interview with Dan Carlisle.

14. Davis, quoted in *Freakout USA* 1, no. 1, 1993.

15. Fields, quoted in McNeil and McCain, *Please Kill Me*, 49.

16. Ibid.

17. Ibid.

18. Ibid.

19. Ibid.

20. Ibid.

21. Kramer, quoted in Kelly, "MC5's Other Guitarist."

22. Kramer, in Guterman, liner notes, *The Big Bang!*

23. Bruce Botnick, quoted in Jac Hoitzman and Gavin Davis, *Follow the Music: The Life and Times of Elektra Records in the Great Years of American Pop Culture* (Santa Monica, Calif.: First Media Books, 1998), 260.

24. Author's interview with John Sinclair.

25. Rick Clark, "The MC5's 'Kick Out the Jams,'" *Mix*, March 2003, 142.

26. Author's interview with Bruce Botnick.

27. Kramer, "Rocket Reducer."

28. Crawford's typical introduction to "Kick Out the Jams."

29. Kramer, "Rocket Reducer."

30. Ibid.

31. Ibid.

32. Author's interview with Bruce Botnick.

33. Kramer, "Rocket Reducer."

34. Holtzman and Davis, *Follow the Music*, 261.

35. Author's interview with Bruce Botnick.

36. Author's interview with Pun Plamondon.

37. Sinclair, *Guitar Army*, 56.

38. Ibid.

39. Ibid., 43.

40. Sinclair, "White Panther Manifesto," November 1, 1968, www.signal66.com/music/lostindc/00_03246.html.

41. Leach, quoted in Peck, *Uncovering the Sixties*, 173.

42. Ibid.

43. Ibid.

44. Sinclair, "White Panther Manifesto."

## Chapter 20

1. Author's interview with Wayne Kramer.

2. Ibid.

3. Ibid.

4. Chris Gray, "Black Mask," *Movement for Anarchy*.

5. Ibid.

6. Ibid.

7. Ibid.

8. Stanley Aronowitz, "Bohemian Eclipse," *First of the Month*, 2001, http://www.firstofthemonth.org/new/new_aronowitz_bohemian.html.

9. Author's interview with Wayne Kramer.

10. Fred Goodman, *The Mansion on the Hill: Dylan, Young, Geffen, Springsteen, and the Head-on Collision of Rock and Commerce* (New York: Times Books, 1997), 170.

11. Ibid.

12. Ibid.

13. Author's interview with Wayne Kramer.

14. Kramer, quoted in Kelly, "MC5's Other Guitarist."

15. Author's interview with Wayne Kramer.

16. Holtzman and Davis, *Follow the Music*.

17. Author's interview with Wayne Kramer.

18. Ibid.

19. Kramer, "Riots I Have Known."

20. Tyner, quoted in McNeil and McCain, *Please Kill Me*, 60.

21. Thompson, quoted in ibid.

22. Author's interview with Wayne Kramer.

23. Ibid.

24. Ibid.

25. Thompson, quoted in McNeil and McCain, *Please Kill Me*, 61.

26. Graham, quoted, ibid.

27. Fields, quoted in Goodman, *Mansion on the Hill*, 168.

28. Landau, quoted in ibid., 168.

29. Ibid.

30. Ibid.

31. Robert Christgau, "The Continuing Saga of the MC5," *Village Voice*, July 5, 1969.

32. Goodman, *Mansion on the Hill*, 169.

33. Sinclair, "The MC5: How the Jams Were Kicked Out."

34. Kramer, interview by Terry Gross.

35. Author's interview with Wayne Kramer.

36. *Argus* (Ann Arbor), February 13–27, 1969.

37. Author's interview with Dennis Thompson.

38. Ibid.

39. Sinclair, "The MC5: How the Jams Were Kicked Out."

40. Ibid.

41. Christgau, "Continuing Saga."

42. Sinclair, "The MC5: How the Jams Were Kicked Out."

43. Ibid.

44. John Sinclair, "The Story of the MC5 on the West Coast," *Creem*, May 1969, 20.

45. Ibid.

46. Author's interview with Dennis Frawley.

47. Sinclair, "MC5 on West Coast," 19–20.

48. Ibid.

49. *Creem*, May 1969.

50. Sinclair, "MC5 on West Coast," 19–20.

51. Ibid.

52. Ibid.

53. Ibid.

54. Mike Walter, "Clover Meets the MC5," http://www.clover-infopage.com/clover12.html.

55. Ibid.

56. Ibid.

57. Ibid.

58. Art Johnson, "MC5 in San Francisco," *Fifth Estate*, April 3–16, 1969.

59. Kramer, interview by Terry Gross.

60. Sinclair, "MC5 on West Coast," 19–20.

61. Johnson, "MC5 in San Francisco," *Fifth Estate*, April 3–16, 1969.

62. Sinclair, "MC5 on West Coast," 19–20.

63. Lester Bangs, "Kick Out the Jams," *Rolling Stone*, April 5, 1969.

64. Graham, quoted in Sinclair, "MC5 on West Coast," 19.

65. Ibid.

66. Author's interview with Dennis Frawley.

67. Sinclair, "The MC5: How the Jams Were Kicked Out."

68. Goodman, *Mansion on the Hill,* 173.

69. Sinclair, "MC5 on West Coast," 20.

## Chapter 21

1. Author's interview with Bill Figg.

2. Scott Morgan, quoted in Unterberger, *Urban Spacemen,* 219.

3. Author's interview with Bill Figg.

4. Ibid.

5. Ibid.

6. Ibid.

7. Ibid.

8. Terry Trabandt, quoted in Marsh and Burr, "The Rationals."

9. Scott Richardson, quoted in Burr, "SRC Music," 12.

10. Author's interview with Gary Quackenbush.

11. Burr, "SRC Music," 12.

12. Author's interview with Gary Quackenbush.

13. Morgan, quoted in Unterberger, *Urban Spacemen,* 220.

14. Advertisement for Detroit Pop Festival, *Creem*, March 1969.

15. "San Francisco?" *Creem,* March 1969, 7.

16. John Rhys Eddins, "Detroit Festival," *Creem,* April 1969, 20.

17. Author's interview with Dick Wagner.

18. Ibid.

19. Ibid.

20. Ibid.

21. Ibid.

22. Ibid.

23. Author's interview with Jem Targal.

24. Ibid.

25. Ibid.

26. Ibid.

27. *Creem,* June 1969, 14.

28. "Früt Rocking On Despite Adversity," *Creem,* April 1970, 20.

29. Eddins, "Detroit Pop Festival," 18.

### Chapter 22

1. Tony Reay, "Jeep—like the Car—Holland—like the Country," *Best of Boy Howdy,* http://groups.msn.com/bestofboyhowdy/tonyreay page1.msnw.

2. Ibid.

3. Ibid.

4. Tony Reay, "Like Pushing a Rubber Giraffe through a Keyhole," rockcritics.com/features/tonyreay_creem.html.

5. Ibid.

6. Ibid.

7. Ibid.

8. Dave Marsh, quoted in Margaret Moser, "Boy Howdy: The Creem Story," *Austin Chronicle* (Austin, Tex.), March 16, 2001.

9. Ibid.

10. Ibid.

11. Ibid.

12. *Creem,* July 1969, 4.

13. Author's interview with Dick Crockett.

14. Author's interview with Dan Carlisle.

15. Author's interview with Dick Crockett.

16. Author's interview with Dan Carlisle.

17. "WABX-FM Gets It On," *Fifth Estate,* October 31–November 13, 1968, 17.

18. Author's interview with Dan Carlisle.

19. Author's interview with Dick Crockett.

20. Connie White, "End of ABX Free Concerts," *Creem,* July 1969, 22.

21. "Jailhouse Rock," *Creem,* September 1969, 11.

22. Various ads and references in *Creem.*

23. Dave Marsh, DeDay LaRene, and Barry Kramer, "The Michigan Scene Today," *Creem,* April, 1970.

24. Described by fan who attended concert, http://ourworld.com puserve.com/homepages/rauk/tstamnis.html.

25. Dave Marsh, *Fortunate Son: The Best of Dave Marsh* (New York: Random House, 1985), 205.

26. Sinclair, "The MC5: How the Jams Were Kicked Out."

27. Ibid.

28. Goodman, *Mansion on the Hill,* 173.

29. Ibid.

30. Sinclair, "The MC5: How the Jams Were Kicked Out."

31. Dennis Thompson, quoted in Thompson, "MC5 Kickin' Out the Jams," 32.

32. Jon Landau, quoted in Goodman, *Mansion on the Hill,* 176.

33. Ibid.

34. Thompson, quoted in McNeil and McCain, *Please Kill Me,* 71.

35. Kramer, quoted in ibid., 71.

36. Author's interview with Dennis Thompson.

37. Ibid.

38. Landau, quoted in Goodman, *Mansion on the Hill,* 177.

39. Sinclair, "The MC5: How the Jams Were Kicked Out."

40. Ibid.

41. Goodman, *Mansion on the Hill.*

42. Sinclair, *Guitar Army.*

43. Sinclair, "The MC5: How the Jams Were Kicked Out."

44. "MC5 on the Cusp," *Creem,* September 1969, 16.

45. Dennis Thompson, quoted in McNeil and McCain, *Please Kill Me,* 72.

46. *Creem,* July 1969, 11.

47. McCollum, "Detroit's Pop Music Landmarks," 1H.

48. *Creem,* September 1969, 2.

49. Ibid.

50. Trial transcript, *State of Michigan v. John Sinclair,* Recorder's Court, Detroit, Robert J. Columbo presiding, July 22–28, 1969.

51. Ibid.

52. Columbo, quoted in ibid.

53. Ibid.

54. Ibid.

55. Ad. Creem, July, 1969.

56. Ibid.

57. Leni Sinclair, quoted in Bill Marvel, "Memories of '60s Rock," *Dallas Morning News,* August 5, 1994, http://sfgate.com/examiner/ee94/woodstockmoments940807.html.

58. Author's interview with Pun Plamondon.

59. Leni Sinclair, quoted in Singer, "Radical Captured 1960s."

60. Author's interview with Leni Sinclair.

61. Ibid.

62. Author's interview with Pun Plamondon.

63. Kramer, quoted in "MC5 on the Cusp," 16.

64. Ibid.

65. Ibid.

66. Tyner, quoted in "MC5 on the Cusp," 16.

67. Ibid.

68. Sinclair, interview by Quinn.

## Chapter 23

1. Jac Holtzman, quoted by Ron Asheton in McNeil and McCain, *Please Kill Me,* 54.

2. Ron Asheton, quoted in McNeil and McCain, *Please Kill Me,* 71.

3. Ron Asheton, quoted in Ralph Heibutzki, "Ron Asheton Revisits the Fun House," *Vintage Guitar,* January 2000.

4. Ibid.

5. Harry Young, "The Stooges on Elektra, 1969–70," http://www.geocities.com/sunsetstrip/palladium/1306/iggy.htm.

6. Jim Osterberg (Iggy), quoted in "Which Mask Are You," *The Big Takeover* no. 49, 2001, http://www.bigtakeover.com/iggy49.html.

7. Ibid.

8. Ron Asheton, quoted in "Wylde in the Streets."

9. Ron Asheton, quoted in Heibutzki, "Asheton Revisits the Funhouse."

10. Ibid.

11. Heibutzki, "Asheton Revisits the Funhouse."

12. "1969 . . . the Stooges," *Creem,* July 1969, 9.

13. Fred Kirby, "Excitement MC5 Keynote—Stooges Make N.Y. Debut," *Billboard,* September 20, 1969.

14. Ibid.

15. Lenny Kaye, "Iggy and the Stooges: Your Pretty Face Is Going to Hell and Back," *Gadfly,* June 1999.

16. Jim Osterberg (Iggy), quoted in Marsh, "Bizarre Music," 32.

17. Ron Asheton, quoted in "Wylde in the Streets."

18. Ibid.

19. Ron Asheton, interview by Gross.

20. Ibid.

**Chapter 24**

1. *Creem,* July 1969.

2. "Carlisle-ABX Split," ibid., 10.

3. "WABX Air Ace Fifth Anniversary," station document, 1973.

4. Author's interview with Russ Gibb.

5. Author's interview with Dan Carlisle.

6. "Russ Buys Eastown?" *Creem,* September 1969, 16.

7. Aaron Russo, quoted in "Battle of the Ballrooms," *Creem,* November 1969, 6.

8. Ibid.

9. "The Mouth," *Creem,* March 1969, 9.

10. Russ Gibb, quoted in "Battle of the Ballrooms," 26.

11. Ibid.

12. "Battle of the Ballrooms," 21.

13. Bill McGraw, "Motor City Journal: Teacher Can't Live Down Tie to Beatle," *Detroit Free Press,* October 12, 2000.

14. Russ Gibb, quoted in ibid.

15. Russ Gibb, quoted in Deday LaRene, "The Walrus Was Paul?" *Creem,* December 1969, 5.

16. Larry Monroe, "The Paul McCartney Death Rumor," 1999, http://www.larrymonroe.com/archive/archive11.html.

17. LaRene, "The Walrus Was Paul?" 5.

18. Ibid.

19. Tom Gelardi, quoted in ibid.

20. McGraw, "Motor City Journal: Teacher Can't Live Down Tie to Beatle."

21. LaRene, "The Walrus Was Paul?" 8.

22. On-line biography of Mike Quatro.

23. Concert ad in *Creem,* October 1969.

24. Barry Kramer and Dave Marsh, "A Fiasco of the Black Arts," *Creem,* December 1969.

25. Ibid.

26. Ibid.

## Chapter 25

1. "The Michigan Bands," in *Creem,* April 1970.

2. Debbie Burr, "Grand Funk Railroad or . . . the Great Train Robbery," *Creem,* December 1969, 12.

3. Don Brewer, quoted in ibid., 2.

4. Terry Knight, quoted in ibid., 12.

5. Roeser, "Tumultuous Times," 44.

6. Ibid., 45.

7. Ibid., 45.

8. Timothy Ferris, "Knight vs. Funk: An End to Brotherhood," *Rolling Stone,* October 12, 1972.

9. Brewer, quoted in ibid.

10. Roeser, "Tumultuous Times," 45.

11. Knight, quoted in Roeser, "Tumultuous Times," 46.

12. Ibid.

13. Robert Hilburn, "Grand Funk Rock's Newest Phenomenon," *Los Angeles Times,* February 9, 1971.

14. Ibid.

15. Knight, quoted in Roeser, "Tumultuous Times," 46.

16. Roeser, "Tumultuous Times," 46.

17. Brewer, quoted in Burr, "Grand Funk Railroad," 14.

18. Roeser, "Tumultuous Times," 45.

19. Brewer, quoted in ibid.

20. Roeser, "Tumultuous Times," 46.

21. Ibid.

22. Burr, "Grand Funk Railroad," 14.

23. *Billboard* magazine, quoted in ibid.

24. Brewer, quoted in Burr, "Grand Funk Railroad," 14.

## Chapter 26

1. Kramer, quoted in "MC5 on the Cusp," 17.

2. Ibid.

3. Ibid.

4. Landau, quoted in ibid.

5. Ibid.

6. Author's interview with Pun Plamondon.

7. Marsh, LeRene, and Kramer, "The Michigan Scene Today," *Creem,* April 1970.

8. Thompson, quoted in Shimamoto, "Dennis Thompson Interview Part Two," I-94 bar.com/ints/thompson2.html.

9. Ibid.

10. Kramer, quoted in Jim Irwin, *The Mojo Collection* (Edinburgh: Mojo Books, 2001).

11. Ibid.

12. Author's interview with Dennis Thompson.

13. Greil Marcus, "Back in the USA," *Rolling Stone,* May 14, 1970.

14. Dennis Thompson, quoted in Thompson, "MC5 Kickin' Out the Jams," 32.

15. "Everyone Benefits," *Creem,* March 1970.

16. Ibid.

17. Ibid.

18. Marsh, LaRene, and Kramer, "The Michigan Scene Today."

19. Sinclair, letter to the *Michigan Daily* (University of Michigan), September 28, 1969.

20. "Michigan Bands," *Creem,* March 1970.

21. George Frayne, "The Story of Commander Cody and His Lost Planet Airmen," http://www.commandercody.com.

22. Ibid.

23. Pat Piper, "Our Man on Twang Climbs the Mountain," *Bay Weekly,* February 21–27, 2002.

24. Ryder, quoted in Marsh, "Bacon on the Paper," 16.

25. Ibid., 16.

26. Ibid., 17.

27. Ibid., 16.

28. Ryder, quoted in "Mitch Ryder: Naked But Not Dead."

29. Marsh, "Bacon on the Paper," 17.

30. Ryder, quoted in "Mitch Ryder: Naked But Not Dead."

31. Ibid.

32. Ibid.

33. Ibid.

34. Ibid.

35. Ibid.

36. Ibid.

37. Author's interview with Johnny Bee.

38. Ibid.

39. Barry Kramer, "Wheels on the Road," *Creem,* August 1970, 34.

40. Ibid., 34.

41. Marsh, LaRene, and Kramer, "The Michigan Scene Today."

42. Author's interview with Dan Carlisle.

43. Marsh, LaRene, and Kramer, "The Michigan Scene Today."

44. "Glantz, Gibb, and the Grande Gang," *Creem,* February 1970, 3.

45. "Rock 'n' Roll News," *Creem,* January 1970, 3.

46. Author's interview with Bill Figg.

47. Author's interview with Richard Stevers.

48. Ibid.

49. Ibid.

50. Ibid.

51. Ibid.

52. Ibid.

53. "Michigan Bands."

54. Dave Marsh, "Iggy Stooge in Sherwood Forest," *Creem,* June 1970.

55. Peter C. Cavanaugh, *Local DJ* (Clarkston, Mich.: Xlibris/Peter C. Cavanaugh, 2001), 161–62.

56. Marsh, "Iggy Stooge in Sherwood Forest."

57. S. L. Duff, "LA Blues," *New Times Los Angeles,* January 20, 2000.

58. Ron Asheton, interview by Gross.

59. Ibid.

60. Ibid.

61. Ron Asheton, interview by Gross.

62. Radio ad for "Wild Wednesday."

63. Debbie Burr, "Savage Grace . . . a Savage Paradox," *Creem,* May 1970, 21–23.

64. Sinclair, "The Lesson of Goose Lake," *Guitar Army,* 253.

65. Ad in *Detroit News,* August 4, 1970.

66. Howard Kohn, "Show Ends but 50,000 to Stay On," *Detroit Free Press,* August 10, 1970, 10a.

67. Lisa Williams, "A Minimum Security Bash," *Los Angeles Free Press,* reprinted in *Creem,* August 1970, 14.

68. Author's interview with Jem Targal.

69. Ibid.

70. Charles Manos, "Youth Survives Fall from Rock Fest Tower," *Detroit News,* August 9, 1970, 2.

71. Kohn, "Show Ends," 10a.

72. Author's interview with Dennis Frawley.

73. Manos, "Youth Survives Fall," 3a.

74. Ibid.

75. Kohn, "Show Ends," 10a.

76. Williams, "A Minimum Security Bash," 15.

77. Sinclair, "Lesson of Goose Lake," *Guitar Army,* 253.

78. Author's interview with Dan Carlisle.

79. Ibid.

80. Milliken, quoted in Charles Manos, "Good-by Rock. . . ," *Detroit News,* August 10, 1970, 3a.

81. Ibid.

82. Kelly, quoted in George Cantor, "Goose Lake Rock Festival Faces Trouble," *Detroit Free Press,* August 12, 1970, 1.

83. Barton, quoted in ibid.

84. Songer, quoted in ibid.

85. Author's interview with Dennis Frawley.

86. Author's interview with Bill Figg.

87. Ibid.

88. Fred Saxon, quoted in forum discussion at www.soulfuldetroit.com.

89. Author's interview with Bill Figg.

90. Morgan, quoted in Shimamoto, "Pirate Music."

91. Author's interview with Bill Figg.

92. Author's interview with Jim Bugnel.

93. Ibid.

94. Ibid.

95. Ibid.

96. Ibid.

97. Terrana, "The Tera Shirma Story."

98. "Get Ready," http://www.superseventies.com/1970_3singles.html.

99. Rivera, quoted in "Beginnings . . . Peter Rivera," http://www.rockforever.com/features/beginnings/begin_07262000.html.

100. Ibid.

101. Ibid.

102. Ibid.

103. Author's interview with Bob Babbitt.

104. Author's interview with Harry Balk.

105. Steve Harnadek, quoted in *Creem,* August 1970, 5.

106. Wayne Kramer, quoted in Guterman, liner notes, *The Big Bang!*

107. Ibid.

108. Murph Murphy, "Interview with Don Brewer," *Music Street Journal,* March 3, 1998.

109. Ibid.

110. Roeser, "Tumultuous Times," 47.

111. Robert Christgau, "Mark, Don, Mel, and Terry," *Newsday,* May 1972.

112. *Detroit Free Press,* May 17, 1970.

113. Farner, quoted in Fred Mills, "Still in a Grand Funk," *Metro Times,* 2003.

114. Author's interview with Dennis Thompson.

115. Dave Marsh and Barry Kramer, "8,000 Celebrate Dylan's Birthday," *Creem,* June 1970, 11.

116. Marsh, LaRene, and Kramer, "The Michigan Scene Today."

117. John Lydon, "Billion Dollar Baby—the Alice Cooper Story," *BBC Music Profile.*

118. Ibid.

119. Furnier, interview by Mike Quigley, *Poppin,* September 1969, http://www.mjq.net/interviews/alice.htm.

120. Lydon, "Billion Dollar Baby."

121. Mark Weisblott, "Alice through the Windshield," *Eye Weekly* (Toronto), June 30, 1994.

122. Furnier, interview by Quigley.

123. Furnier, quoted in Salvatore Caputo, "Alice Cooper Still Likes to Rock, Shock," *Ann Arbor News,* July 20, 1996.

124. Furnier, quoted in McCollum, "Detroit's Pop Music Landmarks," 1H.

125. Furnier, interview by Quigley.

126. Author's interview with Tom Gelardi.

127. Author's interview with Rosalie Trombley.

128. Ibid.

129. Ibid.

130. Rick Vincent, *Funk: The Music, the People, and the Rhythm of the One* (New York: St. Martins Press, 1996), 232.

131. Geoffrey Jacques, "Parliafunkadelicment Thang," *Creem,* October 1970, 27.

132. Clinton, quoted in ibid., 27.

133. Ibid., 26.

134. Clinton interview with J. Eric Smith, 1996, http://www.jericsmith.com/interviews/clintonint.htm.

135. Jacques, "Parliafunkadelicment Thang."

136. Author's interview with Jim Bugnel.

137. Clinton, interview by Smith.

# Chapter 27

1. Author's interview with Pun Plamondon.

2. Jeff Hale, "Linking Woodstock to Antiwar Protest, Again," November 28, 1997, http://lists.village.virginia.edu/lists_archive/sixties-1/0283.html.

3. Author's interview with Dennis Thompson.

4. Lenny Kaye, "Review of *High Time*," *Rolling Stone*, September 22, 1971.

5. Thompson, quoted in Shimamoto, "Dennis Thompson: Phantom Patriot."

6. Marsh, quoted in Peck, *Uncovering the Sixties*, 175.

7. Mills, "Still in a Grand Funk."

8. Ibid.

9. Author's interview with Dennis Thompson.

10. Author's interview with Michael Davis.

11. McNeil and McCain, *Please Kill Me*, 65.

12. Asheton, quoted in "Wylde in the Streets."

13. Bill Harvey, quoted by Fields in McNeil and McCain, *Please Kill Me*, 78.

14. Fields, quoted in ibid., 79.

15. Ibid.

16. *Creem*, July 1969.

17. Seger, quoted in Robert Hilburn, "Bob Seger, Rock's Prodigal Son," *Los Angeles Times*, May 22, 1977.

18. Seger, quoted in ibid.

19. Seger, quoted in ibid.

20. Seger, quoted in ibid.

21. Author's interview with Dick Wagner.

22. Author's interview with Mitch Ryder.

23. Sorenson and McGrath, "Mitch Ryder Interview."

24. Ryder, quoted in Ward, "In Detroit, Mitch Ryder," 30.

25. Ibid.

26. Ibid., 32.

27. Ibid., 30.

28. Ibid.

29. Bill Gray, "15,000 at Ann Arbor Rally to Aid John Sinclair," *Detroit News*, December 11, 1971, 3a.

30. Ibid.

31. Sinclair, quoted in ibid., 3a.

32. Ibid.

33. Author's interview with Leni Sinclair.

34. Marco Trbovich and George Cantor, "A Happy Sinclair Leaves Prison, Free on Bond," *Detroit Free Press*, December 14, 1971, 5a.

35. Author's interview with Leni Sinclair.

36. Trbovich and Cantor, "A Happy Sinclair Leaves Prison."

37. Mother of John Sinclair, quoted in Trbovich and Cantor, "Happy Sinclair Leaves Prison," 5a.

38. Sinclair, liner notes, *Get Out the Vote*, April 10, 1997.

39. Sinclair, quoted in Claudia Lauer, "John Sinclair: Kickin' Out the Blues," *Student Underground*, http://www.thestudentunderground.org/article/.php?issue=378articleid=185.

40. "US vs. Sinclair," discussed in Madison J. Gray, "Gavels for Justice," *Detroit News,* February 9, 2000.

41. Sinclair, liner notes, *Get Out the Vote.*

42. Ibid.

43. Author's interview with Johnny Bee.

44. Vorda, "Interview with Ted Nugent."

45. Nugent, quoted in Ted Finnegan, "Ted Nugent: The Primal Scream," *Where Y'at New Orleans,* http://www.whereyatnola.com.

46. Vorda, "Interview with Ted Nugent."

47. Ibid.

48. Ibid.

49. Ibid.

50. Ibid.

51. Author's interview with Richard Stevers.

52. Author's interview with Wayne Kramer.

53. Author's interview with Michael Davis.

54. Ibid.

55. Ibid.

56. Ibid.

57. Charles Shaar Murray, "Teen Outrage in Croydon," *Creem,* March 1972.

58. Ibid.

59. Ibid.

60. Thompson, quoted in Dan Lovranski, "MC5: Still Kicking Out the Jams," http://www.chartattack.com.

61. Advertisement for Wembley Stadium concert, August 5, 1972, http://makemyday.free.fr/72/mc5_posters_1972_5htm.

62. Author's interview with Dennis Thompson.

63. Author's interview with Wayne Kramer.

64. Ibid.

65. Ibid.

66. Author's interview with Michael Davis.

67. Author's interview with Dennis Thompson.

68. Author's interview with Wayne Kramer.

69. Ibid.

70. Author's interview with Dan Carlisle.

71. Ibid.

72. Ron Asheton, quoted in "Wylde in the Street."

73. Author's interview with Michael Davis.

74. Ibid.

75. Author's interview with Dennis Thompson.

76. Author's interview with Jem Targal.

77. Author's interview with Gary Quackenbush.

78. Ibid.

79. Author's interview with Dan Carlisle.

80. Author's interview with Russ Gibb.

81. "Eastown Shut Down," *Detroit Free Press,* December 11, 1971, 1a.

82. Dave Marsh, "Looney Tunes: Every Picture Tells a Story . . . Don't It," *Creem,* March 1972.

83. Sinclair, quoted in Strausbaugh, *Rock 'Til You Drop,* 101.

84. Author's interview with Pun Plamondon.

85. Eddie Willis, quoted in motion picture *Standing in the Shadows of Motown,* 2002.

## Epilogue

1. Greg Kot, "Devotion Keeps Detroit as Rock City," *Chicago Tribune,* Dec. 18, 2003.

2. Graff, "Detroit's First Promoter of Major Rock Concerts," *Detroit Free Press,* April 6, 1985.

3. Author's interview with Harry Balk.

4. Hank Ballard and the Midnighters Biography. http://www.online talent.com/ballard_biography.html.

5. Sarah Webster, "Michael 'Cub' Koda, 51, Musician, Songwriter," *Detroit News,* July 3, 2000.

6. Author's interview with Dan Carlisle.

7. Vincent, *Funk.*

8. Author's interview with Jamie Coe.

9. Lydon, "Billion Dollar Baby."

10. Ibid.

11. Sam Adams, "Out of the Dark," in Philadelphia City Paper.net, November 14–20, 2002, http://citypaper.net/articles/2002–11–14/movies3.shtml.

12. Author's interview with Russ Gibb.

13. Gordy, *To Be Loved,* 398.

14. Roeser, "Tumultuous Times," 48–49.

15. Mills, "Still in a Grand Funk."

16. Gary Grimshaw biography, http://www.posterplanet.com/grimshaw/index.htm.

17. Author's interview with Gary Grimshaw.

18. Marcus, obituary of Jeep Holland, *Boston Globe.*

19. Johnson, "John Lee Hooker."

20. Alan Neister, "Gonzo with the Wind," http://www.evalu8.org/staticpage?page=review8siteid=2156.

21. http:www.rockcritics.com/interview/davemarsh.html.

22. Gerritt, "David Leone."

23. Author's interview with Barbara Lewis.

24. Mike Zwerin, "Wayne Kramer: Out of Hibernation," *International Herald Tribune,* June 15, 1996.

25. Ibid.

26. Ibid.

27. Author's interview with Michael Davis.

28. Author's interview with Dennis Thompson.

29. Thompson, "MC5 Kickin' Out the Jams."

30. Gohastings.com.

31. "MC5," emusic.com.

32. Gïanluca Tramontana, "MC5 Come Together in London," *Rolling Stone,* March 17, 2003.

33. Alexis Petridis, "Punk Profits," *Guardian,* March 13, 2003.

34. "Michigan Bands," *Creem,* March 1970.

35. "Original MC5 Members to Tour as DKT/MC5," March 23, 2003, http://www.dkt-mc5.com.

36. Heron, "Producer Put His Touch on Singers' Hits," *Detroit Free Press,* February 24, 1984, 11C.

37. Unterberger, *Urban Spacemen.*

38. Author's interview with Bill Figg.

39. Ted Nugent biography, www.tednugent.com.

40. Smith, "Super-Energized Ted Nugent."

41. Author's interview with Harvey Ovshinsky.

42. Bill McGraw, "Motor City Journal: Underground Paper Leaves City, Not Roots," *Detroit Free Press,* September 2002.

43. Author's interview with Bunny Paul.

44. Ibid.

45. Author's interview with Pun Plamondon.

46. Ron Asheton, interview by Gross.

47. Ibid.

48. Brian McCollum, "The Stooges Come Home: New Appreciation, Loyal Fans, and a Phone Call from Iggy Pop Get Them Back Together," *Detroit Free Press,* August 13, 2003.

49. Suzi Quatro Biography.

50. "Mitch Ryder—Naked But Not Dead."

51. Author's interview with Mitch Ryder.

52. Author's interview with Johnny Bee.

53. Ibid.

54. McCarty, interview, *Vintage Guitar.*

55. Ted Nugent, quoted in "Best Live Show," http://www.mitchry der.de/guitarworld.php.

56. Author's interview with Earl Elliott.

57. DeGain, "Hazel Park's Jack Scott."

58. Marsh, "Not a Stranger Anymore."

59. Bob Seger profile, http://members.at.infoseek.co.jf/silverbul let/bio.html.

60. Author's interview with Robin Seymour.

61. "Del Shannon Rock On!" http://dzlc.com/spacebeagle/delshan non.html.

62. "Del Shannon, 1934–1990: Psychiatric Drug Devastates Artist," http://www.cchr.org/art/eng/page20.htm.

63. John Sinclair Papers, Bentley Library, University of Michigan.

64. Frank Provenzano, "The Beat Moves On: Good-bye to Detroit icon," *Detroit Free Press,* October 26, 2003.

65. John Sinclair, quoted in Michael Roberts, "Surviving the Sixties," *Denver NewsTimes,* August 7–13, 1997.

66. Author's interview with Leni Sinclair.

67. Author's interview with Gary Quackenbush.

68. Austin, liner notes, *Daddy Rock.*

69. Author's interview with Jem Targal.

70. Author's interview with Tony Roumell.

71. Adam Stanfel, "The United Sound," *Metro Times,* May 19, 2004.

72. Shimamoto, "In the Trenches."

73. Author's interview with Dennis Frawley.

74. Greg Pederson, "The Great Guitars of Dick Wagner and Steve Hunter," *Vintage Guitar,* February 1998.

# Bibliography

## Books

Bego, Mark. *Aretha Franklin: The Queen of Soul.* New York: St. Martin's Press, 1989.

Bjorn, Lars, with Jim Gallert. *Before Motown: A History of Jazz in Detroit, 1920–1960.* Ann Arbor: University of Michigan Press, 2000.

Boyd, Herb. *Detroit Jazz Who's Who.* Jazz Research Institute, 1984.

Carson, David. *Rockin' Down the Dial: The Detroit Sound of Radio, from Jack the Bellboy to the Big 8.* Troy, Mich.: Momentum Books, 1999.

Cavanaugh, Peter C. *Local DJ: A Rock 'n' Roll History.* Clarkston, Mich.: Xlibris /Peter C. Cavanaugh, 2002.

Churchill, Ward, and Jim Vander Wall. *The Cointelpro Papers, Documents from the FBI's Secret Wars against Dissent in the United States.* Detroit: South End Press. 2nd ed., July, 2002.

Donner, Frank J. *Protectors of Privilege: Red Squads and Police Repression in Urban America.* Berkeley: University of California Press, 1990.

Driver, Jim, ed. *Mammoth Book of Sex, Drugs, and Rock 'n' Roll.* New York: Carrol and Craft, 2001.

Fine, Sidney. *Violence in the Model City: The Cavanagh Administration, Race Relations, and the Detroit Riots of 1967.* Ann Arbor: University of Michigan Press, 1989.

Gavrilovich, Peter, and Bill McGraw, eds. "Detroit Almanac." *Detroit Free Press,* October 13, 2000.

George, Nelson. *Where Did Our Love Go? The Rise and Fall of the Motown Sound.* New York: St. Martin's Press, 1985.

Goodman, Fred. *The Mansion on the Hill: Dylan, Young, Geffen, Springsteen, and the Head-On Collision of Rock and Commerce.* New York: Times Books, 1997.

Gordy, Berry. *To Be Loved.* New York: Warner Books, 1994.

Harris, Sheldon. *Blue's Who's Who: A Biographical Dictionary of Blues Singers.* New Rochelle, N.Y.: Arlington House, 1979.

Hersey, John. *The Algiers Motel Incident.* New York: Knopf, 1968.

Holtzman, Jac, and Gavin Daws. *Follow the Music: The Life and Times of Elektra Records in the Great Years of American Pop Culture.* Santa Monica, Calif.: First Media Books, 1998.

Irwin, Jim. *The Mojo Collection.* Edinburgh: Mojo Books, 2001.

James, Billy. *An American Band: The Story of Grand Funk Railroad.* London: SAF, 1999.

Joynson, Vernon. *Fuzz. Acid, and Flowers: A Comprehensive Guide to American Garage, Psychedelic, and Hippie Rock (1964–1975).* Borderline Productions, 1998.

Keith, Michael. *Voices in the Purple Haze: Underground Radio and the Sixties.* Westport, Conn.: Praeger, 1997.

Mailer, Norman. *Miami and the Siege of Chicago.* Cleveland: World Publishing, 1968.

Marsh, Dave. *Fortunate Son: The Best of Dave Marsh.* New York: Random House, 1985.

Marsh, Dave, and John Swenson, eds. *The Rolling Stone Record Guide.* New York: Random House/Rolling Stone Press,1979.

McLaughlin, David. *Mother's and Others: The Rock and Roll History of Romeo, Michigan.* Lakeville, Mich., 1997.

McNeil, Legs, and Gillian McCain. *Please Kill Me: The Uncensored Oral History of Punk.* New York: Grove Press, 1996.

Merlis, Bob, and Davin Seay. *Heart and Soul: A Celebration of Black Music Styles in America, 1930–1975.* New York: Stewart, Tabori and Chang, 1997.

Murray, Charles Shaar. *Boogie Man: The Adventures of John Lee Hooker in the American Twentieth Century.* New York: St. Martin's Press, 2002.

Obrecht, Jay. *Rollin' and Tumblin': The Postwar Blues Guitarists.* San Francisco: Miller Freeman, 2000.

Oliver, Paul. *The Story of the Blues.* Boston: Northeastern University Press, 1977.

O'Neal, Jim, and Amy Van Singel. *The Voice of the Blues: Classic Interviews from Living Blues Magazine.* New York: Routledge, 2002.

Patterson, Gary. *The Walrus Was Paul.* Nashville: Dowling Press, 1996.

Peck, Abe. *Uncovering the Sixties: The Life and Times of the Underground Press.* New York: Pantheon, 1985.

Poore, Billy, and Danny Gatton. *Rockabilly: A Forty Year Journey.* New York: Hal Leonard, 1998.

Robinson, Smokey, with David Ritz. *Smokey: Inside My Life.* New York: McGraw-Hill, 1989.

Sinclair, John. *Guitar Army.* New York: Douglas Book Corporation, 1971.

Strausbaugh, John. *Rock 'Til You Drop.* London: Verso, 2001.

Thompson, Dave. *Funk.* San Francisco: Backbeat Books, 2001.

Unterberger, Richie. *Urban Spacemen and Wayfaring Strangers: Overlooked Innovators and Eccentric Visionaries of '60s Rock.* San Francisco: Backbeat Books, 2000.

Vincent, Rickey. *Funk: The Music, the People, and the Rhythm of the One.* New York: St. Martin's Press, 1996.

Waller, Don. *The Motown Story.* New York: Charles Scribner's Sons, 1985.

Warner, Jay. *The Billboard Book of American Singing Groups.* New York: Billboard Books, 1992.

Whitburn, Joel. *Top Pop Records.* New York: Billboard Books, 1991.

———. *Top R&B Singles, 1942–1995.* Menominee Falls, Wis.: Record Research, 1996.

———. *Top Pop Albums, 1955–2001.* Menominee Falls, Wis.: Record Research, 2001.

### Articles and Documents

Adams, Sam. "Out of the Dark." *Philadelphia City Paper,* November 14–20, 2002. http://citypaper.net/articles/2002–11–14/movies3.shtml.

Adler, Alan. "Rock 'n' Roll Survivor Still Enjoys Singing His Own Way." *Oakland Press,* March 7, 2002.

Albert, Stew. "Chicago '68 . . . My Kind of Town." http://www.mem
bers.aol.com/stewa/chicago.htm.

"Alice Cooper Biography." *Keno's Classic Rock n Roll.* http://www.keno
.org/alice_cooper_bio.htm.

"Alice Cooper." *Rockin Town.com.* http://www.rockintown.com/cosmet
ics/alice_cooper.html.

Alterman, Loraine. "Underdogs Reach for a Platter Star." *Detroit Free Press,*
October 22, 1965.

———. "Ernie Durham, First Record Hop Man." *Detroit Free Press,* April 9,
1967.

"An American Tragedy, 1967—Detroit." *Newsweek,* August 7, 1967.

Ankeny, Jason. "Russ Gibb Biography." *All Music Guide,* http:// www.all
music.com/cg/amg.dll?p=amg&sql=11:lyarqj7iojda~T1.

Aronowitz, Stanley. "Bohemian Eclipse." *First of the Month.* 2002,
http://www.firstofthemonth.org/new/new_aronowitz_bohemian
.html.

Austin, James. "The Fortune Record Story." Album liner notes. http://
www.lexjansen.com/fortune/.

Bangs, Lester. "Kick Out the Jams." *Rolling Stone,* April 5, 1969.

———. "Of Pop and Pies and Fun." *Creem,* November–December
1970.

———. Review of SRC and Frost albums. *Rolling Stone,* February 7, 1970.

Barnard, Ken. "Berry Gordy Jr.—Detroit's Record King." *Detroit Free Press,*
December 26, 1962.

"Battle of the Ballrooms." *Creem,* November 1969.

"Beginnings . . . Peter Rivera." *Rockforever.com.* http://www.rockforever
.com/features/beginnings/begin-07262000.html.

Bezanker, Paul. Original liner notes. *Daddy Rock: The Legendary Nolan
Strong with the Diablos,* Fortune Records, http://www.lexjansen.com/
fortune/diablos.htm.

Billy C. Farlow biography. http://www.billycfarlow.com/bio.html.

Blanchard, Allan. "Riot at Love-In: Ten Jailed." *Detroit News,* May 1, 1967.

Bledsoe, Wayne. "Rocker Nugent Revels in Goofy Theatrics," Albuquerque Tribune Online, http://www.abqtrib.com/archives/diver
sions/082799_nugent.shtml.

"Bob Seger." http://www.classicbands.com/seger.html.

Bob Seger biography. *Rolling Stone.com.* http:// www.rollingstone.com.

Bob Seger, http://www.classicbands.com/seger.html.

Bolt, Herbert M. "Johnson Sends Five Thousand Troops." *Detroit News,*
July 24, 1967.

Bond, Marilyn. "Rockin' in the Motor City." *Rock and Blues News,*
August–September 2000.

Boyd, Herb. "Cookin' in the Motor City." *Metro Times,* September 17,
1997.

Boyle, Kevin. "After the Rainbow Sign: Jerome Cavanagh and 1960s
Detroit." Speech delivered November, 30, 1999, Walter P. Reuther
Library, Wayne State University. http://www.reuther.wayne.edu/
exhibits/cavanagh.html.

Brackman, Jacob. "The Underground Press." *Playboy,* August, 1967.

Brent, Pam. "Crow's Nest." *Creem,* March 1969.

Bronston, Gary. "Protesters at Chicago Toe Line." *Detroit Free Press,* August
26, 1968.

Bronston, Gary, and Susan Holmes. "Belle Isle Love-In Turns to Hate." *Detroit Free Press,* May 1, 1967.

Bryan, John. "MC5 Kick Out the What?" *Rolling Stone,* October 15, 1970.

Burr, Debbie. "Grand Funk Railroad or . . . the Great Train Robbery." *Creem,* December 1969.

———. "Savage Grace . . . a Savage Paradox." *Creem,* May 1970.

———. "SRC Music Is Like between Easy Rock and Roll and Scary." *Creem,* April 1970.

———. "A Stone for Danny Fisher." *Creem,* February 1970.

Burstein, Jay. "Mitch Ryder Interview." *Official Mitch Ryder Web Site.* August 28, 2001. http://wwwmitchryder.de/tradecenter_interview.php.

Cantor, George. "Goose Lake Rock Festival Faces Trouble." *Detroit Free Press,* August 12, 1970.

Caputo, Salvatore. "Alice Cooper Still Likes to Rock, Shock." *Ann Arbor News,* July 20, 1996.

"Carlisle-ABX Split." *Creem,* July 1969.

Carroll, Ted. "John Lee Hooker: A Tribute." http://acerecoo1.uuhost .uk.uu.net/whoweare/hooker.html.

Christgau, Robert. "The Continuing Saga of the MC-5." *Village Voice,* July 5, 1969.

———. "Mark, Don, Mel, and Terry." *Newsday,* May 1972, http://www.robertchristgau.com/xg/bk-aow/gfunk.php.

Cioe, Chris. "Bob Seger: Hymns from the Heartland." *Musician.* http://www.segerfile.com/earlydays.html.

Clark, Rick. "The MC5's 'Kick Out the Jams.'" *Mix,* March 2003.

Cohassey, John Fredrick. "Down on Hastings Street." *Detroit Blues,* spring 1997.

Collis, John. *The History of Rock, part 24,* 2002. http://www.rockabilly hall.com/JackScott.html.

Cotton, Lee. "The Hawk Rocks Again." *Rock and Blues News,* May–June 1999.

Crook, Max. http://www.maxcrook.com.

Cusimano, Mick. "The MC5: The Last Chapter in Rock and Roll History." *Lollipop,* 1998.

Dahl, Bill. Liner notes, *Rock, Rhythm, and Doo Wop: The Greatest Songs From Early Rock 'n' Roll.* Rhino Records.

———. "Jack Scott." *All Music Guide.* http://www.allmusicguide.com/cg/ amg&token+&sql+11:ygae4j87owaw.

Dean, Peter. "Little Willie John." *R&B Music Primer.* http://www.rhyth mandblues.org.uk/artists/lwjohn.shtml.

"Del Shannon." *History of Rock.com.* http://history-of-rock.com/del shan non.htm.

Denby, Eric. "Wylde in the Streets." *RayGun,* December 1998.

Derogatis, Jim. "An Ode to Rock Criticism's de la Creem." *Chicago Sun Times.* 2000.

DeWitt, Howard A. "Hank Ballard: From Alabama Gospel to the Early Hits." *Rock and Blues News,* August–September 1999.

———. "John Lee Hooker: From Clarksdale to Detroit." *Rock and Blues News,* December 1999–January 2000.

Dillard, William. "Elektra Cleans Up Lyrics on MC5 Cut after Complaints." *Billboard,* March 15, 1969.

Dow, Bill. "Psychedelic Posters Rock: The Art of Collecting." *Hour Detroit*, February 2000.

Dowdy, Earl. "The Amazing Empire on West Grand Boulevard: Million Dollar Music in Four Flats." *Detroit News*, July 25, 1965.

Duff, S.L. "LA Blues." *New Times Los Angeles*, January 20, 2000.

"Eastown Shut Down." *Detroit Free Press*, December 11, 1971.

Eddins, John Rhys. "Detroit Festival." *Creem*, April 1969.

Edmonds, Ben. "Adios, Amigo: Jeep Holland, 1943–1998." *In One Ear*, April 15, 1998.

Ehrmann, Eric. "Kick Out the Jams." *Rolling Stone*, January 4, 1969.

Ellerbusch, Sue. "Bands and Night Spots Become Big Business." *Acorn* (Dondero High School, Royal Oak, Mich.), December 16, 1966.

Epstein, Dan. "A Conversation with Andre 'Mr. Rhythm' Williams." *Ugly Things.* http://www.uglythings.com/andre.html.

"Everyone Benefits." *Creem*, March 1970.

"Falcons, The." *Soulful Kinda Music.* http://members.tripod.com/soulfulkindamusic/falcons.htm.

Finnegan, Kenneth. "Ted Nugent: The Primal Scream." http:/www.whereyatnola.com/ted.shtml.

Finnis, Rob. "Rockin' on Broadway—the Time Brent Shad Story." http://www.acerecords.co.uk/gotrt/2000/apr00/chchd758.html.

"The Fire This Time." *Time*, August 4, 1967.

"First Annual Detroit Rock and Roll Revival." *Creem*, June 1969.

Flores, Michael, "It Came from the Garage! Hideout Records." 1999. http://psychotronic.info/ioam/hideout_records.htm.

Forte, Dan. "Motown's Funk Brothers: The Greatest Hit-Making Guitarists in the History of Pop Music." *Vintage Guitar*, April 2003.

Frayne, George. "The Story of Commander Cody and His Lost Planet Airmen." http://www.commandercody.com.

"Früt Rocking On Despite Adversity." *Creem*, April 1970.

Fulton, Doug. "Gallup Park—Where the Sunday Action Is." *Ann Arbor News*, August 16, 1968.

Gabriel, Larry. "Passage of Decades Brings Power to the Poet." *Detroit Free Press*, June 14, 1995.

Gerritt, Jeff. "David Leone: Managed, Inspired Detroit Rockers." *Detroit Free Press*, October 9, 1999.

Gilbert, Wayne. "Vogue Records, Appealing to the Ear and the Eye." *Southeastern Antiquing and Collecting Magazine.* 2003. http://www.go-star.com/antiquing/vogue.htm.

Ginsberg, Geoff. "Only Fingers Bleed: '70s Guitar Style-Master Dick Wagner." *I-94 Bar.* May 1999. http://www. i94bar.com.

"Glantz, Gibb, and the Grande Gang." *Creem*, February 1970.

Goldberg, Marv. "The Imperials (Great Lakes)." *Discoveries* 149, October 2000.

———. "The Romeos (on Fox)." *Discoveries* 158, July 2001.

———. "The Royals." *Discoveries* 97, June 1997.

———. "The Serenaders." *Discoveries* 98, July 1996.

———. "The Thrillers/5 Jets." *Discoveries* 98, July 1996.

Goldstein, Patrick. "Bob Seger: A Star in His Own State." *Rolling Stone*, July 29, 1976.

Graff, Gary. "Against the Wind." *Detroit Free Press*, May 4, 1986.

———. "Detroit's First Promoter of Major Rock Concerts." *Detroit Free Press,* April 6, 1985.

———. "MC5ER Still Kicks Out the Jams." *Detroit Free Press,* February 11, 1990.

———. "Wayne Kramer of the MC5 Still Kickin'." *Guitar.com.* July 4, 1992, http://www.guitar.com/cda/columncorner/article_display .aspx?ssection=tl8spath=810000007492.

Gray, Bill. "15,000 at Ann Arbor Rally to Aid John Sinclair." *Detroit News,* December 11, 1971.

Gray, Chris. "Black Mask." *Movement for Anarchy.* December 1968.

Greene, Bob. "Bob Seger: Still the Unsung Hero of American Rock." *Detroit Free Press,* April 9, 1986.

Gross, Jason. "Ron Asheton–Stooges Interview." *Perfect Sound Forever.* February 2000, http://www.furious.com/perfect/ronasheton.html.

———. "Interview with Wayne Kramer." In *Perfect Sound Forever.* http://www.furious.com/perfect/mc5/waynekramer.html "Jackie Wilson Biography." http.history-of-rock.com/jackie_wilson.htm.

Gulla, Bob. "The Motor City Madman 'Ted Nugent' Puts Down His Bow to Celebrate the Kill of a New Reissue Campaign." *Guitar,* August 2000.

Guterman, Jimmy. Liner notes. *The Big Bang! The Best of the MC5.* Rhino Records, 1999.

Jacques, Geoffrey. "Parliafunkadelicment Thang." *Creem,* October 1970.

Hageman, Kim. "Mark Farner interview." *New Musical Express,* April 19, 1975.

Halley, Pat. "Plum Street Redux." http://www.prweb.com/releases/ 2004/2/prweb102916.htm.

Handyside, Chris. "Left the Dial." *Detroit Metro Times,* June 9, 1999.

Hart, James. "One Fired, Two Quit in Payola Furor." *Detroit Times,* November 23, 1959.

"Hastings Street Grease: Detroit Blues Is Alive!" http://www.blue-suit.com/html/hastings.html.

Heibutzki, Ralph. "Ron Asheton Revisits the Fun House." *Vintage Guitar,* January 2000.

Heron, W. Kim. "Producer Put His Touch on Singer's Hits." *Detroit Free Press,* February 24, 1984.

———. "The Unsung Heroes of the Motown Sound." *Detroit Free Press,* July 31, 1983.

Hilburn, Robert. "Bob Seger, Rock's Prodigal Son." *Los Angeles Times,* May 22, 1977.

Hodenfield, Chris. "MC5—You're a Revolutionary Group, Aren't You?" *Strange Days,* 1970, http://www.jungle-records.demon.co.uk/bands/ mc5 .htm.

Hohman, Marvin, Jr. "Purging the Zombatized Void with Alice Cooper." *Creem,* July 1970.

Hoover, Barbara. "'Paradise' Is Found in Neighborhood Reunion." *Detroit News,* February 28, 1989.

"Iggy Pop." *Rolling Stone.com.* http://www.rollingstone.com/artist/ bio/_/id/6081/iggypop?pageid=rs.Artistcage&pageregion=artist Header.

"International Free John Sinclair Day promotion." *Rolling Stone,* February 7, 1970.

"Jackie Wilson Biography." http://ourworld.compuserve.com/home pages/DYaros/jwilson.htm.

"Jac LeGoff Fired for Payola Talk." *Detroit Free Press,* November 20, 1959, 1.

Jaggers, Mick. Interview with Mitch Ryder. *Creem,* May 1969.

"Jailhouse Rock." *Creem,* 2, July 1969.

"Jerry Goodwin Recalls MC5." http://makemyday.free.fr/jgrecalls.htm.

"Jim McCarty Interview." *Vintage Guitar,* May 1999.

Johnson, Art. "MC5 in San Francisco." *Fifth Estate,* April 3–16, 1969.

Johnson, Greg. "John Lee Hooker: RIP." *Blues News.* August 2001. http://www.cascadeblues.org/history/johnleehooker.htm.

Johnston, Mike. "Pen Up the Limits: An Interview with Dennis Thompson." *Divine Rights Records.* 1995. http://www.divinerites.com/in_thom1.htm.

Kautto, Peter. "The Ted Nugent Show." *Rock United.com.* http://www.aor-europe.com.

Kaye, Lenny. "Iggy and the Stooges: Your Pretty Face Is Going to Hell and Back." Gadfly, June 1999.

———. Review of *High Time. Rolling Stone,* September 22, 1971.

Kelly, Ken. "An Interview with the MC5's Other Guitarist." *Addicted to Noise.*

———. "Kick Out the Jams, Motherfuckers." *Addicted to Noise.*

Kettner, Klaus, and Tony Wilkenson. "Liner notes," *Such a Rock and Roll Night.* August 2002.

Kinsella, Martha. "The Anti-establishment MC5 and a Local Recording Session." *Detroit Free Press,* November 8, 1968.

Kirby, Fred. "Excitement MC5 Keynote—Stooges Make NY Debut." *Billboard,* September 20, 1969.

Kohn, Howard. "It's Been a Groove—Thousands Leave Goose Lake Early." *Detroit Free Press,* August 10, 1970.

Kot, Greg. "Devotion Keeps Detroit a Rock City." *Chicago Tribune,* December 18, 2003.

Kramer, Barry. "Wheels on the Road." *Creem,* August 1970.

Kramer, Barry, and Dave Marsh. "A Fiasco of the Black Arts." *Creem,* December 1969.

Kramer, Wayne. Liner notes. *Alive Records,* Total Energy Records. March 12, 1999.

———. Liner notes. *The Big Bang! The Best of the MC5.* Rhino Records, March 5, 1999.

———. "Riots I Have Known and Loved." *Pop Smear.* http://www.popsmear.com/popculture/features/24/riotsknown.html.

———. "Rocket Reducer." *LA Weekly,* 1998. http://www.laweekly.com/ink/98/50/reverb-kramer.shtml.

Kubernik, Harvey R. "A Conversation with Mr. Motown, Berry Gordy Jr." *Goldmine,* March 3, 1995.

"Larados, The." www.reflections-music.com/larref.html.

LaRene, DeDay. "The Walrus Was Paul?" *Creem,* November 1969.

Lauer, Claudia. "John Sinclair: Kickin' Out the Blues." *Student Underground.* 2000. http://www.thestudentunderground.org/article.php?issue=378articleid=185.

"Lighting Flash." *Sun-Herald* (Melbourne, Australia), January 6, 2003.

Linder, Douglas, O. "The Chicago Seven Conspiracy Trial." www.law
.umkc.edu/faculty/projects/ftrials/Chicago7/Account.html.

"Local Band Spotlight." *Detroit Free Press,* April 11, 2003.

Lovranski, Dan. "MC5: Still Kicking Out the Jams." *Chartattack.* November
8, 2002. http:// www.chartattack.com/damn/2002/11/0801.cfm.

Lowell, Jon. "Violence on Twelfth—Street of Nightmares." *Detroit News,*
July 24, 1967.

Lydon, "Billion Dollar Baby—the Alice Cooper Story." *BBC1* reprinted.

Manardo, Fred. "56 Arrested in Drug Raids in WSU Area." *Detroit News,*
January 25, 1967.

Manos, Charles. "Good-by, Rock . . ." *Detroit News,* August 10, 1970.

———. "120,000 Youngsters Jam Rockfest." *Detroit News,* August 9, 1970.

———. "Youth Survives Fall from Rock Fest Tower." *Detroit News,* August
9, 1970.

Marcus, Greil. "Back in USA." *Rolling Stone,* May 14, 1970.

Marcus, Richard. "Obituary of Jeep Holland." "Remembering Jeep" Web
Site, http://ennvi.net/jeep/obit/dad.html.

Marion, J. C. "Detroit's Nolan Strong and the Diablos." 2000.
http://home.earthlink.net/~jaymar41/diablos.html.

Marsh, Dave. "Bob Seger, Not a Stranger Anymore." *Rolling Stone,* June
15, 1978.

———. "Concert Master." *Star Polish,* March 25, 2002. http://StarPol
ish.com/features/columns/article.ASP?ID=342.

———. "Heart Full of Soul." *Rolling Stone,* August 24, 1978.

———. "Iggy Stooge in Sherwood Forest." *Creem,* June 1970.

———. "Is It Bizarre Music or Merely Better Music: The Incredible Story
of Iggy and the Stooges." *Creem,* June 1970.

———. "Looney Tunes: Every Picture Tells a Story . . . Don't It." *Creem,*
March 1972.

———. "Put the Bacon on the Paper So the Grease'll Run Off." *Creem,*
November 1969.

———. "Doncha Ever Listen to the Radio . . . How to Remain Obscure
through Better Rock 'n' Roll; Best in the Midwest." *Creem,* May, 1972.

Marsh, Dave, and Debbie Burr. "The Rationals: Your Average High
School Band Seven Years Later." *Creem,* April 1970.

Marsh, Dave, and Barry Kramer. "8,000 Celebrate Dylan's Birthday."
*Creem,* June 1970.

Marsh, Dave, Deday LaRene, and Barry Kramer. "The Michigan Scene
Today." *Creem,* April 1970.

Marvel, Bill. "Memories of '60s Rock's Seminal Movement Remain Strong
for Those Who Went." *Dallas Morning News,* August 5, 1994.
http://sfgate.com/examiner/ee94/woodstockmoments940807.html.

McClure, Sandy. "Adult Theater Owners Facing Brothel Charge." *Detroit
Free Press,* July 7, 1983.

McCollum, Brian. "Detroit's Pop Music Landmarks: From Madonna's
Old Hangout to the Home of Motown Records to the Birthplace of
Punk." *Detroit Free Press,* August 3, 1997.

———. "The Stooges Come Home: New Appreciation, Loyal Fans, and a
Phone Call from Iggy Pop Get Them Back Together." *Detroit Free Press,*
August 13, 2003.

"MC5 On the Cusp." *Creem,* September 1969.

McGraw, Bill. "Fifth Estate Turns Twenty, as Radical as Ever." *Detroit Free Press,* November 22, 1986.

———. "Motor City Journal: Underground Paper Leaves City, Not Roots." *Detroit Free Press,* September 5, 2002.

———. "Paradise Succumbs to Progress." *Detroit Free Press,* February 6, 2002.

———. "Teacher Can't Live Down Tie to Beatle." *Detroit Free Press,* October 12, 2001.

McGuire, Mary Yared. "Memories of Black Bottom Stir as Reunion Nears." *Detroit Sunday Journal,* August 4, 1996.

McLaughlin, David. "A Detroit Legend Reborn." *Jam Rag,* May 2002.

———. "Jack Scott Live This Saturday." *Romeo Observer* (Romeo, Mich.), January 23, 2002.

Meikle, David. "The Golden World Story." In *Soulful Detroit.com.* 2002. Available from World Wide Web @ http://www.soulfuldetroit.com.

Mills, Fred. "Still in a Grand Funk." *Metro Times,* August 14, 2002.

"Mitch Ryder: Naked But Not Dead." 2003. http://www.radio.1.be/programma/cuca/series/ryder_mitch.htm.

Mr. Curt. "Iggy Pop—Turn Around . . . Take a Look at Yourself." *Rock around the World* 11. http://www.ratw.com/issues/11/iggy_pop.htm.

Monroe, Larry. "The Paul McCartney Death Rumor." 1999. http://www.larrymonroe.com/archive/archive11.html.

Morales, Jose. "Up against the Wall, Motherfucker!" *Student Underground* 37, April 2002. http//www.thestudentunderground.org/article.php3?Issue=37&ArticleID=185.

Morris, Julie, and Jenny Nolan. "Sex, Drugs, Rock 'n' Roll, and Plum Street." *Detroit News, Rearview Mirror.* http://www.detroitnews.com/history/hippie/hippie.htm.

Morse, Steve. "Rock Notes." *Boston Globe,* April 3, 1998.

Moser, Margaret. "Boy Howdy: The Creem Story." *Austin Chronicle* (Austin, Tex.), March 16, 2001.

"Motown, Writers Are Out of Tune." *Detroit Free Press,* August 30, 1968.

Murphy, Murph. "Interview with Don Brewer." *Music Street Journal,* March 3, 1998.

Murray, Charles Shaar. "Teen Outrage in Croydon." *Creem,* March 1972.

"Musically Speaking, We're a Hit, Motown Holds Secure Spot in Star's Hearts—and Tours." *Detroit Free Press,* November 28, 1984.

"Nolan Strong and the Diablos." http://members.aol.com/dowop dowah/diabs.htm.

Nooger, Dan. "Devora Brown: The Fortune Teller Speaks." *Goldmine,* June 20, 1986.

Ochs, Edward. "Motor City 5: A Non-stop, Driving Unit." *Billboard,* January 10, 1969.

Olson, Steve. "I Am the Original Caveman in the Year 2002." *Juice.* http://www.juicemagazine.com/tednugentintw.html.

O'Rune, Mush. Review: "MC5—the Roadhouse, July 1970." http://www.pooterland.com/chronicles/1970/mc5_roundhouse/mc5_roundhouse.html.

Osgood, Dick. *Wyxie Wonderland.* Bowling Green, Ohio: Bowling Green University Press, 1981.

Ovshinsky, Harvey. "City Ablaze." *Fifth Estate,* August 1–15, 1967.

Owens, Keith A. "Hastings Street Breakdown." *Metro Times,* July 25, 2000.

Parcellin, Chris. "Let There Be Dark," http://www.d-filed.com/asheton.html.

Pederson, Greg. "The Great Guitars of Dick Wagner and Steve Hunter." In *Vintage Guitar* [magazine online]. February 1998. Available from World Wide Web @ http://www.vintageguitar.com.

Piper, Pat. "Our Man on Twang Climbs the Mountain." *Bay Weekly,* February 21–27, 2002.

Poore, Billy. "Great Scott." *Rock and Blues News.* May–June, 1999.

"Pot Rally Aids Sinclair." *Detroit Free Press,* December 11, 1971.

"The Progress of Progressive Radio." *Creem,* March 1969.

Propes, Steve. "Johnny Otis, the Rock 'n' Roll Years: Doin' That Crazy Hand Jive." *Goldmine,* March 25, 1988.

———. "Lamont Dozier: An Insider's Inside Look at Motown." *Goldmine,* July 20, 1986.

Quigley, Mike. Interview with Alice Cooper. *Poppin.* September, 1969. http://www.mjq.net/interviews/alice.htm.

Quinn, P.T. "Interview with John Sinclair." *Perfect Sound Forever.* http://www.furious.com/perfect/mc5/johnsinclair.html.

Rabid, Jack. "Which Mask Are You?" Interview with Iggy Pop. *The Big Takeover* no. 49, 2001. http://www.bigtakeover.com/iggy49.html.

"Rare Earth Biography." *Encyclopedia of Popular Music.* London: Muze, 2002.

Reay, Tony. "Flash; Beatles New Release Introduced on WABX." *Fifth Estate,* October 31–November 13, 1968.

———. "Jeep—like the Car—Holland—like the Country." *Best of Boy Howdy,* March 2004. http://groups.msn.com/bestofboyhowdy/tonyreaypage1.msnw.

———. "Like Pushing a Rubber Giraffe through a Keyhole." *Rock Critics.com.* 2002. http://www.rockcritics.com/tonyreay_creem.html.

Richards, Rick. "Fortune Records." *Discoveries* 107, April 1997.

Rivera, Pete. "Beginnings (Rare Earth)." In *Voices of Classic Rock* [online magazine]. Available from the World Wide Web @ http://www.rockforever.com.

Roberts, Michael. "Surviving the Sixties: How John Sinclair went from Being a White Panther to a Blues Scholar," http://www.westword.com/issues/1997–08–07/music/music4.html.

"Rock and Revolution." *Blastitude* 13, August 2002. http://www.blastitude.com/13/ETERNITY/rock_and_revolution.htm.

"Rock and Roll News." *Creem,* various issues, 1969–70.

Roeser, Steve. "The Tumultuous Times of Terry Knight." *Discoveries,* February 2000.

Rohnisch, Claus. "John Lee Hooker Biography." July 28, 2001. http://www.sciforums.com/showthread.php?threadid=3345.

Rotenstein, David S. "John Lee Hooker." *Daily News* (Atlanta), April 1992.

"Russ Buys Eastown?" *Creem,* July 1969.

Saal, Hubert. "Kick Out the Jams." *Newsweek,* May 19, 1969.

"A Salute to Motown." *Hitkit,* June 1–15, 1968.

Segal, David. "Musicians Play Deejay: Ted Nugent's Most Influential List." *Washington Post,* 2002.

Sanner, Howard. "Chronology of Ampex Professional Products." http://www.recordist.com/ampex/docs/histapx/ampchrn.txt.

Settle, Ken. "Mitch Ryder, No More Vacations." *Goldmine,* May 20, 1988.

Shimamoto, Ken. "Dennis Thompson: Phantom Patriot." *Addicted to Noise,* March 24 and 28, 1998. http://www.i94bar.com/ints/thompson .html.

———. "In the Trenches with the Guitar Army." *Addicted to Noise.*

———. "Leni Sinclair: Through the Camera's Lens." *I94 Bar,* 2001. http://www.i94bar.com/ints/leni.html.

———. "Pirate Music: The Scott Morgan Story." *Addicted to Noise,* April 8, 1998. http://www.i94bar.com/ints/scottmorgan1.html.

"Shorr Fired by WXYZ; Denies He Took Payola." *Detroit Free Press,* November 28, 1959.

Simon, Tom. "? Question Mark and the Mysterians." [Online article] 2000. Available from World Wide Web @ http://www.tsimon.com/ mysteria.htm.

Sinclair, John. "Coat Puller." *Fifth Estate,* August 1–14, 1967.

———. "Interview with John Sinclair." *Moon Traveller.* October 1998. http://pwl.netcom.com/-jvaughan/art/qa0001010a.htm.

———. Letter to the editor. *Michigan Daily* (University of Michigan), September 28, 1969.

———. Liner notes. *Get Out the Vote.* Alive Records, Total Energy Records, April 10, 1997.

———. "The MC5: How the Jams Were Kicked Out." *Zig Zag,* 1977.

———. "The Story of the MC5 on the West Coast in March." *Creem,* May 1969.

Singer, Christopher M. "Radical Captured 1960s in Photos." *Detroit News,* December 5, 2001.

Smith, Brian. "School's In: Alice Cooper Comes Clean on Celebrity, Booze, and Detroit Rock 'n' Roll." *Metro Times,* October 23, 2003.

Smith, J. Eric. "Interview with George Clinton." 1996. http://www.jeric smith.com/Interviews/clintonint.htm.

Smith, Michael B. "The Super-energized Ted Nugent: It's the Nature of the Beast." *Goldmine,* February 25, 2000.

"Smokey Robinson Biography." http://www .comcast.net/soulex press4/soulbioe.htm.

Sorenson, Al, and Rick McGrath. "Mitch Ryder Interview." *The Georgia Straight.* June, 1970. http://www.rickmcgrath.com/mitchry der.html.

Spencer, Robert. "Sun Ra Biography." December 1998. http:// www.allaboutjazz.com/bios/srbio.htm.

Stanfel, Adam. "The United Sound." *Metro Times,* May 19, 2004.

Stults, Ron. "The Unrelated Segments: The Story of Their Lives." Album liner notes, reprinted March 18, 2000. http://www.cicadelic.com/seg ments.htm.

"Suzi Quatro Biography." http://www.artistdirect.com/music/ artist/bio/0,,481985,00.html?artist+suzi+quatro.

"Suzi Quatro." *Suzi Quatro Web Page.* http://www.comnet.ca/-rina/suzi quatro.html.

Talbert, Bob. "Seger and Me." *Detroit Free Press,* April 28, 1996.

Tamarkin, Jeff. "They Don't Make 'em Any Sweeter—The Skeeter Davis Interview." *Goldmine,* January 31, 1986.

Teegardin, Carol. "John Sinclair: A Long Strange Trip It's Been." *Detroit Free Press,* July 27, 1986.

Teranna, Ralph. "The Tera Shirma Story." *Soulful Detroit.com*. 2002. http://www.soulfuldetroit.com/web03-terashirma/index.html.

Thompson, James. "Detroit's Play-It-Extra-Loud Rock 'N' Roll Scene: Garage Bands Thrived in the Motor City in Mid-60s." *Goldmine*, February 25, 2000.

———. "MC5 Kickin' Out the Jams." *Goldmine*, March 10, 2000.

Trakin, Roy. "Bob Seger: The Creem Interview." *Creem*, September 1986.

"Trans-Love Special." Descriptive essay, 1967. Bentley Library, University of Michigan.

Trbovich, Marco, and George Cantor. "A Happy Sinclair Leaves Prison, Free on Bond." *Detroit Free Press*, December 14, 1971.

Trowbridge, Chris. "Mitch Ryder: Doctor Detroit." *Eye Weekly* (Toronto), November 28, 2002, http://www.eye.net/eye/issue/Issue_11.28.02/music/ryder.html.

Turczyn, Coury. "Dropping the Bomb." *Pop Cult*, 2002. First published in *Metro Pulse*, February 23, 1995.

Uhelszki, Jaan. "The Importance of Being Iggy." *Rolling Stone.com*. July 2001. http://www.rollingstone.com/news/newsarticle.asp?nid=14229&ct=85.

Uhl, John. "Ann Arbor's Had the Blues for Decades." *Michigan Daily* (University of Michigan), September 15, 2000.

"WABX Air Ace 5th Anniversary." Station brochure, 1973.

Walker, Joe Louis, "1998 Blues Estafette Lineup Notes." 1998. *Blues World.com*. http//www.bluesworld.com/estafette98.html.

Waller, Don. "Earth to Cloud Nine: Barrett Strong on 'Money,' Motown, and the Muse." *LA Weekly*, January 15–21, 1999.

Walley, David. "Interview with Iggy Stooge." *Jazz and Pop*, January 1970.

———. "Interview with the MC5." *Jazz and Pop*, March 1969.

Walter, Mike. "Clover Meets the MC5." [online article]. Available from World Wide Web @ http://www.t-online.de/home/clover.infopage11.htm.

Ward, Ed. "In Detroit: Mitch Ryder, No Wheels." *Rolling Stone*, March 2, 1972.

"Wayne Kramer: About the Artist." 2002. http://www.muscletonerecords.com/waynekramer.cfm.

Weinstock, Ron. "Boogie on John Lee." http://www.dcblues.org/articles/hooker.html.

Weisblott, Mark. "Alice through the Windshield." *Eye Weekly* (Toronto), June 30, 1994.

Werbe, Peter. "You Don't Turn in Your Card." *Vintage Guitar*, December 1998.

Whitall, Susan. "R&B Great Reclaims His Fortune." *Detroit News*, December 5, 2002.

White, Connie. "End of ABX Free Concerts." *Creem*, July 1969.

———. "You've Come a Long Way Baby." *Creem*, March 1970.

White, Timothy. "The Loneliness of the Long Distance Rocker." *Crawdaddy*, November 1977.

"Who's Who of the Ministars of the Minispectacle." *Situationist International*, June 1969. http://www2.cddc.vt.edu/sionline/si/whoswho.html.

Williams, Lisa. "A Minimum Security Bash." *Los Angeles Free Press*, reprinted in *Creem*, August 1970.

"Wilson Pickett Biography." *Rock + Hall of Fame and Museum.* 1993. http://www.rockhall.com/hof/inductee.asp?id+167.

Wolff, Carlo. "Fortune Records." *Goldmine,* May 3, 2002.

Wynn, Ron. "Bob Shad Profile." http://www.music.com/ person/bob_shad/1/.

Young, Brian C. "The Making of Runaway." 1998, http//www.delshannon.com.

———. "Max Crook Biography," http://maxcrook.com.

Young, Harry. "The Stooges on Electra, 1969–70." http://www.geocities.com/sunsetstrip/palladium/1306/iggy.htm.

Zwerin, Mike. "Wayne Kramer: Out of Hibernation." *Harold International Tribune,* June 15, 1996.

## Interviews by Author

Ronnie Abner (Peps). July 8, 2002.

Lee Alan, January 26, 1999.

Marc Avery, February 20, 2001.

Johnny (Bee) Badanjek (Detroit Wheels). July 2, 2002.

Bob Babbitt (Funk Brothers). October 22, 2003.

Bob Baldori (Woolies). August 11, 2003.

Harry Balk. August 11, 2003.

Gary Banovetz. April 17, 2004.

Bruce Botnick. November 23, 2002.

Sheldon Brown. January 19, 1999.

Lynn Bruce (Gigolos). June 7, 2003.

Beatrice Buck. July 29, 2003.

Jim Bugnel (Flaming Ember). October 22, 2003.

Dan Carlisle. September 9, 2003.

Jamie Coe. January 21, 1999.

Dick Crockett. February 5, 2003.

Bud Davies, May 19, 2003.

Michael Davis. September 17, 2003.

Larry Dixon, October 7, 1999.

Earl Elliott (Detroit Wheels). August 14, 2004.

Artie Fields. May 29, 2004.

Bill Figg (Rationals). May 13, 2003.

Dennis Frawley. March 15, 2003.

Tom Gelardi. November 22, 2002.

Jack Grenier (Chantones). July 6, 2004.

Russ Gibb. July 23, 2003.

Gary Grimshaw. August 18, 2002.

Bill Hennes. November 13, 2003.

Thomas Hester (Peps). July 8, 2002.

George Katsakis (Royaltones). July 12, 2003.

David Kovarik (Gigolos). June 11, 2003.

Wayne Kramer (MC5). August 2, 2003.

Chris Lena (Underdogs). May 21, 2002.

Barbara Lewis, June 10, 2003.

Tony Micale (Reflections). June 13, 2003.

Harvey Ovshinsky. August 29, 2002.

Bunny Paul, August 15, 2004.

Pun Plamondon. March 26, 2004.

Johnny Powers. August 21, 2003.
Gary Quackenbush (Fugitives, SRC). October 25, 2003.
Tony Roumell (Underdogs). May 18, 2002.
Bill Randle. June 6, 2003.
Clark Reid, March 15, 2002.
Mitch Ryder. August 9, 2003.
Robin Seymour. October 27, 2003.
John Sinclair. July 5, 2004.
Leni Sinclair. August 15, 2003.
Richard Stevers (Frijid Pink). October 27, 2003.
Jack Surrell, December 14, 2002.
Jem Targal (Third Power). September 24, 2003.
Dennis Thompson (MC5). September 30, 2003.
Rosalie Trombley. August 28, 2003.
Dick Wagner (Frost). November 1, 2002.
Gino Washington. February 3, 1999.
Thomas Wearing (Tidal Waves). January 31, 2003.
Tom Wright. March 28, 2004.
Ed Wolfrum. August 14, 2003.

**Miscellaneous**

Bentley Historical Library, University of Michigan, Ann Arbor.
Burton Historical Library, Detroit.
Rusted Chrome, A Tribute to Motor City Rock 'n' Roll: 1966–1972.
http://home.att.net/~s.m.geer/.
Soulful Detroit.com.
Local chart numbers from record surveys of radio stations: WJBK, WXYZ,
    WKNR, and CKLW.

# Selected Album Discography

**Alice Cooper**
*Love It to Death.* Warners, 1971.
*School's Out.* Warners, 1972.

**The Amboy Dukes**
*The Amboy Dukes.* Mainstream,1967.
*Journey to the Center of the Mind.* Mainstream, 1968.
*Migration.* Mainstream, 1969.
*Marriage on the Rocks.* Mainstream, 1970.
*Survival of the Fittest.* Ted Nugent and the Amboy Dukes. Mainstream, 1971.

**Brownsville Station**
*Smokin' in the Boys' Room:* The Best of Brownsville Station. Rhino.

**Commander Cody and the Lost Planet Airmen**
*Lost in the Ozone.* Paramount, 1971.

**Grand Funk Railroad**
*On Time.* Capitol, 1969.
*Grand Funk.* Capitol, 1969.
*Closer to Home.* Capitol, 1970.
*Live LP.* Capitol,1970.
*Survival.* Capitol, April 1971.

**Flaming Ember**
*Westbound No. 9.* Hot Wax, 1970.
*Sunshine.* Hot Wax, 1971.

**Frijid Pink**
*Frijid Pink.* Parrot/Deram Records, 1969.
*Defrosted.* Parrot/Deram Records, 1971.

**Frost**
*Frost Music.* Vanguard, 1969.
*Rock 'n' Roll Music.* Vanguard, 1969.
*Through the Eyes of Love.* Vanguard, 1970.
*The Best of the Frost.* Vanguard, 2003.

### The Funk Brothers

*The Best of the Funk Brothers.* 20th Century Masters/The Millennium Collection, Motown/UMe Material originally released in 1966 under Earl Van Dyke's name.

### Funkadelic

*Funkadelic.* Westbound, 1970.
*Free Your Mind and Your Ass Will Follow.* Westbound, 1971.
*Maggot Brain.* Westbound, 1971.
*America Eats Its Young.* Westbound, 1972.

### John Lee Hooker

*John Lee Hooker.* Blues King Pins Series. Virgin Records America, 2003. Detroit recordings.

### The MC5

*Kick Out the Jams.* Elektra Records, 1969. Reissue on Rhino.
*Back in the USA.* Atlantic Records, 1970. Reissue on Rhino.
*High Time.* Atlantic Records, 1971. Reissue on Rhino.
*The Big Bang! A Best of the MC5,* 2000. Rhino.

### Jack Scott

*Jack Scott's Greatest Hits.* Curb Records.

### Mitch Ryder and the Detroit Wheels

*Take a Ride.* New Voice, 1966.
*Breakout.* New Voice, 1966.
*Sock It to Me.* New Voice, 1967.
*All Mitch Ryder Hits.* New Voice, 1967.

### Mitch Ryder

*The Detroit-Memphis Experiment.* Dot, 1969.
*Get Out the Vote.* Alive Records. Recorded live in 1970.
*Detroit (featuring Mitch Ryder).* Paramount, 1971.

### Parliament

*Osmium.* Invictus, 1970.

### Rare Earth

*Get Ready.* Rare Earth, 1969.
*Ecology.* Rare Earth, 1970.
*One World.* Rare Earth, 1971.
*Rare Earth in Concert.* Rare Earth, 1971.

### The Rationals

*The Rationals.* Crewe Records, 1970.
*Temptation 'bout to Get Me.* Alive Records. Recorded live at the Grande Ballroom in 1968.

### Savage Grace

*Savage Grace.* Warner/Reprise, 1970.

*Second Grace* 2. Warner/Reprise, 1971.
*The Complete Savage Grace.* 33 1/3rd, 1998.

## The Bob Seger System
*Ramblin' Gamblin' Man.* Capitol, 1968.
*Noah.* Capitol, 1969.
*Mongrel.* Capitol, 1970.

## Bob Seger
*Brand New Morning.* Capitol, 1971.
*Smokin' OPs.* Palladium, 1972.
*Back in '72.* Palladium, 1973.
*Seven.* Warners, 1974.

## SRC
*SRC.* Capitol, 1969.
*Milestones.* Capitol, 1970.
*Traveler's Tale.* Capitol, 1971.
*Lost Masters.* One Way Records.

## The Stooges
*The Stooges.* Elektra Records, 1969.
*Fun House.* Elecktra Records, 1970. Reissue on Rhino.
Iggy and the Stooges. *Raw Power.* Columbia, 1973.

## Third Power
*Believe.* Vanguard, 1970.

## The Unrelated Segments and the Tidal Waves
*Where You Gonna Go?* Collectables, 1998.

## The Up
*Killer UP.* Alive Records.

## Compilations
*Friday at the Hideout: Boss Detroit Garage, 1964–67.* Norton Records.
*Michigan Nuggets.* Sabre Records.
*Michigan Rock 'n' Roll.* Seeds and Stems.

# Index

Michigan State Fairgrounds, 22, 206

Midnighters, the, 6–8, 10. *See also* Ballard, Hank

"Midnight Hour," 86

Miles, Buddy, 291

Miller, Larry, 146, 148. *See also* WABX

Milliken, Governor William, 245–46

Mill Valley, 192

Minah Birds, the, 132

"Mind Over Matter (I'm Gonna Make You Mine)," 45–46

Minor Key, the, 35, 58

Miracles, the, 36, 44, 91. *See also* Robinson, William "Smokey"

"Miss Ann," 50

"Miss You," 138

Mitchell, Tom and Grace, 114

Mitch Ryder Show (band), 138. *See also* Ryder, Mitch

Mitnick, Alan, 239

"Misery," 10

"Misery" (Dynamics), 43

Mixed Media (store), 202

Modern Records, 4–5

"Mojo Hann," 132

"Mommy, What's a Funkadelic?" 258

"Mona," 159

Monette, Ray, 97

"Money (That's What I Want)," 33, 38, 76

Monroe, Larry, 113

Montgomery, Bill. *See* Wanted, the

Moore, Charles, 108

Moorehouse, Steve, 271

Morea, Ben, 183–84

Morgan, Michael. *See* Underdogs, the

Morgan, Scott, 76–80, 140, 152, 195, 197, 247, 287. *See also* Rationals, the; Sonic's Rendezvous Band

Morris, Ron. *See* Larados, the

Morrison, Jim, 161, 194

Motherfuckers, the (Up Against the Wall Motherfucker!), 184–87

Mother's (club): Ann Arbor, 76; Romeo, 162

"Motor City, The," 37

Motor City Five, the. *See* MC5, the

"Motor City Is Burning," 180

Motown, 44, 50, 53, 56, 90–95, 97, 248–51, 277. *See also* Gordy, Berry, Jr.

Mount Clemens Pop Festival, 212

Mount Holly Ski Lodge, 77, 141, 240

"Mr. Sandman," 48

Mumford High School, 128

Mump, the, 76

Munford, Jane (Pat), 113

Murphy, Carmen, 36

Murphy, Stoney. *See* Wilson Mower Pursuit

Murray the K (Kaufman), 233

Muscle Tone Records, 285

Mushrooms, the, 139

"Music for My Mother," 258

"My Generation," 105

"My Girl," 94

"My Girl Josephine," 238

"My Heart Went Do Dat Da," 48–49

"My Last Dance With You," 44

"Mystery Man," 199

Mystery Train (band), 291

"My True Love," 25

*Naked Lunch* (Burroughs), 107

Nantis, Jim. *See* Chantones, the

Nathan, Syd, 8, 39

National Mobilization to End the War in Vietnam (MOBE), 170

Nelson, Billy. *See* Funkadelic; Parliament/Funkadelic

"Never Thought You'd Leave Me," 74

Nevins, Al, 30

Newark, N.J., 181

New Bethel Baptist Church. *See* Franklin, Rev. C. L.

Newman, David, 207, 209

*New Musical Express*, 285

Newton, Huey, 181

*New York Times*, 188, 208

Nievelt, Roy, 96

"1969," 215